Studien zur Migrations- und Integrationspolitik

Reihe herausgegeben von

Danielle Gluns, Hildesheim, Deutschland

Uwe Hunger, Münster, Deutschland

Roswitha Pioch, Kiel, Deutschland

Ina Radtke, Potsdam, Deutschland

Stefan Rother, Freiburg, Deutschland

Migration ist eines der zentralen Globalisierungsphänomene des 21. Jahrhunderts. Entsprechend groß ist das Interesse an Fragen der politischen Regulierung und Gestaltung der weltweiten Migration, den Rechten von Migrantinnen und Migranten und der Integration von der lokalen bis zur globalen Ebene. Die Buchreihe ist interdisziplinär ausgerichtet und umfasst Monographien und Sammelwerke, die sich theoretisch und empirisch mit den Inhalten, Strukturen und Prozessen lokaler, regionaler, nationaler und internationaler Migrations- und Integrationspolitik befassen. Sie richtet sich an Wissenschaftlerinnen und Wissenschaftler, Studierende der Geistes-, Sozial-, Wirtschafts- und Rechtswissenschaften sowie an Praktikerinnen und Praktiker aus Medien, Politik und Bildung.

Weitere Bände in der Reihe http://www.springer.com/series/11808

Christiane Heimann

Blessing and Curse of Intra-EU Mobility

Free Labour Movement in Spain, Germany, and the UK

Springer VS

Christiane Heimann
München, Germany

Dissertation, funded by Konrad-Adenauer-Stiftung and Bamberg Graduate School of Social Sciences (BAGSS), Otto-Friedrich Universität Bamberg, 2019

ISSN 2567-3076 ISSN 2567-3157 (electronic)
Studien zur Migrations- und Integrationspolitik
ISBN 978-3-658-31485-9 ISBN 978-3-658-31486-6 (eBook)
https://doi.org/10.1007/978-3-658-31486-6

This Springer VS imprint is published by the registered company Springer Fachmedien Wiesbaden GmbH part of Springer Nature.
The registered company address is: Abraham-Lincoln-Str. 46, 65189 Wiesbaden, Germany

Acknowledgement

First and foremost, I gratefully acknowledge the scientific guidance, support of and discussions with my first supervisor Richard Münch from the very first ideas to the printing of this book. As a member of the Bamberg Graduate School of Social Sciences (BAGSS), the practical advice on scientific writing and career planning of my second supervisor Ariadna Ripoll Servent became equally important to me. Brigitte Münzel's English language editing as well as her moral and organizational support was indispensable to me. She helped me overcome both linguistic and bureaucratic obstacles all the way through my PhD. I am also very glad to be friends with my delightful colleagues Stephanie Beyer and Oliver Wieczorek who brightened up my PhD days.

It was exciting to be a member of BAGSS and profit from all the resources it provided. Therefore my thanks go to its director Thomas Saalfeld and Miriam Schneider. Due to her strict regime, which I highly appreciated, I could always rely on BAGSS. Last but not least, I would like to thank Daniel Odinius who was a very likeable and intelligent office mate and made my office days more pleasant.

Surprisingly, I also left the building. So next to all the members of BAGSS, I would like to thank the Interdisciplinary Research Group on Immigration at the Universitat Pompeu Fabra, Barcelona, the Migration Research Group at the University College, London, and the Institute for the Studies of Societal Issues at the University of California, Berkeley, for having set the stage for very fruitful encounters and discussions. During my research stays abroad, I thankfully received the support of Michael Janoschka, Claire Dwyer, John Eade, Chris Zepeda Millan, Deborah Freedman Lustig, Christine Trost and Martin Sanchez Jankowsky. In particular, Ricard Zapata Barrero, John Salt and Aaron Cicourel provided invaluable scientific guidance when I was a visiting scholar in Spain, the UK, and the US. I hold their advice, encouragement, and hands-on assistance very dear.

At the beginning of my PhD, Jürgen Deller of Leuphana University of Lüneburg and Axel Klopprogge of Strategy For People helped me tremendously getting acquainted with the matter.

Finally, without the willingness of my many interview partners to provide such rich and insightful source material, this work would not have come to be.

Thank you!

For their generous support and funding, I gratefully acknowledge the Konrad-Adenauer-Foundation, the German Excellence Initiative, IPID4all and Büro der Frauenbeauftragten of the University of Bamberg, all of which allowed me to work on my thesis, travel to inspiring places to converse with magnificent people, and helped me survive while doing so.

It goes without saying that this entire project would not have been possible without my parents Annerose and Jürgen Heimann who supported me unconditionally during my PhD and, together with me, endured one or the other strenuous stretch. In this context, I would like to apologize to my father for increasing his blood pressure and bringing him closer to a heart attack by postponing the submission, defence and publication of my dissertation. In contrast and as calm as a clock, my trusted feline companion Mini patiently oversaw me for hours, months, and years toiling on the family's couch, helping me carry the PhD burden. I must admit that she has a lot more "Sitzfleisch" than I. In retrospect, certain people even suspect her to be more suited to do a PhD. Yet I may write these lines today, for which I particularly thank my dear husband Kei Müller who encouraged me, pushed me and forced me mercilessly to hand in this thesis and publish this book.

Done! Thank God this PhD is over!

Christiane Heimann

Table of Contents

List of abbreviations

BA	Bundesagentur für Arbeit
BAMF	Bundesamt für Migration und Flüchtlinge
BDA	Bundesvereinigung der Deutschen Arbeitgeberverbände
BIBB	Bundesinstitut für Berufsbildung
BMAS	Bundesministerium für Arbeit und Soziales
CJE	Consejo de la Juventud de España
CLASS	Centre for Labour and Social Studies
CCOO	Comisiones Obreras
CDU	Christlich Demokratische Union
CEDEFOP	European Centre for the Development of Vocational Training
CoJ	European Court of Justice
CSU	Christlich Soziale Union
DGB	Deutscher Gewerkschaftsbund
EC	European Commission
ECVET	European Credit System for Vocational Education and Training
EQF	European Qualification Framework
EU	European Union
EURES	European Employment Service
FDP	Freie Demokratische Partei
FUNDAE	Fundación Estatal para la Formación en el Empleo
GSCS	General Skills Certification Scheme
HR	Human Resources
IHK	Industrie- und Handelskammer
INE	Instituto Nacional de Estadística
IQ	Integration durch Qualifizierung
IT	Information Technology
JPC	Job Centre Plus
LRC	Lisbon Recognition Convention
NARIC	National Agency for the Recognition and Comparison of International Qualifications and Skills
OECD	Organisation of Economic Cooperation and Development
ONS	Office for National Statistics
PP	Partido Popular
PSOE	Partido Socialista Obrero España
RCN	Royal College of Nursing
SAF	Strategic Action Field
SEPE	Servicio Público de Empleo Estatal
SPD	Sozialdemokratische Partei Deutschlands
UGT	Unión General de Trabajadores
UK	United Kingdom
UKIP	United Kingdom Independence Party
TEU	Treaty on European Union
TFEU	Treaty on the Functioning of the European Union
VDI	Verein Deutscher Ingenieure

Abstract

Since the beginning of the 21st century the European Union (EU) has pursued the strategic goal of deepening both the economic and social integration of the union and its peoples (European Committee of the Regions, 2017). Therefore, the EU has aimed to foster intra-EU mobility to increase its human capital in order to strengthen its economic competitiveness (European Commission, 2018b). However, the common European labour market consists of structurally and culturally diverging economies with regards to their labour market, educational system and migration. Despite these obstacles, member states and EU programmes support intra-EU mobility according to specific labour market needs in certain areas, which leads to the guiding research question of this study: How steerable is intra-EU mobility?

For this purpose, the cases of Spain as a labour emigration country, Germany as a destination country fostering labour immigration and the UK struggling to restrict immigration, are analysed in the aftermath of the economic crisis. An abstract, innovative approach developed by Okolski and Salt (2014) was chosen to analyse intra-EU mobility as fostered by the coincidence of the right place, right circumstances and right people for labour mobility. In order to capture the new phenomenon of politically steered labour mobility, Heimann and Wieczorek (2017) refined this approach. In this book, the approach is first combined with other approaches and then enhanced towards a comprehensive approach of intra-EU mobility.

Highlighting the extent to which member states become the *right place* by implementing intra-EU mobility policies, the harmonisation effects of the supranational EU polity is analysed by applying the World Polity Approach (Meyer, 2005). The implementation of the EU polity into policies of mobility and integration on national level however depends on powerful stakeholders, which differ between the member states. These provide the *right circumstances* that are analysed applying the approach of Strategic Action Fields (Fligstein & McAdam, 2011). Existing theoretical categories such as elite migration (Favell, 2008), the more adventure-driven liquid migration (Engbersen, 2012) and the search for better living and working conditions (Triandafyllidou & Gropas, 2014) have been extended and unified to analyse the profile of *right people* for intra-EU mobility.

In Spain, Germany and the UK data was collected from interviews and group discussions with stakeholders of intra-EU mobility and participant observations. 95 individualised interviews, one group discussion in each country and two participant observations provide in-depth information from multiple perspectives of the stakeholders. Due to this thorough triangulation, the research design ensures a high degree of ecological validity (Mruck & Mey, 2000).

The holistic approach provides insights on how the situation in the member states affects the institutional implementation of intra-EU mobility and how mobile EU citizens navigate these policies strategically. In addition, it offers relevant insights for practitioners and policy-makers alike as the policies and practices of intra-EU mobility are evaluated with regards to their effectiveness for international recruitment and labour integration.

1. Introduction

1.1 EU labour mobility in the aftermath of the financial crisis

One of the European Union's (EU) strategic goals is to close the economic gap on the United States of America and thus "make Europe the most competitive and dynamic knowledge-based economy in the world, capable of sustainable economic growth with more and better jobs and greater social cohesion" (see European Committee of the Regions, 2017). This twofold interdependent ambition – deepening both the economic *and* social integration of the union and its peoples – has provided the frame and the motivation for and supplied the main research goals of this study.

Ever since the formalisation of the Lisbon Strategy in the year 2000 and the subsequent *Programme EU2020*, the EU has aimed to increase its human capital by improving mobility and lifelong learning in order to maintain and increase economic competitiveness (see European Commission, 2018a). The motivation is obvious: On the one hand, an adequate answer is required to the continuously growing differentiation and integration of the global market and the need to foster and develop knowledge and innovation despite changing demographics. This feat must be achieved while maintaining or even increasing current levels of productivity.

To this end, a well-educated, flexible, agile and readily available workforce is of paramount importance. Therefore, the recruitment of (highly) skilled labour has become a significant cornerstone of modern knowledge-based economies. Within the EU, this crucial challenge is met by the concept of *freedom of movement for workers* guaranteed throughout the entire territory of the common market. As a result, intra-EU recruitment has been dramatically facilitated, rendering, e.g., the bulk of the time-consuming visa-related bureaucracy obsolete (see Schmid-Drüner, 2017).

The global economic and financial crisis of 2008 intensified previously existing labour migration flows from the East to the West and generated new unprecedented labour migration flows from the South to North of the EU (Engbersen, 2012; Okolski & Salt, 2014; Triandafyllidou & Gropas, 2014). Whereas East-West migration has been a complex, nation- and destination-specific and often policy-driven matter (e.g. with regard to full labour market access for Polish, Romanian, or Bulgarian EU citizens), South-North migration did not have to overcome any significant obstacles. Southern European countries like Spain have always enjoyed full access to the EU labour market but until 2008 did not witness substantial labour fluxes. However, triggered by the crisis and the subsequent decline of the Southern European economies, this situation changed dramatically. Suddenly, the gradients in economic performance within the

C. Heimann, *Blessing and Curse of Intra-EU Mobility*, Studien zur Migrations- und Integrationspolitik, https://doi.org/10.1007/978-3-658-31486-6_1

European Union became apparent and acted as a catalyst to labour mobility (see Bräuninger, 2014). Due to the straightforward causality of this development and an overall unchanged political and statutory frame, South-North labour migration is the ideal issue for an unbiased, in-depth study of the mechanisms behind and the effectiveness of labour migration between EU member states.

Against this backdrop, this book addresses the question of how steerable labour mobility is for EU member states. Therefore, the study analyses institutional adjustments made in Spain, Germany, and the United Kingdom to steer intra-EU labour mobility in accordance with these countries' economic situation and their labour demand. Spain became one of the major emigration countries, while Germany and the UK became the main countries of destination. The social and economic advantages and disadvantages of intra-EU mobility have been fiercely disputed on the national and the EU level. While Germany actively fostered intra-EU labour recruitment, the UK unsuccessfully tried to control and prevent EU immigration, which finally led to the EU exit.

This study will look into the changes fostering labour mobility, taking into account dominant political framings and institutional processes. While free labour movement for EU citizens was already established in the Maastricht Treaty of 1993 and currently formalised in Article 20 TFEU (see Bux, 2017), only a relatively small number of people seized the opportunity (see Smith & Favell, 2006, p. 23) to migrate across state boundaries in search for work. Therefore, in the framework of the Programme EU2020 as well as in other programmes such as ERASMUS and Leonardo da Vinci, or "Your first Eures Job" and "MobiPro-EU" (see European Commission, 2014a), the European Commission encouraged people to draw on free labour movement in its initiative Youth on the Move (see European Commission, 2014b). It aims at improving education and employability to raise the youth employment rate.

Conceptually, such aims are doubtlessly appealing on the EU-level. In practical terms, however, the proclaimed liberal idea of free labour movement is faced by the non-existence of EU-wide rules for labour mobility (see Bernhard & Bernhard, 2014) including universally valid administrative procedures, recruitment and application practices, immigration and integration policies. Instead, different types of organisational principles of the national labour markets clash on the transnational level. This book aims to offer an insight into recruitment practices and labour integration in a move to inform and bolster the efforts of policy-makers, recruiters, migrants, researchers or any institution involved in labour migration. Ideally, it will raise the awareness with regard to chances and challenges of intra-EU mobility and offer strategies of how to cope with them. Different ways to overcome the obstacles of labour mobility in the EU will be examined in order to show to what extent the principle of free labour movement (see Maciejewski & Dancourt, 2017) in the common European labour market offers employment opportunities for professionals and employers.

1.2 Main research goals, contributions and structure of the book

In line with the motivations mentioned in Section 1.1, the main research goal of this study is to show how steerable intra-EU mobility is so that member states are able to benefit from the common EU labour market. This question is divided in three sub-questions:

- How and why do member states try to foster labour emigration, labour recruitment or prevent labour mobility?
- How do institutional adjustments concerning intra-EU mobility influence labour mobility?
- How do mobile EU citizens navigate the field of intra-EU mobility and its institutions to be able to benefit from it?

In order to carve out answers to the above questions, this book discusses the policies and practices implemented by the labour market institutions in Spain, Germany and the UK.

The following chapter will give an overview of the research design including the theoretical framework and methodological approach. In chapter three, it will be shown how a change in migration policies took place in Spain, Germany and the UK. Chapter four will highlight how labour emigration was fostered in Spain in the wake of the economic crisis. It will be elaborated in chapter five how Germany hails the increasing efforts to recruit professionals internationally as a way to ease the 'demographic crisis'. In chapter six the UK's massive international recruitment efforts will be set in contrast to the political debate on control over immigration that started in the aftermath of the economic crisis, which eventually led to BREXIT. Chapter seven provides insights into the profiles that define the right people for intra-EU labour mobility. The findings of this book will be presented in chapter eight, which analyses institutional changes in each of the member states to steer intra-EU mobility; these findings will be discussed more broadly taking into account practical and theoretical implications. Finally, the book will conclude with a summary of the research efforts undertaken and will offer a brief outlook pointing out future avenues of research investigations.

2. Research Design

This study aims at a holistic approach taking into account the interplay between policies, institutional actions and how they are received by migrants. This perspective offers new insights, as institutions and policies are mostly seen as parts of an existing structure in migration politics and not as actors following their own interests. The same is true for migrants and the way they make use of intra-EU mobility. They are mostly regarded as passive recipients of their particular economic and social environment, but not as strategic actors. Hence, this study combines the interplay of policies, institutions and individuals, taking also structure and agency into account.

The present study addresses the guiding research question as to how different EU member states, namely Spain, Germany and the UK, try to steer labour mobility according to their labour market needs. The idea of steering intra-EU mobility according to labour market needs in the common EU labour market is new as are most of the EU programmes, such as *your first EURES job*, directives such as the *recognition directive,* and the size and number of members belonging to the common EU labour market. Thus, the chances and limits of steering mobility have not been researched so far. Nor has any research been done on how (mobile) EU citizens respond to the services and programmes developed to steer mobility. Since this topic has been unexplored so far, an innovative theoretical and methodological approach is required to carry out this study. Therefore, theoretical approaches of new institutionalism and concepts of intra-EU mobility will be applied to derive as much data of theoretical interest as possible. The World Polity Approach is applied to provide a structural overview of the involvement of institutions and actors in the field of intra-EU mobility on the macro-, meso-, and micro-level and their relation to each other in the different member states. Therefore, in a first step relevant institutional structures of the fields of the labour market, education and migration will be examined to find out the typical structure in the member states before field changes took place in the course of intra-EU mobility. The theory of strategic action fields will be used in order to describe the dominant actors and how they initiate field changes to steer labour mobility along with the actors involved that stabilise the new structure of the field. In addition, theoretical concepts explaining EU mobility from the perspective of mobile individuals will contribute to deriving new hypotheses and categories from the exemplified professions. The findings will be retrieved and combined to enhance the idea of the *three right factors* to provide a theoretical approach that helps to capture the whole phenomenon in a holistic approach.

New Institutionalism is used as modern societies are highly institutionalised (DiMaggio & Powell, 1983; Fligstein & McAdam, 2011; Ganz, 2000; Meyer & Rowan, 1977; Scott & W., 2014), therefore EU harmonisation efforts as well as

C. Heimann, *Blessing and Curse of Intra-EU Mobility*, Studien zur Migrations- und Integrationspolitik, https://doi.org/10.1007/978-3-658-31486-6_2

efforts to steer EU mobility are reflected in institutional structures and processes. In an attempt to steer mobility the member states do not only need to consider the demands and structures of their own labour market, instead, they also need to take into account EU policies and laws, and the motives and strategies of mobile EU citizens. The labour market structure becomes most visible by observing its institutions, such as companies in specific sectors, unions, employment laws, etc. Also, the implementation of EU policies and laws as well as the degree of harmonisation in a certain member state are most obviously represented by its institutions. Thus, the institutional analysis will offer insights into adjustments made by different member states to benefit from mobility according to labour market needs. However, this is not enough to understand how well intra-EU mobility is steerable as it is exercised by mobile EU citizens. In addition, it is therefore important to note how mobile citizens make use of the benefits of intra-EU mobility themselves and how they use the newly developed programmes and services strategically.

This chapter is structured as follows: In Section 2.1, the World Polity Approach gives an overview of the structures including different possible levels. The Approach is used to derive a survey of relevant institutions and actors on each level and their relation to each other for the three member states. Section 2.2 shows the conceptual location of the field of intra-EU mobility and its neighbouring fields, in which the relevant institutions are located and through which the migrants navigate. These structures are examined to identify favourable conditions of the *right place* for labour mobility. The Approaches and concepts described in Section 2.3 are applied to examine the *right circumstances* for intra-EU mobility. The approaches of Strategic Action Fields and the roles of institutions (Section 2.3.1), different types of isomorphism (Section 2.3.2) and the concept of myth, perceptions and framings are used for the theoretical analysis. In Section 2.4, different concepts of mobile EU citizens will be highlighted that help to examine the exemplified professions. Last but not least, an outlook is provided on the following chapters.

2.1 Overview: EU Polity and harmonisation

The World Polity Approach will be applied in order to show how changes in the field of intra-EU labour mobility have been turned into structures within certain member states.

The idea of liberalised labour markets and the competition in the global war for talent was nourished by ideas and myth that diffused into the EU polity via the world culture (see Meyer, 2005). Thus, it will be shown how the myth of international labour migration as a rational instrument to optimise the supply and demand of the labour force was spread by EU policies and diffused in the member states Spain, Germany and the UK. This analysis is based on the assumption that different adjustments have to be made on the macro-, meso- and micro-levels in order to steer intra-EU mobility in the common EU labour market. The general EU polity of the common labour market clashes with the specific policies of migration, labour market and education on the national macro-level. These have evolved historically and are deeply embedded in the characteristic culture of the individual states. This level defines whether a country is the *right place* for labour mobility or not. Therefore, this study will analyse the national implementation of labour market oriented EU policies of intra-EU mobility in the aftermath of the Lisbon summit.

In order to implement these policies into the historically grown structure in the nation states, institutions serve as intermediaries and addressees of change towards EU-wide mobility on the meso-level. This is the level where the *right circumstances* for intra-EU labour mobility are developed. The national macro-level produces a certain meso-level structure that might or might not be favourable for intra-EU mobility. Depending on the historically grown institutional landscape, the extent of institutional adjustments a member state needs to take in order to benefit from intra-EU mobility is defined. On the one hand, various institutions are involved and challenged in this transformation process so that EU labour mobility of professionals becomes practicable. These are institutions of education and training and the labour market, such as universities, companies, recognition bodies, as well as institutions entrusted with migration and integration, such as migrant organisations or integration services. National institutions are important bodies for legitimising and delegitimising political framings. Therefore, they operate as intermediaries between individuals and the state as well as between the EU polity and local values and norms. In this case, important collective actors include, for example, labour unions, employers' associations, immigrant associations and national job centres. On the other hand, it will be examined to what extent individuals found institutions and influence the implementation of increased mobility and lifelong learning. In this context, it will be scrutinised to what extent professionals strive for increasing or adjusting their human capital in order to achieve international flexibility in terms of employability. Therefore, it will be of interest to what extent educational institutions, companies and consultation services encourage professionals to do so.

These institutions are in an intermediary position between the macro-level and the micro-level. From a top-down perspective, they function like an institutional filter implementing policies and spreading political framings within society. From a bottom-up perspective, they work as an institutional filter for individuals establishing collective actors in order to influence the forming of political will and political decision-making (Meyer, 2005).

The micro-level will be analysed in order to identify perceptions, preferences that form certain motives and objectives related to transnational labour mobility that create certain projects of labour migration. On the one hand, micro-level research is included in the study to offer insights into the impact of the EU polity, on individuals. To this end, it will be analysed to what extent politics and organisations influence the perceptions of individuals. Also, it will be examined how individuals navigate the institutional structure strategically according to their own motives and aims. In this context, it will be of interest to establish whether the ways these policies were put into practice are able to meet the political intentions.

The expected institutions on the macro-, meso-, and micro-level have been integrated into Figure 1:

Figure 1: Diffusion process of the EU polity

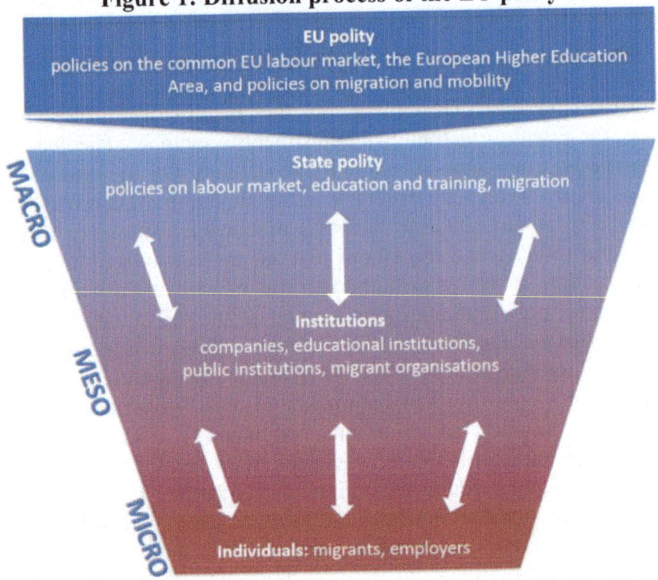

Figure 1 shows the interdependence of perceptions in the world polity, the EU polity, national policies, the institutions involved and of individual migrants. This figure is based on the model of Coleman's bathtub (Coleman, 1990) and its modified version of Stegbauer (2009).

The core of this study will focus on the interdependence between EU policies, national policies, institutions and individual motives concerning labour mobility of professionals obtaining EU citizenship, in this case Spaniards. In order to provide a holistic overview the World Polity Approach (see Meyer, 2005) will be applied to describe the diffusion processes of the common EU labour market. It will be analysed how institutional arrangements in the EU member states Spain, Germany and the UK were implemented to benefit from the common EU labour market. Depending on their specific labour market needs and societal situation they make different use of the harmonised common EU Labour Market as well as of the European Higher Education Area, and policies on migration and mobility.

2.2 Right place: relevant societal fields and their structure

In the following subsection, the concepts of the societal fields involved in intra-EU labour mobility will be explained. Every strategic action field includes different subfields, is part of wider fields, and is related to neighbouring fields (see Fligstein & McAdam, 2011). Three neighbouring fields of intra-EU mobility are of special interest, which are the labour market, culture and education as well as migration and integration. They define the activities in the subfields, which are transnational recruitment and (labour) integration. These fields and their structure determine whether a *place* is *right* for intra-EU mobility. Okolski and Salt (2014) define the *right place* by economic conditions, such as a booming economy and a reluctance among domestic workers to take over certain jobs or accept certain wages, the *labour market* is one important field that needs to be taken into account. Additionally, they highlight favourable public attitudes towards certain immigrants that are pre-existing even before policies promote intra-EU mobility. Those are related to the field of *migration and integration*. Furthermore, Okolski and Salt emphasize the educational expansion and structural mismatches. They link these structural mismatches to the availability of *right people*, however, in this book it is evaluated as part of the structure of member states defining a *right place*. Therefore, the field of *culture and education* will be in focus as producer of these mismatches.

The first neighbouring field is the *labour market*, which determines transnational recruitment/job-seeking strategies as well as international relations of labour and trade unions. The national labour market depends on the shape of national labour markets including policies, economic performance, key sectors, supply and demand of professionals obtaining certain skills as well as the role of unions, the organisation of labour relations, the extent of social and employment protection. All these characteristics are influenced by the extent to which labour markets are liberalised or regulated (Amable, 2003; Hall & Soskice, 2001). On the one hand, this historically grown labour market structure will be examined in order to understand what kind of deficits the specific labour market had developed so far for international recruitment, labour emigration or the prevention of labour immigration. On the other hand, the typical structures as well as the specific labour market deficits influence the way the regulations of the common EU labour market were implemented. Thus, how EU policies with regard to freedom of movement for labour, mobility projects (such as your first EURES job), and the EU labour market institutions (such as EURES) work in a certain member state depends on the specific national labour market structures.

Figure 2: Neighbouring fields of intra-EU labour mobility

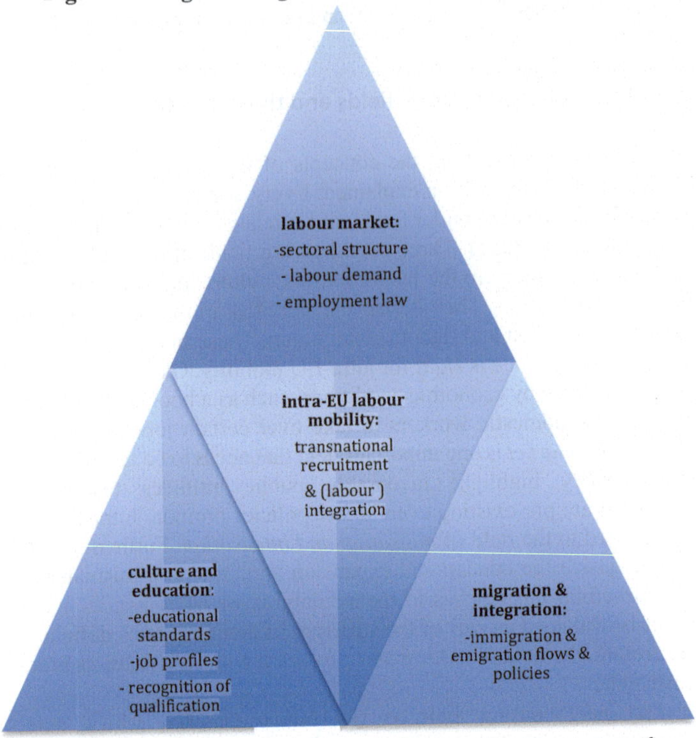

This figure was created by the author and is based on own research.

The second neighbouring field is that of *education and training,* because the transferability of skills and competences strongly determines the benefits of transnational labour mobility. It is influenced both by the system of education and training and the job profiles that vary among the nation-states. Educational systems differ in the extent to which theoretical education and/or practical training is part of the curriculum. Additionally, they are distinguished by the extent to which specialised, standardised or general skills are gained in educational programmes and demanded by employers (Crouch & Streeck, 1997; Hall & Soskice, 2001). Furthermore, the level of internationalisation of higher education determines the global mobility of professionals. Student immigration in a certain member state may facilitate labour immigration, while language skills and international exchange programmes may help labour emigration (see Streitwieser, 2014). These characteristics of the national labour market determine how harmonization efforts of the European Higher Education Area (EHEA)(see Secretariat of the Bologna Follow-Up Group, 2017), the European Qualification Framework (EQF) (see CEDEFOP, 2009) and the Lisbon Recognition Convention (see Council of Europe, 2014a) are implemented on the national level. In the field of intra-EU mobility, the recognition of diplomas, comparability of educational standards, and job profiles influence how actors can shape the field decisively.

The third neighbouring field is *migration and integration*, which facilitates, steers and/or impedes migration for certain groups and individuals. If the same kind of path dependency is assumed for policies and structures of migration and integration as it is for education and the labour market, national immigration and emigration policies and practices will influence future migration policies and practices (see Koslowski, 1998). In this context, historical and cultural ties with other countries affect intra-EU mobility. Additionally, existing ethnic communities and migration networks may facilitate labour mobility and reduce its costs (see Haug, 2008, p. 593ff), analysing ethnic communities (see Pichler & Gruner, 1997; Wilpert, 1992) and migration networks (Goss & Lindquist, 1995; Guilmoto & Sandron, 2001; Stark & Wang, 2002).

Hence, the three neighbouring fields of intra-EU mobility are the labour market, culture and education as well as migration and integration as shown in Figure 2. These neighbouring fields influence the actions in the subfields of intra-EU mobility, which are transnational recruitment and (labour) integration. The structures and processes in the field of intra-EU mobility and its neighbouring fields are analysed with regard to intra-EU mobility in the member states.

Attention is drawn to institutional arrangements and institutions on the meso- and macro-level, which affect the behaviour on the micro-level. Compared to more structuralist points of view, institutions are not only part of a given structure and recipients of policies and societal norms in new institutionalism according to Fligstein and McAdam. Instead, they are able to turn themselves into rational actors to produce and reproduce policies and norms. Thus, institutions are considered critical for the realisation of labour mobility and labour integration. Institutions of relevance to this study include, e.g., employment contracts, wage labour, corporations, organisational institutions, academic disciplines and the educational systems (see Jepperson, 2012, p. 144). Jepperson (ibid., p. 145) defines institutions as follows:

> ***Institution*** *represents a social order or pattern that has attained a certain state or property;* ***institutionalisation*** *denotes the process of such attainment. By order or pattern, I refer, as is conventional, to standardized interaction sequences. (...) Put another way, institutions are those social patterns that, when chronically reproduced owe their survival to relatively self-activating social processes.*

Institutions are established and stabilised as structures or mechanisms of social order, which govern the behaviour of individuals in a certain community or society (see Huntington, 1968, p. 394ff). However, institutions are not merely reproduced by collective action in the strict sense. Instead, routinely reproduced procedures stabilise them until collective action or environmental shocks can prevent these procedures (see Jepperson, 2012, p. 144).

Institutions may assume forms that can be distinguished most clearly by their level of formalisation (see Durkheim, 1982, p. 45ff). There are informal institutions expressed as customs, such as adequate forms of salutation in certain cultural contexts. Furthermore, there are formal institutions, which are based on formalised rules, like employment laws or employment contracts. The most objectified form of institution is an organisation with formal rules, formal structure, defined membership and local embeddedness, such as a migrant organisation, the Ministry of Employment or a company.

Although, institutions do not necessarily need to be formal organisations, most of the institutions examined in this study are formal organisations indeed. However, other informal institutions, such as migrant networks, will also be described.

In section four, the neighbouring fields and their institutions are examined in order to highlight pre-existing structures that provide the framework for changes in the field of intra-EU mobility in order to define the right place for mobility. These are rather consistent macro-structures, which affect the meso-level. Thus, the transitions between these levels are fluid. Generally, these institutional structures represent rather consistent path-dependent institutional arrangements.

Within the framework of these relatively stable institutional structures of the member states, institutions are able to initiate changes.

In order to analyse field changes, the institutions on the meso-level are analysed with regard to the role they take over in the field of intra-EU mobility. Therefore, the theoretical framework of strategic action fields will be applied.

2.3 Right circumstances: shaping the field of intra-EU mobility

In the following section, the perspective on the different institutions forming strategic action fields (see Fligstein & McAdam, 2011) will be described, in which these define the educational standards, job profiles and labour market structures. By doing so, they are able to create the *right circumstances* and thus influence how beneficial free labour movement is for certain member states, companies and labour migrants.

Due the perspective of Okolski and Salt (2014) the right circumstances are provided by societal perceptions, international ways of job search and some kind of matching. Heimann and Wieczorek (2017) show that political framings, transnational recruitment relations and labour integration measures developed by institutions are more relevant in steered forms of intra-EU labour mobility. Thus, the following approaches and concepts will be applied to find out which societal perceptions and political framings are transported by which actors. Furthermore, they are used to find out which international ways of job search and services for the matching of redundant professionals with vacancies are created in the emigration country Spain. Complementary, the transnational recruitment relations and labour integration measures developed by certain institutions in the UK and Germany will be analysed by the theory of Strategic Action Fields.

Hence, Fligstein's and McAdam's approach is applied to analyse how institutions steer labour mobility of qualified Spaniards to Germany and the UK. The basic assumption of this approach is that the actors involved shape the policy field according to their interests. The approach's advantage is a combination of traditional sociological new institutionalism and rational choice institutionalism (ibid., p. 1). The first one takes societal norms, rules and laws into account, while the latter focuses on the behaviour of actors in line with their interests. Hence, by using this analytical instrument, strategic actions are made visible while considering structural conditions.

In this case study, the approach of Fligstein and McAdam is applied to examine the changes in policies and practices of intra-EU mobility in Spain, Germany and the UK as strategic action fields (SAF). These SAFs are theoretical and rather unspecific as they describe a transnational field connecting the labour markets of at least two different European nation states. Here, the focus is on the meso-level, because institutions are formalised most often on the meso-level.

According to the approach, SAFs are the fundamental units of collective action in society, in which individuals or collectives interact while knowing each other (ibid., p. 4). In this case, for example, a Spanish migrant or an employer is an important individual actor, while migrant organisations or employers´ associations are crucial collective actors.

Through their interactions, they produce and reproduce social order on the meso-level. Hence, by taking into account or ignoring the institutional rules, norms, and laws, such as labour contracts, educational standards or diplomas, and employment laws respectively, the actors legitimate certain forms of behaviour. The actors in the SAF share a common understanding about the field's purposes to a certain extent. They know about the relationships in the SAF, its hierarchies and power structures, and its rules. Within the framework of these structures, different institutions like recruiting companies, labour unions, and political parties try to influence other actors strategically to achieve their goals (ibid., p. 16).

2.3.1 Strategic action field of intra-EU labour mobility

The strategic action field of labour migration from Spain to Germany and the UK will be analysed to explain why certain institutions take part in the field and how they shape the field with their strategic actions. To analyse the field of mobility policies and the institutions involved, the development of the field has to be taken into account. Interests of institutions determine whether an institution participates in the field and in which way it facilitates or impedes labour mobility. This structure works like an institutional filter that is able to explain policies and practices of mobility.

Actors in the field can be distinguished by the roles they hold. The approach defines four different roles, which are *incumbents*, *challengers*, *entrepreneurial actors*, and *governance units* (ibid., p. 2ff).

SAFs tend to be stable as long as they fulfil a specific function with respect to other fields in a balanced and interpenetrative way. Nevertheless, different forms of crisis can destabilise them and question the "status quo". While SAFs can find themselves in conflicts as a result of internal processes, it is far more common for a crisis to develop as a result of an exogenous shock emanating from a neighbouring SAF. Only the most dramatic shocks are powerful enough to destabilise related SAFs (ibid., p. 15ff). For the Spanish economy and labour market, the economic crisis is interpreted as such a dramatic event, destabilising the economy, the labour market, and questioning the powerful actors and existing structures. In Germany, the political agenda is described to be dominated by the internal demographic crisis, while in the UK the emergence of an immigration crisis is shown.

In times of crisis, different actors can gain or lose power because the instability of the SAFs may favour a power shift and create opportunities for emerging new actors (see Fligstein & McAdam, 2011, p. 8). The theory of strategic action fields is applied in order to find out who has the power to fuel changes in the field of transnational labour mobility and recruitment. In this study, *power* is defined in the Weberian sense as "the ability of an individual or group to achieve their own goals or aims when others are trying to prevent them from realising them" (Weber, 1925, p. 28). The empirical analysis will show which actors are able to enforce their goals in the field of labour mobility and which actors try to prevent them from achieving them.

Powerful institutions in the field of intra-EU labour mobility are therefore more likely to shape the field of intra-EU mobility and thereby create the *right circumstances* for labour mobility or prevent them.

This subsection will describe the roles institutions may assume to shape the policies and practices of intra-EU mobility. Their roles define whether they proactively shape the field or passively respond to changes in the field.

The SAFs of labour migration from Spain to Germany and the UK will be analysed to explain why certain institutions take part in the field and how they shape the field with their strategic actions. In order to analyse the field of mobility policies and the institutions involved, the development of the field has to be taken into account. In this context, interests of institutions determine whether an institution participates in the field and in which way it facilitates labour mobility (see Fligstein & McAdam, 2011, p. 1). This structure works like an institutional filter that is able to explain policies and practices of mobility.

Actors in the SAF can be distinguished by the roles they hold. The approach defines four different roles, which are *governance units, incumbents*, *challengers* and *entrepreneurial actors*.

Most fields have formal *governance units* that take care of the system's operativeness and control the compliance to rules. These units are internal to the field and differ from state structures, which are external. Internal governance units are created to corroborate the dominant logic and to protect the interests of the incumbents (see Fligstein & McAdam, 2011). In the field of intra-European labour mobility different governance units were detected as decisive during data collection, such as *the Ministries, public administration and civil services, which are concerned with regulating the neighbouring fields, the labour market, culture and education, as well as, migration and integration.*

Those actors, whose views tend to be strongly reflected in the dominant structure of the field, are called *incumbents*. Incumbents are normally well positioned and are quite resistant to pressure from outside, because they possess significant resources and powerful allies in the field. Yet, these advantages may not be enough to secure their position in times of crisis (ibid, p. 5). A significant mismatch of labour demand and supply or a significant increase of immigration can cause such a crisis. Institutions from the fields of the labour market, culture and education, as well as migration and integration will be analysed to identify incumbents.

Challengers usually do not agree with the status quo, but have only limited powers to change the structures in stable fields. Therefore, their influence is limited to certain niches in the field, which they occupy. However, in times of crisis, like the economic crisis in Spain, the demographic crisis in Germany, or the immigration crisis in the UK, they can become stronger and more powerful. The niche they dominate in the labour market may become a whole field (ibid., p. 6).

The success of the interaction between different actors depends on their *social skills,* i.e., the ability of individuals or collective actors to cope with the given structures (see Fligstein, 2001; Fligstein & McAdam, 2011). In an unstable and unorganised and/or emerging field such as that of intra-EU mobility, skilled actors can become institutional *entrepreneurs* due to their social skills (see DiMaggio, 1988). In such an environment, their ability to help, create, and maintain collective identities can be deployed (see Ganz, 2000). These might be institutions offering special social skills for the field so as to fulfil a bridging function between different national labour markets. Actors in the field of intra-EU mobility will be examined to find out the challengers and entrepreneurs.

Institutions obtaining all of the different roles in the strategic action field are involved in the development of institutional adjustments made to facilitate labour mobility and integration from one member state to another. The institutional adjustments are the outcome of strategic power struggles, in which social skills and resources are crucial to interact successfully and stabilise the field. The extent to which these adjustments are made depends on the ability of incumbents, e.g., national educational systems and labour unions, to maintain their position by preventing institutional change or taking a new and active role in it. Furthermore, the strength of the challengers to initiate changes in the field of intra-EU mobility is crucial for the (re-)establishment of norms, rules, and laws. Additionally, governance units assume a key role in settling a renewed social order because they reflect, control, and enforce the interests of the dominant actors in the SAF.

Institutions act and react in relation to each other, once field changes are initiated institutional chain reactions may occur. In order to understand these chain reactions better, the concept of institutional isomorphism complements the mechanisms in strategic actions fields.

2.3.2 Institutional isomorphism in different member states

The concept of institutional isomorphism will be applied in order to show what institutional similarities and differences are produced by the implementation of EU policies in national labour markets. From a top-down perspective, the increased efforts towards harmonisation of the labour market and the educational system in the EU can be interpreted as a diffusion process of the EU polity in the member states. To put the aims for the common EU labour market into practice, which means to increase the human capital by strengthening mobility and lifelong learning, the member states have to adopt similar institutional arrangements.

As described by Weber (1968), rationalisation efforts fuel homogenisation by aiming to increase efficiency via formal structures in order to be successful in the competitive marketplace. International labour mobility for the sake of increased economic competitiveness can be interpreted as such a rational myth. According to Meyer and Rowan (1977, pp 10ff), organizational structures are formed and legitimated by common myths of rationality created in the institutional environment instead of demands for efficiency; these myths lead to institutional isomorphism. If EU policies based on myths of rationality lead to institutional arrangements that facilitate labour recruitment and labour integration in a similar way, they are considered to encourage institutional isomorphism.

The perspective on labour migration as means to increase competitiveness and reduce labour market deficits such as unemployment and labour shortages, which is promoted by the European Commission (see European Commission, 2018b), will be highlighted in this study. It will be shown how institutions adopt similar formal structures, because organisational fields, such as the bureaucracy and administration and professions support myths (see DiMaggio & Powell, 1983, pp 147ff).

Formal organisations form and expand by incorporating structural elements based on myth. Hence, institutions on the national level develop and expand through the implementation of institutional arrangements that facilitate labour mobility. Increasing modernisation leads to an extension of rationalised institutional structures and growth of domains containing them (see Meyer & Rowan, 1977, p. 10). In pluralised, modern societies, the emergence of interest-based associations has risen enormously (see Münch, 1984, p. 298). The government is therefore based on a variety of administrative and decision-making institutions, with the labour market and the educational system combining a broad range of public, private and non-profit organisations related to one another and building complex structural networks. In these complex relational networks, myths originate and spread, especially in environments, where the degree of collective organisations is high and local organisations are struggling for leadership positions. Collective organisations might be part of the industrial relations, such as labour unions or employer associations. Local organisations might be companies that struggle for leadership in the marketplace. In these densely institutionalised environments, myths are deeply rooted and widespread in organisations and society, which increases their legitimacy (see Meyer & Rowan, 1977, p. 10). Therefore, a field is formed by an increase of interactions among organisations, of defined inter-organisational structures, of the information load and information flow among the organisations and the awareness of actors to belong to the field. Accordingly, actors make organisations more similar by trying to change them (see DiMaggio & Powell, 1983, p. 148) Institutional organisations incorporate societally legitimised and rationalised elements in order to maximise their own legitimacy. Meyer and Rowan (1977, p. 11) call this behaviour ceremonial assessment criterion, which is applied to increase the resources and strengthen the survival capabilities of institutions. This means that competition, institutions and organisations (see Aldrich, 1979, p. 265) drive structural isomorphism.

Different processes lead to isomorphism, which are called *coercive isomorphism*, *mimetic processes* and *normative pressures* (see DiMaggio & Powell, 1983).

As member states have to implement directives, guidelines and regulations, EU harmonisation is fostered by coercive isomorphism. *Coercive isomorphism* results from formal and informal pressures that are exerted on organisations by others. In this case, it will be shown how institutions, such as universities, recognition bodies or municipal youth centres are pressured to implement EU policies and put pressure on other organisations. *Mimetic processes* occur in environments of high uncertainty, which encourages copying others. Certain institutional arrangements might be copied from other member states in a highly dynamic globalised market in order to facilitate labour immigration. *Normative pressures* originate primarily from professionalisation and are transmitted through education and professional networks (ibid., p. 150). Universities, employers′ associations and professional unions may transport the need for internationalisation as a necessary asset and turn it into a norm and value.

Commercial organisations and institutionalised organisations implement the same formal structure for different reasons. On the one hand, commercial organisations are under strong output control, their success therefore depending on the management of relational networks, which encourages the realisation of institutional myth. In this case, employers apply new strategies for international recruitment in order to get the professionals they need to fulfil their customer requests. To this end, their success depends on their relationship with recruiters, recognition bodies, etc. On the other hand, the success of institutionalised organisations depends on the confidence and stability achieved by isomorphism in accordance with institutional rules. Therefore, public institutions might be of special importance in order to create this confidence and stability in the newly emerging field of labour migration. The density of collective organisations of society and the leadership of organisational elites creates a highly institutionalised context (see Meyer & Rowan, 1977, p. 16)

However, conflicting institutional rules cause a dilemma between legitimacy and efficiency. Different myths might originate from diverse parts of the institutional environment and are therefore likely to conflict with each other (ibid., p. 17). In this case, the rules of the Lisbon Recognition Convention to recognise comparable diplomas in all EU member states might conflict with the national standards for the professions. Organisations handle these inconsistencies by a decoupling or loose coupling of formal structures and day-to-day work activities (ibid., p. 18). Loose coupling conceals inconsistencies and inefficiencies by minimised inspection, while evaluation by both internal managers and external constituents helps to conceal such inconsistencies. Decoupling is another way to cope with inefficiencies and inconsistencies by "outsourcing" the problematic parts to other institutions. In the case of intra-EU labour mobility highly elaborated institutions might be developed to overcome lacking structural interconnectivity of educational systems and job profiles as well as missing language skills.

In summary, environments that are shaped by a larger number of rational myths generate more formal organisations in which these myths are institutionalised. Organisations that incorporate institutionalised myths are better legitimised, more successful, and likely to survive. Organisational control efforts, especially in densely institutionalised contexts, are devoted to ritual conformity, both internally and externally (ibid., pp 21ff). According to Di Maggio and Powell (1983, pp 154ff), there are certain organisational and field-level predictors, which encourage isomorphic change. In the field of intra-EU labour mobility especially the extent of professionalisation and structuration in a field increases normative pressure to implement the rational myth[1].

However, depending on the national institutional structures, such as the labour market situation, the educational system and migration regimes in the member states, EU policies are implemented differently. Despite all efforts to harmonisation, the interaction of EU polity and national institutions defines whether a member state creates the *right circumstances* for intra-EU labour mobility. Institutional myths are decisive to create certain circumstances. In the case of intra-EU mobility, they might be supported by *societal perceptions* (see Okolski & Salt, 2014) and *political framings* (see Heimann & Wieczorek, 2017).

1 Other field-level predictors will not be addressed to the same extent because the focus is more on structuration, specialisation and professionalisation in the national field of intra-EU mobility. Other field-level predictors include resource centralisation and dependency of organisations from these resources that make isomorphic change more likely and goal ambiguity and uncertainty increases the likelihood of mimetic processes.

2.3.3 Basis of institutional myths: perceptions and framings

The following subsection will describe how institutions use perceptions and framings in order to create institutional myths. Thus, the perceptions and framings they spread are of tremendous importance to influence the field of intra-EU labour mobility.

Institutions use different kinds of resources to influence policies concerning intra-EU mobility and provide resources for labour recruitment and integration. Ian C. Macmillan (1978) defines *influence* as '*the capacity to control and modify the perceptions of others*'. An issue can be seen from a variety of perspectives and interpreted from multiple angles, and it can conflict with various values or concerns. In the case of intra-EU mobility, these might be concerns about brain drain, fears of undermined wage settings, a decreasing educational level or falling quality standards. Conflicting values can be competing forms of solidarity on the local, national and international level. To this end, strategic actors use *political framing* to gain influence and support for their goals. '*Framing refers to the process by which people develop a particular conceptualization of an issue or reorient their thinking about an issue*' (Chong & Druckman, 2007, p. 104). In a political debate, a framing turns out successful, if it *'organizes everyday reality' (Tuchman, 1978, p. 193) by providing 'meaning to an unfolding strip of events' (Gamson & Modigliani, 1987, p. 143) and promoting 'particular definitions and interpretations of political issues'* (Shah, Watts, Domke, & Fan, 2002, p. 343).

Consequently, by dominating the prevalent perceptions in the field, actors are able to legitimise their goals and their measures to achieve these goals. These are ultimately legitimised, when they are legal, in line with normative principles, and when those affected accept the policies and concrete political decisions (see Beetham, 1991).

The debates on intra-EU mobility might express diverse pros and cons in different countries, but they are all rooted in two forms of solidarity. Counter-arguments are based on national solidarity and request for protectionism, while pro-arguments are based on transnational solidarity and favour liberalism. According to Münch (2012, p. 40ff) forms of *transnational solidarity* need to develop in a common EU labour market, which are independent of nationality. A sense of unity was more likely to be bound to people's identification with the nation state and its integrative power. This is based on a common language, culture and ethnos as well as the distinction between one's own national identity and that of others. From this sense of belongingness a social commitment for the greater good of the national society arises, which is especially reflected in the welfare system and its attempts to create equality of results to a certain extent so as to improve the living conditions of those who are less well off. Institutions of the welfare state, which play a role in the common EU labour market, include free education (without financial demands), subsidies, unemployment benefits, social welfare, etc. covered by tax payments. To what extent nationals perceive foreign EU citizens to be eligible for profiting from the welfare state and labour market or to what extent these foreign EU citizens are perceived to contribute to the national welfare state and the labour market influence the debate, societal perceptions (see Okolski & Salt, 2014), political framings (see Heimann & Wieczorek, 2017) and institutional myth (see Meyer, 2005) alike.

The implementation of freedom of movement for labour and the harmonisation of the common EU labour market long for liberalisation. On the national level of the member states, debates may arise that dispute the legitimacy and value of liberalisation versus protectionism. A common EU labour market aiming at creating the most competitive knowledge-based economy, inter alia by increased mobility and lifelong learning as formalised in the Lisbon strategy, implies EU-wide competition for the best and the brightest. Such an economically liberal paradigm can only be legitimised by justifying equality of opportunity over equality of results, which becomes more likely in the increasingly individualised and pluralised societies that depend on the global economy. Institutions of collectively shared welfare might be gradually undermined by these changes. Especially in less liberal but more coordinated market economies, liberal institutions are gradually introduced at the periphery, but not at the core of the labour market. However, the more of these institutional elements are incorporated, the higher is the pressure for a paradigmatic change (ibid., p. 249ff). The incorporation of such liberal elements encourages national and transnational solidarity based on network solidarity and justice in terms of achievement, equality of opportunity and fairness. Hence, non-governmental institutions may play a key role by preventing or establishing transnational forms of solidarity and by mediating between national and transnational forms of solidarity. First and foremost, interest-based organisations, such as cultural organisations, labour unions, trade unions, etc. might play a crucial role opposing, cooperating or outbalancing conflicting paradigms negotiating protectionist interventions versus liberalisation by the government, economic actors and other parts of society.

In order to create a common EU labour market, the national solidarity needs to be overcome or at least weakened and a different basis of in-group and out-group solidarity needs to be established. These are necessary preconditions for *multiple ties and interactions linking people or institutions across the borders of nation states* (see Vertovec, 1999), which is referred to as transnationalism. This minimum definition of transnationalism will be applied in the following study. Many scholars refer to non-governmental institutions and actors as transnational ones (see Faist, 2000; Glick-Schiller, Basch, & Blanc-Szanton, 1992; Pries, 2007), although this concept is rarely ever applied strictly. While governmental institutions such as immigration politics, border controls, etc., always influence cross-border migration, focusing on non-governmental actors might be fruitful depending on the field under review. However, in the case of the transnational field of intra-EU mobility governmental institutions play an important role for cross-border activities due to the supranational politics in the EU that establish the parameters of mobility. Therefore, governmental institutions are explicitly involved in analysing the transnational field of intra-EU mobility.

Institutions use their resources, such as social skills, in the struggle for the predominant framing; it will therefore be analysed how actors use their resources in order to put transnational labour recruitment and labour integration into practice. By doing so, they are able to form structural arrangements steering migration flows within the European labour market. These actors belong to different fields in their nation states, such as the labour market or the educational system.

Depending on their power, perceptions and role, the institutions in the field of intra-EU labour mobility do or do not create the *right circumstances* for intra-EU mobility. National structures in the fields of education, labour market migration as well as institutions and their role in the support or prevention of intra-EU mobility are but one side of the coin. The other side shows how EU citizens respond to the possibilities offered by intra-EU mobility.

2.4 Right people: elite, adventurers or searching for a better life

Thus, on the micro-level, the *people* will be focused in order to gain insights into the specific migration project they pursue. Especially profiles and motives will be highlighted and linked to how the migrants navigate strategically in the field of intra-EU labour mobility.

According to the rudimentary scope of *right place, right circumstances*, and *right people*[2], there are mainly two requirements for the emergence of the right people. Firstly, there is their availability, which means professionals who are redundant in their home country due to a structural mismatch. Secondly, an increase in educational attainment and **intercultural competences/maturity**[3] (see Okolski & Salt, 2014, p. 32) combined with the awareness of freedoms and entitlements ensured by EU citizenship constitute the *right people*. Okolski and Salt themselves claim their scope to be open to capture and unify existing scopes of intra-EU mobility, such as that of the Eurostars (see Favell, 2008) and that of liquid migration. As the scope is rather "raw" it is not only able to, but should necessarily be complemented with findings of other researchers. Thus, in a first step, concepts of the most visible available studies will be applied to enhance the concept of the *right people*. In a second step, the findings in the empirical part of this chapter will be used for further a specification of the concepts.

A significant amount of research has been conducted on intra-EU mobility to analyse motives, professional profiles of mobile EU citizens, favourable conditions and benefits of mobility for the member states. In the following sections, relevant scopes and findings on intra-EU mobility will be highlighted with regard to crisis-induced mobility from Spain.

2 Italic signalizes theoretical concepts applied in this study.

3 Bold signalizes theoretical concepts, which are examined and enhanced in this study

In the 2000s, the freedom of movement for workers and the career opportunities abroad triggered emigration from Spain that was part of an **elite migration** in Western Europe (see Recchi & Favell, 2009). Alaminos Chica and Santacreu Fernández (2010) analysed that the number of highly skilled Spaniards leaving Spain to work in Germany increased dramatically while emigration of unskilled Spaniards was only marginal. These elites possess **high cultural and economic resources and a high market value**, which are transferable to other countries.

In the wake of increasing European integration the motive of adventure-seeking was also established as another form of labour mobility conceptualised as **liquid migration** (Engbersen, 2012) or **intentional unpredictability** (Eade et al., 2007). Based on Zygmunt Bauman's research on *liquid modernity* (see Bauman, 2000) and *liquid lives* (see Bauman, 2013), *liquid migration* conceptualises a new specific form of migration emerging due to legally almost unconstrained intra-EU mobility. This type is characterised by its temporariness, labour migration, legal residential status, unpredictability, individualisation and a migrant habitus of open options and intentional unpredictability (see Engbersen, 2015, p. 7f.).

According to research by Triandafyllidou & Gropas (2014), the reasons for migration during the Spanish economic crisis were, first and foremost, the search for **better working and living conditions**. That might explain that the qualificational and socioeconomic profile is far more diverse in the case of those migrating to Germany during the crisis (see Faraco-Blanco, 2014; Montero-Lange, 2014) than that of the highly skilled Eurostars described by Favell. In particular, the emigrating Spaniards are not as well prepared for international careers. Facilitating intra-EU mobility for skilled but not necessarily highly-skilled people is one of the aims of new programmes, such as *MobiPro-EU* or *your first EURES job*. Thus, labour mobility of those who are not prepared for international careers is fostered. As this is a new and unexplored development, the migration projects of these professionals will be of special interest.

However, according to Tewes and Heimann (2018), a variety of different motives driving Spaniards to emigrate to Germany and the UK can be discerned even during the economic crisis. Additionally, they show that there is usually not one single motive but a combination of different motives, such as career-advancement, partner migration, adventure seeking or job search, which make Spaniards start their migration project. Thus, it seems likely that either elite migration, liquid migration as well as migration of those who search for better living and working conditions takes place in times of crisis.

Certain push factors may accompany the situation in the home country, such as social disorder (see Thomas & Znaniecki, 1958), which was identified in the case of Polish migration to the UK but also in the case of Spanish migration to Norway (see Bygnes, 2017) and was categorised as a state of anomy. Similarly, the complaints about corruption (see Conti, 2011; Triandafyllidou & Gropas, 2014) and social depression (see Tewes & Heimann, 2018) of Spanish migrants in their home country might be indicators of the same factors.

Taking into account the various motives for intra-EU mobility, the differences in economic performances and the political climate in the member states and the heterogeneous professional profiles of intra-EU migrants, Okolski and Salt (see 2014) advocate a new level of intra-EU labour mobility, which explains the emergence of migration flows with the coincidence of the three factors, right place, right circumstances and right people.

In order to relate these three factors, the aim of this study is not only to find and refine categories of intra-EU migrants with regard to their profile and motives, but also to find out how they strategically navigate the institutional hurdles and incentives in the field of intra-EU mobility to benefit from the new institutional structure.

2.5 Outlook on the empirical part and analysis

Before the overarching analysis applying the World Polity Approach can be provided, other theoretical approaches and concepts support the analysis of the different places, circumstances and people.

Firstly, the relevant fields for intra-EU mobility will be analysed in order to find out about steady structures and important institutions. Therefore, the fields of migration, the labour market and education are examined in order to gain insights in the economic performance and the structural mismatch of labour demand and labour supply, which are the most important characteristics for the *right places* for mobility.

Secondly, the *right circumstances* provided by institutional adjustments and isomorphism in order to benefit from intra-EU mobility are examined by applying the approach of strategic action fields of Fligstein and McAdam. This approach is used to show which institutions initiate field changes, and how favourable myth, perceptions and framings are spread to promote intra-EU mobility. Furthermore, the institutional adjustments made to offer the necessary new ways of job search and matching in the emigration countries as well as the recruitment and labour integration in the immigration countries will be highlighted.

Additionally, the strategic migration projects of the mobile people will be examined with regard to different professional profiles. The concept of Okolski and Salt (2014) that points out intercultural competence and maturity as well as the awareness of the possibilities of freedom of movement for workers as determining the *right people* will be enhanced. In this context, taking into account the scopes of intra-EU mobility of the Eurostars and liquid migrants as well as new concepts derived from the empirical findings will be taken into consideration.

2.6 Qualitative Methodology

Qualitative methods are applied in order to investigate the institutional actions and measures of transnational recruitment and labour market integration. Interviews with experts who are representatives of relevant institutions in the field of intra-EU labour mobility as well as migrants form the most important source of information. In this way, in depth information, different perceptions and developments in the field of labour mobility can be captured. Additionally, focus groups and participant observations are applied to validate and triangulate the information about the main challenges, cooperation and disputes among the institutions involved in labour recruitment and labour integration. This holistic approach including perspectives of all relevant actors in the field provides for very high ecological validity (see Mruck & Mey, 2000).. The various activities of institutions and labour migrants are analysed in order to unveil the opportunities and limits created in the different countries and the perceptions, framings and institutional myths they are based on. Thereby, the different ways to implement the EU polity of the common EU labour market, the European Higher Education Area and the freedom of movement of persons and labour will be examined. These developments influence the characteristics of *right people, right places* and *right circumstances* of intra-EU labour mobility.

Applying this approach, interactions in the field and the subjective views and goals of the different actors can be analysed (see Lamnek, 1988). Qualitative methods, such as interviews, focus groups and participant observation, are an adequate tool to analyse underlying interpretative patterns, possibilities of action as well as processes of negotiation and interaction of institutions, its policies and practices. They offer the chance to study the research object closely by taking the context into account, especially the historical circumstances (like the economic crisis in Southern Europe), which provides the necessary ecological validity for case studies and practical issues (see Mruck & Mey, 2000). First of all, institutional experts representing the relevant institutions in the field of intra-EU labour mobility were interviewed and observed in Spain, Germany and the UK. The data collected in this way is analysed to identify labour market structures that shape the *right places* for labour mobility and processes of institutions that create the *right circumstances*. Additionally, Spanish labour emigrants were interviewed, who moved to Germany and the UK, in a move to look at their perspective on the matter and the relevance of certain institutions for their labour migration and integration. Furthermore, the information given by institutions dealing with a large number of Spanish labour emigrants together with the data derived from the interviews with migrants are examined to identify the *right people* for labour mobility as shown by Table 1.

2.6.1 Case selection

Germany, the UK and Spain have been chosen because they have a high migration quota especially from and to other EU countries (see Bräuninger, 2014; see Green, 2014; Kreienbrink, 2010). Nevertheless, they differ significantly with respect to their economy and educational systems due to diverging welfare regimes (see Esping-Andersen, 1998), as well as their market capitalisms (see Amable, 2003). Furthermore, the direction of migration as well as the agenda concerning mobility is either complementary or contrary.

The United Kingdom is the most attractive destination for labour migrants and had the most strongly labour-market-oriented regulation of labour immigration (see Hopkins & Levy, 2012). It was also a "first-mover" in the European Union to seize the opportunity of recruiting (highly-) skilled foreigners according to their labour market needs. Nevertheless, while unemployment rates in the UK have been rising in the aftermath of the economic crisis (Green, 2014), policies on immigration and mobility became more and more rigid.

Table 1: Types of data collection applied per country

Qualitative methods	Spain	Germany	United Kingdom
Interviews with institutional experts	O	O	O
Interviews with Spanish emigrants	-	O	O
Group discussion	O	O	O
Participant observation	O	-	-

Being an export-oriented nation, Germany feels the pressure of globalisation, which is mostly exerted by the thriving economies of the emerging countries. Germany can hardly stay competitive with regard to the total amount of industrial output or the value of exported goods. Symptomatically, Germany had been overtaken by China as the world's most important exporting economy as early as in 2009 (see Monaghan, 2014). Its macroeconomic strategy therefore crucially depends on the ability to produce high-end industrial goods. Since the employable population is decreasing due to the demographic crisis, qualified employees are most important to maintain and reinforce this competitive advantage. To this end, Germany has not only opened its labour market to foreigners but German companies in fact recruit qualified foreigners and receive financial support to do so by the German government.

At the same time, Spain faced the second highest unemployment rate in the European Union after Greece. Especially young and qualified people were suffering from unemployment. Therefore, (highly-) skilled Spaniards emigrated to other European countries, first and foremost to Germany, followed by the United Kingdom, and France (see Bräuninger, 2014).

Therefore, this study analyses institutional adjustments made in Spain, Germany, and the United Kingdom to steer intra-EU labour mobility so as to allow these countries to benefit from the migration flows. How Spain became the main emigration country, while Germany and the UK became the major destination countries for labour migrants will be highlighted. In all three countries the social and economic contributions and costs of intra-EU mobility have been intensely disputed. It will be shown how Germany actively encouraged intra-EU labour recruitment, while the UK tried in vain to control and reduce EU immigration, which finally led to the country's EU exit.

Hence, these countries were selected as they were in different situations with regard to labour mobility and show different institutional structures, while all of them tried to steer labour mobility. Therefore, they seem the ideal case studies to establish the concepts of *right places*.

In order to examine the *right circumstances,* experts from relevant institutions in the field of intra-EU labour mobility were approached. Consequently, the experts were chosen due to their position as directors or specialists of institutions in the field labour mobility. They were individually and systematically selected by a combination of internet research and by snowball sampling. The snowball sampling method should have helped to reach an approximate theoretical saturation for the period of data collection at least for Spain and Germany. In the process of data collection experts increasingly recommended other experts that were already interviewed and decreasingly mentioned new information on the topic. The same can be said for the data collection in the UK with the limitation that relevant public institutions, such as EURES and NARIC, were not willing to give proper interviews but only provided few information via phone and email due to the political explosiveness of the topic. More information about these institutions could only be gathered indirectly from the knowledge of other experts. Nevertheless, a comprehensive and manifold picture could be put together from the data gathered.

In order to gain insights into different migration projects of Spanish professionals in these countries, engineers, nurses, technicians in crafts and trades and graduates of social sciences and humanities were chosen. Engineers, nurses and technicians were chosen as they are highly demanded in the immigration countries Germany and the UK (see Mangelberufe.de, 2018; UK Visa Bureau, 2018). They were selected due to their different skill-levels; graduates of arts and sciences are considered to be highly skilled according to the definition of the European Union as they graduated in a five-year study programme. As those professionals on a medium-skilled level are also highly demanded the nurses and technicians were selected for this purpose (ibid.). Furthermore, Spanish professionals were selected for the interviews, who migrated in the wake of the economic crisis and belonged to the age category of 18-35-year olds. This age group is eligible for the EU mobility programme *Your First Eures Job* (see European Commission, 2014a). Hence, these professionals were chosen to provide insights into the characteristics of the *right people* for intra-EU labour mobility.

2.6.2 Interviews with institutional experts

The main database was compiled from interviews with various stakeholders of intra-EU mobility. Due to differences in approaching the interview partners, they were subdivided into two main groups: institutional experts and migrants. A different approach was chosen because the institutional experts were questioned about their (professional) knowledge of and expertise in the field of labour mobility, while the Spanish labour emigrants were questioned about their biographic experiences. By examining activities of institutions and labour migrants, insights will be gained into the opportunities and limits created in the different countries based on collectively shared perspectives. Similarities and differences within the scope of the EU polity of the common EU labour market, the European Higher Education Area and the freedom of movement of persons and labour will be analysed along with their impact on intra-EU mobility.

The empirical analysis is mainly based upon the knowledge of experts working in different subfields of the policy area of mobility between the EU member states Spain, Germany and the United Kingdom. These experts are able to provide insider information about the implementation and interpretation of norms, rules, and laws concerning labour market mobility.

According to Mieg and Näf (2005, pp. 6–8), the sociological definition of an "expert" is characterised by his or her role in society. In this context, an expert's role is defined by being part in processes of decision- and policy-making in the field of mobility and/or having access to insider information. Consequently, most experts were chosen because of their position in institutions involved in transnational mobility. These experts are either directors of the institutions or specialists in the field of institutional activities concerning labour mobility. Directors were chosen, because they have a broad overview of institutional activities, networks and the organisation's policy. Specialists were chosen, because they provide valuable insights into day-to-day practices. The experts were selected individually in a systematic and labour-intensive process based on the institutions they work at and the positions they hold. Additionally, Spanish labour migrants in Germany and the UK were interviewed to identify their strategies of job seeking and their perceptions of the role of different institutions involved.

In line with the theory of fields, three main fields of strategic action are distinguished for this study. These fields are ideal types developed as theoretical categories in order to distinguish between institutions according to their field of activity. They are categorised as the field of the labour market; culture and education; as well as migration and integration. Consequently, data was retrieved from interviews, homepages and reports of the institutions presented in Table 2[4]:

Table 2: Selection of institutions institutional experts

Labour market	Culture and education	Migration
- Ministries of Employment - European Employment Service (EURES) - Servicio Publico de Empleo Estatal (SEPE) - Job Centre Plus (JPC) - Bundesagentur für Arbeit (BA) - Trade associations - Labour unions - Employers´ associations - Private recruitment agencies	- Ministry of Education and Cultural Affairs - Administrative government institutions, such as Federal Institute of Vocational Education and Training (BIBB) - National Academic Recognition Centres (NARIC) - Universities - Language schools	- Ministry of the Interior - Administrative government institutions, such as Federal Office of Migration and Integration (BAMF) - Migrant organisations - Local advisory centres

In a first step, relevant institutions were deducted from pre-existing knowledge about relevant actors of the labour market, migration and education. Furthermore, in a second step, Internet search was applied to find relevant institutions, and in a third step a snowball system was initiated. The latter two methods were particularly important, as it was not completely obvious or intuitive which institutions take part in the field of labour mobility and how to find them. The first interviews were conducted in 2013, while many of the interviewed institutions or their services concerning mobility were created only recently. Due to the currently developing differentiation and creation of institutions and the services they provided in the field, the output of literature review was limited. Instead, the most fruitful approach to discovering relevant institutions was the information and advice of their collaborators in the snowball approach.

In the end, 66 interviews with institutional experts were conducted between 2013 and 2016, which are grouped in Table 3 by category of institution and countries in which they were based. These experts are bound to supply the most reliable information on institutions and policies, services and practices in the transnational field of labour mobility. Qualitative interviews in Spain, Germany and the UK were therefore conducted with institutional experts to gain insights in the role they play and the activities they carry out in the field of intra-EU labour mobility. The institutions are analysed according to their role as challengers, governance units, incumbents and entrepreneurial actors as well as their activities to adjust to changes in the field triggered by the crisis. By doing so, they shape the

4 These are but a few of the institutions providing the database, it is not a complete list of interview partners.

field and create the *right places* and the *right circumstances* for intra-EU labour mobility.

Table 3: Interview partners classified by Institution

Category / Location	Spain	Germany	UK	Total
Recognition bodies/ Counselling services	3	6	3	12
Employers/recruiters	3	5	2	10
Labour/professional unions, employers' associations, Chamber of Commerce	2	4	4	10
Universities	3	--	--	3
Non-profit/migrant/cultural organisations/networks language schools	4	3	4	11
Scientists, think tanks	3	2	4	9
Public employment agencies	2	2	--	4
Politicians, specialists in ministries or governmental administration on national, regional, local level	3	2	2	7
Total	23	24	19	66

2.6.3 Interviews with migrants

Migrants were chosen by theoretical sampling (see Glaser & Strauss, 1998) in order to develop profiles of Spanish labour emigrants that can be considered the *right people* for labour mobility. In total, 29 interviews were conducted (15 in the UK and 14 in Germany) between 2014 and 2016. The interview partners were aged between 21 and 35, 14 were female and 15 were male as shown by Table 4.

Each country sample covered two engineers, two or three nurses, and three technician, as these are described in more detail as exemplifying professions. Other Spanish labour emigrants with various degrees were interviewed to find out about general issues and for comparative reasons. In doing so, a third group could be detected, which shares common characteristics and is summarized as humanists as they pursue the objective of gaining cultural experience instead of material goods such as salaries. Furthermore they are mostly, although not exclusively, graduates from social studies, humanities and arts. In addition to the interviews, several YouTube tutorials, Facebook tutorials, professional and ethnic forums as well as TV documentations on Spanish labour emigrants were analysed in order to triangulate the information given by the interview partners. Also, all the institutions providing consultancy and/or mediating services such as labour and professional unions, recruiters and language schools, were asked about the reasons of Spaniards to migrate and their profiles. Hence, apart from the interviews with the migrants themselves, two other types of sources were used to corroborate and add information regarding the mobile Spaniards.

Table 4: Sampling of Spanish migrants

	Germany	**UK**	**Total**
Spanish emigrants	14	15	29
Female	6	8	14
Male	8	7	15
Age	23-35 years	21-34 years	
Engineers	2	2	4
Nurses	3	2	5
Technicians	3	3	6
Other professions	Social worker Business graduate Tourist Manager Artist Philologist Psychologist	Lawyer Social worker Real estate actor PhD student Translator 2 Journalist Economomist	14

3. Right places for intra-EU mobility

This chapter analyses the relevant structures for the field of mobility, which represents an intersection of the fields of migration, the labour market and education for each of the three countries under review. It highlights important institutions in the labour market, education and migration before the specific mobility schemes in Spain and Germany were developed, and before the BREXIT vote in the UK. An analysis of the structures at the end of each section helps to understand the deficits on the labour market that led to a crisis and highlights institutions relevant for labour mobility.

3.1 Status quo ante economic crisis in Spain

Firstly, the structures of the relevant fields of migration, education and the labour market are analysed in order to show why Spain was particularly vulnerable in the global financial crisis, which led to high unemployment rates and labour emigration. This is important to understand how Spain became a *right place* for labour mobility as described in Section 4.1. The characteristics of the field of migration are introduced in Section 4.1.1. Section 4.1.2 puts the focus on the labour market, its sectoral structure, employment protection and labour relations. The educational system, its degree of internationalisation and EU harmonisation is outlined in Section 4.1.3. Certain deficits were produced due to the structure of the fields, which led to the Spanish economic crisis as explained in Section 4.1.4. Furthermore, the involvement of relevant governance units and incumbents in policies and practices in the field is shown in a structural analysis in Section 4.1.5.

3.1.1 Status quo ante crisis in the field of migration

The first field under scrutiny is the Spanish field of migration. It is pointed out to what extent governance units tend to be involved in labour migration policies and practices and which incumbents, such as migrant organisations, developed. Attention is drawn to migration practices and policies in the past, which influenced the development towards a labour emigration country as they have an impact on future migration decisions, flows, political frameworks, informative resources and points of contact abroad.

3.1.1.1 Spain and emigration

This section roughly outlines the emigration history of Spain to show that

C. Heimann, *Blessing and Curse of Intra-EU Mobility*, Studien zur Migrations- und Integrationspolitik, https://doi.org/10.1007/978-3-658-31486-6_3

migration has traditionally been a policy instrument to adjust the labour force to current demands during the last century. The migration history that connects Spain to Latin America, but lately also to the European countries, is described in the following part.

Over the past 500 years, Spain has mainly been a country of emigration, which was mostly directed to Latin America, starting with its colonization. Hereby, Spain influenced Latin America's history in a decisive way and established cultural and political ties that persist until today. After the Spanish colonialism, Latin America remained a destination in people's search for better living conditions (see Kreienbrink, 2006, p. 1). At the beginning of the 20th century, Spain was a poor, mainly agricultural country as Spanish industrialisation took place late and slowly compared to the development in other European countries, like the UK. At the end of the 19th and the beginning of the 20th century, modern industry developed only in the textile mills in Catalonia around Barcelona and in the metallurgical plants of the Basque provinces (see Tortella Casares & Núñez, 2014). Due to poverty and starvation in Spain's agricultural society, emigration towards Latin America peaked at the beginning of the 20th century, when 1.5 million Spaniards left for Argentina, Brazil, Uruguay and Venezuela between 1905 and 1913.

After the World Wars and the Spanish Civil War, which took place between 1936 and 1939, another wave of emigration to Latin America followed (see Vilar Ramírez & Vilar, 1999). In the 1940s, 50% of the active population were still working in agriculture and the rural Spanish economy did not recuperate from the war until 1959 (see Tortella Casares & Núñez, 2014). Therefore, 624,000 Spaniards left for America between 1946 and 1958 in search of better living conditions (see Kreienbrink, 2006, p. 1).

Under the dictatorship of Francisco Franco, a second phase of industrialisation began in the 1950s, especially around Madrid, Barcelona and Bilbao. It became fruitful from 1959 onwards, and, together with an increasing tertiary sector, mainly in tourism, Spain's economy started to flourish. Emigration from rural areas to the urban metropolitan cities Madrid, Barcelona and Bilbao set in. This development created negative side effects, like poor ghettos of workers in industrial areas and increasing inequality of wealth and living standards in the rural and the urban areas (see Tortella Casares & Núñez, 2014). Therefore, in the 1960s, the prospering Western European countries became attractive countries of destination, especially for Spaniards from the still agriculturally marked and relatively poor rural areas. This was when the next big wave of outmigration took place towards booming European countries like Germany, Switzerland and France. A range of bilateral agreements with these flourishing European economies reduced the tense labour market situation during this phase of the Franco era (see Vilar Ramírez & Vilar, 1999).

Labour emigration from Spain to these booming economies was especially attractive in the post-war period, because skill requirements were low and earnings relatively high, especially when compared to salaries in Spain. Additionally, workers were recruited for a secondary labour market that did not offer the jobs preferred by the native population and led to the upward mobility of the core workforce in these countries (see Herbert, 2001).

Labour recruitment of these countries stopped with the outbreak of the oil crisis in 1973. From 1960 to 1975, an estimated two million Spaniards migrated to other European countries. Apart from long-term labour migration, seasonal migration, particularly in the agricultural sector, became a labour opportunity authorized by the Spanish government. Therefore, in the 1960s and 1970s, approximately 1.5 million Spaniards migrated to France to work in harvesting jobs (see Kreienbrink, 2010). After the death of the dictator Francisco Franco in 1975 and the following transition to democracy, unemployment rose steadily from 5% to nearly 22% in 1986 and decreased again to 16% in 1990 (see Clemente, 2015).

Due to the high unemployment rates recorded between 1975 and 1990, around 15,000 people per year made use of the *controlled emigration programme* in Spain in order to work in other European countries for less than one year. A majority of these migrants went to Switzerland and a smaller part to France. After Spain´s entry into the European Union in 1986 and the possibility of free labour movement in 1991, the programme became obsolete (Kreienbrink, 2006, pp. 1–2).

For millions of Spaniards, emigration was an option to earn money for better living conditions. More than 2 million Spaniards live abroad permanently, especially in Latin America and other European countries. These Spaniards form a valuable source of support for other Spaniards who decide to emigrate. Spanish clubs and networks abroad are a significant place of contact because they offer information, contacts, accommodation and jobs, as has been described by the interviewed Spanish emigrants.

Spain's migration history seems to facilitate emigration as Spaniards are very well aware of the opportunity of labour emigration. A big part of Spanish immigrants interviewed mentioned that they felt encouraged to emigrate by the experiences made by peers and family members. The interviewed Spanish scientist 1, who is a professor of economics, explained in 2014:

> *For us in Spain, labour emigration is nothing new and not a big deal. We are used to that and see it as an opportunity. Here in Valencia everybody knows someone who is or has been a labour emigrant once. My parents were labour emigrants, my job is rather secure but if this was not the case, I would also consider labour emigration. My daughter learns English, so if the situation in Spain stays the way it is, and I think it will, she will have more labour opportunities if she knows languages.*

However, the characteristics of the emigrants changed during the past decades since the guest worker migration in the 1960s. In the 2000s, Spanish emigration became part of an elite migration in Western Europe (see Favell, 2008), according to Alaminos-Chica and Santacreu-Fernandez (2010). They found out that the number of highly skilled Spaniards leaving Spain to work in Germany and France increased dramatically, while emigration of unskilled Spaniards was only marginal. This elite emigration became possible in the wake of the

Europeanization process and Spain's EU membership. Besides, it is an indicator of a lack of opportunities for the highly-skilled in Spain, as described by Lorca-Susino (2011), which already existed before the crisis.

Thus, in the course of the 20th century, Spaniards emigrated mainly because of poverty and/or a lack of labour opportunities in Spain. Governance units from the labour market have supported labour emigration as a policy instrument to reduce unemployment since the Franco era and after the democratization of Spain. The fact that labour emigration has been a legitimate policy tool to reduce unemployment in the past increases the probability that it will be reused in the future. Nowadays, the combination of the Europeanization process and the lack of opportunities for the highly-skilled provides the premise for becoming a *right place of intra-EU labour emigration* of Spanish professionals. The recent emigrants that arrived in other European or Latin American countries, however, received support from the Spanish diaspora abroad.

3.1.1.2 Spain and immigration

After the country's democratization, the amount of repatriates from the diasporas abroad grew steadily since the 1980s as will be described in the next section. Additionally, it shows how the increase of labour immigrants during the Spanish economic boom since the mid 1990s has contributed to the development of services for (labour) migrants.

There has been a considerable amount of repatriates from Europe of around 15,000 to 20,000 per year, especially since 1980, until the beginning of the crisis. The most probable cause for this development is the retirement of Spaniards who were recruited by the *guest worker agreement* and wished to spend their remaining years in their home country. From the mid-1990s to the beginning of the 21st century the number of repatriates from Latin America also increased steadily from 8,000 per year to about 20,000 in 2004 due to the political and economic destabilisation in many of these countries (see Kreienbrink, 2006, pp. 1–2). These repatriates also became a valuable source of information and support for (potential) emigrants in the wake of the economic crisis.

In general, Spain was a very homogeneous society in the 20th century, because less than 200,000 foreigners lived in Spain until 1981, which was approximately 0.5% of the Spanish population (see Instituto Nacional de Estadistica, 2018c). Since the mid-1980s, Spain has become a destination for *retirement migration* from Northern and Western Europe. Today, Spain is the most popular destination for this type of migration (see Kreienbrink, 2006, p. 4). Especially British pensioners immigrate, who long to spend their retirement in the warm Mediterranean climate (see Rodríguez Rodríguez, 1999).

After another period of high unemployment of between 20% and 25% in the mid-1990s (see Clemente, 2015), the Spanish economy started to grow. These developments contributed to a population growth in Spain. Between 1975 and

2000 the number of foreigners living in Spain rose from 200,000 to 1 million (see Kreienbrink, 2006). Between 1995 and 2007, a period of strong economic growth set in with an annual growth of GDP of 3.5%. This development was triggered by Spain´s entry into the Monetary Union, which resulted in lower interest rates and increasing trust of international investors in the Spanish economy. As a result, the demand for credits for company investments as well as for real estate rose and led to a decline of the unemployment rate to 8% (see Ferreiro & Serrano, 2012).

Along with increasing prosperity, labour shortages of low-skilled workers were noted, as these jobs were no longer attractive for Spanish workers, like the agricultural sector, construction and domestic work. Therefore, the demand for unskilled labour and informal labour increased, which created job opportunities for immigrants in the labour market. Therefore, Spain also became a destination country for Central and Eastern Europeans. In this context, and after the coercive process of the EU's Eastern enlargement, Spanish employers saw the possibility to hire citizens from these nations, who then found new job opportunities in Spain (see Dehesa, 2009).

Due to the historic and cultural relationship between Latin America and Spain, it was easier for Latin Americans to immigrate to Spain than for other third-country nationals. As Spain has always pursued very restrictive asylum policies, a major part of the African immigrants were illegal labour immigrants. Due to the increased demand for labour these illegal African immigrants were tolerated and were given the opportunity to become naturalized during the Zapatero government. These immigrants were willing to work in low-skilled and low-paid jobs in agriculture, construction or the household (see Kreienbrink, 2006, p. 6f.). On the other hand, Spaniards themselves are less and less prepared to work in these sectors as increased prosperity raised their expectations of self-realisation in their job. This development influences job search also during the crisis, as the German recruiter 3 (interviewed in 2016) said:

> *Basically, Spain is also an affluent society and the quality of life is quite high, so that people have relatively high expectations. These relatively high expectations do not necessarily reflect the job offers on the real labour market.*

Thus, labour immigrants took over the less favourable jobs and on account of the economic boom at the beginning of the 21st century, Spain became an immigration country. Between 2000 and 2007, the foreign population more than quadrupled from around 900,000 to 4,500,000 foreigners living officially in Spain, which is equal to 10% of the population (see Instituto Nacional de Estadistica, 2018c). Ferreiro and Serrano (2012) estimate the contribution of labour immigrants in Spain at around 33% of the annual GDP between 2000 and 2007. So Spain profited from becoming one of Europe's most important immigration countries and the right of free movement of workers, which was granted also to the Eastern European citizens since 2004. During this period of economic growth, immigration from other EU countries and Latin America to Spain also rose (see Kreienbrink, 2010).

However, the distribution of immigrants is limited to certain regions. The labour immigrants are mostly attracted by the opportunities offered by the metropolitan regions like Madrid, Catalonia including Barcelona and Valencia, but also in the agricultural areas like Andalusia, Murcia and La Rioja. The wealthy "retirement immigrants" are mostly found on the Balearic Islands, the Canary Islands and along the sunny coasts of Andalusia, Valencia and Catalonia.

Legislation concerning migration was modified several times to keep pace with developments. Debates and measures of social integration of immigrants emerged at the beginning of the 21st century (see Cebolla Boado & González Ferrer, 2008). Since that time, a variety of migrant organisations have developed advisory service on how to achieve legal documents for (illegal) immigrants, assisting immigrants in exploitative employment contracts and general consultation. These services became incumbents of the field of labour migration as they also played an important role in order to provide institutional assistance for emigrants during the economic crisis as stated by public institutions and migrant organisations. Thus, they provided prerequisites for establishing the *right circumstances* for intra-EU labour mobility of Spaniards.

In summary, the democratisation has increased repatriation from the diasporas since the 1980s. From the mid-1990s onwards, labour immigrants from other EU countries also started to enter the Spanish labour market. These immigrants as well as the repatriates may support new Spanish emigrants by giving advice based on their own experiences. Also, Latin America and Africa contributed to a population growth during the economic upswing in Spain. As a result of the immigration wave, organisations for (labour) migrants have emerged that facilitated (labour) integration of foreigners. Once these organisations became established incumbents in the field of migration and integration, they could easily use their knowledge and contacts to support labour emigrants as will be shown later on.

3.1.2 Status quo ante crisis of the labour market

The following chapter is going to examine the labour market situation in Spain before the economic crisis. The focus is on specific labour market characteristics of the Spanish type of the Mediterranean Market Economy (see Amable, 2003). The developments of different labour market sectors, labour relations and the extent of social protection provide insights into strengths and weaknesses of the Spanish labour market and its vulnerability in the economic crisis. Typical sectors, products and financing in Spain are tightly connected to the jobs in demand. Additionally, industrial relations and labour regulations determine who is in a favourable position on the labour market. Furthermore, the social protection supplied by the welfare state is analysed to take into account the risks related to not being employed and the actors covering these risks in times of crisis.

Spain underwent a considerable economic and political transformation in the 20th century, from an agricultural society to an industrial one and from a military dictatorship to a parliamentary monarchy. Unemployment rates in Spain had steadily been relatively high at between 15% and 25% since the democratisation (see Instituto Nacional de Estadistica, 2018b). In 1990, 13.1 million people were employed, which was the highest number of employed workers by then. Between 1997 and 2007, the employment rate rose steadily to 56.2%, which means that ultimately 20.5 million employed workers were registered. This represented 33.6% of the total creation of employment in the euro area, which was mainly financed by cheap credits for company investments and for real estate available after Spain's joining the Monetary Union. So, Spain became the world's 8th biggest economy in terms of GDP before the crisis. This rise of the employment rate can be attributed in particular to an increased participation of females in the labour market and to labour immigration (see Ferreiro & Serrano, 2012, p. 240).

After this summary of the economic development that led to an economic boom in Spain, the next part provides an overview of eligible jobs that were created in Spain during the economic boom. The following sections show that the most important sectors in Spain did not offer an appropriate extent of qualified employment as the supply of highly-skilled people rose along with the educational expansion in Spain. Furthermore, it describes how the liberalisation and flexibilisation of the labour market led to more precarious working conditions, especially for newcomers on the labour market, which are mainly young people.

3.1.2.1 Spain and its economic sectors

While an educational expansion took place in Spain just like in many other countries (see Beduwe & Planas, 2003; OECD, 2009), the main sectors did not proportionally develop the number of jobs needed to match the increased amount of qualified graduates. In services and applied sciences, demand for highly skilled workers increased, but still, also during the economic boom mainly low- or semi-skilled jobs in agriculture, retail, tourism and construction were created.

In Spain, agriculture was still relatively important contributing around 5% to the GDP (see Instituto Nacional de Estadistica, 2017) with a total farm labour force of 1,782,690 persons in 2013 (see European Commission, 2016). Nevertheless, the service sector and the industrial sector expanded over the past 50 years at the expense of the primary sector.

Nowadays, retail, tourism, banking and telecommunications mainly contribute to the GDP in the service sector. Especially the hotel and catering sector has become an important economic factor since Spain has become one of the world's leading touristic destinations (see Santiago et al., 2009, p. 14). The Spanish telecommunication sector also expanded, especially the global player Telefónica, which is represented on the European, the Latin American and the Chinese markets (see The Economist, 2009). The banking sector played an important role offering favourable loans for investments in industry, construction and private housing. During the boom period of the Spanish economy, the banking sector represented 22.3% of the GDP according to Ferreiro and Serrano (2012). The most visible companies on an international level are the BBVA (Banco Bilbao Vizcaya Argentaria) and the Banco Santander (see The Economist, 2009).

The construction industry grew particularly at the beginning of the 21st century and, accounting for 9.5% of the GDP, represented a larger proportion of the economy than in most other European countries (see Ferreiro & Serrano, 2012, p. 240). Besides the locally embedded companies there are also multinational companies in this sector. Especially FCC (Formento de construcciones y contratas) is a global player in construction as is Ferrovial, a leading company for infrastructural projects (see The Economist, 2009).

At the beginning of the 21st century, the industrial sector began to decline and accounted for 20% of the GDP before the crisis. Car manufacturing was the most important industry in Spain, which belongs to the world's top 10 motor vehicle producing countries. Over 80% of the cars produced are exported, which contributes around 5% to the GDP (see Santiago et al., 2009, p. 14). The most important company was SEAT, which is based in Matorell in Catalonia and has been a wholly-owned subsidiary of Volkswagen since 1990 (see Autofácil, 2015). Strongly related to the automotive industry is the industry of metals and metal manufacturers, which was among the major industries alongside machine tools and shipbuilding. Another fairly important industrial sector was energy in which the multinational companies Repsol, an integrated oil and gas company, or Ibedrola, an electric utility company, witnessed substantial growth. Furthermore, chemicals, pharmaceuticals and medical equipment are produced by the Spanish industrial sector (see Santiago et al., 2009).

Additionally, the textile and footwear industry has traditionally been important in Spain since the beginning of the 20th century. Nowadays, first of all Inditex, the world´s biggest fashion group, was representative of the Spanish textile industry on a global level. The flagship store Zara belongs to this group as do the chains Zara Home, Massimo Dutti, Bershka, Oysho, Pull and Bear, Stradivarius and Uterqüe (see Costa & Duch, 2004). The industrial companies are mostly located around Madrid, Barcelona and Catalonia, Zaragoza and the Basque Country (see Dehesa 2009).

All the important sectors influence the skills of professionals in demand and the experience of the Spanish professionals. During the economic boom jobs were created above all in retail, construction, tourism and hospitality, and partly also in applied sciences and financial services. However, there were only little investments in Research and Development, which the Spanish economy was criticised for. The Spanish scientist 2, a professor in employment law and social legislation, said in 2014:

> *Well, many economists and the OECD warned that our boom based on internal consumption and our economic structure is not sustainable.*

> *The demand for a modernization of the Spanish economy and more investments in research and development was often highlighted. (...) Our politicians however, were even proud of creating a boom without creating innovations. They misused the famous quote of Miguel Unamuno "May others invent!" and now we are all paying the prize for their ignorance.*

Hence, despite the fact that Spain had been the 8th biggest national economy before the economic crisis and possesses visible global players, the majority of the Spanish companies were small, non-listed low-tech businesses. In these small low-tech firms, ownership was concentrated and they were mainly family owned (see Arosa et al., 2012). However, not only the economic structure, but also the capitalistic spirit was generally not very pronounced in Spain, as several interview partners explained. The Spanish professor of economics (Spanish scientist 1) said in 2014:

> *Then, there is the entrepreneurial class, which I think that – strictly speaking - in Spain includes but a few protagonists; let's say there are more independently wealthy persons who own a company, but in reality their capacity to run a business, their education and their knowledge of management, including their spirit is low, so to speak, in that they are little innovative, little receptive to be more proactive and to apply more dynamic processes with regard to the productive structure. I think this plays an important part in the weaknesses (of the Spanish economy).*

Nevertheless, during the economic boom and the growing multinationalisation of several Spanish companies, investments in R&D and high-tech increased. Thereby, jobs demanding medium to high skills were created, especially in applied engineering and applied chemistry, which were in demand in construction and infrastructure, energy and telecommunications, pharmaceuticals and medical devices. Additionally, medium and high skills are partly also necessary in services as, for instance, in public administration, tourism and retail (see Santiago et al., 2009). However, the majority of employment created was low- to semi-skilled. In general, small low-tech companies characterized the incumbents of the Spanish economy. Additionally, there was an emphasis on sectors requiring first and foremost low- to semi-skilled workers, such as construction, hotel and catering or retail as well as seasonal workers in agriculture (see Dehesa 2009).

3.1.2.2 Employment protection in Spain

The next section points out that high employment protection has traditionally been a crucial feature of the Spanish labour market. Thus, under the pressure of globalisation Spain rearranged the risks a workforce that is more easily adjustable to the current demand bears towards the young people.

Across all sectors, an important aspect of the labour market is the protection or precariousness that employment contracts provide for the employee, which means either rigidity or flexibility for the employer. Spain is traditionally a country with high levels of employment protection and a less flexible labour market (see Siebert, 1997). It was still relatively rigid in its employment relationships and restrictive regarding the use of temporary work and fixed-term contracts in the early 2000s (see Amable, 2003, p. 126ff.). Prior to the economic crisis, the high employment protection was said to be the main reason for high and persistent unemployment in Europe (ibid., p. 124). It was criticized that the Spanish version of the Mediterranean capitalism with its high employment protection and the seniority principle protected those who are established on the labour market. Thus, employment protection was liberalized in the early 21st century in order to create more flexibility in the labour market and to allow for a faster response to changes in demand. Therefore, more temporary labour contracts were introduced, because a more liberal and flexible labour market was hailed as being more competitive in times of globalization (see Hassel, 2014). Hence, during the economic boom the proportion of temporary work contracts grew significantly so that as many as one third of all employees had a temporary contract (see Santiago et al., 2009, p. 14).

Both the OECD and economists recommended a loosening of the rigid employment contracts and high labour protection so as to create a labour market, which is more flexible to react to changing demands in the globalised economy (see Amable, 2003; OECD, 2010). Naturally, it is difficult to legitimate why employees should lose some of their privileges especially in times of an economic boom. Therefore, temporary labour contracts had been introduced first and foremost for newcomers to the labour market (see Ferreiro & Serrano, 2012), among these many highly qualified young Spaniards, especially those who had finished school recently, while the well-established employees retained their high protection.

3.1.2.3 Wage bargaining and industrial relations

The following part shows that the individual employee has hardly any chance to get support from employee representatives who can protect their rights in the company. Additionally, it points out that neither the state nor employers cover social risks so that the family has to care for the unemployed.

The state intervenes in wage bargaining and industrial relations in the same way as in employment contracts. Labour and trade unions had been rather powerful before the crisis, but they do not negotiate directly with employers or employers´ associations. Instead, labour unions make use of their collective power by lobbying and influencing labour regulations, which makes them an important incumbent of the labour market. Similarly, the employers negotiate with politicians in order to make an impact on political debates and decision-making. Consequently, the state is in a strong intermediary position (see Hassel, 2014). Due to missing links between the managerial and the employee level in the companies, the manager-employee relation was rather conflict-ridden. Neither a centralized, nor a coordinated procedure had been formalised. Instead, the only means to diminish conflicts are high employment protection and contestation (see Amable, 2003, p. 138).

Apart from the regulations, employment policies are limited in every dimension. This includes public expenditure on labour market programmes, employment indemnity, youth programmes and handicapped persons′ programmes (see Amable, 2003, p. 140). Thus, labour integration and the related measures are a task of the individual employee. The same is true for social protection in the rudimentary family-based welfare state of the Mediterranean capitalism in Spain. The state provides only little protection against social risks, like unemployment, invalidity, disability, birth or old age, so that the family and the church traditionally cover social risks (see Amable, 2003, p. 155; López Antuñano, 2009). Consequently, during the economic crisis it was first of all the parents who had to care for the young Spaniards that became unemployed. A major part of them had to move back into their parents' homes, a development which is called boomerang returns (see Lennartz et al., 2016).

3.1.3 Status quo ante crisis in the educational field

The third important field for the analysis of labour emigration and its institutional challenges is the educational system. In this chapter, the educational system of the Spanish variety of capitalism will be described, focusing on the skills and competences produced and the involvement of different labour market institution in the educational field.

3.1.3.1 The system of higher education in Spain

The following section highlights how the Spanish educational system has been modernised and Europeanised in recent decades but still does not meet the requirements of the Spanish labour market.

In the 1990s, the Spanish educational system still displayed all the characteristics of a lagging educational system meeting the requirements of the comparatively low-tech industry. First of all, a high proportion of the labour force had only a primary degree as their highest educational level, while a relatively low percentage of the labour force had enjoyed secondary education. Secondly, unemployment was high for the university-level workforce, although tertiary education provided an advantage on the labour market to a certain degree (see Amable, 2003, p. 167f.). Nevertheless, the Spanish educational system transformed significantly. Not only the government was democratised but also the university system, accompanied by a remarkable educational expansion (see Santiago et al., 2009, p. 11ff).

As in other EU countries, a substantial expansion of the educational sector took place in Spain in the second half of the 20th century (see Beduwe & Planas, 2003). Naturally, this expansion did not continue infinitely, and the number of students stabilized in most countries. In Spain, even a slight decrease has been noticeable when comparing the number of students in the academic years of 1996/1997 and 2006/2007 (see Santiago et al., 2009, p. 29). Two different explanations seem to influence this decrease: On the one hand, the age groups accounting for lower birth rates had reached the age of professional education. On the other hand, higher education was not necessarily required during the economic boom years to obtain a relatively well-paid job. According to several interview partners, this was one of the reasons, why many young people did not attend any educational institutions after finishing school.

During the economic boom a far-reaching framework of governance and quality assurance was set in order to harmonise the Spanish educational system with the European Higher Education Area (EHEA). The various phases of the Bologna process were implemented to adjust the country-specific regulations to the EHEA, including the recognition and accreditation of degree courses and qualifications (see Santiago et al., 2009, p. 54). Thus, the coercive isomorphism harmonizing the educational system spread to the educational institutions in Spain.

Additionally, higher educational pluralism expanded, which means that an increasing number of private universities and non-university institutions were established; a shift of responsibility took place concerning the funding and support of tertiary education from the central government to the autonomous communities; furthermore, the institutions were allowed to design their educational programmes themselves. Institutional autonomy is more and more recognised, with guarantees of academic freedom and self-government. Additionally, the resources for research and development as well as in knowledge transfer increased considerably during the times of the economic boom in Spain. Accordingly, the number of students taking part in higher vocational training increased to around 13% before the crisis thus transforming tertiary education from a school-based, twofold educational system to a more diverse system meeting the demands of the modern labour market (see Santiago et al., 2009). Different tripartite agreements in Spain, collectively represented by the Tripartita foundation, provided assistance to the companies for the definition of needs or training supply in line with the demands of the labour market and the development of a knowledge-based economy. The three parties united in this foundation are the employers´ associations represented by CEOE and CEPYME, the labour unions represented by CCOO, UGT and CIG, and the governmental administration of labour represented by the national job centre SEPE (see Fundae, 2018).

However, there is still room for improvement as OECD researchers criticised several aspects of the educational system: Firstly, there is a risk of disintegration and incoherence combined with overregulation due to the various governing and coordinating centres. Secondly, the university system does not meet the requirements of the labour market. It is mostly academically driven, shows little differentiation and does not meet the diverse needs of the current labour market adequately. There is no appropriate academic labour market and competition is diminished by intra-institutional recruitment and career advancement. The matching of university and non-university sectors is low and student support is insufficiently integrated. Teaching is supply-ruled and is not really linked to the labour market. Employers, industry and trade unions seem to provide limited input to tertiary education policy. Thirdly, the universities' third-mission activities, like external service, training and consultancy as well as continuing education and training were criticised as being weakly developed. Fourthly, Spain's educational system was characterised by average differentiation and medium to high standardisation. There has been limited initiative from either the employers´ or the employees´ side in continuing training. Additionally, the employers' participation in continuing training has been weak and low to moderate in vocational training (see Amable, 2003, p. 169; Santiago et al., 2009) with a low level of complementarity between continuing and vocational training.

In summary, a considerable increase in the number of university graduates has been recorded in the past few decades. At the same time, the system of tertiary education diversified and was harmonised according to the guidelines of the European Higher Education Area (EHEA). However, one of the biggest problems in the two-fold educational system in Spain is that the incumbents, namely universities and companies, do not cooperate. This is why universities produce graduates that do not meet the skills demanded by the companies. These factors complicate the school-to-work transition and the labour market entry of young Spaniards.

3.1.3.2 Internationalisation of higher education in Spain

The next section will describe the low internationalisation of the Spanish system of higher education, while highly-skilled graduates increasingly internationalised to find better working conditions abroad

Another aspect that has become increasingly important in the globalised economy is the educational system's degree of internationalisation. Spain has a long university tradition, as the university of Salamanca is the third oldest university in the world after Bologna and Oxford. The Salamantine model was exported to Latin American universities later on. Due to the historical and cultural relations, most of the international cooperations between universities and the economy are still going on with Latin American universities. Apart from this transatlantic connection, most Spanish universities are rather isolated, despite the harmonisation efforts in the EHEA system (see Santiago et al., 2009, pp. 92–95). Foreign language skills are traditionally fairly low, a deficit produced by the educational system, as the *First European Survey on Language Competences* published by the European Commission (2011) shows.

Generally, the enormous educational expansion along with the loose ties between educational institutions and the labour market seems to fuel the risk of mismatches and over-qualification. Several researchers (see Consejo de la Juventud de España, 2013; Rahona-López & Pérez-Esparells, 2013; Santos-Ortega, 2013) show that, ever since the 1990s, over-qualification has been a reason for a mismatch on the labour market. Obviously, during the enormous educational expansion, the number of jobs for highly-skilled employees did not increase to the same extent and/or the skills of university graduates did not match the skills in demand on the labour market. Therefore, increasingly highly-skilled employees emigrated to find suitable jobs and salaries elsewhere. The elite emigration increased, while emigration of low-skilled workers decreased as Alaminos-Chica and Santacreu-Fernandez (2010) found out. Several interview partners mentioned the lack of opportunities or comparatively low salaries for highly-skilled. A Spanish emigrant in the UK and researcher in the field of economics stated in 2015:

> *Well, this (overeducation) is not a new problem in Spain. It was already the reason for me to emigrate many years ago. In Spain, there are not that many opportunities for those who studied and if there are, you earn far less than you could earn in other countries. So what shall we do? This whole debate about brain drain makes me sick! What shall we do if there are no jobs for us in Spain?*

Amable (2003) also showed that secondary education protected better from being unemployed than a university degree in the 1990s, while at the beginning of the 21st century obtaining tertiary education offered better protection than lower educational levels (see Santiago et al., 2009). A survey by ANECA (2013) unveils that only 10 % of degree holders who graduated in 2000 were unemployed about 5 years later. Furthermore, 77% of the participants found a job within less than a year, and 65% evaluated their job as adequate for their training. This could be interpreted as an effect of modernization in the Spanish labour market.

In contrast, the REFLEX survey (see J. Allen & Velden, 2011) comparing 16 countries shows that five years after their graduation in 2000, Spanish tertiary graduates were the ones with the lowest average salary. Also, García Montalvo (2007) argues that rates of return for university graduates have declined between 1995 and 2002, which might provide evidence of the oversupply of university graduates in Spain.

3.1.4 Destabilisation of the status quo on the Spanish labour market

The weaknesses of the Spanish labour market came into effect, when the financial crisis hit the Spanish economy as an external shock.

In 2007, the financial crisis triggered in the US affected many European countries, but Spain is one of the countries which the financial crisis had the strongest impact on. During the final phase of the electoral campaign at the beginning of 2008, the crisis had not yet reached Spain. The government announced that Spain would soon be in the Champions League of European economies. Although economic experts warned that the crisis would reach the developed European countries including Spain, the conservative government and the socialist opposition dismissed these forecasts as antipatriotic (see El Mundo, 2007). Nevertheless, as a measure of precaution the Spanish government increased spending on the public sector in order to prevent unemployment. The effect of the global financial crisis hit Spain with some delay but nevertheless provoked a longer and deeper crisis than in other European countries. As a matter of fact, the US financial crisis and the following global financial crisis was the first external shock that initiated the economic crisis in Spain (see Ferreiro & Serrano, 2012) with the second one being the Greek sovereign debt crisis in 2009 (see Arghyrou & Kontonikas, 2011). However, these external shocks were only the trigger that revealed economic and labour market deficits, which had already been latently present during the period of the economic boom in Spain. Ferreiro and Serrano (see Ferreiro & Serrano, 2012) explain that the sheer effect of the global financial impact of the crisis was not higher in Spain than in other European countries. They argue that, in 2009, nine member states of the euro area and eleven out of twelve European economies outside the euro area witnessed negative effects of the economic crisis that were stronger than in Spain. One year later, only Greece and Ireland in the euro area, and Latvia and Romania outside the euro area, performed worse in economic terms.

At this point, the deficits of the Spanish economy came to light. Mainly due to the deficits of the Spanish financial system, the fiscal policy and the labour market, Spain was especially vulnerable according to Ferreiro and Serrano (ibid.). The economic boom in Spain relied first of all on the availability of cheap credits and internal consumption, while a high external debt accumulated because of a steadily growing trade deficit. Furthermore, they criticize the cyclical fiscal policy in Spain, which allows for high employment creation during times of economic growth and extensive job losses in times of crisis. In this context, three out of four job losses occurred in the private sector, while one was in the public sector (see Casillas, 2013). The sectors of the labour market were affected differently by the crisis; industry and construction were hit hardest. In absolute values, the manufacturing sector, which showed a decline in its GVA of 16,482 million euros in 2011, was most strongly affected by the crisis, while the construction sector followed immediately behind accounting for a decline of 9.2 million euros (see Ferreiro & Serrano, 2012, p. 244). Due to the high labour intensity of the construction sector, most of the job losses were recorded here with 6 out of 10 dismissed persons having been employed in this sector (see CCOO, 2011; La Vanguardia, 2011). Between 2007 and 2013, more than 3.2 million jobs were cut, which means around 14.5% of the total employment in 2007 (see Casillas, 2013).

Therefore, general unemployment rates between 20% and 26% and youth unemployment rates of around 50-56% were identified between 2012 and 2016 (Instituto Nacional de Estadistica, 2018b). In 2007, 30% of the labour contracts were temporary contracts according to Ferreiro and Serrano (2012, p. 248f.). The destruction of temporary employment represented 83.1% of the total job losses. As a consequence of high employment protection for established employees, the job losses affected first of all those with temporary contracts, which were mostly the younger employees. According to a report of Comisiones Obreras (see CCOO, 2011; La Vanguardia, 2011) in 2011, which is one of the biggest labour unions in Spain, 86% of the destroyed jobs were held by young people between the age of 16 and 29. Young Spaniards were strongly hit by the financial crisis, as were immigrants and women. So when the crisis arrived, these groups proved to be most severely affected by the crisis (see CJE, 2013).

Thus, young graduates were dismissed first, which was one of the major preconditions for Spain to become the *right place* for emigration and to provide the *right people* for intra-EU mobility.

3.1.5 Structural analysis: financial crisis as an external shock

In this section the influence of the Spanish immigration history, the national economic structure and policies were highlighted. The economic crisis in Spain hit a certain institutional structure that made the labour market particularly vulnerable and led to unemployment and eventually labour emigration on the micro-level. This structure and its incumbents in the labour market and the field of labour immigration were described in their historical context in order to show how Spain became an emigration country.

In summary, due to its relatively weak economic development and performance compared to other Western European countries Spain was an emigration country until the Spanish economic boom in the early 21st century. During most of the 20th century, poverty and economic depression made Spaniards emigrate. After Spain's accession to the European Community in the late 20th century, the country's economy experienced an upswing and it became an immigration country, especially for the low- and semi-skilled workforce. During the boom phase, the *coercive* institutional isomorphism of the EU had already diffused to a considerable extent as the Zapatero government supported labour immigration, also from other EU countries, including the Eastern European nations. Subsequently, non-profit organisations and public services developed labour integration measures for immigrants, which could be reversed during the crisis to assist labour emigrants. Since the 1950s, the various Spanish governments employed migration policies according to their labour market needs.

The twofold educational system is nowadays mainly composed of Bologna-certified universities and small companies that provide training on the job. Although a small but increasing part of higher vocational training develops, universities and companies are still the incumbents of the school–to-work transition. In Spain, high-tech areas expanded during the past decades, such as in IT and the automotive sector. Yet, more efforts would have been necessary to create a knowledge-based economy that absorbs the amount of highly skilled graduates produced by the educational expansion. There were a lot of *right people*, which means qualified professionals, available on the Spanish labour market for recruiters from abroad. Even during the economic boom, mainly low and semi-skilled jobs were created in construction and services, which led to an influx of mostly low- and semi-skilled immigrants from the EU, Latin America and North Africa. The economic structure offered only limited opportunities for highly skilled professionals who became more numerous due to the educational expansion. This mismatch on the labour market led to an emigration of elites in the late 20th and early 21st century. Free labour movement in the EU facilitated this kind of labour mobility. The principle of free labour movement as well as the harmonisation efforts of the educational system within the scope of the European Higher Education Area paved the way towards creating the *right circumstances* for intra-EU labour mobility, which came into effect most obviously during the economic crisis. In this context, the *coercive isomorphism* and its diffusion to the educational institutions in Spain became evident.

Figure 3:
Status quo of the Spanish market economy and the effects of the crisis

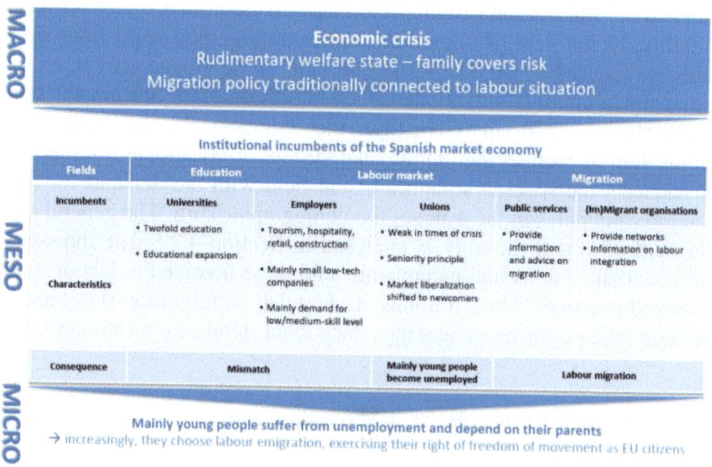

This figure was created by the author and is based on own research.

The jobs created in the boom period were mainly based on cheap credits and internal consumption. Accordingly, the global financial crisis hit the Spanish labour market hard as it stopped the availability of cheap credits abruptly and national consumption slowed down. In the institutionalised industrial relations in Spain, employees did not have the opportunity to negotiate their contracts or dismissal individually or company-based via employee representatives. Labour unions as an incumbent of the labour market represented the employees politically but were not involved in companies to defend the rights of the individual employees against their employers. The seniority principle combined with *liberalised* precarious labour contracts for newcomers led to the dismissal of mainly young people, immigrants and women. Thus, the financial crisis was an *external shock* that revealed the structural deficits of the Spanish economy. As Okolski and Salt (2015) claimed, precarious working conditions and unemployment of young graduates foster mobility and made Spain the *right place* for labour emigration. In this situation, the principle of free movement of workers and the harmonisation of educational systems in the EU, which were coercively implemented, gave young workers the opportunity and prepared them to some extent for labour mobility in the EU as summarised by Figure 3

3.2 Status quo ante demographic crisis in Germany

The following section highlights the structures leading to a high demand for skilled and highly-skilled labour in Germany, especially in view of a demographic shift. To this end, the developments in the relevant fields of migration, the labour market and the educational system in Germany are described, which form the field of mobility. In the field of migration, former immigration and labour migration policies are focused in Section 4.2.1. The field of the labour market, its sectoral structure and labour relations are described in Section 4.2.2. Section 4.2.3 outlines the educational field in Germany, the educational expansion and EU harmonisation as well as the unique dual system of vocational training. Section 4.2.4 connects the specific structure of the field with the demand for (highly-) skilled job candidates in the wake of the demographic shift. The general structure of the field of labour mobility is analysed in Section 4.2.5 that shows to what extent governance units and incumbents tend to be involved in labour migration policies and practices. Thus, it points out how labour migration flows are related to the economic performance and the educational standards in Germany.

3.2.1 Status quo ante crisis in the field of migration

Attention is drawn to migration practices and policies in the past causing the development into a labour emigration country as they have an impact on future migration decisions, flows and political frameworks. Previous labour migration and institutions created points of contact that can be resurged.

First of all, migration practices and policies in the past are targeted in the next section in order to underline to what extent governance units in Germany tend to be involved in the field of migration historically. At the same time, previous transnational recruitment relations are described to show how they affect subsequent migration policies and practices. In the wake of the German (im-

)migration history, incumbents in the field of migration developed such as migration networks and organisations that are introduced in this section and that became relevant during the recent phase of transnational recruitment.

3.2.1.1 From German emigration to guest worker immigration

The following part shows how Germany changed from an emigration country at the end of the 19th century to an immigration country in the 1950s. It is highlighted how the German government developed bilateral agreements on labour recruitment to satisfy the labour demand in Germany. Additionally, the next section describes the special role of Spanish guest workers in terms of labour integration and its contribution to the recent immigration wave from Spain. The Spanish guest workers influenced the way in which Spanish immigrants are perceived in Germany. Additionally, they created incumbents in the field of migration, such as Spanish networks and migrant organisations.

Germany had become an emigration country in the wake of violent conflicts and starvation during the 1950s. As a result of political instability, constant wars, religious conflicts and famines, Germany had been an emigration country for centuries. Between 1820 and 1920, six million Germans emigrated, most of them to the USA. Emigration decreased when the industrialisation brought economic success to the German Empire. At that time, more foreigners immigrated to Germany as compared to Germans who emigrated, because it was relatively easy for foreign workers to find employment in the booming centres of the coal and steel industry.

Before and during World Wars I and II, many people fled the country, mainly to neighbouring European states, the United States and Latin America. During World War II, the forced employment of foreigners was a measurement to provide the necessary workforce in agriculture and the heavy industry.

After 1945, Germany was characterised by immigration, which affected the population structure sustainably. This development was caused by the forced mobility of different groups of people, like refugees, people expelled from their homeland through territorial exchange and other so-called displaced persons. At this point already, the number of people rose who lived in Germany but had transnational relations to other (European) countries due to relatives and cultural connections abroad (see Bundeszentrale für politische Bildung, 2005). Since 1955, resettlers from diasporic communities in the Soviet Union also raised the number of German citizens with an immigration background.

Economically, the post-war years were dominated by the reconstruction of the country, but in the 1950s the economy started to boom, which was called the *German economic miracle*. Germany became a booming economy showing growth rates of 12.1%. This increased prosperity led to higher consumption and a flourishing agricultural and industrial sector in Germany. Due to automatisation entering the industry, especially low-skilled workers were in demand for the production lines. The unemployment rate decreased from 11% to less than 1% in 1961. In order to deal with upcoming labour shortages, the federal government recruited temporary foreign workers. During this boom Germany introduced a programme of controlled labour immigration for the first time (ibid.).

In 1955, the first *Agreement on the Recruitment and Placement of Workers* was negotiated with Italy. Soon afterwards, further agreements followed with Greece and Spain in 1960, Turkey in 1961, Morocco in 1963, Portugal in 1964, Tunisia in 1965, and Yugoslavia in 1968. These are more commonly known as *guest worker agreements,* which implies the temporal limitation of the recruitment programme and its labour contracts. This opportunity was seized by 14 million foreigners, who were mainly employed as unskilled and semi-skilled workers in industrial companies, working shifts on the assembly line (see Herbert, 2001). Spanish workers were among the first to be recruited and the (labour) integration of Spanish guest workers was assessed very positively in Germany (see Thränhardt, 2005).

On the one hand, the guest worker agreements offered many relatively well-paid jobs that did not require special training or even language skills. Hence, the guest worker agreements offered an opportunity to make money for everybody who was willing to immigrate. In Germany, foreigners received the same labour contracts and employment rights as the domestic employees, which were significantly above the standards in their home countries. On the other hand, the lack of training, non-recognition of foreign certifications and language deficits limited the guest workers to the lowest wage categories and the most unattractive tasks. By doing jobs that Germans considered unattractive, they did not compete with the German core labour force at times of labour shortages. Instead, they supported the upward mobility of the German core workforce to more qualified positions (see Bundeszentrale für politische Bildung, 2005). Summarizing, the guest worker recruitment offered a chance for the recruited workforce, because earnings were relatively high, especially when compared to the salaries in their home countries, while skill requirements were low. At the same time, the recruited foreigners supported an upward mobility of the German core workforce, which increased the wealth and status of the domestic employees.

Immigration of guest workers was stopped abruptly in 1973, when the oil crisis involved recession and price shocks. On November 23, 1973, the recruitment ban (Anwerbestopp) became effective. Although the guest worker agreements were designed to offer time-limited employment opportunities, 3 million guest workers did not return to their home countries. Some of them stayed, fearing that once they had left, they would not be able to return. Those who did not return to their home countries settled down in Germany and made use of the right of family reunification (see Herbert, 2001).

Furthermore, a substantial number of Spaniards, who had come as guest workers stayed in Germany. One year after the guest worker agreement had been signed Germany had already become the second most important destination country for Spanish emigrants in Europe (see Thränhardt, 2005, p. 95). The

Spanish immigrants turned out to be the best integrated ethnic group of guest workers. A prominent indicator of integration are the intermarriage-rates, which show the proportion of Spaniards married to partners from other nationalities. Spaniards displayed a very high intermarriage rate of 81.7 % in 1997, which is far above the rates of the other big immigrant groups in the same year (Italian: 42,2%; Turkish 13,5%). According to Thränhardt (2005, p. 97f.), intermarriage rates are a suitable indicator to measure the ability of a long-term, transgenerational assimilation because the descendants are cultural natives of the immigration country. During the interviews with experts from institutions of the labour market, migration and politics it became even clear that many of those are cultural natives of both countries. Among the interviewed experts working for migrant organisations, the government, public services, companies and recruitment there was a significant number of second generation immigrants, who were bilingual and studied and worked both in Spain and Germany.

This is proof of the educational success of the second generation of Spaniards in Germany. Additionally, it underlines the advantage of the high proportion of Spanish children taking part in voluntary Spanish classes besides their compulsory education (which was at 97.2% in North Rhine Westphalia in 2001) (ibid., 2005, p. 106).

But it was not only the second generation, but also the Spanish guest workers themselves who were very successful in their labour market integration when compared to other nationalities, although their qualifications and language skills were low. Around 70% of the Spanish immigrants needed to retrain, among all ethnic groups of guest workers they were best able to make use of promotion opportunities within the companies they worked for (see Breitenbach, 1985, p. 73f.).

Generally, the Spanish immigrants showed the highest integration skills of all guest worker groups. These positive experiences made with Spanish immigrants in Germany provide strong arguments in favour of the recruitment of Spaniards. This applies, above all, in the wake of the educational expansion in Spain, which is likely to improve the individual opportunities of labour integration of new immigrants due to their skills and knowledge.

Thus, in the 1950s, Germany became an immigration country, when the government developed bilateral agreements on labour recruitment to meet the increased labour demand, which was created by the economic boom. The guest worker agreements were negotiated with several countries, however the Spanish guest workers did remarkably well when it comes to integration into the labour market and the German society. This is why the Spanish immigrants enjoy an outstanding reputation with German labour market institutions and the German governance units. The guest workers and their descendants who have meanwhile been established in Germany created Spanish networks and migrant organisations. These Spaniards in Germany became important for the new Spanish labour immigrants in the 21st century, because they provide assistance for labour integration (see Chapter 4-7).

3.2.1.2 From a non-immigration country to international recruitment

This section shows that labour migration also became a policy instrument in times of unemployment in Germany. It describes how governance units and incumbents of the field of the labour market and migration were involved in supporting these policies.

In the 1990s, Germany suffered from relatively high unemployment rates, which were caused by global recession as well as the structural transition of Eastern Germany from a centrally planned economy to a market economy after reunification (see Hinrichs & Giebel-Felten, 2002). Thus, after the collapse of the Soviet Union in 1990 labour immigration was very low, while especially the resettlers from the former Soviet Union immigrated to Germany. Instead, labour emigration was fostered in the 1990s, so emigration rates have constantly hovered between 600,000 and 700,000 per year. Ever since, immigration rates have been the reason why the population size remained relatively constant at around 80 million, while mortality rates exceeded the birth rates and emigration rates did not decline (see Bundesamt für Migration und Flüchtlinge, 2013, p. 13). Public employment agencies supported the outgoing professionals, as was stated by the interview partners from the public employment service Bundesagentur für Arbeit (BA). Interview partner 2 of the BA, who works in international services and representation abroad, said:

> *Well, in the last decades our focus was Outgoing. That means, our task was mainly to retain German citizens into employment abroad.*

At the beginning of the 20th century, the first policies were introduced again to use labour immigration and international recruitment in order to attract highly-skilled employees for the German IT-sector. These specialists were considered extremely relevant for the knowledge economy in the 21st century. Therefore, the government of Gerhard Schröder introduced the Green Card for IT specialists. Between 2000 and 2003, 14,876 Green Cards were awarded, which was less than previously expected due to the declining market in the IT sector during these years (see Bundesamt für Migration und Flüchtlinge, 2013).

Nevertheless, at the same time, Germany did not allow labour market entry for the new Eastern European member states from 2004 until 2011. In this period the world-wide economic crisis of 2007 also affected Germany. Under difficult economic conditions labour immigration, especially from less prosperous countries, was considered to be a threat to German prosperity causing wage dumping, and erosion of social and employment standards. In accordance with EU law, Germany had to allow Eastern EU citizens to its labour market since 2011 due to the coercive isomorphism that spreads from the EU level to the member states. In the meantime, Germany had recovered from the crisis. Its economy started to boom and the demographic shift led to a declining workforce. Hence, the German labour market finally opened up for immigration and international recruitment.

Along this line, the action programme for the contribution of labour migration for securing skilled labour of 2008 (="*Beitrag der Arbeitsmigration zur Sicherung der Fachkräftebasis*") was developed along with related changes of employment regulations (=*Beschäftigungsverordnung*). These were introduced to facilitate labour immigration and were relevant further steps to open up the labour market for the immigration of skilled labour (see Loeffelholz, 2013). These developments were the first steps towards a new period of labour recruitment policies and practices. They show one of the main characteristics of German migration politics, which is steered labour migration depending on the economic situation.

In this context, Spanish professionals came into focus once again due to the good experiences made with the Spanish guest workers in the past (see Montero-Lange, 2014). They themselves and their descendants employed at public institutions and private companies offer language skills and contacts, which facilitate the recruitment as described by and confirmed in the interviews conducted with experts (see also Chapter 6).

In summary, labour immigration and emigration has traditionally been a policy instrument to adjust labour market needs in Germany. Spaniards are perceived as extraordinarily suitable for labour recruitment and social integration in the German society. In the past decades, the Spaniards established in Germany formed networks and organisations offering support for the recruitment of Spaniards due to their cultural skills, language skills, etc.

3.2.2 Status quo ante crisis of the labour market

The next section highlights the most important sectors in Germany and their high demand for skilled and highly-skilled labour force to show why professionals are recruited from abroad during times of economic boom and a demographic shift. Additionally, it describes the role of trade associations and labour unions in industrial relations.

3.2.2.1 Sectoral structure

This part shows that Germany is an export-oriented market economy with an important industrial sector which has made great efforts to keep pace with the modern knowledge economy in a globalized world.

Although industrialisation took place relatively late in Germany, the German economy caught up rapidly with the pioneers, Great Britain and France. As early as in 1910, Germany was among the leading industrialised nations together with the UK and the US.

This fast industrialisation process was supported by an alliance between industrial entrepreneurs and aristocratic landowners. The production of coal, steel, machines and machine tools, chemicals, electronic equipment, ships and, subsequently, motor vehicles was emphasized during the late 19th and the 20th centuries. Well-organized business, labour and farm associations collaborated and created the specific structure of the German Coordinated Market Economy (CME). The strong core of the industrial sector outlasted the two world wars (see Hall & Soskice, 2001). Nowadays, Germany remains a global leader in manufacturing and technological innovation. Therefore, Germany is Europe's most strongly industrialised country and generated global players originating in industries such as automotive manufacturing, machinery, precision equipment, heavy automotive, technology and software. The German industry contributed 28.1% to the country's total GDP, and employed 24.6% of the entire labour force (see Statistisches Bundesamt, 2018a). The German industry is famous for its quality products which maintain their high standard by incremental innovations (see Hall & Soskice, 2001).

The country is traditionally strong in the field of industrial products and displays high export rates in mechanical engineering and automobiles. Germany is the world's fourth-largest producer and the largest exporter of cars. Out of the 500 most important stock market listed companies, 37 are headquartered in Germany. Many of these belong to the industrial sector, and often they are automotive companies or related to the automotive industry, like Volkswagen, Daimler, BMW, Bosch, MAN, Siemens, BASF, Thyssen Krupp. There are also several global players in the pharmaceutical sector, like Bayer and Merck. In the clothing and footwear sector, Adidas and Puma count among the world's largest stock market listed companies. Germany also produces household and consumer goods for the international market (e.g. the Henkel AG & company). Besides, German companies are strong in the electronics and energy sector, such as Infineon or E.ON (see Forbes, 2018).

The German service sector accounted for 71.1% of the country's GDP and employed 73.8% of the national labour force (see Statistisches Bundesamt, 2018b). Thanks to its highly skilled labour force it is ranked third in the provision of services among all exporting nations. Additionally, it is ranked first in skill-intensive services. This includes technical services and IT-services like the global player SAP. Furthermore, financial and insurance services belong to these skill-intensive services, which are provided by the global players Commerzbank and Deutsche Bank or Munich Re and Allianz (see Forbes, 2018).

This part showed that Germany is an export-oriented market economy with an important industrial sector producing high quality products. Additionally, it described the development towards a modern knowledge economy providing skill-intensive services. These high quality products are developed by incremental innovations, which require a (highly-) qualified workforce and a long-term cooperation among stakeholders of the labour market, which is addressed in the next section.

3.2.2.2 Incumbents: Companies and unions

The following section describes why the planning horizon of German companies is rather medium to long-term and outlines its implications for the role of qualifications and skills on the labour market.

Corporate banks or corporate shares traditionally secure companies´ financing in CMEs. In the coordinated market economy in Germany, the cooperation between companies is supported by institutional settings, which are established either by the state or by other organizations (see Hall & Soskice, 2001, p. 22ff). Therefore, the German companies are usually not entirely dependent on publicly available financial resources. Stakeholders and their capital are relatively "patient", which allows for investments in projects that generate returns only in the long run (see Sachverständigenrat für Wirtschaft, 2013; Thelen, 2004). On the one hand, this allows for the development of high quality products by incremental innovation. On the other hand, in times of economic recession, German firms are generally supportive to subsidies so as to avoid losing skilled workers during economic hardship. The same was true during the economic crisis, when companies and the government subsidized short-term work in industry to avoid layoffs due to the poor order situation. This cooperative atmosphere is supported by the internal structure of the firms. The top management has to take the interests of the stakeholders into account. This means that decision-making in Germany is based on a consensus between supervisory boards, including employee representatives, major shareholders, managers as well as major suppliers and customers (see Hall & Soskice, 2001).

Industrial relations in Germany tend to be strictly regulated as compared to other countries. The state provides protection for employees by employment laws that cover dismissal, health, safety at work, holidays and working hours. There are also relatively powerful labour unions and employee representatives. In Germany, employee representatives are part of the advisory boards and therefore involved in major decisions taken by the top management. On the German labour market there are labour unions that are organized in sectors and regions under nationwide umbrella associations. They are strong employee representatives and powerful socio-political incumbents able to negotiate with employers' associations and politics. These protect and defend the rights of all employers.

However, in recent years a liberalisation and flexibilisation has taken place with regard to labour contracts, which has involved more temporary employment and less job security, especially since 2003. This was when the government of Chancellor Gerhard Schröder introduced the labour market reforms in the framework of the Agenda 2010. The very positive development of the German labour market is commonly attributed to a favourable situation of the global economy and increased competitiveness of German companies due to these labour market reforms (see Petz, 2013).

Thus, the economic crisis, which peaked in June 2009 in Germany, affected the positive economic and labour market situation only briefly and not sustainably (see Sachverständigenrat für Wirtschaft, 2013, p. 302). Since 2005, the share of the working population has risen constantly and has peaked at 43.87 million people in January 2017 (see Statista, 2018a; Zeit Online, 2017). Hence, the number of employees liable to pay social insurance contributions rose to 31 million (see Vollmer, 2015, p. 11), while the number of unemployed citizens declined from 4.86 million to 2.9 million between 2005 and 2014. In 2016, the unemployment rate dropped below the mark of 2.7 million for the first time since 1991 (see Zeit Online, 2017). The general unemployment rate fell to 6.1% (see Statista, 2018a) in December 2016, although there are relatively high regional differences (see Vollmer, 2015, p. 13). Owing to the positive economic performance, the economic crisis was overcome quickly and labour demand in Germany has been on a constant high level since 2010; labour market experts predicted that it will continue to rise in the future (Sachverständigenrat für Wirtschaft, 2013, p. 312). The flourishing economy in Germany was likely to attract workers from other EU countries while freedom of movement is granted.

Not only the demand for workers but also the demand for skills and qualification requirements rose over the past few decades. The percentage of employees in the different economic sectors changed significantly. While the number of employees in the primary and the secondary sector decreased, the relevance of the service sector increased significantly. Business-related services gained particular importance including, for instance, market research, financial services or consulting. Therefore, the general trend was towards knowledge-based occupations that require increasingly high skills and qualifications (see Allmendinger & Ebner, 2006, p. 232). This development indicates that Germany has evolved towards a knowledge-based economy with a relatively high demand for highly qualified professionals, while the demand for low-skilled workers diminished (see Vollmer, 2015, p. 13).

The developments, cooperation and labour contracts are rather based on medium to long-term relations. Labour and trade unions are an important incumbent in the labour market, therefore employment protection is relatively high compared to more liberal market economies such as the UK. Also, qualifications and skills requirements of German companies tend to be high so that they are able to produce high quality products and successive innovations in Germany.

3.2.3 Status quo ante crisis in the field of education

The following part shows the unique German educational system, which provides and demands professionals that are highly specialized and standardized. It describes how a broad range of incumbents in the educational field created a variety of defined skills, knowledge and competences related to certain job profiles.

3.2.3.1 Educational expansion and its effects

In the following section, the educational expansion and the Europeanisation of the German system of higher education is described, while taking into account unintended side-effects that complicate the school–to-work transition and the match of graduates in the German labour market.

As in other developed countries, a significant educational expansion has taken place in Germany since the 1950s. In 1960, only 6% of all school leavers obtained a university entrance qualification and this number included hardly any women. More recently, in 2011, 35% of school leavers had acquired a university entrance qualification (see Geißler, 2014). Consequently, during the same period the enrolment at universities grew tremendously from 6% to 23%. In addition, enrolment grew from 2% to 15% at the universities of applied sciences. According to OECD research (see Schleicher, 2012), an estimated 42% of young people in Germany were expected to enter academic study programmes, and an estimated 30% of young people were expected to graduate in 2012. This was, however, still below the OECD average of 62% entering studies and 39% graduating from academic study programmes. Although the number of university graduates rose significantly, the OECD constantly criticised that other OECD countries yielded notably more university graduates than Germany (ibid., p. 2).

Nonetheless, a university degree is ever less bound to guarantee a successful career in Germany and in other developed countries, which has been described as the elevator effect by Beck (see Beck, 1986, p. 122). This effect explains the paradox of simultaneous devaluation and revaluation of university degrees as a result of the educational expansion. On the one hand, a university diploma is an increasingly important prerequisite for a career, but on the other hand, the value of university diplomas decreased in view of the greater number of university graduates entering the labour market. In several modern societies potential employees nowadays need to obtain a university degree to take up certain careers that did not require a university diploma in previous generations. In more and more areas tertiary education has therefore become a prerequisite for labour market entry, while it is less and less a guarantee for a promising career.

Additionally, the number of graduates in the humanities, arts and social sciences also rose along with the increasing number of university graduates, hence in a discipline that does not provide a concrete professional profile. Therefore, the share of the population obtaining a degree offering unspecified skills has increased , which makes the transition from education into the labour market more difficult; this will be described more specifically in Chapter 5. Furthermore, ever since the implementation of the Bologna process, which aimed at harmonizing the European Higher Education Area, employers have faced some irritations, according to their own statements. While the "Diplom" was replaced with the "Master", and the "Bachelor" degree was newly introduced, it turned out more difficult for employers to assess the meaning of these new certificates, as has been stated by the interviewed employers and labour unions from all fields and sectors (see also

Chapters 7). German recruiter 1, who worked in the human resource (HR) department of a big multinational corporation before being self-employed in this field, said in 2015:

> *Ever since the Bachelor and Master degrees have been introduced, the titles have become incomprehensible. The variety of titles seems to be unlimited and all of them have fancy names, but you can hardly guess what the titles stand for. They are extremely specialised and it is even hard to find out what the major subject of this degree is.*

So, the *coercive isomorphism* of the educational system's EU harmonisation provoked irritations on the national level.

This passage described the educational expansion, which brought about an increased amount of degree holders on the German labour market. At the same time, the degrees were de- and revaluated, which involved decreased career opportunities for university graduates. In a coercive process the German system of higher education was harmonized, which weakened the signalling effect of university diplomas. Both the elevator effect and the transition to the Bachelor and Master system complicate labour market entry for university graduates.

3.2.3.2 Dual system

The next section underlines the importance of standardised and specialised job profiles obtained by vocational training, the dual system, which combines theoretical learning and practical skill development. It addresses the shortage of professionals meeting these requirements for the job profiles of the dual system and the difficulty of recruiting workforce from abroad for these jobs.

However, Germany´s educational landscape is complemented with a huge sector of vocational training, which combines practical and theoretical skill development. This type of skilled labour is trained in the country's dual apprenticeship system, which is operated jointly by the social partners and chambers for certain trades, crafts or professions. The involvement of employers in developing training curricula ensures that apprentices acquire the required skills and that the certifications received upon graduation match a specific portfolio of skills, which is transferable and can easily be recognised by employers (see Crouch & Streeck, 1997). The number of trainees graduated from vocational training has remained relatively stable since 1995 at around 13-14% (see Geißler, 2014; Schleicher, 2012), while the OECD average is at around 10%. Furthermore, an estimated 21% of young people in Germany were expected to take up a vocational training programme, which was 4 percentage points above the OECD average in 2012 (see Schleicher, 2012).

Overall, vocational training in the dual apprenticeship system is still the most promising education in Germany to avoid unemployment during a person's professional life as it strengthens employability (see Heidemann, 2012, p. 11; Kettner, 2012, p. 63; OECD, 2017). This is why many of the shortage occupations in Germany require a degree of vocational training. Demand in these professions increased due to the decrease of citizens at employable age combined with the educational expansion, which raised the proportion of university graduates (see Beck, 1986). However, the unique educational system including a variety of specialized and standardized training courses containing practical hours, complicates the recognition of foreign competences matching a German job profile (Chapter 6). The interviewed German recruiter 1 said:

> *The major difference is that the dual system in Germany does not exist in other countries. That means, in Germany there are qualified professionals that are practically trained, while elsewhere they are theoretically educated. The different education also leads to different job profiles.*

This diversified educational system is one of the reasons why the percentage of young people between 15-29 years who are not in education, employment or training (NEET) is at 12% only and did not increase during the global recession in Germany (see Schleicher, 2012, p. 2). Moreover, Germany is the only country in which unemployment declined on all educational levels in recent years.

Germany shows a structured and standardized educational and training system, which produces a variety of concrete specialized job profiles. Therefore, educational certificates have a strong signalling effect on the German labour market. German employees are trained to develop specialized skills, while companies rely on their highly qualified staff to fabricate high quality products. The German government supports cooperation between companies as well as between companies and educational institutions. This increases the matching of degrees and job profiles on the labour market in Germany. Also, the collaboration between science and companies is institutionalized, which makes a fruitful transfer of technology possible (see Hall & Soskice, 2001).

This kind of educational landscape and cooperation between educational institutions and other actors of the labour market is conducive to the high quality of products as it is grounded on formalized qualification requirements on all levels. Therefore, Germany has a relatively high share of qualified specialists among its entire labour force when compared to other OECD countries; the share of qualified employees among the labour force was at 86% in Germany in 2016 and is estimated to rise in the future (see Wehrhahn & Sandner Le Gall, 2011). This is not only true on high-, but also on the medium-skilled levels both in practical and theoretical terms. Thus, companies in Germany enjoy a comparative advantage in incremental innovation and diversified quality production (DQP) (see Hall & Soskice, 2001). This means firms continuously improve products through permanent though minor alterations and, in this way, achieve high quality standards and a lead in technology, often in niche markets (see Crouch & Streeck,

1997). This strategy requires a workforce equipped with the necessary industry or company specific skills to understand products and processes and thus detect areas for improvement. As an incentive for workers to specialise, job tenures are long and employment protection is rather high.

Traditionally, German companies were prepared to invest in training their staff because they were interested in committing their staff permanently to the company so that training investments paid off in the long or medium run (Hall & Soskice, 2001). Generally, Germany displays a high demand for skilled employees due to the country's focus on the production of high quality goods and knowledge-based services. This demand is met by a unique educational system providing highly specialized and standardized education that leads to formalized job profiles on all levels of qualification. Nevertheless, the high demand for skilled and highly-skilled labour is a favourable precondition for joining the global war for talent.

The past section highlighted the role of the German dual system producing standardised and specialised job profiles by vocational training. These combine theoretical learning and practical skill development in order to provide a qualified workforce able to fulfil practical tasks. Employers, employers' associations, labour unions, trade associations and the Chamber of Industry and Commerce are incumbents of this kind of education and develop job profiles cooperatively. Due to the educational expansion professionals in crafts and trades have become particularly demanded in the knowledge economy since more people chose to study.

3.2.4 Internal crisis: demographic change in Germany

The neighbouring fields of intra-EU labour mobility show an increased demand for skilled and highly-skilled professionals in the wake of the boom of the knowledge-based economy in Germany and first attempts to open up the German labour market for the immigration of professionals. At the same time, labour market experts and demographers predict a declining availability of labour force in Germany.

As in most other European countries, a significant change in size and structure of the population took place in Germany, which is now most commonly described as *shrinking* and *ageing*. A country's population size and structure depend on birth rates and mortality as well as on immigration and emigration. The first two items are considered natural population dynamics, while the latter two are called population movements.

The demographic change is the result of social change influenced by institutional transformation processes such as changing values, norms and behaviours. Due to a modification in the socio-cultural framework the demographic structure has changed sustainably (see Wehrhahn & Sandner Le Gall, 2011).

One of the major reasons for this development was the implementation of modern contraceptives in the 20th century, which reduced birth rates from 2.5 children per woman in the 1960s to 1.5 children per woman today (see Bundesamt für Migration und Flüchtlinge, 2013; Statistisches Bundesamt, 2018c). The increased number of childless adults along with the decreasing number of large families having three or more children and the rising age of women giving birth for the first time, which is currently at 29 years, are indicators of the changing fertility in Germany (see Statistisches Bundesamt, 2015). Additionally, life expectancy rose permanently over the past few decades due to increased prosperity, medical progress and improved sanitary conditions. Thus the current life expectancy was predicted to be 77.7 years for newborn males and 82.8 years for newborn females (see Statista, 2018b).

Labour market researchers describe various effects of the demographic change. In order to examine the consequences for the labour market the most relevant age group of people between 20-64 years has been in the focus. Labour market researchers claim that the current and future shrinking and ageing of the population will challenge the national economy because the baby boomer generation of the 1950s and 1960s has now reached retirement age. A great number of employees will soon leave the labour market and the following generations showing low birth rates are not able to fill this gap. Especially, the lower birth rates recorded in the 1970s and 1980s cause an imbalance between those who leave and those who enter the labour market (see Statistisches Bundesamt, 2018c). The overall potential of the labour force is currently about 45 million people. This number includes the working population, the number of unemployed and the so-called *hidden reserve*. The latter covers people, who are jobless but do not show in the unemployment statistics (see Vollmer, 2015, p. 16).

However, labour demand is not only influenced by the population development. It is also influenced by labour market participation and the achievements of the educational system, etc. (see Heidemann, 2012, p. 11), while labour supply depends on economic trends and determines the number of employees (filled labour demand) as well as the number of vacancies provided by the companies (unfilled labour demand) (see Kettner, 2012, p. 63). Generally, there is a great willingness among employers to hire employees due to the good economic situation. Therefore, as result of the shrinking and ageing population different fears arise. The crucial problems debated in this context are the collapse of the tax-funded social security system and the economic slowdown due to the limited availability of labour. With regard to the social security system, especially the pension scheme is concerned when proportionally less tax contributors have to compensate for a growing number of beneficiaries. In an ageing society this is certainly problematic for the health care system, which has to face increasingly more people in need of care. It also affects the social infrastructure and the field of basic public services. While schools are closed due to decreasing birth rates, there is a higher need for senior residencies and day care facilities (see De Lange et al., 2014, p. 189). Thus, not all sectors are affected by the current labour situation to the same extent. There has been a shift of skills in demand on the

German labour market as a result of the increasing mechanisation and globalisation. Additionally, occupational tasks have changed in the economic sectors, which must be ascribed to the fact that the manufacturing activities, but also jobs in civil service decrease, while business-related and knowledge-based skills have reached historically unprecedented values (see Bundesministerium für Arbeit und Soziales, 2013; Heidemann, 2012, p. 14). Therefore, not only have the skill-intensive sectors become more and more important, but the skill level in demand in the companies is also rising. Generally, four levels of qualification can be distinguished: academic employees, employees with advanced further vocational training, employees with a vocational degree, and employees without a professional degree. There is an increasing demand for university graduates and a decreasing demand for low-skilled workers, while those who have completed some kind of vocational training are most demanded on the labour market.

Predictions are different for the development of the labour supply in the upcoming years. Although various studies unfurl different scenarios, all of them agree on that the amount of university graduates will rise in the next few years, which is underlined by the increasing number of university entrants (see Bundesministerium für Arbeit und Soziales, 2011, p. 29). Yet, the highest demand for employees will remain on the level of vocational degrees. However, there is a general demand for professionals in Germany, which triggered a new wave of politically controlled labour recruitment, as is described in Section 4.2.

3.2.5 Germany as the right place for labour immigration

In this section the status quo ante demographic crisis was highlighted in order to show how Germany became the right place for labour mobility. Figure 4 shows that the demographic shift has a high impact in Germany due to the demand for skilled and highly-skilled professionals. Furthermore, it shows that unions and migrant organisations create resources for labour immigrants.

As a result of the boom and the shrinking population Germany opened up for labour immigration and recruitment again. Traditionally, Germany has been steering labour migration since the 1950s in order to meet labour market demands. During the economic boom in the 1950s and 1960s, the so-called guest worker agreements represented the first attempt of politically controlled labour immigration, which was well-received. At the end of the 20th century legal opportunities for labour immigration became rare due to a recession, instead governance units fostered labour emigration, among those the public employment service (BA). Thus, Germany has a long tradition and much experience in steered labour migration, which is adjusted to the economic situation. While the effects of the economic crisis were still noticeable in Germany, access was denied to Eastern EU citizens. As late as in 2011, they were granted freedom of movement for workers due to the *coercive isomorphism* in the EU.

Since the beginning of the 21st century, the order level of German quality products has been positive and exports are flourishing. In view of the economic boom in Germany and the decreasing population at an employable age, Germany has a high labour demand and low unemployment rate. Especially skilled and highly skilled professionals are in demand, above all in the industry and the health care sector. The mix of declining birth rates during the past decades and the higher willingness to recruit led to a lack of professionals in recent years.

Due to the shrinking population at an employable age and the grown qualification requirements it has become more difficult for employers in specific sectors, such as MINT-subjects and health care professions, and in certain regions, such as Southern Germany and various other areas, to find suitable job candidates.

Figure 4: Economic boom and demographic shift in Germany

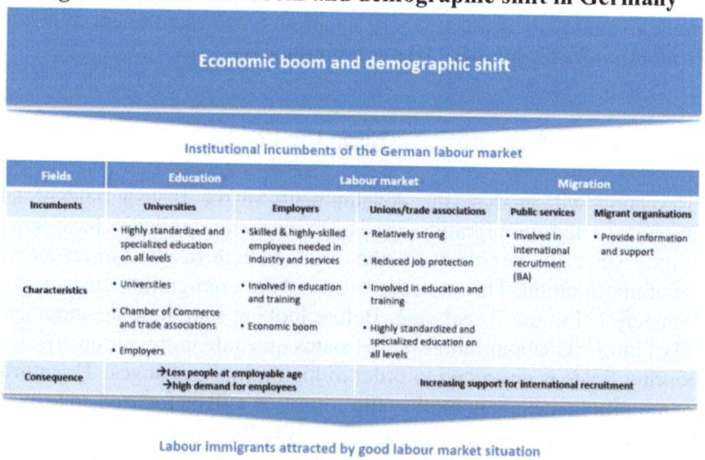

Figure 4 shows the impact of the demographic crisis and its influence on labour immigration while taking the characteristics of the field of education, the labour market and migration into account and highlighting their incumbents. This figure was created by the author and is based on own research.

The German labour force itself includes an increasing amount of university graduates and a very high amount of skilled and highly-skilled professionals, who represent around 86% of the entire labour force. Germany has a highly structured, standardized and specialized educational system on all levels. The latter provides educational certificates, which have a high signalling effect in the labour market and match defined and specialized job profiles. As there is an institutionalized cooperation between companies and educational institutions, education in Germany tends to be more practical and oriented to the labour market and the jobs it provides than in other countries. This educational structure complicates labour market entry for newcomers, especially those from abroad. Consequently, the *right people* for labour immigration to Germany are likely to be skilled and at least willing to acquire special and practical skills. Generally, Germany can be considered to be the *right place* for labour immigrants, who obtain the skills in demand. In this context, it is easier for EU citizens to immigrate due to the freedom of movement for workers, which diffused to the member states by *coercive isomorphism*. However, the coercive process of harmonisation in higher education already caused irritations on the national labour market, which are likely to aggravate on the international level. The status quo ante in the German market economy that led to the demographic crisis is summarised in Figure 4.

The Southern European member states suffered extremely from decreased consumption and unemployment, while Germany showed increasingly favourable labour market conditions. For Spaniards, in particular, there is also a vast potential that can be exploited to assist in labour integration and recruitment to create the *right circumstances* for intra-EU labour mobility.

3.3 Status quo ante immigration crisis in the UK

This section will analyse the developments in the British field of labour mobility before the immigration crisis. Immigration policies have changed significantly since the beginning of the 2000s, which resulted in an enormous increase of immigration. This increase triggered the immigration crisis in the UK and ultimately led to the Brexit vote. Before looking into these developments in the field of intra-EU labour mobility, the status quo ante immigration crisis of the neighbouring fields is described in order to highlight the changes. Therefore, the fields of migration, the labour market and education will be focused on to examine changes leading to the new policy agenda of the British immigration crisis and finally to the BREXIT vote. The structures of these fields provide insights into the conditions of intra-EU mobility, which show why the UK was the *right place* for immigration. In Section 4.3.1, immigration from the Commonwealth and the EU is highlighted. Section 4.3.2 deals with the labour demand in the British sectors and the open labour market. The educational system, its internationalisation and its high numbers of student immigrants are outlined in Section 4.3.3. Structural arrangements of these fields provide insights into the conditions of intra-EU mobility, which show why the UK was the *right place* for immigration (Section 4.3.5), before the immigration crisis emerged (Section 4.3.4).

3.3.1 Status quo ante crisis in the field of migration

The following section highlights the long immigration history of the UK, which is closely connected with its colonial history. It shows that immigration policies for citizens of the Commonwealth have become stricter during the 20th century, while the UK has become more open to labour immigration from EU countries in its Europeanisation process. In more recent history, Polish immigrants form a considerable and visible group of labour migrants in the UK. During the last decades the UK developed immigration policies closely adjusted to the British labour market needs. However, these efforts to create labour market adjusted policy measures were undermined by freedom of movement for workers, which caused unprecedented immigration flows leading to an immigration crisis.

3.3.1.1 Field of labour immigration and the Commonwealth

The next part shows that the UK was especially attractive for citizens from the Commonwealth due to the historic migration relation between these countries. While the UK was open to citizens from the Commonwealth until the middle of the twentieth century, it became more and more restrictive and focused on labour recruitment.

As early as in 1830, wealthy British families brought workers from India to the United Kingdom (see BBC News UK, 2018). Britain had experienced migration already before the middle of the twentieth century, but usually inflow was low and temporary. For a long period, people from the former British colonies enjoyed privileged treatment with regard to immigration, but only a small number of people born in the former colonies of Australia, New Zealand, Canada and South Africa actually immigrated to Britain. Thus, they were more or less insignificant in demographic terms, yet had an economic and cultural impact. All citizens from the Commonwealth were free to enter the United Kingdom without any visa requirements (see Hansen, 2000), as the British Nationality Act of 1948 granted the subjects of the British Empire the right to live and work in the UK. Therefore, Commonwealth citizens were not subject to immigration control; the Home Office estimated the net influx from the former colonies at about 472,000 immigrants between January 1955 and June 1962, which were mostly young males (see Green, 2006). Due to the high number of migrants the conservative government started to control immigration in 1962. At the beginning, the Labour Party criticized these measures as being driven by populism and racism, but the effects of the right to family reunion became obvious when the Labour Party formed the government in 1964. On average, two to four family members followed each immigrant. Thus, in 1965, the Labour Party gave up on the idea of open borders and intensified immigration controls (see Hansen, 2000). Consequently, stricter immigration controls for Commonwealth citizens followed from 1962 onwards.

In fact, the new immigration controls resulted only in a moderate decrease of immigration from the Commonwealth. In the 1960s, around 75,000 citizens from the former colonies were admitted to the UK every year. In 1971, the conservative government decided to treat the citizens from Commonwealth countries just like all other foreign citizens. Only people with British grandparents still enjoyed privileges concerning immigration. On average, around 72,000 Commonwealth immigrants per year were admitted to the country in the 1970s, and about 54,000 per year in the 1980s and at the beginning of the 1990s. The measure to cut the privileges of Commonwealth citizens with regard to immigration entered into force in 1973, when the United Kingdom opened its borders to labour force from the European Economic Area (EEA) (see BBC News UK, 2018; Green, 2014).

Hence, since the UK opened its labour market to EEA citizens in 1973 restrictive politics towards immigrants from third countries have continued both under Labour and conservative governments. The aim was to reduce immigration in general and to decrease the number of asylum seekers in particular. Nevertheless, from 1998 onwards, numbers began to rise substantially. In 1998, net migration from the Commonwealth leaped to 82,000 and continued to grow, peaking at 156,000 in 2004, before it started to decline again (see Green, 2014).

In order to steer immigration according to the economic needs a major change was introduced to immigration politics in the UK in 2002, which was called the Nationality, Immigration and Asylum Act. Several measures were implemented to favour the immigration of highly skilled professionals to boost the knowledge-intensive British service economy (see Cerna, 2011). This was called the Highly Skilled Migrant Programme (HSMP), which was replaced by a five-tier immigration law in 2008 (see Hopkins & Levy, 2012). The law's aim was to secure the necessary labour force for the British knowledge economy, while a generation of low birth rates had reached employable age, and the generation of high birth rates was about to retire. Before the introduction of the five-tier immigration law 80 different paths to immigration had existed. The first tier regulates the immigration of highly skilled people. The second tier legalises the immigration of skilled workforce, such as nurses, teachers or engineers. The third tier covers the regulations for low- and semi-skilled workers, although this tier has never been practically implemented. The fourth tier applies to students, and the fifth one to *working holidaymakers*, sports professionals and musicians. While immigration policies were more and more made to match the labour demand in the UK, work and formal study became the main reasons for immigration and increased enormously, while asylum seeking decreased significantly (see Green, 2014).

Thus, on the one hand, in the phase of on-going Europeanisation the UK became more and more restrictive towards third-country nationals and increased the focus on labour market adjusted immigration. This development also affected people from the former colonies, while EU citizens gained privileges.

3.3.1.2 Field of labour immigration in the Europeanisation process

Until the 21st century, immigrants from EU countries were mainly qualified and not in the focus of politics. This situation changed when the Eastern European states joined the common European labour market.

Ever since, the immigration of EU citizens has been highly disputed. Especially the Polish population in the UK has risen significantly since Eastern Europeans have been granted the right to enter the labour market. The UK census noted a constant increase in the annual influx of Polish people peaking at 826,000 in 2014 (see Green, 2014). The Polish people were attracted by better earning possibilities in the UK, while other countries such as Germany were still restrictive towards the immigration of Eastern Europeans. Additionally, established Polish immigrants in the UK helped the newcomers to settle. During the Second World War, hundreds of thousands of Poles were stationed in Britain, and the Polish Resettlement Act of 1947 offered citizenship to 200,000 Polish soldiers who did not wish to return to a Poland being dominated by the Soviet Union. As a result, the Census recorded 162,339 Poles living in Britain in 1951. The UK also introduced a guest worker scheme after the war so that a considerable number of Eastern Europeans were actively recruited for the British labour market (see Burrell, 2006). The existing Polish community in the UK also provided a supportive network for new Polish immigrants in the 21st century. Thus, Polish immigrants found similarly favourable conditions and support due to transnational networks in the UK as the Spanish did in Germany.

The increase of immigrants from the Commonwealth since 1997 and of (Eastern) European labour immigrants since 2004 has led to an enormous growth of the foreign-born population in the UK between 2001 and 2011, namely from 4.6 million to 7.5 million. This dramatic growth of migration can partly be ascribed to the policy line that favoured international recruitment to *attract the best and the brightest* under the Labour Government of 1997-2010 (see Hopkins & Levy, 2012). A political debate concerning the global war for talent paired with scenarios of the expected decrease of the labour force created a beneficial climate for international recruitment. Therefore, a perception of the need for international recruitment and labour immigration spread in Britain (see Okolski & Salt, 2014, p. 28f.). Although the British government set a policy framework for labour immigration, governance units were less actively involved in recruitment than in Spain or Germany. Due to its liberal market economy the role of recruitment agencies is far more pronounced than the involvement of public institutions (see ibid., 2014, p. 31; and also in Chapter 7). The existence and importance of a highly professionalized, specialized, very competitive and dense recruitment industry involved in transnational mobility was regularly highlighted by the interviewed experts of the British labour market. As interviewed expert 4 from a British trade union put it in 2016:

> *Recruiters? Yes, there are a lot of recruiters involved searching for professionals from abroad. Actually, I wonder what all these recruiters are doing? Is there really so much work to do for all of them? I think this country does not need all of those guys. For my taste, there is some redundancy.*

The active recruitment industry and the open policies for labour immigrants led to a massive increase in the level of migration after 1997, which is unprecedented in the country's history, reaching a net migration of three million (see Office for National Statistics, 2018a). It was supported by policy incentives aimed at the international recruitment of professionals and the unrestricted entry of Europeans. Interview partners from former Commonwealth countries regularly criticized the shift from privileging Commonwealth citizens over European citizens. Interviewed expert 2 from a labour union in the UK was a national of a Commonwealth country. In the interview this expert said in 2016:

> *Those professionals from my country need to meet much higher standards than those from the EU. In terms of education they (professionals from expert's home country) need to satisfy more criteria and a higher score in the official English test is required to get recruited. Although their education is much better (than those of EU immigrants) as well as their English skills because in my country English is an official language... If you ask me, this is pure racism!*

This quote shows that prioritizing EU citizens may not find legitimation among established immigrant groups from third countries. Instead, it may lead to a competition among different ethnic groups. The protest against privileging EU citizens may become even more efficient as a big part of immigrants from the Commonwealth are naturalized in the UK (see Blinder, 2017), which gives them the right to vote.

The open immigration policies were meant to support the British knowledge economy and to secure the necessary labour force while demographic changes in the native society were predicted (see Hopkins & Levy, 2012). In this context, the UK became the *right place* for intra-EU labour mobility due to its labour immigration policies. The huge amount of immigrants following the liberal labour immigration policies shows the *normative isomorphism* of the necessity of international labour recruitment for modern knowledge based economies. While privileges were given to EU citizens, they were removed from citizens from the Commonwealth, which led to a competitive situation between different immigrant groups.

3.3.2 Status quo ante crisis of the labour market

The following part shows that measures fostering labour immigration became effective, because the labour market offered favourable conditions. The more flexible and open labour market structures are outlined as an advantage for international recruitment besides the English language.

3.3.2.1 Sectoral structure in the UK

Firstly, the sectoral structure of the British economy is outlined as well as its impact on innovation and labour relations.

In the middle of the 18th century, the process of industrialization started in the United Kingdom and was accompanied by an increased efficiency of the agricultural production. As early as in 1840, less than 30% of the workforce were employed in the agricultural sector, while it was still two thirds on average in the rest of Europe. During the 19th and 20th centuries, the industry acquired even greater importance when compared to agriculture. Since the end of the 1950s, the British economy has transformed from an industrial to a service economy (see Sturm, 2009). Compared to other OECD (2017) countries, the UK is exceptionally strong in knowledge-intensive services, such as telecommunication, banking and insurances, research and development as well as services to companies. In contrast, sectors with weak growth rates, such as agriculture and low-tech manufacturing, are less successful in the UK compared to the average of OECD countries. The most relevant economic sector employing around 77% of the Britons has been the service sector, especially in the fields of banking, insurance and reinsurance, as well as financing. The City of London is among the world's most important financial centres alongside New York and Tokyo. In 2005, 43% of the transactions in international equity trading took place in London. In 2004, 28% of the GDP were produced in financial and business services. While growth in industry stagnated, the financial sector has grown significantly faster than the British economy in general (see Sturm, 2009, p. 2).

The United Kingdom has been a pioneer in privatisation, liberalisation and deregulation, which have spread throughout the European single market. The UK belongs to the liberal market economies (LME) following the principles of supply and demand. In LMEs, companies depend on their shareholders in the stock market. Consequently, UK companies have to generate rising profits and continued positive growth prospects. Furthermore, the companies need to respond fast to market demands and changing economic trends. Therefore, top managers in liberal market economies like the United Kingdom have the capacity to act unilaterally. Thus, new strategies can be enforced faster and more easily. Accordingly, liberal market economies have a comparative advantage in radical innovation, i.e. the development of entirely new products or production processes (see Hall & Soskice, 2001).

In order to succeed with a radical innovation strategy, firms need to be able to alter their production capacities quickly so as to produce novel products or provide new services. In LMEs, this strategy is facilitated by fluid labour markets and a workforce endowed with high levels of general skills acquired in formal educational institutions such as schools and universities. Fluid labour markets allow firms to easily adapt their workforce in line with new products because of the low job security they offer. International recruitment was fostered to meet the demand for highly-skilled professionals for the knowledge-based service economy quickly (see Cerna, 2011). Due to the high rate of fluctuation and short job tenures, companies and workers do not tend to invest too much into specific skills (see Hall & Soskice, 2001). Therefore, international recruitment and labour integration could more easily *diffuse* in a *process of isomorphism* among British labour market institutions as the risks of failed investment are lower than for employers and employees in Germany.

3.3.2.2 Labour relations in the UK

In order to ensure the liberal open labour market in the UK, labour protection is relatively low and labour unions comparatively weak, which will be shown in the next section. The hire and fire principle also has an impact on the investments made in skills by employees and employers in the UK.

In liberal market economies, companies prefer to hire employees possessing high levels of general skills and train them for specific tasks in-house. General skills complement this strategy because they reduce the costs of in-house training. Companies are mainly financed by stock markets, a measure that requires them to ensure current profitability rather than maintaining market shares (Hall & Soskice, 2001, p. 30ff).

Employers' associations are far less powerful in the UK than in Germany and therefore less able to influence political decision-making. On the one hand, the deliberate goal of politics had been the creation of a liberal deregulated market ever since the government of Margret Thatcher (1979 to 1990). On the other hand, the employers' associations are not in a position to collectively organize themselves, because interests vary widely between multinational companies (MNCs) and small and medium-sized enterprises (SMEs) in the UK. The same conflicts separate the industry and the service sector as their attitudes vary widely with regard to the government's role for the economy, such as in the case of governmental subsidies. Especially financial services, which is the most important sector in this field, takes a different stance on this topic as compared to other parts of the service sector. Furthermore, the umbrella organisations of corporations play a minor role in tariff policy (see Sturm, 2009).

Apart from the public sector, labour unions are also relatively weak in the United Kingdom. Wages are negotiated on the company level. Shop stewards play the most important role in negotiations about wages and labour conditions on the employer side . This most recently developed type of employee representation is most common in the UK today. The proportion of the workforce organized in labour unions diminished over the past decades from around 54% in 1979 to around 29% in 2007. In the public sector, labour unions are still an incumbent as 60% of the labour force were organized in unions in 2007, while only 20% of the labour force in the private sector are members of labour unions (see Sturm, 2009, p. 2). Thus, in the public sector, such as the health care sector, which will be highlighted in more detail in Chapter 7, the trade and labour unions are influential, while negotiations and disputes are settled individually in the private sector. This affects also the newcomers on the British labour market. While Spanish immigrants were able to get support from the labour unions to exercise their rights in Germany, Spanish immigrants in the UK painted a different picture of the unions in the UK. A member of the *Oficina Precaria* in London, which is a Spanish migrant network offering support to those in precarious working conditions, said in 2015:

> *Well, here in the UK everything is negotiated on an individual basis. So, if you are a professional who earns well and is important to the company, you can negotiate your salary or you can sue your employer if he is bullying you or doesn't pay your salary. To do so, you need to be able to bear the costs. In the case of precarious workers, they cannot bear the costs and there is no official instance to protect or defend their rights as employees. In case of bullying or if their salary is not paid, they just leave the employer if they can't stand it anymore.*

Several Spanish immigrants interviewed in the UK reported about precarious job experiences, in which employers abused their power and they just left the contract, knowing that their last salary will be lost. This phenomenon seems to occur ever more frequently, since precarious working conditions have increased since the economic crisis.

Especially the financial sector in London, which is the country's economic motor,was affected by the international financial crisis. The banking crisis had an impact on economic growth and caused unemployment in the UK. Banks cut back on lending, which meant that it became more difficult for firms to obtain credits to finance investments. As a result of the declining investments, lay-offs occurred not only in the financial sector, as consumer confidence dropped and the demand for goods decreased. Companies reacted by laying off workers due to a decrease in consumer demand. Thus, unemployment resulting from the banking crisis was primarily attributable to lacking demand. In the UK, job losses were witnessed in the financial sector, with banks laying off staff to reduce costs, but the greatest part of the unemployment was identified in other sectors, which were indirectly affected by the banking crisis.

During the recession of 2008 to 2013, unemployment rose from around five to eight per cent, which was less than expected. The reason was the flexible labour market, in which a growth in under-employment based on zero hour contracts[5] and part-time work absorbed those who would have become unemployed otherwise. Hence, the amount of people working in precarious labour conditions increased (see Booth, 2016).

Nevertheless, due to the low unemployment rate, its stable economy, the open labour market and active international recruitment the UK became the *right place* for labour immigration.

5 The term zero-hour contract is used for a contract between an employer and a worker according to which the employer is not liable for any minimum working hours, while the worker is not compelled to accept any work offered (ACAS advice and guidance 2017). It is often used in the agriculture, hotels and catering, education, and healthcare sectors. Such contracts are designed to enable on-call shift scheduling practices.

The labour market's flexibility softened the expected effects of the crisis on the unemployment rate. Instead of suffering from unemployment, a growth of under-employment based on zero-hour contracts and part-time work raised the amount of people working under precarious conditions. Due to the open labour market, efforts of international recruitment, the English language and the stable economy during the economic crisis, the UK became the *right place* for intra-EU labour mobility.

3.3.3 Status quo ante crisis in the field of education

The following section highlights the particular characteristics of the educational structure in the UK, its incumbents and its relation to labour immigration.

3.3.3.1 Educational system in the UK

The impact of the flexibility of the British labour market was already mentioned influences the extent to which companies and employees invest in skill development through education and training as outlined in more detail in this section.

Based on their demand for general skills and the focus on current profitability, British firms are more likely to oppose training measures and to support international recruitment instead, because they need to match their staff rapidly to customer demand. Furthermore, due to the high fluctuation rate training is seen as a long-term investment with uncertain benefits for the companies. In view of their focus on profitability British companies are therefore generally more hesitant to make uncertain long-term investments (see Hall & Soskice, 2001). Hence, international recruitment can offer a valuable opportunity to hire adequate professionals at low costs as stated by the British recruiters. The success of British companies is usually not based on long job tenures during which specialized skills are developed for their comparative advantage, as is the case in Germany. Additionally, the UK's educational system does not produce certificates having the same high signalling value the German employers can rely on. The relatively low employment protection allows for dismissing and hiring workers at low costs. Nevertheless, employment levels are high across the United Kingdom for all levels of attainment. Those groups of the population having a secondary or post-secondary non-tertiary qualification as their highest level of education display unemployment rates below the OECD average, for both general and vocational qualifications (see OECD, 2016).

The British educational system is decentralized and organized differently in England, Wales, Northern Ireland and Scotland. However, it is centrally organized within the different UK member countries and therefore more clearly structured than the German one. Typically, the British educational system is subdivided into school-based education and training on the job. As in most other nations, there is no training combining standardized theoretical and practical training over several years, such as the dual system in Germany. Instead, the UK has the second highest graduation rate among all OECD countries at 54 % following Iceland, while Germany, for instance, accounts for a graduation rate of 31%. The high graduation rate is a result of a larger proportion of adults with bachelor degrees as compared to other OECD countries. In 2015, 43% of the 25-46 year olds had a tertiary qualification in the UK, which is above the OECD average of 36%, while the proportion of professionals with a master degree was similar to the OECD average of 11%. Additionally, children born to foreign parents are more likely to attain the tertiary level of education than those with native parents, which is in contrast to most other OECD countries (see Jacobs, 2017).

Adults with a higher level of education are less likely to be unemployed in the UK, and unemployment rates for each attainment level are among the lowest in OECD countries. However, many university graduates do not necessarily meet the skill requirements of the labour market (see K. Allen, 2015). On the contrary, a great number of those who participated in tertiary education in the UK are often considered over-qualified. The figures of the European Social Survey (2016) show that 58.8% of employees in the UK worked in jobs below their skill level between 2004 and 2010. Since 2004, this number has risen significantly from 40% to nearly 60%. This proportion of over-qualification is comparatively high and only exceeded by Greece and Estonia in Europe, while countries having a strong tradition of vocational training, such as Germany, the Netherlands or Slovenia, only feature 10% or even less graduates in non-graduate jobs (see Tobin, 2015).

The mismatch in the UK is accompanied by high tuition fees in tertiary education. Expenditure per student in the UK is above the OECD average at each level of education, but it is particularly high on the tertiary level. In part, this is due to an increase of tuition fees between 2008 and 2013. Looking at the proportion of public funding in relation to private sources, one will establish far more private financing in the educational system than in most other OECD countries, especially in tertiary education. In England, high tuition fees are charged. Nine out of ten tertiary students who graduated in 2014/15 were indebted, because they had to take student loans of more than 30,000 US dollars. The OECD (2016) considers the availability of public student loans and loan repayment conditions to be relatively favourable. Nevertheless, the British government estimates that 45% of the university graduates will not reach salaries allowing them to pay back their student loans (see Allen, 2015).

Hence, British tertiary education is most expensive for students when compared to other European countries, and the high investments in education seem to pay off less and less. This is one reason why an apprenticeship system has been developed by the British government. Besides, especially the industry has established a demand for professionals on the medium skill level (see Department of Education, 2018). Interviewed expert 4 from a trade union in the British industry that develops vocational training said in 2016:

> *We noticed that our industry has a high demand for people obtaining practical skills, which do not meet the qualification of an engineer. Now we try to develop specialized vocational training as you (addressing the German interviewer) have it in Germany. Of course, we can't implement the same system because our labour market and its historical developments are different, we have to adjust it to our system.*

According to OECD (2016) research, people having acquired a vocational degree are least likely to get unemployed and show the highest employment rates in the UK as well as in Germany. The lack of vocationally qualified professionals and the high job security offers a niche for foreign professionals, especially those who obtain good qualifications in crafts and trades, such as the Poles (see Chapter 7).

Although the educational system obviously does not meet the current skill requirements of the domestic labour market in the UK, British universities are regularly ranked among the top universities worldwide. The support given to science and innovation enjoys high priority in the UK. British universities offer attractive labour conditions and attract highly skilled people from all over the world. Government funding for science aims at strengthening international competitiveness and the creation of jobs for this group of professionals. Generally, research is geared towards economic growth, and political discourse focuses on market needs and employment. Thus, the responsibilities for universities and research are divided between the Ministry of Education and the Department of Trade and Industry. In order to support cooperation between science and economy in high technology sectors, Catapult Centres have been founded, based on the model of the German Fraunhofer Institutes. The United Kingdom belongs to the leading nations worldwide with regard to science and research.

3.3.3.2 Internationalisation of higher education in Britain

Due to their prestige and the universal language, British universities attract international students from all over the world.

International students represented around 18% of all tertiary students in the UK in 2014, which is three times as much as the OECD average of 6% and the second highest percentage after the United States (19%).

The higher the levels of tertiary education, the higher is the attainment of international students: It is about three times higher than the OECD total for students in both bachelor or equivalent programmes (14% compared to 5%) and master programmes (37% compared to 12%), International students account for 42% of all students in doctoral or equivalent programmes, which is significantly above the proportion for OECD countries as a whole (27%) (OECD, 2016). Hence, a high level of internationalisation can be discerned in tertiary education due to student immigration, which is attributable to the renown of British universities and the fact that English is the no. 1 language in the world. These international students raise the availability of highly skilled labour force on the British labour market and support the knowledge-intensive service economy in the UK. Interviewed Spanish immigrant 2 (age: 25) in London was once a student immigrant before coming back to the UK to find a job there. She was particularly successful on the British labour market as she worked part-time at a public youth centre and did a PhD in anthropology. In an interview in 2015, she highlighted the increase of job opportunities obtaining a British Masters degree from one of the British top universities:

> *Well, I did my Masters degree at the University College London. I had to pay high tuition fees in order to graduate there. In general, I think Spanish universities are not worse, at least the one where I studied. In the end, I paid for the name and the fame of the university, but I do not complain. Due to the Masters certificate from UCL, I have a good job here and a PhD scholarship.*

Most probably many student immigrants from abroad try to follow the same strategy. The advantage of English as a widespread and universal language is a favourable condition for student immigration as it broadens labour opportunities.

The job profiles, which are determined by a general set of skills, combined with the high number of foreign students in Britain and the training on the job provided by employer have facilitated the integration and recruitment of foreign professionals in the UK. Therefore, the *isomorphism* of international recruitment and labour integration did not produce the same amount of institutional change then in the case of Germany. Thus, Britain became the *right place* for intra-EU labour mobility.

3.3.4 Outlook: British immigration crisis

In this section a brief outlook roughly describes the basic arguments and developments that influenced the BREXIT vote. It summarizes how the social gap in the UK led to a perceived immigration crisis in view of the experiences of the financial crisis and the huge immigration wave of the last two decades.

As described earlier in Chapter 4.1, an unprecedented increase of immigration has been witnessed in the UK in the past 20 years (Green, 2014). The open labour market, the English language and favourable economic conditions as well as policy incentives for the international recruitment of professionals contributed to this development. Labour immigration was supported by politics and society at the beginning of the 21st century for the reason of fighting the demographic shift and attracting the best and the brightest. The public opinion changed in the aftermath of the financial crisis, when unemployment rose slightly and the number of precarious jobs increased significantly.

At this time, critique of immigration grew as immigrants were considered to threaten the social cohesion, the cultural integrity and the economic prosperity of the British population (see also Chapter 7). These opinions were discussed in the media and among established parties. The immigrants were collectively accused of being a burden to the British welfare state due to benefit tourism and the costs they and their children produce by participating in the British educational system. Furthermore, they were blamed for causing wage dumping, unemployment and more precarious working conditions for British citizens. A big part of the British citizens also saw their cultural identity threatened by increased immigration. The Aurora Development Index (2017) reports that 56% of the British interviewees felt their local culture threatened by ethnic minorities. 24% of the interviewees still thought migrants took jobs away, and 34% said migrants took more from society than they contributed (see The Guardian, 2017). In this discussion immigration from EU countries was a particularly disputed topic as it was not controllable due to the freedom of movement for workers in the Common labour market.

As these attitudes were spreading, Prime Minister David Cameron promised to reduce net immigration at his re-election in 2010 (see Migration Observatory, 2015). He could not reach this goal, amongst other things because he could not prevent EU citizens from labour immigration due to the freedom of movement for workers. The rising criticism of immigration while more and more immigrants entered the labour market, finally led to BREXIT.

A group of researchers from the London School of Economics explain the spreading of opinions with risen social and economic inequalities among the British society since the market liberalisation under the Thatcher government in the 1970s. They found that those citizens who favoured BREXIT tended to be older and poorer than those who preferred to keep the UK a part of the European Union. Hence, they claim that the consequences of a market-driven capitalism are partially responsible for anti-EU and anti-immigration attitudes that finally culminated in the BREXIT vote.

In summary, the unprecedented immigration wave in the last 20 years, and the widening social gap among British citizens led to an anti-EU and anti-immigration attitude among big parts of society.

3.3.5 Structural analysis: UK as the right place for labour mobility

In this section the influence of the Europeanization process, the national policies and the incumbents in the field of labour immigration were highlighted in order to show how the UK became so attractive as an immigration country, but lost the support for labour immigration of a decisive part of its citizens. The freedom of movement for workers encouraged high numbers of labour immigrants due to the institutional structure of the labour market, characterized by an open labour market that has a demand for general skills. Additionally, established migrants and networks provided support for immigrants. However, due to increasing precarious working conditions for British citizens, immigration lost support on the micro-level.

The UK became especially attractive for (EU-) immigrants due to its economic stability and its open labour immigration policies. Britain was among the first countries to open its labour market for Eastern European citizens. Although, the financial sector was most important for the British service economy, unemployment only increased from around 5% to 8% between 2008 and 2013 and dropped steadily in the following years to around 4% in 2018 (see Office for National Statistics, 2018b). The prosperity and open structure of the British labour market and its famous educational system provided the basis for triggering a huge wave of labour immigration.

The British educational system is internationally renowned and the English language attracts student immigrants that are well prepared for the UK labour market after their graduation. In the two-fold educational system, universities and companies are the main incumbents. The universities and other educational institutions focus the theoretical knowledge.

The flexible labour market makes companies only willing to invest a minimum in human resource development due to the high fluctuation caused by the hire and fire-system. In this system it is advantageous to develop general skills to increase the range of job opportunities on the British labour market. The demand for general skills and the use of company-specific in-house training is far more favourable for labour immigration than the German system of standardized and specialized job profiles. Additionally, due to the two-fold system and the depreciation of blue-collar work, the UK has a demand for practical skills, which created a niche for certain labour immigrants, as the "Polish plumbers". As the British labour market is highly deregulated, labour and trade unions are only powerful incumbents in the public sector, so labour unions are only a contact point for native and immigrant workers in this area.

Due to the open labour market, the high number of student immigrants, the demand for general skills and practical skills the immigration-friendly policies were well received. The British citizens supported these policies as the public opinion and the political leaders expected labour immigration to boost the British knowledge economy and to secure the necessary labour force in times of a demographic shift. Therefore, an immigration law adjusted to the current labour demand was developed for third-country nationals in the early 20th century, which affected first of all the immigrants from the Commonwealth countries, which are historically connected to the UK. Particularly the Polish workers welcomed the early opening of the British labour market for Eastern Europeans. Private recruitment agencies facilitated labour immigration of EU citizens and third-country nationals. Meanwhile they are incumbents of the labour market that developed a highly competitive and dense recruitment industry.

All these structures and developments on the British labour market made the UK the *right place* for intra-EU labour mobility, which was unrestricted in contrast to the immigration of third-country nationals. The open labour market, active international recruitment, the English language and the stability of the economy during the economic crisis attracted workers from abroad. As general skills are more helpful to get hired than specialized ones and in-house training is provided by the recruiting company, it tends to be easier for newcomers to enter the labour market than in more regulated labour markets such as the German one. These characteristics combined with the high number of foreigners educated in Britain makes the UK the *right place* for intra-EU labour mobility.

Figure 5: Status quo ante BREXIT in the British market economy

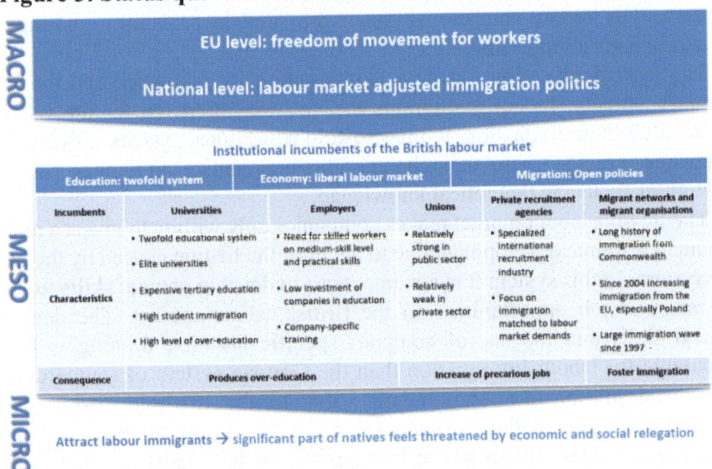

Figure 5 shows the impact of the liberal immigration policies in the UK on the British citizen while taking the characteristics of the field of education, the labour market and migration into account and highlighting their incumbents. This figure was created by the author and is based on own research.

Nevertheless, there is also a flip side of the British labour market structure and its developments. The educational system is not able to yield graduates that meet the demand of the British companies. Tertiary education is very costly and does not pay off for approximately two thirds of the British employees as this is the proportion of those overeducated for the requirements of their job. Furthermore, the flexibility of the British labour market diminished the effects of the crisis but led to a growth of under-employment and precarious working conditions. These recent trends have increased the social gap between poor and rich, which has widened ever since the market liberalisation in the 1970s. Therefore, a decisive part of British citizens evaluates immigration as a threat to the UK's social, cultural and economic prosperity. In particular, EU immigration was criticized as being uncontrollable due to the right of freedom of movement for workers. However, not only native Britons were among the critics, but also immigrants from the Commonwealth complained about being discriminated while EU citizens were privileged.

The anti-immigration and anti-EU framings developed at a time of increasing precarious working and living conditions formed the starting point for field changes that culminated in the BREXIT vote. The status quo ante BREXIT in the British market economy is summarised in Figure 5.

4. Creating the right circumstances in Spain

The external shock of the financial crisis led to a destabilization of the labour market. The next chapter shows how institutions cope with the effects of the economic crisis in the fields of education, labour market and migration. The actions triggering field changes on the part of challengers, governance units, incumbents and entrepreneurial actors in the field of labour migration in a move to shape its policies and practices of mobility are highlighted. By implementing policies and practices, they created the *right circumstances* for intra-EU labour mobility of Spaniards. Therefore, Section 5.1 analyses the socio-political debate on labour emigration, which resulted in the *dominant framing* and the subsequent actions. The young people are challengers, who initiated the new policies on labour mobility. Therefore, they are the first group to be examined so as to make it possible to understand the development of the field. The subsequent reactions of governance units, namely the Ministry of Employment, the public employment agencies and municipal youth services are outlined afterwards. Section 5.2 highlights how incumbents of the field of labour mobility implemented the policies by developing new services for *international job search* and *transnational matching* of job candidates in Spain and vacancies abroad.

4.1 Actions and Framings of recruitment in the field of mobility

The following part addresses the development of framings that legitimize or delegitimize intra-EU labour mobility in the Spanish economic crisis. In this situation young people in precarious working conditions challenged the status quo in the field of mobility and were able to initiate field changes, as will be described in Section 5.1.1. Afterwards, the governance units and their (re-) actions are focused to analyse the implementation of policy changes in the transnational field of labour mobility in Section 5.1.2. Political framings for policy changes are the starting point to create or remove the *right circumstances* for intra-EU labour mobility.

4.1.1 Challengers of the status quo[6]

Due to temporary labour contracts and easier dismissal, those most affected by the economic crisis were the young people in Spain who were unable to see a future in their home country. They displayed the highest unemployment rates and

6 With regard to governance units, only the collaboration of the German and the Spanish governments will be described, as there were no bilateral agreements between the UK and Spain

C. Heimann, *Blessing and Curse of Intra-EU Mobility*, Studien zur Migrations- und Integrationspolitik, https://doi.org/10.1007/978-3-658-31486-6_4

therefore started to express their dissatisfaction and raised awareness for the precarious working and living conditions they were facing.

40.2% of the young people between 16 and 29 did not participate in the labour market in 2012. This high number reflects the difficult transition from school to work. The majority of these under 30 year-olds, were in education or training. At the same time, unemployment affected 26.6% of the population under 30. Hence, only one third of this age group had a job (see Consejo de la Juventud de España, 2013, p. 4). Due to the high youth unemployment rate it can be assumed that the high percentage of those under 30 in education was not only a strategy to increase the chances on the labour market, but also to avoid unemployment.

Furthermore, young employees are often in a precarious labour situation, which is underlined by the relatively high rate of part-time contracts (27.5%) (ibid, p. 6). In general, 23% of the under 30s are underemployed, which proves that there is a large potential of unused labour capacity available in this age group. In concrete terms, this means that their working hours are not sufficient in relation to their availability to work, their economic needs and the average working hours in similar jobs. Additionally, the instability of employment among those between 16 and 30 years had been growing. 46.9% of them have temporary labour contracts, of which 43.8% are valid for less than one year. Another alarming aspect in times of a higher level of education is that Spain shows a high proportion of over-education. 53.9% of young people under 30, who are not enrolled in study or education programmes, are overqualified. This problem is even more pressing among women accounting for a rate of 59.1% compared to men of the same age group (49%), and also for those between 30 and 34 years amounting to a rate of 56,2% (ibid.).

The precarious conditions, including reduced working hours and short-term contracts, impede long-term planning, establishing own life projects like moving out, marrying or starting a family (see Triandafyllidou & Gropas, 2014). These poor prospects mobilised masses to protest on the street and in public spaces in 2011 and 2012. According to the interview partners in Spain, this was the time, when it became evident that the economic crisis in Spain was more than just a short-lived phenomenon. The atmosphere changed as people lost hope and became increasingly desperate.

In the international media these demonstrations were called the Spanish revolution (see Varsavsky, 2011). The aim of the protests was to raise awareness for the deplorable state of affairs. They criticised the social, economic and political problems in the country. Among other aspects, like credit regulations and corruption in Spain as well as the austerity policy of the European Union, the protesters criticised especially the high employment protection for the older employees and the easy dismissal of the younger age groups as well as the lack of job opportunities for qualified professionals in general. On May 15, 2011, protests in 58 Spanish cities were organised via the Internet and supported by 200 associations. On that day, the movement decided to organise itself centrally outside the Internet and it was named after its date of birth: 15M (see Beas, 2011).

The movement is independent of political parties, unions and worldviews. Several demonstrations followed, like the one on June 19th, which took place in 80 Spanish cities. Protest camps were installed in the big cities, like Madrid and Barcelona (see Flock, 2011). This movement was also called "Los indignados" (= the indignant) after a book by the resistance fighter Stéphane Hessel (2012) with the original title "indignez-vous!", who invokes resistance against financial capitalism.

When "the indignant" formed their protest movement in 2011, the general unemployment rate in Spain was at ~23% and the youth unemployment rate at ~44%, according to the National Institute of Statistics (2012). At that time, Chancellor Angela Merkel offered a perspective for unemployed Spaniards to escape the crisis and work in Germany. In January 2011, she gave a speech in Spain claiming that Germany had a demand for 100,000 engineers due to labour shortages. Although she had to correct the number downwards to 10,000, this information spread ubiquitously in the Spanish media (Delgado, 2011; Roth, 2011). Intended or not, she "raised a storm" of potentially emigrating Spaniards seeking for information at all kinds of public services, employment services, labour and professional unions, as well as German language schools according to the statements of these institutions. Interview partners working at these institutions stated that unemployment, irregular or illicit labour were the foremost and nearly exclusive reasons for international job search. Those desperately looking for a job were eager to find out how to get the jobs the German Chancellor was talking about. They put enormous pressure on these institutions to offer information and advisory service on international mobility.

In the following three months the number of students learning German at the Goethe Institutes in Spain rose by around 35%, according to the German newspaper "*Die Zeit*" (Müller, 2012) so that German became the second most popular language after English. The interview partner 1, who organized recruitment fairs and informative events on labour immigration to Germany, working for a German cultural non-profit organisation in Spain reported about an information event on working conditions in Germany in 2014:

> *[...] when the magazine "Spiegel" spread the news that she (Angela Merkel) said Germany was looking for so many professionals. This was at best a misinterpretation but it was widely spread in the media. The event we offered afterwards was completely booked. People were like mad and we had to close the room; the event was even transmitted outside as a live video stream, because there was still a general run on this topic.*

The youth's interest in these events indicates that Angela Merkel's speech did not only raise the awareness of the young people towards labour mobility. Instead it also shows that the perception of labour mobility as a chance to escape the economic crisis in Spain diffused among those unemployed or in precarious working conditions.

The EU, especially the free movement of labour in the EU (Article 20 TFEU) and harmonisation efforts of the common European labour market provided favourable conditions for labour mobility (see Maciejewski & Dancourt, 2017). Free movement of labour became particularly viable as other EU member states were in a similar economic situation, i.e. suffering from labour shortages. Germany became the major destination for intra-EU labour mobility, because it coped with the crisis exceptionally well and German companies started to search for professionals on the Spanish labour market. In 2012, German employers offered approximately 57% of all registered job advertisements in the European Employment Service (EURES) according to the annual report of SEPE in 2012 (see Servicio Público de Empleo Estatal, 2012) Therefore, Germany offered more jobs than all other EU countries together. Apparently, German companies were not the only ones trying to benefit from the labour force potential in Spain. However, German companies were most actively recruiting from the Spanish labour market.

Hence, German companies but also other foreign companies appeared as challengers of the status quo in the Spanish field of labour mobility by applying new recruitment strategies. They not only underlined the perception of labour mobility as an abstract possibility, but converted it into a realistic chance.

4.1.2 Governance units: Ministries of Employment

The pressure of young Spaniards, who were unemployed or in a precarious labour situation, attracted attention to these problems both nationally and internationally. Due to pressure from the bottom it became a political issue, as *the lost generation* itself blamed the government for their bad labour situation and the bleak future prospects.

One of the responses was to facilitate labour emigration in order to support (young) Spaniards to find decent working conditions and to escape unemployment and precarious living conditions. Two years after Angela Merkel's speech, who supported the international recruitment of employers, a memorandum between the German Federal Ministry of Labour and Social Affairs and the Spanish Ministry of Employment and Social Security was signed in Madrid as one of the measures to deal with labour shortages in Germany and unemployment in Spain. By signing this memorandum on May 21st, 2013, both governments agreed on the recruitment of five thousand Spaniards for the German labour market per year. The Spanish Minister, Fátima Bañez, based the memorandum on transnational cooperation and labour migration as a solution to youth unemployment: "more collaboration means more opportunities for everybody, in this case (...) for the youth" (see Ministerio de Empleo y Securidad Social, 2013). The then German Minister Ursula von der Leyen highlighted the aim to help the unemployed Spanish youth according to the idea of a Common Europe using "free labour movement". Jointly the two Ministers emphasized the political framing of labour mobility as a chance for the youth provided within the framework of the EU and the "free movement of labour" to legitimize the Memorandum.

In the case of German companies, recruitment was supported by the programmes "MobiPro" and "job of my life", which were designed as a *first-aid* package for the unemployed youth in Spain, while helping to reduce labour demand in Germany. Therefore, the programme aimed at recruiting suitable job candidates. The first group, targeted by "job of my life", covered young people under 35 who held certain qualifications that are defined as scarce skills. Scarce occupations were found in the health sector, like nurses and doctors, as well as in the technical field like engineers, plumbers, etc. (see Mangelberufe.de, 2018). The second target group, covered by "MobiPro", included young people between 18 and 27, who were not in education, employment, or training (NEET) and are therefore called *ninis* (the "neither-nors") in Spain. They were offered to participate in a two- or three-year apprenticeship to learn a profession. Financial support was provided for travel costs, salary, a lump sum for removal costs, preparatory language courses for the recruited in the country of origin and accompanying courses in Germany. The Spanish-German policies on transnational labour mobility were in line with EU politics aimed at increasing the employability of EU citizens within the strategy Europe 2020 (see European Commission, 2018a). The interviewed representative 1 of the Spanish Ministry of Employment stated:

> *We affirm that at least we (...) do not oppose new migration. We are not worried about all these questions, like Brain Drain. They do not concern us, because in the end the focus is on the field of free labour movement, in which people exercise their rights. And in collaboration with our partners we try to specifically target this issue.*

This quote shows that the freedom of movement for workers, which was implemented by the EU in a *coercive process* diffused deeply into Spanish politics. The Spanish opposition however took a different stance on this topic. In April 2013, the Spanish media and the opposition accused Fátima Báñez (Partido Popular) of stimulating the "Brain Drain" and forcing young Spaniards to become "economic refugees"(see 20minutos, 2013; El Mundo, 2013; Publico, 2013). Despite the interpretation of labour emigration as economic exile causing Brain Drain, most of the interview partners assess fears of Brain Drain as overestimated, as do researchers like Bräuninger (2014) or Santos Ortega (2013). The latter shows that media articles addressing the Brain Drain[7] quadrupled between 2008 and 2012. Nevertheless, he evaluates this phenomenon as a diversionary tactic to avoid active dispute about the real problem, namely the helplessness to decrease unemployment. The Brain Drain argument contrasted the framing of "labour mobility as a chance", providing a counter argument. This counter argument was

7 Original term in Spanish: fuga de cerebros

spread by the opposition and the media, which triggered a political and public debate. Afterwards, politicians, who commented on the topic of labour emigration, had been most strongly criticised in the media. It was a sensitive issue, because the need for international labour mobility was caused by the failed economic policy in Spain. In response to the harsh critique, politicians started to avoid the topic of labour emigration according to the statements of the interviewed experts from politics, science and public. The interviewed politician 2 in Spain said in 2014:

> *Emigration politics are on a level of communication that is the less you talk – the better.*

However, the mobility programmes were very well received by the young Spaniards and implemented by public employment services to ensure their feasibility and quality. The German programme "Mobi-Pro" was designed to be part of the pilot project for the EU-wide programme "your first EURES job". Due to the success of the pilot projects that facilitated labour mobility (see European Commission, 2018b), the EU-wide programme started in 2014 having a similar design as Mobi-Pro. Specifically young people up to 35 years are eligible to obtain support in finding a job, traineeship or apprenticeship in another Member State. Just like Mobi-Pro, it is geared to the vacancies that are hard to fill, and which are defined individually by the member states. It is open to young candidates and employers of the EU-28 countries, Norway and Iceland and to all candidates, who are nationals and legal residents of those countries. In order to promote these mobility programmes the homepage of the Spanish Ministry of Employment announced job offers in Germany and information on the labour market. Due to the enormous demand the information given on the homepage was extended step by step. Several topics such as living conditions, sectoral distribution and recognition procedures were added and different countries were included with their labour market data, including non-EU member states.

All these developments raised awareness for the possibility of intra-EU labour mobility and labour emigration in general, although especially the governance units but also other labour market institutions were first and foremost facilitating mobility to Germany due to the Memorandum and the subsidies. The enormous interest in the programmes and the high demand for information on labour mobility show that the political framing of labour mobility as a chance became accepted. Hence, the combination of masses of unemployed, young and well qualified people and the demand for skilled labour in other countries, especially Germany, along with the freedom of labour movement provided the availability of the *right people* from Spain.

4.1.3 Framing of intra-EU mobility as a chance

In the wake of the economic crisis the Spanish economy and the labour market became unstable, which led to high general unemployment and even higher youth unemployment. This economic recession formed the starting point for field changes, when young people started to protest against unemployment and precarious working conditions and created the movement 15M. Finally, they began to search for jobs internationally, especially, after a speech by Angela Merkel in Madrid offering jobs for Spaniards. This speech raised the awareness for and the interest in jobs abroad for which young Spaniards seeked information.

However, the changes in the field of intra-EU labour mobility do not follow a clear bottom-up process. And this even more so since the Memorandum on the recruitment of Spanish professionals is a bilateral agreement between Spain and Germany. It was *framed* as a chance for unemployed youth and as a cooperation between EU countries. The high unemployment rates and missing alternatives, triggered emigration. Thus, the *counter-framing* of the opposition – the Brain Drain argument – attracted some attention, but did not initiate any significant institutional action.

Table 5: Role of institutions for policy changes in Spain

Institutional Role	Institutions	Strategic action	Framing/Perception
Challengers	15M	Look for and apply new ways of job search	Precarious living and working conditions in Spain
Governance units	Ministry of Employment	-Memorandum and agreements on recruitment -Announce job opportunities	Intra-EU mobility as a chance
	Opposition	Develop counter-argument	Brain Drain

Hence, labour mobility as a chance for young people became the dominant framing and legitimized the recruitment relation to Germany and other countries facing labour shortages. The roles, strategic actions and framings spread by the most relevant institutions that initiated the changed labour emigration policies is summarised by Table 5.

4.1.4 Governance units: implementation of mobility structures

In order to fully tap this potential the government relied on different public institutions to put the policies concerning labour mobility into practice. The next section shows how they facilitated international job search and labour emigration of unemployed Spaniards for labour markets abroad to enforce the new policies.

In doing so, they promoted the *framing* of intra-EU mobility as a chance and *the new ways of international job search* as it will be described in the next part.

4.1.4.1 Public employment agencies (EURES, SEPE, BA)

The success of the programmes of intra-EU mobility was only possible due to the involvement of employment services. Especially, the public employment services belong to the governance units that are heavily involved in working on intra-EU mobility as a chance for young people. These are necessary, because international mobility offers new opportunities for employers and employees, yet there are still high hurdles to overcome. First and foremost, there are language barriers and cultural differences, which are the immanent challenges of international mobility.

The employment agencies link foreign employers and Spanish job candidates since both of them lack the knowledge about different educational systems, job profiles, and labour market structures in the other country. The employment services establish contacts using their knowledge about the cultural norms and institutional structures in Spain and other countries. They do so by connecting the Spanish public job centres with foreign public job centres. This enabled the employment agencies to respond to both the needs and conditions on the Spanish as well as the foreign labour markets. In order to connect the national labour markets public employment agencies on different local, national and European levels collaborate. In the cases of Spaniards leaving for work in Germany and the UK, it is based on the collaboration of the European Employment Service (EURES), the German employment service Bundesagentur für Arbeit (BA) and the Job Centre Plus (JCP) in the United Kingdom, and the Spanish employment service (SEPE). These employment agencies organize recruitment fairs, round tables and offer information and consultation services to bring employers and job candidates in touch with each other. According to their own statements, they do not only provide information for employees, but also for cultural institutions and language schools, local public services, labour unions, chambers of commerce, universities and migrants′ organisations in Spain. In this context, they circulate information on living conditions, the labour market situation, sought after profiles in different countries as well as existing mobility programmes. The Spanish EURES employee 1 explained in 2014:

> *In Spain, our task is to promote our activities and recruit candidates. Therefore, we collaborate closely with universities, professional unions, (...). We also search via the Internet and use certain professional forums in order to spread our activities and to be able to find the sought after profiles. (...) We put a lot of effort in promoting recruitment and therefore in building networks that help us promote the events.*

In these networks, the institutions spread the advantages of a common European labour market and its benefits for different member states and their citizens according to the labour market situation. In doing so, they promote the *institutional myth/framing of labour mobility as a chance by using their social skills*. Knowing about the cultural norms and institutional structures in Spain, the employment services did not only offer information, but also supported recruitment tasks, like the pre-selection of candidates, job interviews, or the organisation of preparatory language courses. As interview partners in Spain state, they played a key role in raising the acceptance and trust by expanding the visibility of the public institutions and their activities in the field of international recruitment.

However, the involvement of public employment agencies in facilitating intra-EU mobility depends strongly on the labour market situation and the political perspective on the issue of labour immigration. While the British public employment agencies withdrew parts of their commitment in facilitating intra-EU mobility, German public employment agencies at the same time increased their recruitment activities. Therefore, the German public employment agencies worked closely together with the Spanish ones. For this reason, the Bundesagentur für Arbeit (BA) opened a branch in Madrid in 2014 to improve the cooperation between both labour markets according to BA-employees (see Anerkennung in Deutschland, 2018).

Along with the promotion of the programmes of mobility, the public employment agencies work on assuring the quality for both the employer and the job candidate. On the one hand, they try to preselect adequate job candidates for the employers. On the other hand, they receive direct feedback from the job candidates if the labour situation in the company did not live up to their expectations.

There are risks on both sides, when either the selected job candidates or the employers do not meet certain criteria. On the one hand, the employer has to face the risk that job candidates were selected, but when it came to moving to the other country, they did not take this step or they quitted the job soon after. This is especially costly for employers, when they finance international recruitment, language courses and training measures, which are a major investment that only pays off in the long run.

However, there are also certain risks involved for the job candidate. In both the UK and Germany there were reports of instances, in which employers did not keep their promises. The main issues were that employers promised to organise accommodation or to offer an apprenticeship or qualified work but when the job candidates arrived, they were not given accommodation or had to do unskilled work without any prospects of education and training. Other negative feedback given by the job candidates referred to the jobs' locations, which were often in rural areas, far away from the next city and having a poor infrastructural connection to other places.

Therefore, the public employment agencies in Spain saw their role in promoting the job offers from abroad and creating, maintaining and restoring trust in the mobility programmes and procedures of international recruitment. By doing so, they spread the framing of labour mobility as a chance for the unemployed youth and helped to expand transnational networks, which are to a great extent connected by employment agencies. In this context, *coercive* as well as *normative isomorphism* is witnessed as the institutions implement policies and practices and promote the idea of intra-EU labour mobility and the idea of the common EU labour market.

4.1.4.2 Municipal Youth Services

Similarly, other public services started to supply general information and advice on international mobility. They provide all those interested in international labour mobility with all kind of information, i.e., geographical and climatic conditions, career opportunities, language and cultural characteristics, health insurance and social system, unemployment benefits, etc.

Due to the high demand created during the crisis, municipal youth services increased their services on issues of international mobility. The extent to which demand for counselling services rose was illustrated by expert 2 in 2014 who was in a leading position and responsible for the department of international mobility at a municipal youth centre in one of Spain's biggest cities:

> *We created advisory centres in the different districts of the city in order to offer a space where young people can make their demands, and we from the City Hall can give answers to these demands. From this point of view, we collect demands of all types. At the moment, work-related issues are most frequently asked about. In second position, there are education-related issues, academic and non-academic, education and training in general. Spare time-related issues follow in third position. And then, there is already international mobility, which is combined with tourism and occupies the fourth position. And there are a lot more topics following on the list, but to be honest, while a few years ago international mobility occupied only position nine or ten, it is now ranked fourth. Thus, in the past few years, demand has risen enormously for this type of necessity among the young people, who are moving to perform some kind of mobility in order to work, to study or for volunteering. So, here we are offering this service, this youth advisory service.*

At the headquarters of this municipal administration and service alone, the number of employees working in the field of international mobility quadrupled due to the high demand for consultancy services on this matter.

Public services have broadened and specified their services quantitatively but also qualitatively. Not only has the number of advisors increased significantly, but also the variety and specificity of informative events. In order to spread their activities among young people public services announce them on their own homepage and make use of social media. The municipal service interviewed offered 10-15 informative events a year, which are held in all districts of the cities on a rotating basis. The advisors in the districts organize these events. In this context, the platform "Eurodesk" is an important platform for the public institutions offering networks and information sources. It is a pan-European network of more than 1000 youth professionals working with Eurodesk in 34 countries to raise awareness for and facilitate mobility opportunities among young people (see Eurodesk, 2018). Advisors in Spain explained that they establish contacts with possible destinations and obtain information for the young people from Eurodesk. Additionally, advisors from Eurodesk in the destination countries support the Spanish advisors when they deal with a complicated case or have more detailed questions. In the municipality interviewed, the first campaign on international mobility for young people was started in 2013. In that year, workshops took place offering specific information on eleven countries. Furthermore, thirteen workshops were organized in which embassies, consulates or representatives of different delegations or countries were contacted in order to give them the chance to talk directly about the opportunities their country was offering.

According to the internal statistics of the public institutions, young people looking for work were mostly interested in where to find work in their profession independent of the destination country. However, information on English-speaking countries was most strongly in demand, especially the United Kingdom and Ireland. Furthermore, information on jobs in Germany and France was also much sought after; due to the wide spreading of the English language in these countries, the Netherlands and the Scandinavian countries also turned out very popular. Outside the European Union, the United States, Canada, South America and Australia were most in demand due to the English language spoken there. Among the South American countries Brazil, Chile and Argentina were the ones young people were most interested in as destinations for labour emigration.

The public advisory services on international mobility distinguish their young clients by four age groups, which are minors under 18 years, and adults between 19 and 24 years, 25 to 29 years, as well as 30 to 35 years. The biggest group they attended to were those between 19 and 24 years as most of the mobility schemes provided by municipal youth services target this age group, such as *Erasmus+*, *Leonardo da Vinci*, etc.

Across all these age groups, there is growing interest in international mobility. The profile of people having a defined professional aim is growing according to the local advisors, but most of the people plan a stay in order to improve their language skills. The expert 2, head of the department of international mobility at the interviewed municipal youth service, offered a twofold explanation:

> *We hypothesize that the increased mobility, the demand for mobility,*

> *is attributable to two reasons. The one which is most visible in the communication media is the necessity to find a job, which is not available here but in other places outside the country. This surely is one part, but there is another part, which never appears in the communication media and which might also be an issue of high importance in the decisions of the young people to give international mobility a try, which is the level of globalization we have in the world at the moment. The young people are discovering this as an opportunity that did not exist before. So, this mobility becomes increasingly natural compared to what it was 30 years ago, when in fact all the mobility that occurred was purposeful and forced. We think that currently there is also a part that is forced but there is also a part, which is growing, which has grown with the crisis but would also have grown without the crisis and that is the part of being keen on educational experience or volunteering or work abroad, with the idea of returning, or with the idea of visiting the world, or with the idea of enjoying the maximum of possible experiences in this globalized world.*

So, apart from finding a job, the main objectives of international mobility stated by the municipal youth service is to gain international experience and to increase language skills. This motive was also mentioned by most of the interviewed Spanish immigrants. Hence, the political framing of mobility as a chance for the unemployed youth was supported by a diffuse perception of international mobility as a chance to gain experiences, get acquainted with foreign languages and cultures, and travelling. All interview partners highlighted the opportunities provided by the European Union, which shows the *normative* diffusion of the idea of a common EU labour market and its opportunities provided by intra-EU labour mobility. They emphasised the increased ease of international mobility and thus take part in the process of spreading the idea of labour mobility as a chance in the Spanish society.

Summarizing, in the wake of the economic crisis several institutions started to facilitate labour emigration either on behalf of the government or due to pressure from unemployed Spaniards. These institutions provide resources, which supported intra-EU mobility and labour emigration in general. In this context, public institutions created a field of labour mobility and emigration, which was able to realize the policies introduced by creating the *right circumstances*.

4.1.5 Governance units: promoting new job search strategies

In the wake of the Memorandum, the *framing* of labour mobility as a chance was spread and promoted by governance units in the field of the labour market. On demand of the young Spaniards governance units in Spain supported international *job search*. Firstly, the *Ministry for Employment* announced job opportunities and informed about labour market and living conditions abroad. Secondly, *public employment agencies*, such as SEPE and EURES in *Spain promoted the opportunities of intra-EU labour mobility* and *built networks* with different institutions of the labour market in Spain and abroad. In doing so, they informed about possibilities as well as points of contact for *international job search* and, and *spread the framing*.

Thirdly, municipal youth services, broadened and deepened their activities with regard to intra-EU mobility and promoted the *framing of labour mobility as a chance for the youth*. The role of governance units in creating new ways of job search is summarised by Table 6.

Table 6: Role of governance units in creating new ways of job search

Institutional role	**Institutional action**	
Public employment agencies	-promote international job opportunities -establish networks	→ spread framing → offer new ways of international job search
Municipal youth services		

Although mobility was politically steered it was not a definite top-down process as perceptions towards EU mobility recently seemed to change among young people towards *using the freedom of movement in the EU to gain experiences*.

In this context, the governance units created a favourable framework for labour mobility, which was important for creating the *right circumstances*. While the *framing* and the new *ways of international job search* were developed in the interplay between young Spaniards as challengers and governance units, such as the Ministry of Employment, EURES, SEPE and the municipal youth services, other institutions created an institutional filter for the *matching* of Spanish job candidates and foreign employers. Those institutions, their actions and roles are highlighted in the next section.

4.2 Strategic actors: practices of the recruitment industry

After outlining the field changes initiated by the challengers and the governance units, the following section shows how other institutional incumbents of the labour market, education and migration joined the field of intra-EU labour mobility subsequently. They did so for strategic reasons by participating in the new field in order to make money and/or secure their survival by gaining prestige or new fields of activities as will be described in the following part. Entrepreneurial actors initiated the recruitment industry and therefore the practices of transnational labour mobility that offered the connecting points for Spanish institutions. Both entrepreneurial actors and incumbents provide a necessary function for the *matching* of Spanish job candidates and vacancies abroad as outlined below.

4.2.1 Entrepreneurial actors: recruiters

The raised awareness of chances of international mobility and the growing number of those willing to emigrate combined with financial support from abroad for recruitment has also led to the emergence of a variety of private mediators. These are entrepreneurial actors making money by assuming a bridging function between the Spanish labour force and the German labour market.

During the crisis, these mediators in the private sector emerged in Spain offering recruitment services and/or support finding and applying for a job, language courses, etc. Mediators usually have social skills qualifying them to facilitate mobility and seize the opportunity to make profit by offering specialized services. Business consultancies working in trading, language schools, or international human resource consultants obtain these social skills because they possess the necessary language skills, business contacts and know-how. The human resource managers of big international companies that look for job candidates on the Spanish labour market also belong to this category of recruiters.

The recruiters provide individual services depending on their clients, the professions or the sector and the service tasks provided. Due to the novelty of the field of skilled labour mobility, the interviewed Spanish international recruiters recently became professionalised recruiters, often due to social skills or knowledge, such as contacts or language skills in the recruiting country, which were not necessarily gained expressly for this purpose. Several recruiters in Spain worked in a job in one of the neighbouring fields of labour mobility, such as education, migration or business before they started international recruitment. However, some became recruiters more randomly, which is exemplified by a statement of the Spanish recruiter 3:

> *Well, I have a daughter, who is a nurse and when she finished her study programme she couldn't find a job here. Therefore, as I knew English, I helped her to do everything that had to do with the inscription in the Nursing and Midwifery Council and helped her to find work in the UK. Afterwards, another friend came who was also unemployed and was looking for work and I did the same. So, that was how it started and finally I said "Well, then I will start to do that for profit", because I was dedicating my time, my money, my calls to help other people. Then, little by little, I did it like that. I work from home and I am self-employed. I have my office in the garage of my house and have been doing this for some years. I founded the company three or four years ago but I started a bit earlier helping other people and so on. So, as there was high demand, well, I decided to dedicate myself to this as it provides a lot of satisfaction to help other people who are in the same situation as my daughter, who are lost and do not know what to do. Obviously, it is a company dedicated to the crisis. (...). Now, there is a necessity.*

This statement also shows the typical perspective the recruiters have on their clients and international labour mobility. From their point of view, they are driven by their economic and social necessities and perceive labour mobility as a chance they want to seize. The increased emergence of private agencies for international recruitment on the Spanish labour market is an indicator of the *institutional isomorphism* towards putting the idea of the common EU labour market into practice.

Although the range of public services for questions on international mobility has increased in number and specialization, the emigrating Spaniards seem to prefer the services of mediators from the private sector. Spaniards interested in foreign job opportunities suppose that the private institutions offer more "trustworthy" job advertisements, as stated in the interviews with public services and professional unions. Therefore, they often prefer to pay for recruitment services instead of using the public or private ones that are for free because they expect them to offer better service. Paradoxically, according to migrants, public and private employment centres, but also migrant organisations, the black sheep of international recruitment are more likely to be found among the recruiters charging the job candidates for job placement. A typical dubious business model is that recruiters charge a significant but still affordable amount of money for recruitment services and guarantee an adequate job placement matching the job candidates' qualification. Once the applicants have left Spain, they find themselves working in an unskilled job for a fast-food chain. This practice seems to be a common strategy of dubious recruiters from the UK offering mediating services. Ironically, at least during the time of data collection between 2013 and 2016, the fraud practices of parts of the private recruitment agencies did not increase the trust in public employment agencies. Instead, the belief in increased quality of a recruitment service that is offered for-profit was strengthened.

However not only the recruiters from abroad, but also the Spanish employers destroyed the trust in fair labour relations. Especially during the crisis, incorrect behaviour of Spanish recruiters and employers seemed to be standard. Therefore, Spanish jobseekers are used to fraud and false promises, which complicates the work of foreign recruiters. Several interviewed migrants, migrant organisations and labour unions in Spain told stories like the following of the male recruiter 1 from Germany in 2013:

> *During the complete recruitment procedure we try to inform people in a transparent, fair and open-minded manner, putting all our cards on the table, as we would also do it in Germany with the German applicants. We do not work according to the slogan "The applicants have no other choice, so they have to come anyway". No! Instead we want to inform them clearly and honestly. The reactions to that were interesting because many of the candidates are not used to that in Spain, not at all. Not at all! However, they are generally not used to that in Spain, but even less so in a Spain in crisis. Also, they are not used to it from foreign, in many cases, dubious recruiters. They are not used to receiving a confirmation of receipt. They are not used to receiving a letter of refusal. They are not used to a recruiter*

calling them and getting in touch with them. There is a considerable amount of young ladies among the applicants and I notice to some extent, that they are suspicious and wondering "Who is that? What does he want?" Or whatever... because they are not used to being treated in a decent way, which is standard for us.

I was in Madrid in March and talked to various job candidates. They told me that mostly when they applied for a job they received no response at all or they heard empty promises over and over again, when they asked about the state of the application procedure. However, they never got to receive some real information about what will happen next. Partly, the people got a job offer and afterwards nothing happened. When they asked for the job, they heard empty promises again that maybe they would get the job half a year later.

Similar stories were told by the Spanish emigrants interviewed. Most of them experienced exploitation as well as unfair and indecent treatment by Spanish employers. These conditions on the Spanish labour market make it difficult for foreign recruiters to build trust in the services they offer, although reliable recruiters may guarantee the quality, efficiency and success of transnational labour mobility. Therefore, they usually collaborate with other institutions, which are well established in the neighbouring fields of education, labour market or migration. They provide the crucial social lubricant *trust* to make the *right circumstances* work effectively.

4.2.2 Incumbents of the field of labour migration

The following institutions play an important role when it comes to supporting international job search and the preparation of international recruitment and labour integration abroad. Subsequently, it is outlined how these incumbents support the *matching* between employers abroad and job candidates in Spain by establishing contacts, giving information and providing knowledge on labour market issues, recognition of education, social benefits, cultural characteristics, or they offer language skills as described in this section.

4.2.2.1 Language schools

In conjunction with international recruitment and labour mobility, the demand for language courses in Spain skyrocketed during the economic crisis. They are the main recipients of demands for preparatory services and thereby fulfil an important function for the *matching* of job candidates in Spain and employers abroad

Before the crisis, English was the most demanded language and became even more popular during the crisis. German became the second most demanded language because of the good economic situation and the MobiPro-EU programme, while French, as the language of the neighbouring country, was in third position (see Cruz-Martin, 2012). As the owner 1 of a private German language school in Spain put it:

> *Today there is a high demand for studying the German language in Spain. This has various reasons: the crisis; the fact that there are no jobs; and you always have to give an added value to your curriculum. There are people who are looking for work in Germany or in another German speaking country. Other people are working here but for some reason or other they do not exclude living in Germany for a job or they just would like to have more formation for themselves.*

According to the interview partners in Spain, the same holds true for other languages. Due to the increased demand, language schools increased the amount of language courses and broadened their services. Besides the standard language courses that teach vocabulary, grammar and day-to-day topics, new and more specified language classes were developed, such as courses focusing on terminology in certain sectors or geared to particular professions. Other courses aim to impart the German or English culture in order to prepare those who choose to live abroad for particular features of the local mentality. Furthermore, language schools offer workshops on how to write a proper CV and how to do a job interview in a specific foreign country. Both are essential stepping stones on the way to finding a job abroad and differ from country to country concerning both chronology and content.

Since the onset of the economic crisis and the increased demand for information on labour emigration language schools have also been offering workshops on where to look for jobs. Accordingly, they give information on institutions, home pages, release job announcements and/or provide information on living conditions. However, due to the high demand, several language schools also developed advisory and mediating services. They established contacts with international recruiters and check and collect job announcements for Spanish customers looking for a job abroad and/or preselect job candidates for foreign recruiters. The interview partners at language schools have a different perspective on their clients than the experts at municipal youth services. They miss the appreciation for international experiences in their clients. Instead they state that their clients feel forced to emigrate. The owner 1 of a German language school explained:

> *I went abroad and for me it was a luxury to work in Germany because when I went abroad all these facilities we have today did not exist and for me it was a luxury that I was able to go and work abroad. What happens now is that also all the communication media emphasize that it is not a luxury but a necessity and they present it as something bad. But it is not bad! Believe me it is not! All the experience you may have made abroad*

> *will serve you for all your life, personally or professionally. And a lot of people are not aware of that. However, there are already all those public and private institutions that emphasize how bad it is in Spain and that our people, our youth have to go to work abroad. Instead they should have a look at the other side of the coin: Alright, even if it is a necessity but now there are a lot of European programmes and there is hardly any barrier in the internal Europe, therefore it is much easier to find work nowadays. And in the end, the truth is that there are few people who really want to go. And that is surprising to me.*

This quote shows that those working in language schools perceive labour mobility as a chance because they themselves are or were "internationally mobile professionals". This attitude was also found in the interviews with other interview partners from language schools. Thus, they transport the framing of labour mobility as a chance for young professionals to improve their working and living conditions to their clients in a process of *normative isomorphism*.

Due to the labour demand in Germany and the subsidies for labour mobility offered by the German government, especially the demand for German language classes rose enormously compared to the level of demand before the crisis (see also Spiegel Online, 2012). The German language schools interviewed in Spain reported that their business is flourishing, so that they increased the number of classes, their service portfolio and their staff. Among other subsidies, the German government funded preparatory language courses in the home country of up to 120 hours. These subsidies were intended to offer the opportunity of labour emigration also to those Spaniards, who had no German language skills before. First of all, private language schools seized the opportunity to earn money by providing specific courses, advisory and mediating services, but also public ones broadened the variety of their services. Hence, language schools started to participate in the field of international labour mobility offering new services in order to make their institution more profitable. By doing so, they supported the diffusion of the political framing and the individual perceptions of labour mobility as a chance. The high demand for language courses also shows that international labour mobility had become a legitimized option in the economic crisis, despite the Brain Drain criticism. However, not everybody who chose this option perceived international mobility as a chance. Instead, a considerable group of labour emigrants felt forced to leave the country for better working and living conditions as was explained by the interviewed language schools.

4.2.2.2 Labour, professional and trade unions

Unions were addressed by their affiliates as well as by recruiters as points of contact in order to provide information on concrete labour market topics or certain professions or sectors.

In general, during the economic crisis labour unions lost a large portion of their influence as social partners in labour relations. Labour unions were traditionally relatively strong in Spain before the crisis since the (so-called) Moncloa Pact became effective in 1978, which was part of the democratic transition in Spain (see Ministerio de Economía, 1977). Ever since, the labour unions have had a strong institutionalized power on the political level, as they could use their collective power by lobbying and negotiating with politicians to influence political debates and decision-making (see Hassel, 2013).

The interviewed experts from the labour market mentioned various factors accounting for the diminished power of labour unions in the wake of the economic crisis. First and foremost, the bargaining power of labour unions is shrinking in times of mass unemployment. When labour supply itself becomes problematic because of high redundancies as compared to demand, labour unions have no means to exert pressure on employers. Additionally, the unemployed have hardly any financial means or other reasons to pay the membership fees of labour unions. Therefore, the biggest labour unions in Spain, which are UGT and CCOO, lost 44% of their members during the economic crisis (see Triper, 2015). Furthermore, several corruption scandals of labour unions affected their credibility in the public eye (see elEconomista.es, 2013).

A major change between the social partners corrupting the institutionalized power balance in the labour relations was driven by new legislative regulation. In line with the liberalisation efforts implemented since the 1980s, the socialist party loosened the provisions for dismissal protection in 2010 during the government of Jóse Luis Rodríguez Zapatero (see Suárez-Corujo, 2017). However, a much more radical liberalisation took place in 2012 when the conservative government of Mariano Rajoy was in charge. Their labour market reforms made it easier for employers to hire employees under more precarious conditions offering more temporary contracts. The new regulations decreased the protection against dismissal and especially collective dismissal became much easier while there were cuts in the welfare system, e.g. in the pension, health and social system (ibid.).

In the face of the enormous unemployment rates of 20-25% (see Clemente, 2015; see Instituto Nacional de Estadistica, 2018a) during the economic crisis many people, who were unemployed or working in precarious labour conditions, approached labour and professional unions to seek information and assistance for labour emigration. Therefore, it became a new field of activity for these unions to provide or facilitate advisory services or contacts to recruiters. According to the interviewed unions, the general multi-sectoral labour unions that act on the national level give general advice on employment opportunities in different countries and regulations of social legislation, which should be taken into account, like conditions of eligibility or expiration of Spanish social, unemployment and health care benefits, while living abroad.

Professional unions or unions for certain sectors or crafts offer more specific information and contacts. Labour unions and professional unions introduced mediating services for Spanish professionals, companies and recruiters. According to their own statements, the labour unions react to the requests of members and non-members and want to assist them as much as possible, as it is their main task and objective to make a solidary contribution. The latter was very difficult in a situation with high unemployment rates, when the labour unions lost big parts of their institutional influence and lost reputation due to corruption scandals. As there were very limited means available for the labour unions to help the unemployed find a job on the national level, they expanded their services to provide information and contacts on working abroad, especially in the EU. Therefore, participation in the field of international labour market integration, which can be considered a subfield of labour mobility, was a strategy to avoid losing even more members and to legitimate their existence. The following statement by executive 1 from a Spanish labour union mirrors the relevance of intra-EU labour mobility for the unemployed, the information service they offered to different societal parties, but also the existential fear of the labour unions:

> *The option to go abroad is big. If you do not have a job here you can go abroad as we are in a common space on the EU level. It is limited to EU citizens and we benefit from this advantage. So you have to make use of this mobility here, while for others it is very complicated to go abroad and work there. Even if not everybody wants to work abroad, we are lucky to have this chance. Therefore, we from the labour union do our utmost to assist affiliates and non-affiliates alike. We also serve people like you (referring to the author). We give information on that matter to a lot of people from different organizations. You can rely on us because we think that if we can make a contribution, it will always be useful, you know. Whatever you need, you have my contact details and I am always at your disposal whenever necessary. We make a solidary contribution and keeping us alive will serve all of us.*

This quote shows that unions provided contact and information to assist their affiliates but also to gain new fields of activities in order to secure their survival.

The professional unions are a strategically important contact point for recruiters for various reasons. Firstly, they have the possibility to spread vacancies among a high number of suitable job candidates, not only among their members, but they also have mailing lists and personal contacts with relevant educational institutions and alumni associations. Secondly, they offer contacts with relevant platforms, in the media (tv) or trade journals, which recruiters can use to inform about vacancies, but even more so, about job requirements, recruitment procedures, working conditions, salaries and companies in the potential destination countries. By facilitating these contacts with the recruiters, they help them gain credibility and seriousness in the eyes of the professionals. In this way, the professional unions create trust into those offering the opportunities of labour emigration and into international mobility itself among possible job candidates. Thus they establish the precondition for making the institutional changes in the field of labour mobility the *right circumstance* by being well received and working adequately.

Labour unions and recruiters collaborate as they profit from each other's contacts and social skills. The recruiters gain trust in their services and access to suitable job candidates by collaborating with labour unions, while the labour unions, in their turn, gain prestige and new fields of activities after having lost power and status. By doing so, both recruiters and labour unions secure their survival by profiting from the demand for services related to international labour mobility. Therefore, they benefit from the perception of labour mobility as a chance for unemployed Spaniards and spread the framing of this matter. Additionally, unions offer valuable resources in the form of contacts to a pool of job candidates offering a specific job profile in demand. Hence, the efficiency of the *matching* process between job candidate and employer is increased.

4.2.2.3 Universities and other educational institutions

The same is true for universities and educational institutions. Therefore, universities and training academies that qualify their students in the fields sought after in other countries, also take part in the field of international mobility in various ways. They are often contacted directly by companies or recruiters or by the public employment agencies on behalf of these companies. Private universities tend to be more responsive and more committed when it comes to establishing and maintaining contacts with companies and recruiters. Several recruiters confirmed this tendency, which was also experienced during the participatory observation. In the framework of the participant observation, the private university contacted responded immediately, and the first meeting of the recruiters and the university staff took place one day after the first approach was made. During the meeting the facilities were shown to the recruiter and the author by the Dean, the university lawyer, the head of teaching and the head of international relations at the university. In this way, general information was given by the staff concerning the practical training the curriculum, the number of students, the tuition fees, and so on. Afterwards, during lunch at the university canteen, the basic points of the future cooperation were discussed. During the whole meeting, the tour and during lunch all staff members attended, were available for questions and raised relevant issues for their field of activity. Obviously, the university staff was interested in giving a good impression of the university and in clarifying the most important issues for starting cooperation. Within one or two days, the university staff sent a first draft for formalizing the recruitment relation meeting the universities' regulation. In this context, the national standards had to be considered, as well as the conformity with international standards such as the regulations in the European Higher Education Area (EHEA) and the Bologna reform.

In the participatory observation, the public university proved to be much more tardy and the administrative bureaucracy worked very slowly. It took the recruiter, who established the contact, half a year to fix an appointment, as the Dean was not responsive. According to the information given by various recruiters and public employment agencies, public universities seem to be more responsive and more engaged the higher their reputation is. The higher degree of commitment shown by the private universities and by public ones with a high reputation can be interpreted as a sign for them being more concerned about economic needs and a good reputation in public awareness. It was also confirmed by recruiters and unions that universities belong to recruitment networks.

Cooperation with universities is especially suitable for establishing long-term relationships. Therefore, it is most adequate for companies that have a constant high demand for job candidates in a certain professional field. Hence, cooperation between a university and a company can be regarded as the basis of a sustainable recruitment relationship. If both parties are willing to invest limited efforts in maintaining the relationship, it may turn into a lasting cooperation based on personal contacts between the university staff, the recruiters and their core customers. In this way, trust may increase between the parties involved that help to prevent the escalation of intercultural misunderstandings and other potential conflict situations. These are serious issues determining the success of all forms of transnational cooperation that were commented by most of the interview partners from public and private institutions as well as migrants.

A variety of measures can be taken jointly in order to corroborate the cooperative relation, as the universities are not only able to spread job announcements but have the possibility to include opportunities for international mobility or the preparation of international mobility into their curriculum. They do so by integrating preparatory language courses into their range of courses. These do not only impart general language skills but also the specific professional terminology. Additionally, the universities are able to integrate internships abroad into their curriculum, which account for the mandatory practical training. Both language courses and internships abroad provide students with the necessary ECTS credit points. For the recruiting companies, the big advantage of this cooperation is a step-by-step familiarisation of the students with the foreign language, culture, working and living conditions in the specific country.

Together with the recruiters the university are able to organize special recruitment fairs, information events, workshops and seminars to simplify international recruitment. In the different recruitment events students and graduates are able to receive information directly from different sources such as the university staff, recruiters, employers and establish most valuable contacts with students and graduates, who have worked in the envisaged country of destination before.

Compared to most of the other advisory and mediating services, the universities, which maintain cooperative relations with companies, offer a very coherent and specific form of preparation for labour emigration. It is mostly tailored to the specific needs of students and graduates of a certain profession and their needs at every stage of their career development.

Thus, the universities and companies control and improve the quality and suitability of the courses and events offered by the university as well as the training measures in the companies and the recruitment procedure. The job candidates can therefore rely on the purposeful design of the different educational opportunities and the job offers facilitating international mobility. This increases the successful matching of Spanish job candidates and employers abroad.

In order to gain prestige and new students universities enter the field of transnational mobility and start to cooperate with companies or recruiters that, in turn, profit from increasing credibility and contacts with students. The latter suggest cooperation and offer internships as well as jobs to secure a long-term potential of labour force for themselves. In doing so, they create the *right circumstances* for intra-EU labour mobility on the Spanish labour market. Both recruiters and educational institutions ensure their survival by collaborating in the field of transnational recruitment. Furthermore, the cooperation between Spanish universities and German employers and recruiters is an indicator of the *institutional isomorphism* in favour of the common EU labour market.

4.2.2.4 Non-Profit-Migrant organisations

Several of the non-profit organisations and services that had recently been established in order to assist the integration of immigrants in Spain started to offer assistance for Spanish labour emigrants during the crisis.

The advisory services on labour emigration became necessary due to Spain's abrupt change from being an immigration country to becoming an emigration country again and the demand of Spaniards planning to leave for labour opportunities. The migrant organisations in Spain were initially founded to give advice for labour immigration offering support and integration measures for immigrants, as the number of immigrants to Spain had risen enormously in the decade before the crisis. During the crisis their services were less frequently used as immigration reduced, while emigration increased. However, several relevant topics for labour immigrants are similar to the issues labour emigrants have to face, such as the procedures for recognition of diploma or the availability of networks that might be of assistance. Thus, these non-profit organisations used the social skills they had already acquired and extended their field of work to Spaniards likely to emigrate. Advisory services were developed for labour emigration in collaboration with other non-profit organisations, labour unions and public advisory services cooperating in the field of labour immigration and integration. By doing so, they responded to the changed demand and secured their survival by participating in the field of labour emigration.

Comparing the different institutions in Spain with regard to their perspective on the clients using their advisory and mediating services, the people asking for advice from the migrant organisations seemed to be the least prepared ones. According to the migrant organisations themselves, they had no or very little language skills. They hardly ever informed themselves about labour opportunities, hurdles, legal requirements and legal conditions. As stated by the interview partners from non-profit organisations, the vast majority of their clients did not obtain a degree in one of the professions sought after in other countries. This was why they did not meet the requirements to be sponsored by employers or foreign recruitment programmes. On their own account, they had to invest money for language courses, travelling, removal costs, and recognition of certificates, which mean enormous expenses for someone who is unemployed or works under precarious conditions. The non-profit organisations on international mobility were aware of the difficulties and of the limited capacities of the unemployed seeking help. They reported that most of the clients entered the advisory services with high expectations but were disillusioned by the advisors about their job opportunities abroad. This was depicted most clearly by expert 1 working for a Spanish non-profit organisation, who said:

> *It's frustrating, because my job is to destroy dreams.*

Additionally, most of them seemed to search for low-skilled and low-wage jobs in the country of destination. The interviewed migrant organisations stated that most of their clients went abroad for jobs they could also have found in Spain. The expert 1, employee of a migrant organisation, obtained a lot of approval by representatives of other advisory services when she said in a group discussion:

> *Many of them go abroad for a job as a waiter, a cook's mate or a chambermaid. Well, common! With a little effort they could get the same job here. I do not understand why they go abroad for doing cleaning jobs!*

The experiences gained by the migrant organisations show two conflicting aspects. On the one hand, there were the high expectations the unemployed or precariously employed Spaniards had with regard to international mobility, but also the limits of international labour mobility became obvious. Labour demand abroad, subsidies and international recruitment mean a chance for those professionals who match the sought-after profiles in the knowledge-based globalized economy. For others, labour opportunities might be as bad in Spain as anywhere else. Hence, the framing of transnational labour mobility as a chance was spread by institutions among wide parts of the society and thereby also created deceptive illusions, which proves that an institutional myth had been developed.

4.2.3 Analysis of field changes: ways of job search and matching

This section showed that not only governance units, such as the Ministry of Employment, public employment agencies and public youth centres supported international *job search* and the matching between employers abroad and job candidates in Spain. Recruiters also emerged as entrepreneurial actors to make profit by fulfilling the bridging function between the Spanish labour market and the one abroad. They were necessary as the institutional transnational hurdles were hard to manage for employers and job candidates themselves. The actions of recruiters as entrepreneurial actors and incumbents creating new ways of job search and matching job candidates and employers is summarised in Table 7.

Recruiters provided the vacancies of employers abroad. In order to find suitable job candidates they often worked together with incumbents of the fields of education, migration and the labour market, such as language schools, universities, other educational institutions, labour unions and migrant organisations. These incumbents created information services and established contacts as a reaction to the demand of those unemployed or in precarious working conditions. In doing so, they created new *ways of international job search*. While the entrepreneurial actors connect the Spanish labour market with labour markets abroad to make money, the incumbents seek to secure their survival by taking part in the field of labour emigration.

Table 7: Actions of entrepreneurial actors creating new ways of job search and matching job candidates

Institutional role	Institutions	Ways of job search	Matching
Entrepreneurial actors	Recruiters	Spread jobs announcements at public employment agencies and incumbents	Individual matching of job candidates and employers
Incumbents	Educational institutions (universities & institutes)	Announcements via mailing lists or notice board	Matching of profile and vacancies
	Labour unions		
	Language schools	Contacts to recruiters Assistance in the application procedure	Individual matching of job candidates and employers
	Migrant organisations	General information	

Entrepreneurial actors and incumbents fulfil a function of preselection and thereby contribute to a successful *matching* and *recruitment* of individual job candidates for employers abroad. While the recruiters *recruit* employees for certain professionals, incumbents mostly try to *match* job candidates with job opportunities abroad.

Language schools and migrant organisation deal with a rather broad variety of job candidates seeking for a qualified job abroad. Therefore, they offer individualised services depending on the profile of the candidates and the assistance they need during the application procedure.

Migrant organisations, however, rather offer a advisory service to people who are either not professionally qualified, who do not possess the skills in demand abroad, or who do not seek international mobility for professional reasons.

Furthermore, educational institutions, including universities, and labour/trade/professional unions match candidates obtaining a specific job profile with employers from the same sector searching for precisely this profile. They spread vacancies via mailing lists, facebook or noticeboards.

As the probability of matching is very high, approaching these incumbents to find a job abroad is the most promising way of international job search. Nevertheless, this is not an option for all professionals because unions and educational institutions are more likely to have established recruitment relations with employers abroad, if they offer a pool of candidates in demand abroad.

4.2.4 Creating the right circumstances for intra-EU mobility

The institutional changes in the aftermath of the Spanish economic crisis are summarized by Table 8. During the time of data collection, the policy agenda in Spain was dominated by the economic crisis, which caused the second highest unemployment rates in the EU after Greece. Young Spaniards who were most strongly affected and lost their future perspectives, exerted pressure on governance units and other institutions, applied new strategies of international job search and demanded for information on labour mobility and emigration. This development was supported by a *changing perception* of migration in Spain. Labour migration was increasingly seen as an opportunity rather than a necessity. This suggests a normative diffusion of the advantages of labour market liberalisation in the common EU labour market.

In response to the protest movement and the demand for information on labour mobility of the young Spaniards who were unemployed or in precarious working conditions, the Spanish Ministry of employment built up a policy framework facilitating intra-EU mobility. In the first place, these policy developments were also supported by the German Ministry of Employment and its financial support in the framework of the German recruitment programme MobiPro-EU (see Bundesagentur für Arbeit, 2013). This bilateral agreement was formalised in a Memorandum and paved the way for the successful implementation of the EU-wide programme "Your first Eures job" (see also European Commission, 2018b). However, the Spanish Ministry of Employment did not only develop new policies, but also announced, spread and informed about labour opportunities abroad by means of public services. In order to legitimize these programmes the government framed labour mobility as a chance for the unemployed youth. Although they had to face the counter-argument given by the opposition of labour mobility producing

Brain Drain and economic refugees, the *framing* of labour mobility offering job opportunities became widely accepted.

The implementation of the emigration policies was rendered possible by governance units, such as the efforts of EURES and public employment agencies, which promoted the opportunities of labour emigration, especially intra-EU mobility, on behalf of the government. Therefore, they are key actors in putting the new policies on labour mobility into practice, raising awareness for the chances of transnational labour mobility and giving legitimation to the political framing. Additionally, public services offered assistance for labour mobility due to the political agenda and the citizens' demand. Thus, municipal youth services began to offer advisory services for intra-EU mobility supported by the Eurodesk network (see also Eurodesk, 2018). Hence, a *coercive isomorphism* of institutions promoting and facilitating intra-EU labour mobility and offering *new ways of international job search* is witnessed. The involvement of governance units increased the trust in the mobility programmes, which is mentioned as one of the most important preconditions for intra-EU mobility.

Recruiters were the main entrepreneurial actors from the private sector that initiated the development of a recruitment industry in Spain by using the social skills they possessed, such as knowledge of languages, knowledge about the labour market and business contacts in both labour markets. They seized the opportunity to earn money by transnational recruitment of Spanish professionals who were redundant on the Spanish labour market.

Subsequently to the German government, private language schools participated in the recruitment industry to make profits. Due to the high demand for information also other incumbents of the labour market, such as labour and professional unions, non-profit organisations, public language schools and job centres took over their new role as advisory services in order to facilitate job search and/or labour integration abroad. They helped spreading the framing of labour mobility as a chance for the unemployed youth in Spain and supported the selection of suitable candidates. Additionally, offering advisory services became a strategy to regain influence and increase prestige for unions and universities by tapping a new field of activity. In addition, migrant organisations and cultural institutions, which offered integration measures for immigrants before the crisis, began to use their knowledge and contacts in order to prepare Spaniards for labour integration abroad. In doing so, they provide an institutional filter for the selection of job candidates and their matching with the vacancies abroad. Thus, in a *mimetic process* a broad range of for-profit and non-profit organisations created advisory and mediating services to participate in the field of labour emigration in order to secure their survival in times of high economic uncertainty. However, the successful promotion of the opportunities provided by international mobility partly also created the myth that labour mobility was an option for everybody, which led to false expectations as it is mainly a chance for certain professional profiles that are sought-after.

In this way, a field of intra-EU labour mobility was created by institutions from the neighbouring fields of education, labour market and migration, which provide the right circumstances for labour mobility. The field consists of the subfields of international labour recruitment and labour integration. In the interplay of the institutions participating in the field an institutional myth was created claiming that international labour mobility was an option for everybody to achieve better labour and living conditions. A necessary prerequisite for the development of this field was the availability of the right people, which means a great number of skilled professionals that are in demand abroad.

Table 8: Analysis of the status quo in the Spanish field of intra-EU mobility

Policy Agenda	**Economic crisis**		
Labour Market	**Unemployment**		
Institutional Role	Institutions	Institutional Myth/perceptions/ framings	Strategic Action
Challengers	Young Spaniards organised in 15M	Labour mobility as a chance	Labour emigration • Demand information • Put pressure on governance units and other institutions → Demand new ways of international job search
Governance units	Ministry of Employment Opposition Public employment agencies • EURES, SEPE, BA Municipal youth service	Labour mobility as a chance (government) Vs. Brain Drain and Economic refugees (opposition)	• Memorandum • Your first EURES job • Announce and spread labour opportunities • Consultation service → Create framing of "labour mobility as a chance"
Incumbents	Education • Universities • Institutions of education and training Labour market • Labour/ professional/ trade unions Migrant organisations	Labour mobility as a chance (educational and labour market institutions) vs. labour mobility as an illusion (migrant organisations)	Specialised consultation service • created on demand of potential emigrants • created to regain power • created to increase prestige → Assume filter function for *matching*
Entrepreneurial actors	recruiters	Labour mobility as a chance	• To earn money and secure survival → Bridging function for matching

Different institutions show different perspectives on their clients, their preparedness, motives, their chances on the transnational labour market, their profiles, etc. The reason for these different assessments is the self-selection of potential labour emigrants who chose the institutions. Therefore, in the following part, the relationship between types of professionals, their motives, chances and profiles will be discussed.

5. Creating the right circumstances in Germany

After analysing the field changes and framings that supported labour emigration policies in Spain, the changes in Germany will be highlighted that led to new recruitment policies. Internal changes on the labour market caused by the ageing society involved a destabilisation of the labour market. Section 6.1 shows how employers challenged the status quo by lobbying the government to introduce recruitment programmes. The way in which the employers' associations and the Ministry of Employment created a favourable framing for international recruitment is highlighted. In Section 6.2, the implementation of new policies by institutions, which develop recruitment practices is outlined. The welcome and recognitions culture that was created by institutions in the fields of education, migration and the labour market is described in Section 6.3.

5.1 Actions and Framings of recruitment in the field of mobility

The following part addresses the introduction of policies and practices facilitating labour recruitment. This section analyses the socio-political debate on the demographic shift and its effects on the labour market, which created the dominant framing to legitimize recruitment and subsequent actions. In order to meet the upcoming challenges institutions acted strategically in the fields of labour market and migration. The employers that are challengers, who initiated the new policies on labour mobility, are examined first (Section 6.1.1) to enable an understanding of the development of the field, while the reactions of governance units are addressed subsequently (Section 6.1.2). Thus, this section outlines how employers and governance units developed framings and actions that created the *right circumstances* for intra-EU labour recruitment in Germany.

5.1.1 Challengers of the status quo: employers

The employers played a crucial part in promoting international recruitment as a solution to the demographic crisis and labour shortages, according to the interview partners. As will be described in the following part, they started to create a *framing* legitimizing international recruitment.

The idea of international recruitment emerged in the economic field and was enforced particularly by the employers. From their viewpoint, the shortage of skilled professionals is tightly linked to the demographic crisis (see BDA, 2015). "*Deutschland stirbt aus.*" (=Germany dies out) (Grossarth, 2010) or "*Prognose für 2030: Deutschland schrumpft und vergreist.*" (=Forecast for 2030: Germany shrinks and ages) (Spiegel Online, 2013). These are the regular headlines in Germany´s newspapers, and the debate on demographic change is omnipresent. According to several labour market experts, constantly rising job offers meet a

C. Heimann, *Blessing and Curse of Intra-EU Mobility*, Studien zur Migrations- und Integrationspolitik, https://doi.org/10.1007/978-3-658-31486-6_5

declining workforce. Hence, labour shortages have become a core topic with regard to the labour market. Worst-case scenarios were painted which saw the wealth of the German society at risk if the labour supply could not be guaranteed, because Germany as a successful business and industry location would then suffer a significant decline of its competitiveness (see Vollmer, 2015, p. 20).

In order to corroborate their argumentation, the employers use expert knowledge provided by recognized labour market experts, such as Prognos (2013), a company offering economic research and business consultancy. Prognos published figures on the future development of the labour force in Germany in the next century, predicting an enormous lack of labour force of 1.7 million by 2020 and of 4 million by 2035.

These studies support the framing used by the employers, who identify the supply of labour force as a labour market deficit. According to Brücker et al. (2013) from the Institute of Employment Research, the German labour market is facing labour gaps, which means temporary labour shortages in certain regions and sectors. These labour gaps affect especially professions in MINT subjects, e.g. engineers and mathematical, physical, chemical, biological sciences, or the health care sector, hospitality and certain kinds of technicians (see Mangelberufe.de, 2018). A periodical study by Ernst&Young, called Mittelstandsbarometer (2016), found out that 49% of the medium-sized businesses in Germany suffer from a loss of revenue due to labour shortages.

Internationally recruiting companies that were interviewed and the employers´ association state that employers suffer from the demographic crisis in certain sectors. Member 1 of the executive board of a big company with various branches and several hundreds of employees, explained:

> *In certain areas, you have to fish at the bottom end of the labour market. You have to employ people you would not usually hire. Consequently, there is a lot of fluctuation, because they leave, or you have to get rid of them, or they stay away because of illness, because it is people you would not employ normally.*

Based on the framing of the changing demography, the Confederation of the German Employers' Associations, *Bundesvereinigung der Deutschen Arbeitgeberverbände* (BDA), recommends various steps to safeguard and train the potential of employees (see BDA, 2015). Most recommendations propose measures referring to the labour relationship between employers and employees in Germany. These measures include, for instance, the improvement of education and training, the preservation of employability, the efficiency of recruitment strategies, the flexibility of working hours, extending working life, and the optimization of the matching between employer and employee. Additionally, the BDA states that the national labour force is not enough to cover the job vacancies. Thus, their recommendations include a section dealing with the international recruitment of (highly) skilled professionals to cope with labour shortages and the demographic crisis.

By contrast, the German Trade Union Federation (DGB), who is an incumbent of the labour market, states that the employers are part of the problem. The Federation criticizes that low starting salaries, limited labour contracts, the lack of reconciliation of job and family, poor training conditions and the overall low level of attractiveness of the employers were the main reasons for mismatches and labour shortages. The DGB uses a framing that focuses on an unused potential of employees. They argue that the improvement of education and training as well as of the working conditions is more appropriate than international recruitment. In this sense, the DGB evades the framing of the demographic crisis, which is linked to the employers′ argumentation. Furthermore, the Federation fears that international recruitment is employed as a measure to reduce standard wages, employment rights, and employers' investments in their employees in addition to promoting the exploitation of foreign employees (see Deutscher Gewerkschaftsbund, 2018). The labour unions therefore provided a counter-argument to international recruitment. They offer an alternative framing of international recruitment fostering wage dumping, exploitation and lower investments in education and training. In their view these developments lead to decreasing salaries, standards of employment protection and training also for the German labour force.

Economic interest groups used expert knowledge in the form of reports like those provided by Ernst&Young and Prognos, which legitimize international labour recruitment by claiming that there was a demand for more labour force. These reports offer arguments that are translated into political framings by the employers' association and support the development of the *right circumstances* for international labour recruitment. This perspective of the employers′ association shows that the liberal idea of international recruitment in the common EU labour market for increased competitiveness in the global war for talent was supported and spread among the employers.

5.1.2 Governance units: demographic strategy in Germany

The government turned out to be a strong ally for the employers to translate their interests into *politically legitimized framings* as well as policies and practices that facilitate and steer intra-EU labour mobility to Germany. The next part outlines how the Ministry of Economic Affairs, the Ministry of Employment, the Ministry of the Interior and the public employment agencies jointly supported the development of policies for international labour recruitment in order to create the *right circumstances* for labour immigration from the EU.

Together with the German Ministry of Employment and the Ministry of the Interior, the BDA and the DGB jointly developed a *demographic strategy for economy and growth* (see Bundesministerium des Innern, 2018). Involving a broad range of labour market agents in the development of the policies increases the chances of getting their support for putting the policies into practice. Their joint efforts are reflected in the statement of Carmen Eugenia Barsan, the BDA's legal expert concerning labour migration:

> *One has to ensure that one taps fully and really effectively into the domestic potential first, and then it is a matter of the immigration of professionals.*

Hence, the German government developed certain policies and programmes in order to attract (highly) skilled professionals from abroad. In an endeavour to prevent skill shortages individual measures were defined along five paths of securing employment (*5 Sicherungspfade für Beschäftigung*).

First of all, this concept targets both the better utilisation of the national labour force and the immigrants. Paths 1-4 aim at activating and developing the endogenous potential of the labour force, such as labour market participation of women, elderly people, reintegration of the unemployed, investments in education and training, equal opportunities, etc. (ibid., p. 4). The fifth path focuses on the exogenous potential and its valorisation. On the one hand, concrete measures were developed to improve the integration of immigrants into society and the labour market for those who already live in Germany, for example by offering occupation-related language courses. On the other hand, Germany tries to attract (highly-)skilled professionals from abroad (see Vollmer, 2015, pp. 14 & 21).

In this context, especially intra-EU mobility is focused due to the possibility of labour migration within the Common European labour market, but also recruitment from third countries was facilitated. Thus, these pathways of securing employment show how the employers were able to penetrate the economic policies and how their demand for international recruitment diffused to other institutions. This shows how labour market experts and employers spread the idea of the global competition for talent in a process of normative isomorphism from one flourishing economy to the other.

Thus, within the framework of the *demographic strategy for economy and growth,* international recruitment is promoted as part of Chancellor Angela Merkel's responses to easing problems evoked by the demographic crisis. The former chief economist at the Federal Office for Migration and Refugees (BAMF), Dr. Hans Dietrich von Loeffelholz, who currently conducts accompanying research concerning the implementation and effect of the Blue Card, emphasizes the relationship between migration and the labour market. Based on his experiences as former head of the `Economic Migration and Integration Research Unit for the evaluation of legal measures for effective control of migration´ at BAMF, he states:

> *(...) that migration politics and integration politics on the one side and labour market politics and economic politics on the other side belong together and must be matched.*

On the one hand, the recruitment of professionals aims to reduce labour shortages in certain sectors. On the other hand, the immigration of (highly) skilled, (high-)earning young professionals contributes to reducing the tax deficit in an ageing society (see Brücker et al., 2013). In this regard, the German government adopted a framing that linked the demographic crisis with labour shortages. Contrasting the employers' perception, it emphasised the demographic crisis rather than labour shortages.

The idea of international recruitment as a response to labour shortages was politically implemented in 2012 when the coalition of conservatives and liberals was in power. This economically more liberal government supported international recruitment to increase economic competitiveness. In terms of economic policy, the German government used the framings provided by the German employers to distinguish itself from the social democrats. The interview partners from politics and governmental institutions highlight in particular the role of the Liberal Democratic Party (FDP) and its former Minister for Economic Affairs, Philipp Rösler, who raised the employers' framings to political discourse (see Neurer, 2011). Based on the German employers' framing of international labour migration as a solution to the demographic crisis and labour shortages, the German government developed the programme *MobiPro-EU* (see Bundesagentur für Arbeit, 2013). It provided 139 million euros for the recruitment of young, skilled EU-nationals in shortage occupations and for individuals willing to complete an apprenticeship of 2-3 years. Recruiters state that the German government offered financial support of up to 40,000€ to recruiting companies for every recruited employee from another EU member state. This financial support was designed to cover travel costs, salary, a lump sum for removal costs, preparatory language courses for the recruited in the country of origin and accompanying courses in Germany. In response to the demographic crisis, the coalition of conservatives and liberals, which is close to the employers, initiated and enforced the programme MobiPro-EU. Thus, the liberal party adopted the argument of the employers, which legitimizes international recruitment.

In contrast, the social democrats considered international recruitment the last resort in their endeavours to deal with labour shortages. They widely shared the framing of the DGB, which emphasized the education and training of young people, the reconciliation of family and job as well as the employability of the ageing workforce (see SPD, 2012). Since 2014, when the government changed to a coalition of Social Democrats and Christian Democrats, the programme MobiPro was only eligible for apprenticeships, and financial funding increased more than fourfold. Benefits supporting the international recruitment of professionals were suspended, while the Social Democrats' demand for more investments in education and training for the youth was expanded to international recruitment. In contrast to the former line of argumentation, the call for more investments in education and training was no longer concentrated on the German labour force alone, as interview partners from politics and governmental institutions stated. The Social Democrats linked their arguments to the solidarity with the unemployed youth in Southern Europe and supported international recruitment. Hence, the government related the framing of the demographic crisis with transnational solidarity with the unemployed Spaniards in the form of subsidies and programmes like MobiPro and Job of my life in order to create the *right circumstances* for international labour recruitment

Several agreements on the federal level were developed between German and Spanish Federal States in order to put the bilateral agreement into practice. Such agreements and letters of intents were formalized between the federal states of Catalonia and Baden-Württemberg, Hessen and Madrid, Bavaria and Madrid, the Basque country and Bavaria, as well as Lower Saxony and Valencia. Based on these federal agreements, networks and initiatives developed and cooperative relations were started on the municipal and the regional level between companies and associations. The interview partners from the Ministries regard these federal agreements as the starting point of all operative actions. This is why the majority of job candidates supported by the programme MobiPro-EU were Spaniards as stated by recruiters.

The programme was designed for a total duration of 3 years, from 2013 to 2016. However, the funding was consumed in 2014 already, which proves that the programme was well received in the aftermath of the EU crisis. Bräuninger (2014) specified the positive effects of labour migration for Germany and Spain in quantitative terms. According to his calculations, 10% of the economic growth in Germany in the years before 2014 could be attributed to labour immigrants from the GIPS (Greece, Italy, Portugal, Spain) and Eastern European member states. Not only the destination countries, but also Spain profited from labour emigration in various ways. Firstly, many unemployed Spaniards got a job and were paid according to their qualification. Secondly, emigration eased the tense labour market situation in Spain. According to Bräuninger, the unemployment rate, which was 26.1% in 2013, would have been 8 percentage points higher without labour emigration. Hence, the reduction of unemployment helped to save public spendings in Spain.

So, generally both labour mobility and the programmes facilitating intra-EU mobility were assessed positively. The German programme Mobi-Pro was designed to be part of the pilot project for the EU-wide programme "your first EURES job" (see European Commission, 2018b). Due to the success of the pilot projects that facilitated labour mobility, the EU-wide programme started in 2014 with a similar design to Mobi-Pro. Specifically young people up to 35 years are eligible to receive assistance in finding a job, traineeship or apprenticeship in another member state. As Mobi-Pro, it is open to vacancies that are hard to fill, which are defined individually by the member states. It is open to young candidates and employers of the EU-28 countries, Norway and Iceland and to all candidates, who are nationals and legal residents of those countries. The European Employment Service (EURES) implements the activities so as to ensure their feasibility and quality.

The German government acted as an advocate of employers legitimizing international recruitment as a strategy to reduce the negative effects of the demographic crisis such as a diminished population at employable age and increased tax revenues due to the growing elderly population that is eligible for retirement pension and public health care. On the other hand, Spain and other Southern European countries found themselves in a similar situation due to the economic crisis, which was marked by redundancies of labour force and increased spendings on unemployment benefits. Hence, the framing of the demographic crisis and solidarity with the unemployed youth abroad helped to provide a basis to create the "*right circumstances*" for international labour recruitment. In the German social market economy the idea of fostering international recruitment was easier to sell in combination with a charitable purpose stressing transnational solidarity across Europe.

5.1.3 Framings of demographic crisis and labour shortages

In Germany, employers and employers' associations initiated field changes by lobbying. They challenged the status quo according to which companies traditionally provided education and training for sustainable long-term relationships between the employers and the employees. The employers demanded support for international recruitment of employees from the government and claimed to suffer from the demographic crisis, not being able to fill in vacancies and meet the demands of their customers. The employers found support by using expert knowledge in the form of reports, which legitimize international labour recruitment by claiming a demand that cannot be met by natives alone. This perspective of the employers′ association shows that the employers internalised the liberal idea of international recruitment in the common EU labour market for increased competitiveness in the global war for talent.

The German government patronized the employers' goal to open the labour market for international recruitment. However, the government's argumentation focused rather on other negative effects of the demographic crisis. On the one side, the diminished population at an employable age and the increased tax revenues due to the growing elderly population that is eligible for retirement pension and public health care, were mentioned. On the other side, the complementary situation in Spain and other Southern European countries was highlighted, facing redundancies of labour force and increased spendings on unemployment benefits. In this context, the *framing of the demographic crisis and solidarity with the unemployed youth abroad* provided a legitimized starting point for international labour recruitment. In the German social market economy support for international recruitment was easier to legitimize combined with the charitable purpose of transnational solidarity across Europe.

The roles and framings spread by the most relevant institutions that initiated the recruitment policies is summarised by Table 9.

Table 9: Role of institutions for policy changes in Spain

Institutional role	Institutions	Framing
Challengers	Employers' association	Labour shortages
Governance units	Ministry of Employment	Demographic crisis
	Opposition	Wage dumping and corrosion of social standards

Consequently, employment agencies were able to promote the programmes by taking charge of their practical implementation. They established networks to facilitate the matching of German companies with job candidates abroad. Hence, they spread and *legitimized the framing of international recruitment as a necessity for the German labour market and as help for young unemployed suffering from the crisis*. Therefore, they were decisive for the *normative diffusion* of international recruitment as an economic necessity for competitiveness in the knowledge-based German market economy.

5.2 Institutions creating the right circumstances for recruitment

5.2.1 Governance units: public employment services

One of the most important institutions for creating the *right circumstances* were the Employment services. Employment services are crucial when it comes to implementing the new policies. They assume several functions such as assessing the demand for professionals, promoting the new programmes and facilitating information and contacts with regard to labour migration and integration.

A variety of studies on the topic of labour shortages were published that offer in part contrasting evaluations of the labour market situation in Germany (Brücker et al., 2013; see Bundesamt für Migration und Flüchtlinge, 2013; Ernst&Young, 2016; Prognos, 2013; Vollmer, 2015). They use different measurement methods to quantify shortages. Besides the more quantitative and structural reasons for the skills shortages, the qualification of the job candidates needs to be taken into account. In all OECD countries, there are certain structural discrepancies between the educational system and the labour market (see OECD, 2017). However, the discrepancy varies in as much as there is a mismatch between the qualification of the labour force and the vacancies available. The mismatch in its most extreme form means that no suitable job candidate can be found for the specific vacancy, while job candidates cannot find a job because their skills are not in demand (see Heidemann, 2012, p. 4). Apart from the unemployment rate and the vacancies in a certain region, the time span it takes to find a suitable candidate is also included in the analysis of labour shortages (see Bundesagentur für Arbeit, 2014). All these aspects have been considered in the list of skills shortages published by the Bundesagentur für Arbeit (see Mangelberufe.de, 2018). It is revised every six months and shows the professions in demand for which a publicly funded subsidy can be provided.

Altogether, no general and nationwide labour shortage could be detected in Germany. Nevertheless, there are bottlenecks concerning skills in certain sectors and regions. First and foremost, labour shortages exist especially in the South, but also in specific regions of the East and the North of Germany, where the time until a vacancy can be filled is relatively long (see Czepek et al., 2015, p. 2f). Besides the regional labour shortages there are special sectors and professions that are affected by a skills shortage. Particularly in the MINT-subjects - which summarize mathematics, informatics, natural sciences, and technology - finding suitable job candidates is regarded as problematic. This is true both for academic and non-academic professionals, especially in engineering, electrical engineering, information technology, data processing, plumbing, sanitary, heating and air-conditioning sector (see Bundesagentur für Arbeit, 2014, p. 3). Apart from these technical professions, a significant labour demand is reported in academic and non-academic health care professions such as medicine and nursing, while the shortages seem to be most severe in geriatric care (see Czepek et al., 2015, p. 3).

Apart from assessing the level of demand, the recruitment activities are a rather new task of the employment agencies because of the labour market situation in the past few decades, as executive employee 2 of the BA explains:

> *Due to the labour market situation we witnessed in the past few decades, international placement was focussed on the task of "outgoing". There were redundancies of labour force and the aim was to ease the situation on the German labour market. Hence, interested people who were unemployed on the German labour market were transferred to a job abroad. This was the traditional direction and task of international placement. In the past years, this situation has changed because the labour market situation has changed in Germany and will continue to do so even more in the wake of the demographic change. So, the task of "incoming", the opposite of what we have done for decades, has gained increasingly in importance because of the grown demand for skilled labour, which is not easily covered by the national potential of labour or of those unemployed. This is why the Bundesagentur für Arbeit, the ZAV (International Placement Services = Zentrale Auslands- und Fachvermittlung), changed its strategy in order to offer support by recruiting foreign job candidates. Basically, it was a reaction of the Bundesagentur für Arbeit, the ZAV, to the changed internal labour market situation.*

However, in order to be able to recruit foreign professionals for these vacancies, the first task is to promote the new recruitment programmes, provide information and establish contacts in Germany and abroad. To this end, the BA established consultation hours in Poland and the Czech Republic, and since 2014 a foreign branch has been opened in Madrid, as Eastern and Southern Europe have most been affected by youth unemployment since the economic crisis. However, the focus is on Southern Europe, especially Spain, because not all countries in crisis featuring high youth unemployment rates are equally willing to support "outgoing" of professionals, as has been stated by experts from the BA and politicians. Germany and Spain have a cooperative relationship due to the good experiences made in Germany with Spanish guest workers, and also due to the good relations between the two conservative politicians, the Spanish President Mariano Rajoy and the German Chancellor Angela Merkel. Thus, executive 2, who worked in a leading position in international job placement at the BA explained what is important concerning recruitment agreements:

> *It depends on the political situation in these countries. It depends on those who rule in these countries and their governments' perspective. We enjoy an excellent collaboration with Spain. With regard to Greece, this is more difficult. Their government says „No, we need our people in our country", and I can totally understand that. I would never criticize that. The political ideology is important and also .... well, you know, we in Germany have had kind of a difficult history in Europe during the past century.*

In Spain and other collaborating countries, employment agencies provide information and contacts for German employers and job candidates since both of them lack the knowledge about different educational systems, job profiles, and labour market structures in the other country. In Spain, the principal tasks are to provide information about and facilitate labour migration and labour integration. Isabella Christina Rothermund, director of the only foreign subsidiary of the German employment service, the Bundesagentur für Arbeit (BA), located in Madrid, states:

> *The principal task is still consulting on living and working conditions in Germany, the description of job opportunities (...), assistance in questions of mobility, but also opportunities concerning education and training in Germany.*

In order to connect the national labour markets, public employment agencies on different local, national and European levels collaborate, such as the European Employment Service (EURES), the German employment service (BA), and the Spanish employment service (SEPE), according to their own statements. These organisations offer general initial consultancy services on labour emigration or hold information events. They provide information about living conditions, the labour market situation, sought after profiles in different countries as well as existing mobility programmes. These public employment services also supply information and contacts to institutions that facilitate labour integration. To this end, a *welcome and recognition culture* has been developed in Germany and several institutions provide information in different languages (see Loeffelholz, 2013). Thus, according to their own statements, the Federal Office for migration and refugees (BAMF), the Federal Institute of Vocational Education and Training (BIBB) and the Network Integration Through Qualification (IQ), the Chamber of Commerce, the Conference of the Ministers of Education and Cultural Affairs, as well as professional chambers in the federal provinces provide consultancy and information regarding the educational system and recognition of qualifications. Additionally, labour unions instruct interested parties on employment law and working conditions. All these institutions are part of the established networks and contacts of employment agencies.

In this network, the institutional agents spread the idea of a Common European Labour Market and its benefits for different member states and their citizens depending on the labour market situation. Isabella Christina Rothermund (BA) says:

> *I think a really big topic not to be underestimated is that of communication, networking and public relations.*

These employment agencies organize recruitment fairs, round tables and offer information and consulting services to bring employers and job candidates in touch. According to the job centres and recruitment agencies themselves, they do not only provide information for employees but also for cultural institutions and language schools, local public services, labour unions, chambers of commerce, universities and migrants′ organisations. Consequently, they circulate information regarding living conditions, the labour market situation, and sought after profiles and advertise existing mobility programmes. According to their own statements, the challenge is not only to promote the new policies abroad, but also among their own ranks in the BA and other relevant labour market institutions in Germany.

Apart from the promotion of recruitment, the public employment agencies also supervise, support and control the mobility programmes. Also, funding the recruitment of unemployed young people from abroad in order to fill vacancies in Germany seems reasonable, though it is by no means automatically successful. Several thousands of Spaniards were recruited in the framework of the programme Mobi-Pro, but the dropout rate was about 30%, as employees at the Bundesagentur für Arbeit stated.

There are risks on both sides, when either the selected job candidates or the employer do not meet certain criteria, mainly but not only in a subsidised programme such as MobiPro-EU. On the one hand, the employer had to face the risk of job candidates being selected, taking part in the subsidised German classes in Spain, but then leaving the programme MobiPro-EU when it came to moving to Germany. In the first phase of the programme, it turned out to be problematic that there were no sanctions for quitting the programme halfway, as was stated by public employment centres in both countries. Obviously, German politicians and employers were too optimistic as regards the attractiveness and willingness of unemployed Spaniards to work in Germany, as several public employment agencies in both countries reported. This is a major issue as international recruitment, language courses and training measures represent an enormous investment, which will only pay off in the long run.

In the case of Mobi-Pro EU, there were some obstacles that damaged the reputation of the programme and recruitment for the German labour market in general. One of these instances took place in Erfurt in 2013, when 120 Spaniards arrived expecting to get accommodation and to start a paid apprenticeship (see Fromm, 2013). However, after having finished their German classes in Spain, they arrived in Erfurt to find none of these promises realized. As a result, the Spaniards contacted the Spanish media to draw public attention to their situation. Afterwards, various actors of the labour market put a great deal of effort into solving the problem, first and foremost the local Welcome Centre, but also labour associations, employers, the Spanish and the Thuringian Ministries of Employment. Nevertheless, the reputation of the programme and the recruitment of German employers were severely damaged. According to public employment agencies and recruiters, it became much more difficult to recruit people from Spain and they had to invest a lot of energy in explaining the situation and restoring trust both in the programme and the job offers in Germany.

Another incident happened half a year later after the German government had been newly formed in 2014, when the coalition between the conservatives and the liberals was replaced by a grand coalition between the conservatives and the social democrats. The new government cancelled the subsidies for the recruitment of professionals, while increasing the funding for apprentices. Thus, they created a situation in which a great number of Spaniards who had been promised a job in Germany, refunding of their travel expenses as well as a preparatory language course, were suddenly asked to pay these expenses out of their own pocket. Taking into account that most of these Spaniards suffered from unemployment and precarious working conditions anyway, this represented a financial burden, which turned out too high for most of them. Many of the Spaniards affected by a situation created by the changed political circumstances in Germany felt deceived. Nevertheless, most of them received the subsidies in the end when a deadline was fixed to ensure that those who were already participating in the language courses or had completed them were not left out in the cold. However, this change in the programme also damaged the prestige of the programme and the trust in Germany and German correctness, which had been proverbial in Spain before these incidents.

Employment agencies promote the programmes by taking charge of their practical implementation. They facilitate international recruitment for companies and job candidates by bringing together different actors and institutions from the labour market in Germany and abroad. By doing so, they spread and legitimize the political framework of international recruitment as a necessity for the German population and the labour market situation. In this context they play an important role in the normative diffusion of international recruitment as an economic necessity for competitiveness in the knowledge-based market economy. Additionally, they control, supervise and assess the programmes steering labour mobility in order to create and maintain trust in the programmes.

5.2.2 Entrepreneurial actors

Due to the high labour shortages in Germany, and encouraged by the subsidies given by the government especially in the framework of MobiPro-EU, international recruiters emerged, which take over the role of entrepreneurial actors. They seize the opportunity to make money and assume a bridging function between the labour markets.

These recruiters may be Human Resource Managers from multinational companies (MNCs). International recruitment is nothing new for MNCs as their business is as internationally oriented as their staff. Due to their value and prestige, they are attractive employers for professionals from all over the world. Therefore, the international recruiters, who emerged recently to handle recruitment of Spanish professionals for German employers, are in the focus of attention. There are different types of mediating services depending on the steps they take in the recruitment procedure. The most common strategy among those recruiting from Spain for the German labour market is to offer the complete bridging service, which means that the recruiters maintain direct personal contacts with all parties involved and are responsible for all steps in the recruitment procedure. Hence, they organize and launch the first job announcement, the (pre-)selection of job candidates, trips for internships and trial periods, language classes, etc. until the employment contract has been formalized, and often even beyond that point. In this case, they are involved in developing (labour) integration measures in the company and language courses in Germany and assist in recognition procedures. In this context, they collaborate with employers, professionals, labour unions, universities, public job centres, language schools, recognition bodies and municipal services depending on their tasks and their recruitment strategy. This is why they need to have a broad range of social skills and social contacts in both the recruiting country and the home country of the professionals, which include business contacts, language skills, knowledge of the labour market and labour market structures as well as awareness of the most important actors in the field. Depending on the customers' needs, the sector and the profession, these recruiters carry out the whole procedure and assume full responsibility for all details. Recruiters who offer the complete procedure pursue different strategies on how to do their business. Some acquire companies as clients in the destination country first and search for the job candidates that could fill theses vacancies afterwards. Others select job candidates first, who match the sought-after profile and acquire the clients having suitable vacancies afterwards. Nevertheless, the first strategy is more common.

The complete bridging function was more often witnessed in the case of recruitment for the German labour market than for the English labour market. On the one hand, this is due to the language barrier, as English is more common as a foreign language in Spain. On the other hand, since recruitment activities are a relatively new feature and developed rather fast, structures and contacts still need to be established as recruiters are still widely inexperienced in recruiting labour force from Spain. The mediators usually possess good social skills qualifying them to facilitate mobility, and so they seized the opportunity to make profit by offering specialized services. However, they only developed the recruitment service recently. Mostly, they worked as business consultancies in German-Spanish trading, at German language schools or with international human resource consultants before, as we learned from the interviews. This is where they acquired the necessary social skills such as knowledge of the language, business contacts and know-how.

The bigger challenge for German recruiters is to find employers who are willing to invest in international recruitment, while it is relatively easy for them to find proper job candidates. This is the case because international recruitment involves high costs and high risks. Employers have to invest several tens of thousands of euros depending on the portfolio of services demanded and yet there is no security for them to find an employee who commits himself or herself permanently. There is a high demand for job candidates, especially in SMEs, which typically do not have any experience in recruitment or labour integration of international staff.

The subsidies offered by the German government for the programme MobiPro-EU were one measure to overcome certain obstacles and remove hurdles like language barriers and distance. Recruiters state that the German government offered up to 40,000€ of financial support to recruiting companies for every recruited professional of a shortage occupation covering travel costs, salary, a lump sum for removal costs, preparatory language courses for the recruited in the country of origin and accompanying courses in Germany.

However, the appropriateness of these measures is questioned by some of the interview partners. Some of them even regard these subsidies as subsidies for German language schools in Spain, and not as subsidies to facilitate labour emigration. It is true that language schools were in great demand thanks to these subsidies and recruiters from private and public employment agencies as well as migrant organisations and educational institutions mention a specific problem that arises in this situation, as stated by the German private recruiter 4:

> *Well, we are not friends of subsidies, and as we are not friends of subsidies because we have made a lot of bad experience, I would even let myself be carried away into stating "subsidies are counterproductive to what they subsidise". () Well, for me, MobiPro and also your first EURES*

> *job are subsidy programmes for Spanish language schools. A subsidy programme for people whose intentions to work are not very serious - to formulate it in a diplomatic way - but it is not an instrument to sustainably foster migration of qualified professionals to Germany. Well, we do not believe in that.*

In 2014, the subsidies for the recruitment of professionals within the framework of MobiPro-EU were cut, but the programme your first EURES job was introduced, which offers less financial support. Since then, recruiters, employers and/or job candidates need to pay language courses out of their own pocket, which means a high investment. Additionally, trial periods are mostly no longer involved in the recruitment procedure.

All recruiters and public employment agencies state that it is very important to clarify, whether the job candidates are interested in a permanent commitment in Germany. They have developed different strategies to identify the motivation of job candidates and the goals they pursue by opting for labour mobility. One of the interviewed recruiters developed a psychological test in order to assess the ability of mobility and adaptation in cooperation with scientists from the subjects of psychology, economy and education. Even this recruiter stated that he would select the job candidates much more carefully in the future in view of the high dropout rate, which is around one third of the participants of MobiPro and which is even higher among the nurses. According to the employment agencies and recruiters, the employers tended to perceive Spanish job candidates as longing for the jobs provided by German employers, which turned out to be a misjudgement. Recruiter 1 used a metaphor to explain the situation:

> *It is not as if you have a job to offer, all the Spaniards would queue for getting, or as if the new Iphone was sold at an Apple Store, but that is what employers expect them to do...*

The hype concerning labour emigration to Germany decreased in Spain, when the first obstacles to labour mobility emerged during recruitment and labour integration.

The recruiters' view with regard to international labour recruitment differs widely from the framings of the government. They got the impression that only a very limited number of employers are willing to recruit staff from abroad, and only few professionals from abroad are willing to emigrate for a job. From their experience, first of all a small number of highly skilled people is willing to use intra-EU labour mobility. This supports the view of Favell (2008) claiming that intra-EU labour mobility is mainly used by a European elite instead of becoming a mass phenomenon across all social classes. According to the recruiters, companies tend to underestimate the obstacles, costs and risks of international recruitment. An *institutional myth* was created promising an unlimited availability of high potentials from abroad or highly motivated skilled professionals, who do not require investments concerning education and (re-)training.

While employers regularly underestimate cultural and language issues, they overestimate the attractiveness of German companies and Germany as an immigration country. Both professionals and recruiters tend to overestimate the advantages and underestimate the possibilities of international labour mobility and recruitment. The German recruiter 4 explained their position in this area of tension as follows:

> *The term "Fachkräftemangel" (=skills shortage) is a political term. There is no Fachkräftemangel. The employers want to recruit certain professionals under certain conditions, and these conditions are below the market rates. So if you pay salaries below the market value and you cannot afford to hire a skilled professional in Germany, then you are affected by a skills shortage and you look for a Spaniard. There you come across the unrealistic expectations of the Spaniards, who would like to work at BMW in Munich and earn 80,000 € a year, but the only job you can offer is in Saxony, 50km away from Dresden, with a starting salary of 40,000€.*

Entrepreneurial actors emerged, encouraged by the financial support offered by the government. Their ability to fulfil a bridging function between the labour markets is based on their knowledge of both labour markets. The recruiters explain illusions of international recruitment as being fast, cheap and easily providing suitable candidates or even high potentials as being an institutional *myth*, which spread among German employers. This can be evaluated as a by-product of the normative isomorphism of the efficiency and advantages of international recruitment that is related to the debate on the global war for talent.

5.2.3 Interim conclusion: status quo of labour recruitment

International recruitment was first of all supported and promoted by employers from the economic field. The employers represented by the employers' association BDA used expert knowledge in the form of reports as those provided by Ernst&Young (2016) and Prognos (2013) to corroborate their argumentation of a need for international labour recruitment. By doing so, they put pressure on institutions of the labour market to participate in the global war for talent and actively enforced the *normative isomorphism* of this idea. From the employers' stance, the shortage of skilled professionals is tightly linked with the demographic crisis. The German Trade Union Federation, which is an incumbent of the labour market and the social democrats (SPD), had a different perspective on the topic. They warned against wage dumping and exploitation of foreign workers.

However, the coalition of liberals and conservatives acted as an advocate of the employers' interests. They took over the argumentation and linked it more closely to the demographic crisis and its negative effects on their political agenda, and therefore included international recruitment in the *government's demographic strategy*. Thus, the employers' perspective diffused into economic policies of the government, which was legitimized by the negative effects of the demographic crisis, which are a diminished proportion of the population at an employable age and increased tax revenues due to the growing elderly population that is eligible for retirement pension and public health care. At the same time, Spain and other Southern European countries were in a complementary labour market situation showing enormous unemployment rates in the wake of the economic crisis. Due to the good relations between Germany and Spain a memorandum concerning recruitment on the national level, followed by agreements on the Federal State level, were signed. Hence, the framing of the demographic crisis and transnational solidarity with the unemployed youth in Europe legitimized the creation of the *right circumstances* for intra-EU labour recruitment.

The most important governance units to develop the *right circumstances* are the governmental employment agencies. They promote the programmes and facilitate international recruitment for German companies and foreign professionals by linking labour market institutions in Germany and abroad. To do so, they spread and legitimize the framing of international recruitment as a necessity for the German labour market. Furthermore, they control, supervise and assess the mobility programmes steering labour mobility. The international recruitment activities of BA and EURES show the *institutional isomorphism* of the need to participate in the global war for talent.

The economic boom in Germany and the economic crisis in Southern Europe combined with the subsidies provided by MobiPro-EU encouraged international recruiters to take over the role of entrepreneurial actors. Many of these had worked in other businesses before but seized the opportunity to make money by introducing a new business model. Their increased emergence is an indicator of the *institutional isomorphism* of the global war for talent. They were enabled to do so because of their social skills and the contacts they established in the different labour markets, which form the basis for assuming a bridging function between the labour markets. Thus, they are in an intermediary position between the foreign job candidates and the national employers and their interest.

However, they tend to regard the need for international labour recruitment due to skills shortages as well as the interest of (unemployed) Southern European professionals as overrated. From their point of view, German companies tend to overestimate their attractiveness to foreign professionals, while foreign professionals overestimate their international market value irrespective of their qualifications. They describe the creation of an *institutional myth* of international recruitment as a fast, cheap and easy way of recruitment.

Both private recruiters and public employment agencies encountered difficulties in selecting the *right people* for labour mobility. This issue will be discussed in more detail in the following sections. A summary of this analysis is provided by Table 10.

Table 10: Analysis of the status quo of the field of labour recruitment

Policy Agenda	**Demographic crisis**		
Labour Market Agenda	**Skills shortage**		
Institutional Role	Institutions	Institutional myth/perceptions/framings	Strategic Action
Challengers	Employers (BDA)	Labour recruitment as a necessity to ease skills shortages	• Lobbying
Incumbent	Labour unions (DGB)	Labour recruitment as a necessity to ease the demographic crisis	• Providing and spreading a counter argument
Governance units	Ministry of Employment Opposition Public employment agencies: • EURES, SEPE, BA	Labour mobility as a necessity (government) vs. Wage dumping exploitation (opposition)	• Memorandum • MobiPro-EU • Your first EURES job • Announce and spread the programme
Entrepreneurial actors	Recruiters	Demand for professionals and interest in labour immigration as a myth	• Bridging function for international recruitment • Earn money and secure survival

5.3 Status quo of labour integration: developing a Recognition Culture

The success of the international recruitment of professionals depends strongly on the extent to which educational achievements and professional skills are transferable from one country to the other. Thus, to support the integration of foreigners and people obtaining foreign diplomas on the German labour market a *Welcome and Recognition Culture* was developed to make use of the potential of those obtaining foreign degrees and to reduce the skills shortage.

The Federal Office for Migration and Refugees (2013, p. 20) describes *Welcome Culture* as a set of attractive conditions which are designed to form a welcoming and recognizing society for all new arrivals and legal immigrants.

Recognition Culture is described as the recognition and appreciation of the potential of all people living in Germany with a migrant background, by the receiving society (ibid.)

The concepts of *Welcome and Recognition Culture* originate from the economic field. They were originally developed to reduce skills shortages. The idea then spread from the economic sector to public administration and society (see Bertelsmann Stiftung 2014, p. 94) to create the *right circumstances* of labour immigration for the *right people*, namely professionals in demand.

5.3.1 Governance units: creation of a Recognition Culture

The administrative bodies are usually the first entities foreigners get in touch with in a receiving country. Therefore, a *Welcome and Recognition Culture* was introduced in these institutions, especially with the relevant immigration authorities and residents' offices, which are supposed to be the first contact points for immigrants.

In order to create a welcoming service for immigrants, the employees' language skills were enhanced besides setting up flexible opening hours and accessible contact partners (see Alichniewicz et al., 2014, p. 23f.). The task force (see Loeffelholz, 2013) entrusted with establishing a *Welcome Culture* at the Office for Migration and Refugees designed various practice-oriented recommendations. These include advisory service via email and phone provided by a multilingual permanent contact person complementing the face-to-face service offering relevant information for immigrants. In order to put this aim into practice, the number of people working in civil service and having an immigration background was increased. In doing so, the potential of language skills and cultural sensitivity among the population was used and increased.

The Welcome and Recognition Culture is accompanied by efforts to improve collaboration between different public authorities and other institutions that participate in the process of immigration (see Alichniewicz et al., 2014, p. 23f.). However, the programme job of my life stimulated the recruitment of (highly-) skilled Spanish professionals. Although the financial sponsorship has been cancelled, the recruitment of (highly-) skilled people is still going on. Public institutions in Germany offer more and more information in Spanish and other languages. The websites of the Federal Employment Agency (BA), the Office for Migration and Refugees (BAMF), the Federal Ministry of Education and Research (BMBF), and the Federal Ministry of Labour and Social Affairs (BMAS) offer information on the recognition of diplomas, guidelines on how to gain access to the German Labour Market, how to prepare for job interviews, etc.

These developments were initiated and accompanied by several EU policies seeking to harmonise education and categorise job profiles so as to facilitate mobility and to evaluate professional skills. Being part of the Bologna Process, the Qualification Framework of the European Higher Education Area (EHEA) (see Secretariat of the Bologna Follow-Up Group, 2017), and the Lisbon Recognition Convention (LRC) (see Council of Europe, 2014b) are elements of these harmonisation efforts. The Qualification Framework aims at improving the comparability of qualifications and skills in the EU, while the Lisbon Recognition Convention stipulates that educational attainment must be recognised unless the national institution in charge can prove substantial differences. Hence, the harmonisation of the EU educational systems and mutual recognition of qualifications are enforced by *coercive isomorphism*.

Due to the demographic changes in the knowledge economy, which increases the demand for (highly) skilled professionals (see Braun, 2012, p. 1ff), Germany tries to increase the utility of the qualifications of immigrants. This makes it possible to recruit workforce more effectively from abroad and to benefit from the potential of those who already live in Germany (see BDA, 2010; Braun, 2012; Müller-Wacker, 2017). Thus, in Germany the Lisbon Recognition Directive, which had to be implemented until 2016 (see Bundesministerium der Justiz und für Verbraucherschutz, 2018; Council of Europe, 2014b; Sommer, 2015), was implemented in the *Federal Recognition Act*, which came into force on April 1, 2012. It aims at improving the evaluation and recognition of foreign qualifications. Ever since, labour immigrants have the legal right to have their foreign qualification assessed. The recognition law is an omnibus act, in which the legal framework for recognition is provided in order to ensure transparency and fair labour integration for people who obtained foreign qualifications (see Knuth, 2012, p. 130ff).

Although the new regulation concerning recognition aims at facilitating professional recognition and labour integration, there is a high complexity with regard to responsibilities and requirements in Germany. Generally, there are two types of professions, which are categorized as regulated and non-regulated professions. Only for the regulated professions is the formal recognition a necessary precondition for being allowed to work in this profession in Germany. In non-regulated professions, no formal recognition is required by law (see Bundesamt für Migration und Flüchtlinge, 2015, p. 2). In technical terms, the recognition of regulated professions is called *de jure-recognition*, while the recognition of non-regulated professions is called *de facto-recognition* (see Brussig et al., 2009, p. 3).

On the one hand, regulated professions are either professions in which meeting a certain standard is necessary for safety reasons or to prevent clients, patients or children from any damage, such as in health care or the social sector. This includes medical doctors, nurses and midwives, paramedics and teachers amongst others. On the other hand, occupations in which self-employment is usually aimed at are regulated, such as hairdressers and bakers (see Bundesamt für Migration und Flüchtlinge, 2015, p. 1).

Apart from the regulated professions, there are the non-regulated professions that do not require any formal recognition as a prerequisite. However, the labour immigrants have the chance to apply for an assessment of equivalence. Their skills and qualifications are compared to a profession of reference in Germany that is closest to the occupation in the home country. Though it is not essential, the certificate of equivalence raises the possibility for the applicant to obtain entry to the labour market. Employers are able to evaluate the foreign qualifications through a transparent assessment of skills and qualification obtained abroad.

Furthermore, in some cases the legally protected title for the occupation can be received thanks to the assessment of equivalence. Such a legally protected title is, for instance, the German title *Ingenieur* (see Bundesamt für Migration und Flüchtlinge, 2011). Engineering has a long tradition in Germany and the former academic degree *Diplom Ingenieur* had a high signaling effect all over the world. However, in other countries many professions are entitled to call themselves *engineers*, which would be named technicians or mechanics in Germany and require a lower qualificational level only. In order to prevent the erosion of the symbolic value of the title engineer and of the high standards of skills and qualification the engineers obtain, the title is legally protected. Nevertheless, a foreign engineer is able to work as an engineer without using the title *Ingenieur* (see Kowalewski, 2015). None of the interviewed Spanish engineers had applied for recognition of the title. However, the title may probably be useful for working as a business consultant or self-employed or when the labour immigrant originates from a country where educational standards are supposed to be significantly lower than in Germany.

The subdivision of regulated and non-regulated professions only comes to bear when recognition is a prerequisite for working in a certain profession, while the responsibility for recognition procedures is still confusing. For the recognition of regulated professions the responsibility is divided between authorities on the national level and on the level of the Federal State. The national level is responsible for the recognition of medical doctors, lawyers and civil servants. On the Federal State level, professions such as nurses, teachers, and engineers are recognized. For non-regulated professions the assessment is provided by the responsible Chambers of Trade and Industry or other authorities (see Sommer, 2015, p. 150). Since 2014, the recognition law for all 16 federal states has come into force and since 2016 the recognition directive has had to be implemented on the national level (see Anerkennung in Deutschland, 2018). In what way and to what extent these laws were put into practice by the different institutions involved in Germany will be examined in the following section.

5.3.2 IQ network: support for recognition and labour integration

The complex structure of responsibilities, the different recognition procedures between regulated and non-regulated professions etc. increase the demand for advisory services. Therefore, an important institutional actor providing advisory service, contacts and training measures for all kinds of professionals was created, which is the network IQ (see Integration durch Qualifizierung, 2018).

As both the recognition procedure and the structure of responsibilities of recognition bodies are rather complex matters, the network *Integration through Qualification* (IQ) has supported the recognition procedure since 2011. It is financed by the Ministry of Employment and Social Affairs and the European Social Fund and provides three different types of services, according to the network members' own statement. First and foremost, they offer advisory service for labour immigrants concerning the recognition of qualifications. Secondly, they provide retraining possibilities for all those who do not hold qualifications matching one of the job profiles in Germany. Thirdly, they offer courses to enhance intercultural sensitivity and intercultural competencies for civil services, such as Bundesagentur für Arbeit or municipal immigration services.

The main activity of the network Integration through Qualification is the advisory service regarding the recognition of qualifications. During the first three and a half years since IQ started, more than 80,000 consultations have been conducted, as was stated by the expert interviewed at IQ. The expert reports that the first challenge for the advisory service is to find a suitable profession of reference in the German educational system to match the foreign qualification. There are many educational degrees and professions in other countries that do not correspond to the job profiles of a certain profession in Germany. If no adequate profession is found, the most similar one is chosen as a reference. For example, one of the Spanish immigrants interviewed obtained a degree in wood processing, which is a rather general education in the field of wood working. However, it does not match the specific job profiles and training of either a carpenter, a timberman or a cabinetmaker as the defined reference professions in Germany.

Having selected the matching reference profession, IQ provides the contact addresses of responsible recognition bodies. In view of the complex structure of recognition bodies in Germany, this is the next hurdle for many labour immigrants. These bodies are organized on different levels: on the national level, such as NARIC; on the level of the federal states for health care professions; and at the Chambers of Industry and Commerce (IHK) for crafts. According to labour immigrants, migrant organisations, labour unions, recognition bodies and employers, the complex organisation of recognition bodies is one of the biggest hurdles along with the recognition procedure itself.

The second task is advising on retraining, which is a rather new service. It aims at offering advice on how and where to find employers or seminars that may either help to get a certificate of recognition or an assessment of qualification that matches a certain profession of reference. IQ also offers retraining measures for certain professionals and qualification measures to increase the general employability by further training or retraining measures(see Integration durch Qualifizierung, 2018). As application procedures, labour market structures etc. in Germany usually differ profoundly from those in the country of origin, IQ also offers *bridging measures* for labour immigrants, who seek orientation in the labour market. Participation in the qualification measures offered by IQ is free of charge.

The first two fields of activity, consultation and qualification, address the labour immigrants, while the target of the third task of intercultural training are multipliers in civil services, such as immigration authorities, residents' registration offices, recognition bodies, Bundesagentur für Arbeit, etc. In doing so, IQ aims to increase the intercultural sensitivity and competences of these institutions. On the one hand, the measures are intended to prevent discrimination of immigrants and raise awareness of their special needs and particular situation, such as more information in easier wording or their native language, information on (labour) integration measures, etc. On the other hand, the network IQ promotes its services and possibilities of labour integration, which is part of its public relations policy. Among other tasks, the network staff raise awareness of the different levels of professionalism or rather lack of professionalism at certain recognition bodies. As the Federal Recognition Act only came into force in 2012, there are still some problems pending concerning its practical implementation. According to the network IQ, the recognition procedure is not applied as required by the law in certain Federal States. Hence, in some Federal States it is easier than in others to receive professional recognition. The expert 1 interviewed at IQ explained:

> *In the federal coordination process, we also try to find out, what actions are still required. The Federal Recognition Act has not been implemented in accordance with the law by some federal states or recognition bodies. One of our tasks is to raise awareness of these issues in public. The law came into force three and a half years ago, which is not that long. First, it was implemented on the national level and the federal states followed. Bearing that in mind, the recognition bodies still have to gather more experience. In this context, their professional standards vary widely. Well, we are still optimistic. Both the law itself and the recognition procedure are relatively complex and the topic is not completely trivial. Considering that, it has already been implemented reasonably well, but some issues still need improvement.*

The differences existing between various recognition bodies, provoked some kind of recognition tourism that has been described by Sommer (2015). Thus, one of the IQ network's tasks is to raise awareness of those issues so as to initiate changes towards more professionalisation and the provision of more information by putting pressure on the responsible authorities.

In order to meet its tasks properly, the network IQ collaborates with different institutions from the labour market, culture and education as well as migration on the national level. Their partners include the Ministry of Employment and Social

Affairs, the different IQ advisory services in the Federal States, the different employment agencies of Bundesagentur für Arbeit, and educational institutions that provide several of the qualification measures of IQ; increasingly, companies are also gained as collaboration partners along with recognition bodies and institutions involved such as the Chambers of Commerce or the Ministry of Health on the Federal State level, migrant organisations and refugee agencies.

Summarizing, IQ is a network that supports labour integration of professionals having acquired a degree abroad. They give advice to these professionals, provide training measures and contacts, offer supervision for public institutions and are involved in public relations. All these measurements show the high institutional efforts of and the deep *normative isomorphism* that aims for making labour integration feasible. However, from a different stance it also indicates the structural inefficiencies of labour migration and labour mobility.

5.3.3 NARIC: evaluation of foreign degrees

In Germany, the central body for the recognition of foreign degrees is the National Agency for the Recognition and Comparison of International Qualifications and Skills (NARIC), which is part of the Central Office for Foreign Education in the Secretariat of the Standing Conference of the Ministers of Education and Cultural Affairs in the Federal Republic of Germany.

This institution has existed since 1905 with its main task being the analysis of foreign educational systems in order to provide information for recognition bodies in the federal states, for individuals and employers. In order to assist the recognition bodies NARIC provides a database containing expert opinions several examples of which have been shown here so far. The assessment of foreign educational systems has always been the core activity of the Central Office for Foreign Education in the Secretariat of the Standing Conference of the Ministers of Education and Cultural Affairs. In the wake of the Lisbon Recognition Convention the field of activities broadened, as was explained by the expert 1 in a leading position at NARIC:

> *The main activities of NARIC are the analysis and evaluation of foreign educational systems because before you can furnish any information about a certain foreign degree, you need the necessary information regarding the foreign educational system and you need to get this information, which is the task of NARIC. We collect this information in our database. This is our tool to make the information accessible to private individuals and employers. Based on the information collected, our fundamental mission is to carry out certain services and tasks for the recognition bodies on the Federal state level. The authorities on the federal state level have the right to demand an expert opinion. In your interview guidelines you also asked about changes in our field of activities. Well, providing the expert opinions was the original task but*

that has changed in the meantime, after the second big task was added in 2010, which is the assessment of foreign university degrees.

The Lisbon Recognition Convention stipulated that educational attainment must be recognised unless the national institution in charge can prove substantial differences. Before 2010, only regulated professions were recognized. NARIC in Germany has also evaluated foreign diplomas of non-regulated professions since 2010. This includes a broad range of degrees in humanities, social sciences and MINT subjects. Since 2010, the number of applications for evaluations of diplomas from Portugal, Spain, Italy and Greece, has increased significantly according to the expert interviewed at NARIC. Furthermore, the number of employees also increased significantly by around one third.

In order to meet their tasks of analysing and evaluating educational systems and diplomas, NARIC Germany has been embedded in a comprehensive network of NARICs in other countries. A large number of desk officers work at NARIC looking after the evaluation of the educational system abroad. These desk officers possess language skills and have lived in a certain country for a longer time; they also maintain personal and institutional contacts in these countries.

According to its own statement, NARIC Germany collaborates with the Federal Foreign Office, the German Academic Exchange Service (DAAD), universities, the Federal Ministry for Education and Research (BMBF), the Federal Institute for Vocational Education and Training (BIBB), the Cologne Institute for Economic Research (IW), the network Integration through Qualification (IQ) and the portal for foreign professional qualification (BQ).

Although NARIC is the central national recognition body, other recognition bodies also exist. The recognition body for several professions is the *Landesprüfungsamt* on the federal state level; amongst others, the recognition of nurses is provided by the *Landesprüfungsamt* (see Sommer, 2015). Furthermore, the recognition of professions trained in the dual system of vocational training is provided by the responsible *Chambers of Industry and Commerce*.

5.3.4 Incumbents: recognition of vocational training

The Chamber of Industry and Commerce (IHK) is the recognition body for all professions that obtain their degree in the dual system of vocational training in Germany. The main recognition body in Nuremberg, IHK-Foreign Skills Approval (IHK-FOSA), is in charge of the recognition of qualifications for 77 out of 80 IHKs, as was stated by the interviewed expert. There are specialists, who are fluent in 23 languages and possess comprehensive knowledge about technical and professional matters. Thus, they are able to provide detailed information in the foreign professionals' mother tongue and can gather information directly from foreign Ministries and educational institutions.

This recognition body has been in charge since April 2012, when the federal recognition law came into force. Since that date, the demand for advisory service and recognition procedures has risen continuously. The interviewed experts supposed that the increasing number of clients may be ascribed to the fact that it took some time for the word to spread among potential clients. As there was no possibility of recognising qualifications before, it was first of all required to make this chance known to foreign professionals, employment agencies, administrative bodies and relevant immigration authorities. Additionally, many professionals waited until first experiences had been made with professional recognition before deciding to start the recognition procedure themselves.

According to the interviewed expert, most of the clients seeking recognition came from the sectors of electro technology, metal technology, IT and office occupations. The main question asked by the clients was whether recognition was a precondition to work in their corresponding profession. However, none of the professions the Chamber of Industry and Commerce is responsible for is a regulated profession. IHK-FOSA is commonly referred to as a recognition body providing recognition procedures. IHK-FOSA provides equivalence assessments comparing the foreign qualification and skills to a reference profession in Germany although in a formal, legal terminology, as strictly speaking, the term recognition can be used only for regulated professions.

Even though the equivalent assessment is not a necessary precondition for labour market entry, employers have increasingly been asking for a certificate of equivalence ever since it has been possible to assess foreign skills, as was reported by the recognition body. This is especially true in safety-relevant professions with a high demand for precision, such as aircraft technicians. For the employers, the certificate of equivalence ensures that foreign professionals have acquired the skills necessary for the job profile in Germany. However, employers and experts from the metal-processing industry assume that the possibility to receive a certificate of equivalence is not a hurdle, but rather increases the willingness of employers to hire foreign workers because the certificate guarantees transparency of skills.

Thus, the certificate facilitates labour market entry, which is one reason for professionals to apply for the certificate. Another one is to ensure payment in line with the collectively negotiated union rate. Hence, the chance of professional recognition reduces exploitation of foreign workers, wage dumping and underpayment. A third reason for professionals with an immigration background to strive for a certificate is to raise their self-esteem. Even people who have lived in Germany for decades and do not plan to work in the profession they once graduated in abroad, apply for recognition of their qualification. Employees at recognition bodies explain that in a world in which people mostly identify with their profession, they felt worthless when they came to Germany and their diploma was suddenly considered useless. Hence, there are also immigrants who only want to get the certificate of equivalence for themselves, and not for reasons of employment.

If education and training or the job profiles in the foreign country do not match the German standards, a partial recognition is issued. In most cases in which a partial recognition is issued, it is practical training that is missing. According to the interviewed expert from IHK-FOSA, nearly all labour immigrants applying for recognition are lacking practical training, as the dual apprenticeship system in Germany is unique. In other countries, practical terms are rare and only trained at school, while the trainees are only allowed to watch the working processes in the companies during their education, as was explained by the recognition bodies. The labour immigrants are enabled to gain practical experience by doing internships, etc. Working experience gathered in the country of origin or another foreign country can be acknowledged. Usually, the theoretical part of the education does not represent a problem in the assessment of skills. The application for the recognition of qualification and skills can already be sent while the candidate is still in his/her country of origin. As the German job profiles form the reference categories for the approval of equivalence of skills, professions that do not exist in Germany cannot be recognized. One example in the case of Spanish labour immigrants is the profession of a *tourist guide*, which has a formalized job profile based on a specific education in Spain that does not exist in Germany, as was reported by the interviewed experts.

However, there is also a significant part of immigrants, who do not apply for the assessment of equivalence. Some do not necessarily want to work in the profession they graduated in, either because they never really liked their job or they suffer from health issues that do not allow them to work in the job anymore. In addition, the non-negligible costs of 420€ prevent many of those who do not really need the certificate from applying. In the case of IHK-FOSA, there is no difference in the assessment procedure of qualification certificates between different EU citizens or third country nationals[8]. Language skills are not included in the assessment of skills as the recognition body IHK-FOSA is not allowed to assess language skills according to the Federal Recognition Act (see Bundesministerium der Justiz und für Verbraucherschutz, 2018). In this context, IHK-FOSA assesses the skills based on the applicants' education and working experience and compares them to the German profession of reference; equivalence of qualification is granted independently of any language proficiency of immigrants. However, most employers expect German language skills and consider them a necessary precondition for a candidate to take up the job. This is why most clients are fluent, as was reported by the interviewed expert 1 from IHK:

> *Surprisingly, they (speaking about clients) speak German relatively well, even when they arrived only three month ago. They are really very, very well prepared and those who are not completely fluent, are accompanied by someone, who is able to translate if necessary.*

8 This is not a unique feature for Germany, the same is true in Spain for non-academic professions.

Due to the twofold structure of education and training as well as the competences of the federal states, there is a high complexity of the structure of recognition bodies and recognition procedures in Germany. Therefore, a broad range of institutions is involved in advisory services, recognition and training measures concerning labour integration.

5.3.5 Interim conclusion: status quo of the Recognition Culture

A Welcome and Recognition Culture has been developed in German institutions providing information in different languages and fostering integration (see Loeffelholz, 2013). Amongst others, the Goethe-Institute and the Federal Office for Migration and Refugees (BAMF) offer special language courses for professionals to teach them the technical terminology and what is considered professional behaviour in a specific job. They provide essential, highly country-specific and non-transferable social skills bound to the national context. The Federal Institute of Vocational Education and Training (BIBB), the Network Integration Through Qualification (IQ), the Chamber of Industry and Commerce (IHK), the Conference of the Ministers of Education and Cultural Affairs (NARIC) as well as the recognition bodies in the federal states provide consultancy and information on the educational system and recognition of qualifications. The broad range of institutions involved mirrors the complexity of the recognition procedures in general, and in Germany in particular. The development of the different recognition bodies proves how the *coercive isomorphism* of granting EU-wide professional recognition was implemented in Germany. However, it shows how complex the process of institutional diffusion was in Germany due to the different structural levels on which professional recognition is organised.

The network Integration through Qualification (IQ) was created in 2011 to support labour integration of professionals obtaining foreign degrees. IQ plays a crucial role due to the complex structure of recognition bodies and recognition procedures in Germany. The network offers advisory service and supplies information and orientation to all kinds of labour immigrants, no matter what qualification they have obtained. Furthermore, IQ offers training measures for foreign professionals and employees of recognition bodies, employment agencies and immigration offices. As part of its public relations activities, IQ raises the awareness of chances and issues of labour integration. IQ is financed by the German Ministry of Employment and the European Social Fund. In order to meet the task of labour integration IQ collaborates with a broad range of institutions from the fields of labour market, culture and education, and migration. On the one hand, the activities of IQ show the high efforts and investments in Germany to make labour integration work; on the other hand, it also shows the structural inefficiencies that are often accompanied by free movement of labour in practice.

NARIC is the central national recognition body for degree holders with a foreign university degree. Among other things, the assessment of the qualification of engineers, humanists and social scientists is provided by NARIC. Its main task has been the evaluation of foreign educational systems ever since 1905. Since 2012, assessments of equivalence have also been provided by NARIC. In order to meet its tasks it collaborates with a broad range of institutions, as do other recognition bodies and advisory services.

Table 11: Status quo of the German Recognition Culture

	IQ	NARIC (ZAB)	IHK
Qualification	all	Degree holders	Dual system of vocational training
Professions (examples)	all	Engineers, humanists, social scientists	Technicians, such as plumbers, electricians, mechanics
Responsibility	Nation-wide	Nation-wide	Nation-wide, except three regions
Main tasks	- Advisory service - Training measures - Public relations	-Evaluation of foreign education systems - Assessment of equivalence	- Advisory service - Assessment of equivalence
Recognition	Contacts with recognition bodies or retraining	Assessment of equivalence	Assessment of equivalence
Collaborators	- Ministry of Employment and Social Affairs - Different IQ advisory services in the Federal States -Bundesagentur für Arbeit - Educational institutions - Companies - Recognition bodies - Chambers of Trade and Commerce (IHK) - Ministry of Health on Federal State level - Migrant organisations - Refugee agencies	- NARIC abroad - Federal Foreign Office - German Academic Exchange Service (DAAD) - Universities - Federal Ministry of Education and Research (BMBF) - Recognition bodies - Federal Institute of Vocational Education and Training (BIBB) - Cologne Institute for Economic Research (IW) - portal for foreign professional qualification (BQ)	- Foreign professionals, - Employment agencies, such as BA - Administrative bodies - Relevant immigration authorities - Foreign Ministries and educational institutions - Federal Institute of Vocational Education and Training (BIBB)

The Chamber of Industry and Commerce (IHK) is the recognition body for all professions achieving their degree in the dual system of vocational training in Germany, such as plumbers, mechanics and electricians. The main tasks of the IHK include advisory service and assessment of equivalence for non-regulated professions. The IHK has a broad range of collaborators, especially from the labour market. Most often, when the equivalence of the professional qualification could not be assessed, the candidate lacked practical training. In some cases, no equivalent could be found in the list of German reference professions. This shows hurdles and mismatches due to issues of structural interconnectivity.

However, it is remarkable to note that foreign technicians seeking assessment of equivalence are very well prepared with regard to language skills, although neither do these professions seem predestined for an international career, nor are language skills part of the assessment.

Table 11 summarises the development of a Recognition Culture in Germany is part of the efforts to create the *right circumstances* for intra-EU labour mobility.

5.4 Status quo of labour integration: Welcome Culture by incumbents

Apart from the recognition bodies, several other institutions are involved in labour integration. In the following part, the efforts of companies, labour and trade unions as well as migrant organisations will be highlighted.

5.4.1 Companies

The new policies concerning immigration first of all aim at securing skills and providing professionals for German companies. To this end, it is very important to integrate foreigners at their workplace, which is, in the first instance, the task of the hiring company itself. The companies are usually interested in binding the professionals to the company permanently. In the skills-intensive labour market in Germany, training on the job is necessary to impart specialized and company-based knowledge. Hence, hiring a new employee will only pay off after a while, especially when financial investments were made for transnational recruitment. Therefore, many recruiting companies create a welcome culture in order to prevent return migration (see Alichniewicz et al., 2014, p. 26ff).

In doing so, they offer support for labour integration and personal contacts at the workplace. One of the interview partners, who is employed by a educational institution doing research on labour integration and developing labour integration measures, summarized a broad range of integration measures offered by companies:

> *With regard to integration, there are quite a lot of different measures available, especially in the initial phase. In the first round (of recruitment), the focus is on personal contacts, and job candidates are picked up personally at the airport. Of course, this depends on the company and the organisation. Especially at smaller facilities, the boss or manager was welcoming the new employees personally. At the beginning in particular, a lot of support was offered. I think, in the second round, there were more initiatives, in which established employees work as mentors and provide specialist assistance to support the newcomers in*

> *their professional tasks. Additionally, they offer assistance outside the workplace such as opening a bank account, search for an apartment and so on. There is a lot of support like that. Then, there is the question of companies that might be able to offer apartments themselves. This is often the case in big cities, where the search for apartments is difficult.*
>
> *Besides, there are language courses, of course, which are mostly financed by the companies and language proficiency on the level of B2 is the common standard required, but these skills need to be enhanced. Employers also organise dinners for the employees or events of intercultural exchange. Some offer trainings for intercultural competences, (...), working material in the language of the new foreign employees or they use the language competences or migration background of their staff.*

However, there is a wide variety of integration measures that can be differentiated according to smaller and bigger companies, as was explained by employers, recruiters and educational institutions. In the smaller ones, more personal assistance is normally provided, which also involves the management or bosses of the company. In the bigger enterprises, labour integration is part of the responsibilities of human resource departments. Thus, certain subdivisions of the management are in charge of integration measures, which are rather formally organised. The integration measures provided also depend on the sector and the field of activity of the country as well as the local situation of the company in an urban or rural area.

Multinational corporations (MNCs) are more likely to hire highly skilled professionals from abroad, as was reported by trade unions, employers' associations, recruiters and educational institutions. The professionals hired by MNCs are usually well prepared, know about their market value and have good English language skills. English is often sufficient for a professional in a top position as long as he or she does not have staff responsibilities towards hierarchically lower employees who do not speak English. In Multinational Corporations we usually find an international environment, which means there is an international business culture influenced by the English speaking countries of the Western world. Such an environment demands limited integration efforts of those who grew up in the European Union. This is one of the reasons why labour mobility across Europe is easier to accomplish for those who are highly skilled since English spreads as the working language in companies operating on an international level. These MNCs are often headquartered in big cities, where different ethnic communities are located anyway. Hence, the foreign professionals are easily able to establish social contacts with other nationals from their home country.

However, especially in SMEs in more rural areas, immigrants enjoy more personal contact with the colleagues and the population. Employers are often involved in the search for a job for spouses and the family. Informal networks and personal contacts of employers and colleagues are important resources when it comes to facilitating (labour) integration in smaller companies and in more rural areas, as recruiters explained.

However, all efforts regarding the labour integration of foreigners need the acceptance of the German workforce. According to the recruiters, especially in fields where salaries are moderate and the workload is high, employees criticize investments in labour integration, and calls for using the money for other purposes might arise.

Generally, the companies interviewed put a lot of effort in the labour integration of the Spaniards they recruited. All the employers interviewed stated that they assigned mentors, paid for language courses and helped the Spaniards to deal with the bureaucracy. They were highly motivated to successfully integrate the Spaniards in their company. It is self-evident that those companies who put high efforts into labour integration are more likely to offer themselves for being available as interview partners. Nevertheless, especially the employers in the health care sector were not able to retain the Spaniards recruited until it paid off for them. Despite their own economical constraints, the employers mostly knew about the circumstances the Spaniards faced in Spain and were driven by believing in doing a good deed by hiring them. Additionally, the German employers interviewed usually invest in their staff, however, they also rely on a sense of commitment of their employees towards the company. That is why the interviewed employers from all sectors felt personally concerned if the Spanish employees quit their labour contracts at an early stage.

All these integration measures are only developed in companies that have a demand for foreign professionals. Usually, these are MNCs and/or companies that encounter difficulties in finding adequate job candidates in Germany. The integration of foreign professionals is a rather new matter for small and locally oriented companies, and their integration measures mostly rely on personal relations. MNCs, in turn, are more experienced in integrating foreign professionals and have developed some kind of formal procedures and measures of integration.

5.4.2 Migrant organisations

Additionally, labour unions and non-profit organisations instruct interested parties on employment law and working conditions in Germany.

First of all, Spaniards in Berlin, who offer assistance to other Spanish labour immigrants facing precarious labour conditions, created Spanish migrant and non-profit organisations. Their aims and activities are rooted in the movement of *Los indignados* in Spain, which created *15M* in Madrid. The most important Spanish migrant organisations in Germany are *15M, Marea Granate, Oficina Precaria* and *Grupo de Acción Sindical.*

Marea Granate (=Maroon Wave) is a transnational non-partisan organisation created by Spanish emigrates and their supporters in Spain and abroad. They call themselves the maroon wave referring to the colour of their passports and the migration flow triggered by the economic crisis in Spain.

Oficina Precaria was formed to assist Spaniards in precarious working conditions. It was first established in Madrid during the economic crisis to assist those in precarious living and working conditions, but Spanish emigrants transported the idea of the network to a range of countries of destination, such as Germany, Austria, England, Scotland, France and the Czech Republic. In Germany, their first office was opened in Berlin in 2013 and another one followed in Munich in 2016.

15M grupo de acción sindical (GAS) was also formed in Berlin and cooperates with German labour unions to assist Spaniards in difficult employment situations. All these organisations have developed over the past few years. In 2014, they experienced high visibility when articles in *El País* and *Der Spiegel* reported on the exploitation of Spaniards in Germany and on the group *acción sindical*. In the aftermath of their appearance in the media, they received a lot of help from supporters in Spain and Germany. They have grown into an effective organisation collaborating with labour unions in Germany. Meanwhile, there are also branches in Hamburg and North-Rhine Westphalia.

The emergence of these Spanish organisations in Germany is an indicator of the increased immigration of Spaniards as well as of the institutional isomorphism taking place in the common EU labour market when intra-EU labour mobility rises.

All these groups found a lot of support from other local migrant organisations, Spanish networks, Spanish cultural clubs, Spanish Facebook groups, established Spaniards (especially the children of Spanish guest workers), but also from the Spanish embassy in Berlin and the Spanish consulate in Munich. All these actors offer assistance in legal issues and bureaucratic procedures in one way or another concerning employment law, social benefits, insurances, etc. Additionally, migrant organisations offer language courses, information on how to apply for a job and on employment contract regulations. Partially, the integration measures offered by these institutions are sponsored by the German and/or Spanish Ministry of Employment, the European Social Fund and/or donations. Hence, these organisations show a considerable self-interest in promoting the neediness of their clients as it secures their own survival.

It is self-evident that only Spaniards in difficult social and/or economic situations get in touch with these migrant organisations. The role of these institutions is crucial for these immigrants, because several interview partners offering integration measures state that it takes 3-4 years to become established on the German labour market for most Spaniards who have been neither recruited via the programme MobiPro, nor belong to a shortage occupation or highly skilled elite (see also Faraco-Blanco, 2014).

It is not by chance that these groups were created in Berlin, because Spaniards were strongly attracted by the multicultural metropolitan city, which is still relatively affordable compared to other big cities in Germany. Those who come to

Berlin are mainly interested in adventure-seeking, as has been derived from the interviews with Spanish immigrants. They apply a low-key lifestyle migration (see O'Reilly, 2014; Tewes & Heimann, 2018) and belong to the type of intentional unpredictability mobility (see Eade et al., 2007; Garapich, 2016), which is partly combined with benefit tourism. As they are poorly prepared for labour mobility and poorly informed about the labour market, they only find work in the low-skilled and low-wage sector. The head of a Spanish migrant organisation 1 in Berlin explained:

> *The biggest problem is that these people (Spaniards) are not prepared at all although they had planned to come to Germany, especially those in Berlin. I talk a lot about Berlin because I think it is a bit different here. When I go to Germany, it is important to know where I would like to live, and Berlin is one of the cities, where most people come to. They have a look at the living costs for the first month in Berlin, however, they did not attend any language course in Spain and they did not ask for information about how to find a job, what kind of job, the unemployment rate in Berlin, how can I get recognition of my qualification – am I able to work at all with the degree I hold. Many people come with false expectations and then it is difficult to find a job. Many end up in precarious labour conditions, in hospitality and have hardly any time for language courses. The situation is difficult. Additionally, for the Spaniards contacts in the community are important. Thus, they often stay in the Spanish community and do not build up any networks, which are necessary to find a job. I would say, the main problem is that many of them do not have a clue and no plan about what steps they need to take to find a job here, only illusions and false expectations of the chances in Germany. Once being in Berlin it is difficult to live in another city. Berlin is very multicultural and open compared to other German cities. People feel free and well and live with or know other people with the same migration background and they have some fun. Generally speaking, it is an experience and people do not know how long they will stay in Germany. They do not ask „Should I search (for work) somewhere else". That might happen after 1.5 or 2 years only.*

Compared to other parts of Germany, there is no labour shortage except in the healthcare sector and the low-wage sector, according to migrant organisations and educational institutions in Spain. Nevertheless, the Spaniards stay in Berlin due to its lifestyle and its big Spanish community, doing occasional jobs, mini-jobs and illegal work in Berlin.

However, they present themselves as having been forced to emigrate and call themselves economic refugees on their websites and in their campaigns. This creates a political framing used by 15M and most institutions originating from 15M to highlight the bad labour situation for the youth in Spain and abroad as well as the EU's austerity politics.

5.4.3 Labour, trade and professional unions

The effectiveness of *GAS* is supported by the strong labour unions in Germany, which are organised in a sectorial, cross-sectorial and nationwide manner. The corporatist system in Germany favours this kind of collaboration because strong labour unions are able to defend the rights of employees even if they are not members of the union. Additionally, there is a structure of work councils and employees' representatives in companies that provides assistance and information for employees in need. In order to protect especially those immigrants from other EU countries, the German Trade Union Federation (DGB) created the project *faire Mobilität*, which aims to implement fair working conditions and salaries for labour immigrants from other EU countries. The German Ministry of Labour and Social Affairs and the Ministry of Economic Affairs and Energy support the project. At the beginning, the project was focused on assisting labour immigrants from Central and Eastern Europe. Due to the increasing amount of Spanish immigrants, the programme's target group was extended to include the needs of the Spanish community. In order to inform Spaniards and protect them from exploitation, the German Trade Union Federation published a manual on German employment law in Spanish. The clarification of employment laws prevents the Spaniards from being exploited and the Germans from having to experience wage dumping. Labour, trade and professional unions do not only assist foreign workers in case of exploitation, precarious working conditions and issues concerning employment laws, but they also share their experiences with political actors to maintain the social, economic and educational standards. Thus, by participating in the field of intra-EU labour mobility unions develop new fields of activities, attract new members, maintain employment standards and secure their survival.

Representatives of labour and trade unions also inform job candidates abroad, especially in Southern Europe, about vacancies in certain regions and shortage occupations in Germany. Their aim is to create more transparency and provide information. They are, however, not involved in any recruitment or placement activities. The representative 2 of a German trade union said:

> *We also have representations in other countries. We call them circles of friends, it is like a foreign branch and I was in the South (Southern countries of the EU) several times to speak about the German labour market. I told them how you can enter the labour market and how you can get a job, what is the structure of a curriculum in Germany, what is an internship etc. in order to increase the transparency, because we had noticed that there is an increasing number of enquiries from abroad on how to enter the German labour market. Recently, I also designed a little graphic representation to showcase how you can enter the German labour market, one for EU citizen and one for third-country nationals.*

In this context, the trade and labour unions play an important role for the labour integration of foreigners, which is their main activity with regard to intra-EU labour mobility. In doing so, they spread the framing of intra-EU mobility as a chance and raise awareness of the *right people* on how to prepare for intra-EU labour mobility.

5.4.4 Interim conclusion: status quo in the field of labour integration

A *welcome and recognition culture* has been developed by different German institutions in order to create the *right circumstances* for labour immigration (see Loeffelholz, 2013).

Companies recruiting foreign professionals developed a broad range of integration measures depending on the sector, size and commitment. These measures include language courses, training on the job, welcome events and parties or mentoring. Integration measures go beyond mere working relationships. Additionally, help is offered with bureaucracy, search for apartments or job search for dependents. These measures are, however, only provided for professionals in shortage occupations. In order to integrate the foreign professionals the companies collaborate with migrants, recognition bodies, recruiters and employment agencies. In doing so, they promote labour mobility as a chance. However, these high investments do not necessarily pay off and employers are regularly disillusioned about the lacking sense of commitment of the Spanish employees.

Migrant organisations establish contacts with other migrants and supply information about employment law and social benefits. The labour immigrants, who contact the migrant organisations, are mostly in precarious working conditions and did not prepare themselves for labour migration. Spanish migrant organisations in Germany are assisted by the Ministry of Employment in Spain, the Spanish embassy and consulate in Germany. Additionally, established Spanish immigrants as well as the descendants of guest workers contribute their social skills. Due to their language skills obtaining fluency in Spanish and German, and their knowledge about the institutional structures these established Spaniards in Germany provide important resources to create the *right circumstances* for Spanish immigrants. Together with the media they transported the political framing of exploited economic refugees from Spain.

Labour, trade and professional unions offer information about the labour market situation, employment law and job search in Germany. In order to attract and inform professionals from EU states in crisis, trade unions and professional unions also travel abroad and launch this information, especially in Spain and Italy. This applies, however, only for unions in sectors where shortage occupations were identified. The German Trade Union Federation, and more specifically its project *faire Mobilität* (see Deutscher Gewerkschaftsbund, 2018), aims at improving the working conditions for intra-EU immigrants by supplying information and assistance to those in precarious working conditions. The unions collaborate with migrants, the German Ministry of Employment, the Ministry of Economic Affairs, and Bundesagentur für Arbeit. In this regard, the unions promote intra-EU labour mobility as a chance for foreign professionals and the German economy, while ensuring the standards of employment rights, which is part of creating the *right circumstances* for intra-EU labour mobility. By participating in the field of intra-EU labour mobility, they gain and maintain influence, members and therefore secure their survival.

In Table 12, the incumbents and their efforts for creating a Welcome Culture are summarised. These incumbents invested their social skills in retraining Spanish professionals in terms of language skills and German job profiles. To this end, they provide resources enabling the inclusion of Spaniards to make them the *right people* for the German labour market. In this way, institutions legitimize the framing of the *recognition and welcome culture*.

Table 12: Status quo of the German Welcome Culture

Activities	Companies	Migrant organisations	Labour, trade, professional unions
Labour integration measures	- Language courses - Training on the job - Welcome events - Mentoring	- provide contacts with others - provide information about employment law and social benefits	information about - labour market situation and employment law - how to find a job in Germany - how to apply
Clients/ target group	Shortage occupations	Foreign workers in precarious working conditions	Shortage occupations
Collaborators	- Migrants - IHK - Recognition bodies - Recruiters - Bundesagentur für Arbeit	- Migrants, - Ministry of Employment Spain - Established Spanish immigrants - Descendants of guest workers	- Migrants - Ministry of Employment Germany - Ministry of Economic Affairs - Bundesagentur für Arbeit
Myth, framings, perceptions	cheap, easy and fast way to hire suitable employees and high potentials → loyalty of employees	economic refugees exploited abroad	Labour mobility as a chance for professionals in shortage occupations

6. Removing the right circumstances in the UK

This chapter shows how an anti-immigrant framing was spread that finally led to the BREXIT vote. Section 6.1 outlines the way in which UKIP created an anti-immigrant framing that was taken over by the conservatives. In section 6.2 the actions of public and private recruiters show why the aim to reduce net migration could not be met by the government. Finally, Section 6.3 addresses the question as to what extent policies were implemented to set higher hurdles of labour immigration for EU immigrants and which integrations measures of incumbents such as companies and unions were available for labour immigrants. An overview of the strategic actions in the field of labour mobility is given in Section 6.4.

6.1 Strategic actions: anti-EU-immigrant framings and perceptions

In the next section, the development of a counter-reaction to the high and ever increasing number of immigrants in the UK is analysed. It outlines the anti-immigrant perception that came up and was voiced and spread by UKIP. UKIP related immigration to several social and cultural issues in the UK. The next section shows how UKIP challenged the status quo in the UK and how the governance units in the field reacted by trying to remove some of the *right circumstances* it had created to attract foreign workers.

6.1.1 Challenger of the status quo: UKIP

Since the end of World War II, the United Kingdom has become a popular immigration country. Most immigrants arrived from the former colonies, but more recently immigration from the EU has also increased significantly (see Full Fact, 2018). This development can be ascribed to the active policies of international labour recruitment and the economic crisis in other member states.

The substantial numbers of immigrants coming to the UK over the past 20 years triggered both a public and a political debate. This was the result of a strategic economic policy of the Labour party government under Tony Blair, which promoted labour immigration of EU citizens and international recruitment from third-country nationals . For the latter, contingents were set up for the recruitment of professions, in which a demand for labour force had been detected and that had been labelled shortage occupations (see UK Visa Bureau, 2018). Additionally, as one of the first EU countries the UK lifted all legal barriers to immigration from the Eastern European member states Poland, Estonia, Hungary, the Czech Republic, Slovakia, Slovenia, Latvia and Lithuania (2013). Thus, immigration has become one of the crucial topics on the political agenda since the economic crisis, which coincided with the enormous increase of immigrants. Although Britain was also hit by the crisis, it was affected to a much lower extent

C. Heimann, *Blessing and Curse of Intra-EU Mobility*, Studien zur Migrations- und Integrationspolitik, https://doi.org/10.1007/978-3-658-31486-6_6

than many other European countries. While the UK showed an unemployment rate of around 8% in the aftermath of the economic crisis, Spain featured an unemployment rate of around 25%. Additionally, it recovered relatively fast, as the unemployment rate in the UK went down to around 4% in 2016, while it reached around 18% in Spain at the same time, which is the lowest value since the outbreak of the crisis (see Clemente, 2015; Office for National Statistics, 2018b). Although most immigrants were still third-country nationals (see Full Fact, 2018), the stability of the British economy during the economic crisis led to a noteworthy amount of immigration from the EU, especially from Eastern and Southern Europe.

Nevertheless, the number of Britons working in precarious conditions, suffering from underemployment and limited employment rights due to zero hour contracts and/or part time work grew to around 22.2% (see Booth, 2016). Therefore, the domestic population's perception towards immigrants changed. Labour immigrants were increasingly regarded as a threat to British jobs. The United Kingdom Independence Party (UKIP) exploited this situation of increased immigrant numbers and the economic and financial crisis in the EU to create an anti-European, anti-immigration and xenophobe climate by spreading a populist and far right rhetoric. Immigration became a controversially disputed topic in the United Kingdom. Three main issues addressing benefit tourism, wage dumping and the housing problem raised the political sensitivity for the topics of immigration and Euro criticism, which became completely entangled (see Springford, 2013). Additionally, the conservative government of Prime Minister David Cameron, who promised to limit net migration to 100,000, did not keep their promise as net migration stabilized at around 250,000 per year. During the election campaign, UKIP and the Labour party criticized the conservatives for not keeping their electoral promise. David Cameron himself justified his failure by claiming that neither EU immigration nor emigration were controllable. He blamed EU immigration, which augmented in the aftermath of the economic crisis, and the fact that emigration reduced, while the British economy recuperated from the crisis (see BBC News UK, 2016). In this context, it was ignored, however, that the immigration of third-country nationals still constituted the biggest part of immigrants and could be reduced. However, David Cameron's justification was gladly adopted by UKIP as it corroborated their euro critical, xenophobe and anti-immigration arguments. The reason for their focus on EU immigration only was explained most vividly by the interview partner 2, working at a think tank close to the conservative party in 2015, i.e. before the UK elections:

> *Looking at the published opinions, you get the impression that the issue of migration is solely an intra-European topic. This is most striking if you look at the facts given by research studies, such as that from UCL (referring to Dustmann & Frattini, 2013). More than half of the immigration is non-European but that's no topic at all, nobody wants to mention it. This is a mystery to me. Of course, it is related to the idea of the Commonwealth, "We are one big community. We cannot deny entry.*

What would that look like? That's out of place!" Scapegoating the EU instead sounds reasonable, because all those in Brussels are crazy anyway and you can easily blame them. This is okay, but not for others. The facts are not relevant. There is an enormous discrepancy between reality and debate in the migration debate. And this will become even worse. If I was UKIP, I would dwell on this topic, because it feeds diffuse fears of foreign infiltration and loss of sovereignty. If you read the message that 75% of all legislative amendments in Britain are attributable to decisions taken in Brussels (catch line spread by UKIP in a poster campaign in 2014; see Bundeszentrale für politische Bildung, 2014)*). How is this related to the migration debate? Not at all in the first place, but it fits with the impression of "Those in Brussels decide what happens in the UK". This is not only a British phenomenon, but in the framework of the migration debate it seems to say, "We cannot fix this problem, because those in Brussels force us to keep our borders open".*

In addition to the enormous number of immigrants, and the general discontent with regard to the EU, the government came under particular pressure by UKIP after the elections for the British delegates to the European Parliament (see Clark, 2014), in which UKIP gained the majority of votes in May 2014.

UKIP increased its popularity further by legitimizing their Euro criticism and EU-immigration critique by fostering fears of benefit tourism from EU states in crisis. They used the temporary controls established to stem immigration of EU citizens from Bulgaria and Romania since January 2014 to fuel the fears of uncontrolled immigration and benefit tourism (see Sparrow, 2013).

Hence, the enormous inflow of immigrants in the 21st century led to a counter-reaction of perceiving EU immigration with increased scepticism.

6.1.2 Governance units: reactions of the conservative party

Additionally, the high amount of Southern Europeans, especially Spaniards, who have immigrated since the economic crisis, increased the subjective threat level sensed by British citizens, which intensified when the Romanian and Bulgarian citizens were given the right to move freely in the EU and to enter the EU labour market.

In 2013, Spanish immigrants formed the second largest immigrant group after the Chinese. However, while most of the Chinese immigrants were studying in the UK, the Spanish immigrants were mainly labour immigrants (see Office for National Statistics, 2017). Anxieties of uncontrolled mass immigration from Southern and Eastern European member states were created not only by UKIP but also by the conservatives (see Dominiczak, 2013, 2014). This climate was described as follows by the interview partner 2 working at a think tank close to the conservative party:

> *All Romanians and Bulgarians want to come, and what happens if they all emigrate? It is an absurd idea, but January 2015, when the 7-year period for the new EU member states ended (for further information see European Commission, 2006), it caused phobic reactions. The news programmes and newspapers sent journalists to the harbours, such as Dover, to document how thousands of Bulgarians and Romanians poured into the country with a plastic bag under their arms. Unfortunately, they didn't get these pictures because it did not happen. It showed how emotional this topic has been treated and how irrational it was to believe that all Bulgarians would travel to London. Such an absurd idea, but this was the image created: that all these citizens would come to London. You are smirking and I am smirking but the people had this idea in mind, and it was fuelled by the bad economic situation in many other EU member states. The concerns regarding migration did not imply that 20 million Germans or Norwegians would immigrate, but rather those from Spain, Portugal, Greece, etc. due to their critical situation. In this context, you look at continental Europe, at all those who are worse off than we are, thus it is believed that they all want to come to us and masses are construed in the minds of people and in the published opinions. The topic is inflated to a dimension, which it does not have in fact.*

Hence, the topic of EU-labour immigration was often discussed more emotionally than fact-based. Nevertheless, on both sides, far right and liberal, perspectives brought up serious arguments for and against EU-labour immigration, which will be presented and discussed in the following part. The main issues addressed were the economic effect of immigration, especially for those in lower income groups, and the cost of health care, social benefits and education for immigrants as well as the intensifying housing shortage.

In the deregulated British labour market, employers and recruiters seem to face a demand for foreign labour immigrants. Therefore, experts for the British economy from the Centre of Research and Analysis of Migration (CREAM) highlight the positive effects of recruitment and the labour demand in the British economy, especially in certain professions (see Dustmann & Frattini, 2013) such as nurses, doctors, engineers and plumbers. Thus, as long as the market is not regulated and the labour market absorbs the newcomers, recruitment and labour immigration will continue. Lately, a side effect of labour immigration inched to the centre of attention, which is the effect on the social security system and the health care system. This is an issue appearing only in the debate about intra-EU mobility because the non-discrimination principle of the EU law does not allow for a limitation of social benefits for citizens from EU member states (see Fontanella Khan et al., 2013). The government of David Cameron aimed to ban newly arriving immigrants from benefits such as tax credits and social housing for a period of four years in order to prevent immigration for the reason of benefit tourism (see Government Digital Service, 2018; The Week, 2015). This government debate concerning the abuse of social benefits of EU immigrants fuelled the BREXIT debate (see CLASS, 2014).

A general problem, which is exacerbated by immigration, is the housing shortage, especially in metropolitan cities like London (see Springford, 2013). On the one hand, immigrants are claimed to have higher birth rates than locals and would therefore help to diminish the demographic change that leads to a lack of a necessary rejuvenation of the British society. However, while the population is growing, the tense situation on the housing market becomes even more severe, which leads to a disproportionate growth of rents and real estate prices as compared to salaries (ibid.). Besides the increased demand for housing, another argument regarding the costs of immigration is the participation of immigrant children in the mainly government funded educational system. The third argument refers to immigrants as a burden to the National Health Service (NHS) and is similar to the housing and education argument. All these aspects assume that immigrants contribute less by tax paying than they benefit from government funded services. In a move to ensure that immigrants do not benefit more from the government than they serve the country, David Cameron aimed at limiting the possibility of them receiving tax credits. Tax credits were introduced as a form of social redistribution allowing benefits for low-paid workers while providing incentives to participate in the labour market (see Nardelli, 2015). There are two types of tax credits, which are child tax credits (CTC) paid to families with children, and working tax credits paid to people earning lower incomes. The amount claimants receive depends on their age, the hours worked, the number of children and whether they apply individually or as a couple (see Government Digital Service, 2018; Nardelli, 2015). The recipients of working tax credits receive a minimum of £1,960 per year. Child tax credits include a combination of a flat payment of £545 per year up to £2,780 per child. Tax credits aim at reducing the number of the working poor, while giving incentives to work and support to lower income families. The UK had around 7 million working families with dependent children in 2014 of whom 2.7 million received tax credits. Hence, nearly 40% of the working families with children in Britain rely on tax credits. From 2013 to 2014, the British government spent £29.7bn, which was around 13.5% of the UK´s welfare budget. The vast majority of these expenditures was given to families seeing that 4 million out of the 4.6 million recipients of tax credits have children (see Nardelli, 2015). In this context, it is argued that immigrants are more likely to work in the low-skilled sector and have more children than the domestic population. Thus, they are eligible for tax credits as they are more often working in jobs that are not attractive for the home population. Due to the prosperity gap between the UK and other EU countries, including the minimum wage, even low-skilled jobs in the UK are more attractive for some immigrants than skilled work in their home countries (see Springford, 2013). As the 5-tier immigration system facilitates immigration of (highly-) skilled third-country nationals, while discriminating low-skilled workers (Hopkins & Levy, 2012; see UK Visa Bureau, 2018), it is argued that immigrants working in the low-skilled sector are more likely to come from the EU. Hence, in political debate the question is raised as to whether EU immigrants profit disproportionally from the welfare system, as they have free access to the health care system, to the government funded educational system (while third-country nationals need to pay higher tuition fees and have high costs of health insurance), while they contribute to a lesser extent to the tax revenue due to the tax credits they receive (see Springford, 2013).

Different studies tried to obliterate these arguments. Amongst others, a study by the Centre for Labour and Social Studies (see CLASS, 2014) shows that 11% of the immigrants and 17% of Britons live in social housing. So, the average immigrant is less likely to live in social housing than the locals.

Responding to the accusation that immigrant children meant a burden to the educational system, Dustmann and Frattini (2013) stated that the better school attainment of immigrant children (see OECD, 2017) would balance out the costs of education. Their argument is that these children were more likely to obtain good jobs and pay high taxes to "pay back" the government's investment. However, this idea is based on the hypothesis that immigrant children will stay in the UK, which is an uncertain prediction regarding the future behaviour of this group. On the other hand, there is also a high percentage of foreign students (also from EU countries), who bring money to the UK by paying tuition fees and increasing consumption. It is still uncertain, however, to what extent this number would drop if EU students lost their privileges, such as having to incur lower tuition fees than third-country nationals.

With regard to the worries about the costs of immigration, the CLASS study (2014) says that immigrants would not use the services provided by the NHS as extensively as the Britons and only 0.1% could be contributed to health tourism. Another counter-argument is that immigrants are on average younger than the domestic population and therefore less likely to demand services.

All these calculations do not, however, offset the benefits Britons receive in other EU countries, such as the retirement migrants in Spain who profit from the Spanish health care system (see CLASS, 2014) or British children or students attending schools and universities in other EU countries. Apart from the legal perspective of EU laws, these arguments show that it is very complex - not to say impossible - to establish exactly the profits or costs of immigration for the British government, the British economy and the British citizens both now and in the long run. Furthermore, the evaluation of granting privileges such as social benefits and health care services to citizens of other EU member states depends on how the possibility of enjoying the same privileges in other countries is rated. The arguments given by UKIP and the conservatives in the political debate implicate that immigrants seem to be more likely to profit from the UK than this is the case the other way round due to the fact that the UK is one of the most prosperous countries in Europe.

The controversy of arguments shows how divergent the perceptions on immigration and the EU became in Britain and how difficult it seems to make a solid cost-benefit calculation. Ultimately, these perceptions have become a matter of perspective in a normative and controversial emotional debate, in which economic facts are of secondary importance only. Instead, it shows that immigrants are not supposed to belong to the British society to an extent that allows them to profit from public goods. Thus, the national solidarity among Britons is stronger than transnational solidarity with foreigners. In this context, the public and political debate spread and transported the framing of intra-EU mobility as a threat to the prosperity of the Britons.

6.1.3 Framings of anti-immigration and Euroscepticism

UKIP started an anti-immigrant and anti-EU movement by spreading the perception of (EU-) immigrants as a threat to British prosperity. UKIP represented a counter-reaction that developed as a result of the high and ever increasing number of immigrants in the UK. The right-wing party gained popularity by legitimizing their Euro criticism and EU-immigration critique by increasing fears of benefit tourism from EU states in crisis. A normative and controversial emotional debate was triggered that did not ground in economic facts. It rather showed that immigrants were not seen as part of the British society that allows them to profit from public goods. Having come under substantial pressure by this movement, the governance units took over several of the arguments of UKIP and promised to reduce net immigration. Doing so, the British government legitimized the framing of (EU-) immigration as a threat as summarised by Table 13.

Table 13: Institutions and framings of EU immigration in the UK

Institutional Role	Institution	Framing
Challenger	UKIP	(EU-) immigration is a threat to British prosperity
Governance units	Conservative Party (party in power)	EU immigration uncontrollable → Reduce net immigration

6.2. Status quo in the field of recruitment

Having outlined the changed perceptions and framings towards (EU-) immigration, the following section will highlight the main actors in the field of labour mobility. Public employment agencies and private recruiters are focused in order to show why the government was not able to reduce labour mobility.

6.2.1 Governance units: public employment agencies

As a consequence of the political aim to reduce net migration the involvement of public institutions in offering advice or assistance for labour mobility and immigration was withdrawn or reduced.

During the years when liberal recruitment policies supported international recruitment, the public institutions such as public employment agencies also offered advisory and recruitment service. This changed after the political aim was postulated to reduce net migration. Therefore, the services offered by EURES in the UK diminished more and more in the years prior to BREXIT. While EURES UK was not willing to give any information on their services, EURES consultants in Spain and Germany stated that the number of EURES consultants in the UK had been reduced. Additionally, the tasks of the remaining consultants were shifted towards activities other than orientation and advisory services for foreigners seeking work in the UK in the wake of the anti-EU-immigration debate. EURES advisor 1 in Spain stated:

> *The fact that a country does not invest as much human recourses and technicians for the international intermediary service, such as EURES, shows the political intention of a country or its current political situation (with regard to intra-EU labour mobility).*

Thus, EURES advisors abroad noticed that cooperation with their colleagues working in the UK has become more difficult or unlikely. This is an obvious consequence of the aim to reduce net immigration and especially also the immigration of citizens from EU member states in crisis, who are eligible for social and health care benefits.

However, even if the EU citizens did not receive any assistance from the public institutions in Britain, they still obtained the right of freedom of movement for workers. Hence, they still had the unrestricted permission to enter the country and the labour market as long as employers were willing to hire them.

6.2.2 Incumbents: private recruitment agencies

While public employment agencies withdrew their involvement in international recruitment both on the national and the European level, the recruitment industry in the private sector was still intensely and proactively recruiting professionals from abroad.

Recruitment agencies have become highly professionalized and competitive since the open immigration policies of the Blair government. So the former entrepreneurial actors became incumbents of the labour market ever since liberal labour immigration policies have shaped the status quo. The recruitment industry in the UK was *"driven by tough competition, enormous pressure and fear"*, as was stated by one of the interviewed recruiters. This is especially true for sectors and professions with a high demand, such as the health care sector, which is urgently in need of doctors and nurses. Interviewed recruiters stated that the competition for professionals was very fierce and the demand so high that they could not offer their services to new customers. Hence, recruiters were under high pressure to find enough professionals to satisfy the demand of their customers so that they might run the risk of being driven out of the market.

British recruiters are highly specialised in terms of professions and recruitment tasks, but do not focus on certain recruitment countries as do their German colleagues. This can be attributed to the fact that the language barrier is lower. Lately, the international recruiters had to intensify recruitment within the European Union. The recruiters and employers interviewed stated that due to the claim to reduce net migration the government removed several occupations from the shortage occupation list and/or the minimum wage required for hiring those foreign professionals was increased to an extent that could hardly be met by the particular profession. Interview partner 1 from a trade union in the health care sector explained it for the case of nursing:

> *I don't know whether you're familiar with the UK's migration policy, but you've got tier two general, which is where the majority of nurses will get their visas from and the employers get approval that they can recruit from outside the European Economic Area. And for some time, nurses have been taken off that list and are no longer recognised as a shortage occupation. So we've been trying to campaign to get back on the list. Recently we actually did get back on that list and now they're doing another review at the moment and we're just waiting to find out what will happen. Another thing we are concerned about is that they've done reviews of tier two in general, and they've said that they want, ah, occupations on that list if they earn I think it was 30k or more. Most nurses don't earn that amount; especially when they are starting in the NHS or coming from overseas, their starting salary will be close to 21,000. And they could therefore be disadvantaged, which means that employers might not be able to recruit from overseas, and they will have to recruit from within the European Economic Area.*

Thus, the opportunities to recruit third-country nationals were limited, which forced recruiters to focus their recruitment activities on the EU member states. In this context, recruitment from the member states in crisis became especially attractive due to the availability of professionals, who were out of work. By concentrating on the EU they secured their survival and could uphold their business models while the demand of employers for foreign professionals did not shrink. In order to connect efficiently with the foreign labour markets in other member states, they do not fulfil the whole bridging function as the intermediaries of the German labour market do. Instead, in the UK, a particular kind of labour division is found in the type of international recruitment services, as has been derived from the data provided by the interviews.

One part of the procedure is carried out by recruiters in the recruiting country that provide the vacancies mostly offered by regular customers. These recruiters have established contacts in different countries, like in Spain, where they cooperate with other recruiters who provide advisory service for certain professionals; preselect the job candidates for the foreign recruiters; and provide contacts to language schools, etc. This twofold type of recruitment was witnessed more often in the case of British than in the case of German recruitment. At the beginning, the missing social skills on the British labour market prevented the Spanish recruiters from recruiting directly for British employers. Later on, the British recruiters prevented them from entering due to the fierce competition. Thus, in the case of Spanish recruiters who preselect job candidates for certain professions in the UK, the language and knowledge of the structures in the UK seem to present a lower hurdle for recruiting directly than the fact that established British recruiters strategically prevent them from entering the recruitment industry. Additionally, British employers obviously do not trust in foreign recruitment agencies, as recruiter 3 for health care professions from Spain reported:

> *I try to find my own hospitals but most of the time I work as an intermediary for agencies there, who have the jobs but do not have the nurses and, the other way round, I have the nurses but no jobs. Then, they usually claim to have recruited the nurses, although in fact, I did. Well, but it's like that. Having read in the press that there are many hospitals that do not find nurses and spend loads of money on agencies I contacted various portals there. Then, I wrote a lot of mails offering my service, introducing my company and offering a much lower tariff. They didn't even reply. Well, I do not know if they are really interested in solving their problem. I think there is a sanitary collapse, which is very important. I have good references because I placed a lot of people and I do select candidates, which is important and I did not achieve to have my own hospitals in the UK as direct clients.*

The dense recruitment industry is not only a phenomenon of the health care sector, although this is where labour shortages seem to be most severe. Similar experiences were reported by language schools as well as labour, trade and professional unions from different sectors, such as health care, construction, industry and engineering in Spain that offer intermediary services. They stated that they only were in contact with British recruiters but not directly with employers.

In any case, if one recruiter offers the full recruitment service or if there is a specific kind of labour division with regard to the service provided both in the home and the destination country, job candidates usually do not pay for placements; instead, the employers pay the recruiters for their services. Some of the private employment agencies work as temporary employment agencies, as was explained by Spanish immigrants and migrant organisations. In these agencies, the professional is an employee of the temporary employment agency that withholds a certain percentage of the professional's salary whenever he/she is in employment.

Others are private recruiters that recruit a particular number of certain professionals and receive money for every job candidate they recruit for the employer. The interviewed Spaniards and migrant organisations recommend using this type of recruiters because they guarantee skill-adequate placements and the costs of recruitment are borne by the employer. How fast and successful the recruitment services operates, depends rather on the sector, the profession and the professional skills than on the recruiter, as was explained by recruiters, trade unions, migrant organisations and migrants. In the health care sector, great number of recruiters are competing due to high demand for nurses and doctors, while Spaniards and Spanish migrant organisations report that it is very hard to find a job in the UK in the IT sector. This situation might be ascribed to the fact that British companies in the IT sector either tend to recruit Indian professionals or that IT jobs in the UK are attractive for IT professionals from all over the world, which makes it harder for Spaniards to enter the labour market.

There are also further types of recruitment agencies that Spaniards and Spanish migrant organisations in the UK warn against. They mention agencies offering to find a job for Spanish professionals for a certain amount of money. Once the Spaniards have arrived in Britain, the agency has arranged job interviews at the typical fast-food chains for service, kitchen and cleaning jobs. Often additional services are offered by these agencies, such as searching for accommodation, applying for the national insurance number, which is necessary to work in the UK (see Harris et al., 2014), etc. Generally, Spanish immigrants and migrant organisations claim that it was not necessary to use these agencies as the services provided could be easily fulfilled by the Spanish immigrants themselves. Thus, in the interviews Spanish immigrants in the UK often talk about these services as fraud, although they knew exactly what the services they paid for included. In many cases, they had false ideas about the kind of job they could achieve by using this kind of mediating services. They chose them in order to limit uncertainty and gain security, however, afterwards they mostly regretted having used these services. A member of the Spanish migrant organisation Oficina Precaria in London explained:

> *I don't know, I think it is difficult to take the first step. The step to go to some place and so you get a bit more security (using these services). They abuse this. (...) In reality they abuse your missing knowledge or precariousness. In this context, they easily abuse the right.*

Doubtlessly, the business concept of these agencies is to profit from the lack of knowledge of Spanish/foreign immigrants. However, in the liberal British service economy, they offer a service that assists foreigners to overcome insecurity and missing social skills, such as a lack of information, missing language skills, missing contacts, etc. There might also be agencies that raise illusions by giving misleading information. Nevertheless, it regularly happens both in the UK and in Germany that immigrants knew about the conditions and contracts they signed before, but claimed afterwards that they had been cheated into something. Mostly, these immigrants did not inform themselves and are not satisfied with their situation after emigration. In this case it seems easier for the immigrants to blame others, such as recruiters, employment agencies or employers, than to take over responsibility themselves.

Summarizing we can say that even after the political aim of reducing net immigration had been proclaimed, labour immigration and international recruitment were facilitated by recruitment agencies and employers. While recruitment from third countries became more difficult, recruitment from EU countries, particularly from the states in crisis, was intensified. Hence, recruitment agencies as incumbents of the labour market, such as recruiters and employers, contradicted the new policy line by continuing recruitment as before.

6.2.3 Status quo in the field of labour recruitment

The status quo of the liberal immigration and recruitment policies in the UK was challenged by the United Kingdom Independence Party (UKIP). In particular, they spread anti-immigrant and anti-European framings that claimed to limit the labour market entry for EU citizen. In order to extend their potential electorate, the conservatives took over certain arguments of UKIP. They therefore supported the diffusion of the myth of endangered prosperity in the wake of immigration and promised to reduce net migration. Consequently, after the conservatives won the elections in 2015, EURES and other public employment centres reduced the availability of the *right circumstances* for labour recruitment by decreasing their advisory and recruitment service for labour mobility and immigration to help to achieve this goal. Nevertheless, the mere existence of EURES is a sign of the *coercive institutional isomorphism in the EU*, which took place to facilitate intra-EU labour mobility in the common EU labour market.

Despite the fact that public institutions decreased their involvement in international recruitment, the demand of employers for foreign workers did not slow down in spite of the policies of reducing net migration. Thus, recruitment agencies applied international recruitment with the same intensity as before. Accordingly, the recruitment practices in the liberal market economy remained unaffected and legally ensured by the EU principle of freedom of movement for workers. Therefore, the limited effectiveness and lack of structural interconnectivity between labour market/immigration policy and labour market/immigration practices can be assessed as one of the factors leading to the BREXIT vote. This shows how deeply not only the idea but also the habit of international recruitment had been institutionalised and *diffused* to the major actors of the labour market. The institutions involved, their roles, actions and framings are summarised in Table 14.

6.3 Status quo in the field of labour integration

In the following part, institutions and their role for the labour integration of immigrants are examined. It is shown that in the UK far less institutions are involved in the labour integration of migrants than in Germany, as the language barrier is lower, the labour market is more open and more centrally organized, and responsibilities are shifted rather to the individual than the collective.

Table 14: Status quo of the British field of labour recruitment in the UK

Policy Agenda	**Immigration crisis**		
Labour Migration Agenda	**Reduce net migration**		
Institutional Role	Institutions	Institutional myth/perceptions/framings	Strategic Action
Challengers	UKIP	anti-EU, anti-immigrant arguments	Populism Spread anti-EU, anti-immigrant arguments Put established parties under pressure
Governance units	Conservatives		Follow goal to reduce net migration
	EURES		Reduce involvement in recruitment and advisory service
Incumbent	Recruitment agencies	Demand for professionals	International recruitment Bridging function Earn money and secure survival

6.3.1 Governance units in the field of labour integration: NARIC

The British National Agency for the Recognition and Comparison of International Qualification (UK NARIC), which is the authorized recognition body in the UK, plays a major role in the labour integration of foreigners.

It is officially in charge of the recognition and comparison of international qualifications and skills on behalf of the British Government. UK NARIC provides services for individuals, who want to study, work or settle in the UK. In contrast to NARIC in Germany, the organisation not only offers services with regard to professional recognition but also on visa and immigration law.

Furthermore, UK NARIC provides assistance to universities, colleges and employers in terms of international recruitment and international applications for professional and educational careers. Just like NARIC in Germany, UK NARIC collects information about international education systems and qualifications in an online data bank and provides access to stakeholders.

Additionally, UK NARIC supports member organisations by coordinating various online trainings, events and conferences. It also offers advanced research and consultancy for employers, skills councils, awarding bodies, education authorities and governments (see NARIC, 2018).

Contrary to NARIC in Germany, the British NARIC is also designated to prove the comparability of professions in crafts and trades within the one central organisation ECVET (see European Commission, 2018c), which is the responsibility of the Chamber of Trade and Commerce in Germany. Only regulated professions are treated separately in the UK, such as nurses or doctors that have to apply for recognition at the Nursing and Midwifery Council (see Nursing and Midwifery Council, 2018) and the General Medical Council respectively (see General Medical Council, 2018). Individuals, groups or other entities may request applications and receive information and advice in English. Therefore, they already need advanced language skills in order to achieve recognition. The relatively high level of language skills also facilitates their labour integration into the British labour market.

Once all the necessary documents have been submitted, NARIC commits itself to completing the evaluation procedure within 10-15 working days and to informing the applicant if more processing time is required, for example when greater efforts are needed to receive information on the specific educational system. During the procedure the adequate training and qualification is first assessed with regard to the occupational or professional role in the country of origin, and is then compared to a profession of reference. If NARIC identifies sufficient similarities for ensuring the comparability of the foreign qualification with a British profession or qualification, a NARIC Statement of Comparability and a NARIC Certificate will be issued (see NARIC, 2018).

It is most probably due to the sensitivity of the issue of labour immigration during the period of data collection that UK NARIC was not poised to give an interview on the topic of labour mobility from Spain. However, the institution supplied some information by mail and provided links to other institutions and web pages on which information on related topics could be found.

The interviews with Spanish labour immigrants in the UK revealed that none of the professionals - apart from the technicians - requested a certificate of comparability from NARIC. Spanish technicians stated that an evaluation from NARIC was a precondition for applying for a GSCS card, which was needed to be contracted by employers for qualified work and decent salaries. The Spanish technicians 1 in the UK explained:

> *You need to get your certificates recognized at NARIC in order to obtain a GSCS card (General Skills Certification Scheme Card). Without that you only get the worst low-paid jobs as an unskilled labourer.*

The nurses were the only professionals interviewed, who needed to acquire professional recognition from the Nursing and Midwifery Council to be allowed to work in their profession. For all other professionals from the fields of engineering, social sciences and humanities, professional experiences and social networks seemed to outweigh certificates of education and training. As the interviewed engineer 2 stated:

> *In fact, if you have the experience and you can prove that you know what you know in the job interview, I think it (formal evaluation of diploma by the Recognition Body NARIC) is not important.*

All interview partners who applied for recognition (nurses and technicians) were capable of requesting recognition on their own, and none of the recruiters or employers stated to be asked to provide assistance. Although the required documents are the same in both countries, German recruiters and employers regularly reported to support the application process. This discrepancy could either be caused by language issues and/or the problem of missing personal initiative from the job candidate's side if recruiters offer (too much/a lot of) assistance, as was described by recruiters.

6.3.2 Incumbents in the field of labour integration

Besides the designated institution for the recognition and evaluation of skills and qualifications, there are also other institutions involved in the labour integration of foreign workers. In Britain, the most important ones identified for Spanish immigrants were companies, unions and migrant organisations in the form of institutional organisations or web-based networks.

6.3.2.1 Companies

British companies, which frequently hire migrant workers, have formalized routines of labour integration measures. Bigger companies offer regular induction events, in which the organisation is represented, safety issues are discussed, basics of employment laws and cultural habits are explained along with the work of trade unions in sectors in which they are relevant such as in health care or construction.

Furthermore, companies usually take into account a period for training on the job in which the newly hired people are prepared for their tasks. In this context, experienced colleagues fulfil the role of mentors. In hospitals the most formalised and standardised induction could be witnessed. In this context, experienced colleagues fulfil the role of mentors. Spanish nurse 1, who operated a professional forum, explained:

> *It is more or less the same everywhere. In theory, you arrive at the firm and you get an assigned mentor, who is with you in this redundant period. Well, this mentor should show you the dynamics of the firm, the documentation, the routines and how everything is done in general so that you learn how to work here, in all details.*

Those induction procedures seem to be frequently and routinely applied in companies that regularly recruit a significant amount of foreign workers. Also, established workers having foreign language skills help the newcomers to the company to get settled and translate the relevant terminology for them. Public institutions encourage and support applying this kind of labour integration measures by offering information and best practice examples online (see Integration up North, 2018). However, the extent to which these measures are applied depends on the company, the sector and the profession, as was explained by Spanish nurse 1, the operator of the professional forum:

> *Well, to be honest theoretically everything sounds very nice, but it does not always work out in the same manner. It is true that I had colleagues, who had made very bad experiences because their firms had a severe shortage of manpower. Thus, in my case they left me alone from the very first moment. Well, then you eventually feel a bit overburdened. No? There is also the case that there is a person to show you everything, but well everybody is different, every person has his/her own character, and it's complicated. Not everybody is capable of instructing others, I don't know. There are also cases in which persons, who are not properly instructed in being a mentor or who are not prepared to instruct or who lack empathy, find it difficult to empathize with somebody who came from another country. Probably you don't get everything because of the rapidity of the language. They do not feel it. Or sometimes a great number of Spaniards arrive at once and at the beginning they are very patient, but then there is a moment when they are saturated and lose their patience. Of course, it is obvious if you have to do your work and additionally you have to instruct someone, but there is no time, they indicate that you should do whatever you want. And well, it depends on the type of person you get, you know, if it's a nice, patient and good one, well, that's it.*

Despite the formalised and routinely applied induction, Spanish immigrants in the professional forums mention that learning by doing was the way how they learned most about the skills required, their tasks, organisation and the differences to the Spanish system. The induction seems to be a measure of labour integration for skilled workers (such as nursing), while low skilled (in hospitality and catering) and highly skilled staff (in engineering) solely had the chance of learning by doing. Also, the acquisition of language skills was the responsibility of the individual job candidates/employees interviewed and was not supported financially, by special company leave or in any other way. In this context, the Spanish immigrants generally reported a "swim or sink" approach on the part of their superiors and employers.

Thus, bigger companies that routinely recruit foreign workers offer induction and mentoring programmes. In companies employing workers from different countries more frequently a welcome culture has already become a formal matter of fact, which shows how deeply labour integration of foreign professionals has *diffused* into the routines of British companies. Nevertheless, its appropriateness and effectiveness depends on how professionally it is implemented.

6.3.2.2 Labour and trade unions

In contrast to Germany, Spanish immigrants in the UK reported that unions were only important to those working in the public sector. All other Spanish immigrants and Spanish migrant organisations stated that, according to their experiences, work-related issues were either negotiated individually between employer and employee or had to be settled in court. However, this was only an option for the highly skilled candidates, as other immigrants did not have the necessary resources to negotiate or to bear the costs of legal proceedings.

This is different in the public sector, as has been stated by trade, labour and professional unions from this sector. Especially in the health care sector, unions are strong and influential with regard to society and government decisions. Thus, among all the professions exemplified here, nursing unions were most important and visible when it comes to being involved actively in issues concerning labour recruitment and integration of foreign professionals.

British nurses are approached by the unions already at university with the student nurses programme to attract them to the unions. Immigrant nurses are likewise approached at an early stage already after immigrating to the UK, namely during their induction process at the hospital they start to work at. During this induction process the union had a slot in order to explain what the union in the UK is and does along with the advantages of joining the union.

Generally, trade and professional unions claim that immigrants in the UK (as in Germany) join unions for the same reasons as domestic people. These include mainly improving their practice, getting better access to guidance around professional issues, joining professional forums, influencing the work of the labour union and government decisions, or having a sort of insurance in the case of problems at the workplace. Nevertheless, the likeliness of becoming a member is different for non-European and European nurses in general, and Spanish nurses in particular, as a leading representative 3 of a trade union illustrated:

> *Non-Europeans have a higher propensity to join the union, more than the European nurses, so you see, if there are twenty Philippine nurses, it's*

> *likely that fifteen to twenty of them will join, while when I see kind of ten Spanish nurses, I'm looking to get hold of one of them to join the union, sometimes nobody will. Yeah, so I don't know why, but I always assume that the union in Europe, in Spain, and in all European countries are kind of the same. So they will know what a union does, and they will be more open to acceptance of trade unions also in this country. You'd expect them to be joining the union more frequently. I suppose it depends also on the level of vulnerability they feel, they always stay two or three years and then they'll leave again. They don't think it's worth the time, whilst non-European migrants intend to stay longer and settle in this country, I think 95% of them settle here and have longer working contracts. So they feel that they have a need for the union seeing that most of them feel rather vulnerable, because of recent changes in the UK immigration law. So that's the kind of difference in this context.*

The union stated that the three most important nationalities immigrating to the UK to work there were Spanish, Portuguese and Italian, though less of the latter in the past few years before BREXIT. They were less likely than non-EU immigrants to commit themselves to the unions as they consider their stay temporary. Due to the principles of free movement of workers and their eligibility for benefits related to their status as EU citizens, they feel secure at their specific workplace and in the UK in general. Additionally, their EU citizenship makes them feel free to move back to Spain or another country, which is claimed to be one of the major reasons why they do not actively participate in unions. Not even when significant changes for nurses from EU member states were looming, e.g. when the English language test was introduced as a necessary requirement for recognition, or before the BREXIT vote, did they see any need to join. BREXIT is especially supposed to impose substantial restrictions on the privileges of EU workers with regard to their free movement, health care and social benefits. However, European nurses in the UK hardly participate in any union activities related to this topic, as the interviewed representatives 3 of a union reported:

> *So, the Europeans will weigh those advantages (EU freedoms, social and health care benefits), when the UK gets out of the EU. We want to inform our members, especially the European members, about these matters including the personal impact this might have on them, so that they understand what it means to them. In this way they could, you know, pressure their own government to oppose the EU exit in Brussels, and all this stuff. But I suppose that in all those issues they will only become aware when they are directly affected, when it's too late (laughing). So in terms of those issues, those political issues, we are trying to educate them and to get them engaged. We are trying to show them the need to be engaged. There might be something from them mentally lacking or in how we approach it from our perspective as a union. We might not be doing it the right way. I don't know, or the other way around, there might be some disengagement from EU workers, from Spanish workers, for all these kinds of politics that are happening within the EU, they're not interested.*

> *I suppose, because they are young, that might have some kind of, you know, effect on them and they say "this is nothing for me". They think that it will not affect them now, because they are young, they can move anywhere they want to go, and they can do whatever they want to do at that age. So the demography, especially of the Spanish nurses that we're getting, is that of a rather young group of people.*

Thus, Spanish nurses not only show a very low probability of joining the labour union in the UK with a membership rate far below that of other, especially non-EU, immigrants, but they hardly participate in any activities campaigning to secure their job, free labour market entry and privileges in the UK. It was hypothesised that this might be ascribed to the fact that Spanish nurses consider their stay as being only temporary and, also, that they are mostly young and feel free to move on to another place. Hence, taking the freedom of movement for workers for granted could lead to not appreciating this principle anymore. Actually, most of the highly skilled Spaniards interviewed thought about moving on to another EU country if the conditions in the UK changed, while those working in skilled and low skilled jobs rather considered returning to Spain in the case of BREXIT. Only one of the interviewed Spaniards definitely evaluated his stay in the UK as a permanent project.

Summarizing, at least in the public sector, unions offer a lot of assistance to immigrant workers and are willing to listen to their concerns in order to campaign for their issues. However, hardly any Europeans and especially Spaniards actively or passively participated in unions, which is different for non-EU immigrants, who are more likely to stay long-term. In contrast, in the private sector of the British liberal market work-related issues are usually settled individually between employee and employer or in legal proceedings, according to the experiences made by Spanish immigrants. This seems to be an option for skilled and well-earning immigrants only, while those who are in precarious working conditions do not seem to have any lobby.

6.3.2.3 Migrant organisations

For those in precarious labour conditions, migrant organisations offer support, especially Oficina Precaria in London. Other web-based migrant networks provide general assistance for all Spanish immigrants in the UK.

The web-based communities created Spanish networks, which provide information and support for others who plan to emigrate to the UK and also those who have already done so. Spaniards ask all kinds of questions about living and working conditions in the UK in these communities, while their already established compatriots give advice, post job announcements or promote Spanish clubs and events. Thus, these networks also help to establish social contacts outside the virtual world. These Spanish communities facilitate labour mobility to

Britain and labour integration and encourage Spaniards at home to follow the example of the emigrants, as was explained by the Spanish immigrants and those who run the homepages. The first incentive is, however, mostly provided by job opportunities for skilled candidates; otherwise, the Spaniards might have been inspired and attracted to London by random social contacts, loose ties and indirect social relations. News about existing job opportunities reached them by word of mouth. Those working in precarious working conditions felt particularly attracted to seizing the opportunity of informal networks, such as social contacts offering accommodation.

A branch of the Oficina Precaria was opened in London, which offers information and assistance for Spanish immigrants in the UK. Most enquiries come from immigrants in precarious working conditions seeking information about labour contracts and employment law. Oficina Precaria in London reports that most of those seeking help are ill informed about the labour market and employment conditions in the UK and are not aware of the differences to labour contracts and employment laws in Spain. They report about exploitation on the labour market, especially in the field of zero hour contracts. However, they only can provide information. In contrast to the Spanish migrant organisations in Germany, they are not able to establish contacts with labour unions, politicians or lobby groups or any governmental or nongovernmental assistance. Oficina Precaria states that there is no support for immigrants in low-skilled and low-wage employment in the liberal labour market. Hence, those who find themselves in unbearable exploitative working conditions simply quit the job taking into account that their salary for the last weeks/month will not be paid. Migrant organisations and migrants themselves explain that Spaniards take over low-skilled precarious jobs in order to pay their rent and improve their language skills, while hoping to obtain a better job in the future thanks to the social skills they have acquired.

Migrant organisations state that the skilled, well earning migrants/workers, such as engineers, are able to negotiate individually or to sue their employers if issues arise, but labour, professional or trade unions play a minor role in the private sector. As Spanish immigrants in precarious working conditions do not have this option, they seek help from the Oficina Precaria, once conflicts with their employers arise, which happens frequently, though not only, due to missing language skills, as representative 1 of Oficina Precaria explains:

> *Normally, conflicts with the employer are the main issues. They are in a situation in which they will be dismissed and do not know what will happen to their holidays, or they do not know if they are adequately paid. They ask how to handle certain situations. Those are the conflicts, which depend on the type of work, of course, and they recur, such as: "May I take the holidays or not?" "My managing director is bullying me and calls me at eight in the morning that I have to be at work at 8.30. Where can I file a complaint if my managing director does that? Who is on the next higher level?" Well this is an issue if you go to another country; it is not that easy to go to the human resources department. You feel a bit ignorant*

or isolated. Then, it is more difficult to talk about your problems in another language, which is not your mother tongue. This prevents many people from expressing their problems. So the people swallow, swallow, swallow and in the end the conflict intensifies and often under conditions which are difficult.

Most of the consultation of Oficina Precaria is provided by online services, which is operated by a group of (mainly) young Spanish women, who hold a university degree. They are not and have not been in precarious working conditions in the UK according to their own statements, but are aware of the problems other Spaniards face in Britain. Therefore, they want to help those who are less fortunate. They educated themselves in employment law by searching for information on the different topics other Spaniards seek advice about, as representative 4 of them said:

The Oficina Precaria in Madrid is a group of people, who are very well prepared. This is completely distinct because it developed from the movement 15M. We are people who have various types of education. Right now, we have people here in the department in the UK, who work on the topic of housing, the topic of zero-hour contracts, but we all work in completely different fields, which have nothing to do with the topic of employment or counselling. This is something we do in our spare time.

Generally, the group of Oficina Precaria in London is less effective than the groups in Madrid and Germany as they do not receive any help from governance institutions or other incumbents of the labour market, such as unions. Therefore, they are not embedded in the national structures of the labour market and do not have domestic advocates to represent their issues.

Another kind of web-based assistance that was created in this context are professional forums or YouTube tutorials for certain professions, and in particular shortage occupations. They were developed by the Spanish immigrants themselves to discuss, collect and offer information on job opportunities, recognition, etc. Therefore, many professional forums, Facebook groups, YouTube tutorials giving advice for emigration and labour integration into the UK for certain professions popped up.

In conclusion, there are several internet-based communities and professional forums offering advice and information on working and living conditions or more specific work-related topics for Spanish labour immigrants. These structures also exist in Germany, but they are far more important in the UK where public institutions hardly offer any consultation services. Apart from these organisations, the Oficina Precaria offers services for Spaniards in precarious working conditions online or in person. However, their work seems to be less effective than in Germany, because it is not supported by strong labour unions campaigning for them in the UK. Still, the emergence of Spanish migrant networks and non-profit organisations in Britain is an indicator of *institutional isomorphism* throughout the European Union.

6.4 Analysis of the strategic action field: status quo of labour integration

In the UK, far fewer institutions appear to be involved in labour integration, which is obviously caused by the global spread of the English language, the open labour market, the central organisation of relevant governance institutions and the emphasis on individual responsibility, which seem to create the *right circumstances* for labour integration.

The designated recognition bodies are clearly structured according to their responsibility, such as NARIC or the Nursing and Midwifery Council, which is a *right circumstance* for acquiring recognition. Skilled professionals need relatively good English skills to be recruited and/or to obtain recognition in those professions, in which employers demand recognition. Nevertheless, only regulated professions like nurses, doctors, and sectors that need to consider certain safety standards as, for example, the construction sector, presuppose recognition. For the vast majority of university degrees, however, practical experience is more important than recognition. Thus, the signalling value of a university degree seems to be generally overestimated in the transnational context. Apart from the complexity of the institutional landscape of the *German Welcome and Recognition Culture,* the stronger emphasis of shifting responsibilities of labour integration to the employee instead of the employer and recruiter seems to either preselect independent and autonomous job candidates and/or forces them to become independent, which creates the *right circumstances* for labour integration.

Especially bigger companies - though not only multinational corporations - experienced in hiring foreign professionals apply formalized routines of induction to acquaint the foreigners with the working culture and organisational structure. Firms are encouraged to do so by public institutions, although labour integration is ultimately a matter of the employee and the company. Firms regularly offer mentoring programmes that aim at instructing the foreign professionals in their daily tasks during the first working period. While this concept is generally a *right circumstance* for labour integration, Spanish immigrants regularly reported that it was poorly implemented due to missing professional or personal abilities of the mentor and/or high workload and time pressure.

Spaniards in precarious working conditions reported that there was no representative institution defending their rights, such as the project “faire Mobilität” of the German Trade Union Federation. Skilled workers claimed to have the option to negotiate and settle work-related issues individually or in legal proceedings. In the public sector, the unions are taking migrant workers and their concerns into account. Nevertheless, only comparatively few European immigrants tend to join and actively take part in union activities. Instead, due to the variety of alternatives and the temporary planning horizon they do not integrate themselves to an extent that would make them willing to fight for their rights.

Several internet-based communities and professional forums provide information on working and living conditions in the UK. Their role seems to be even more pronounced in Britain than in Germany due to the drop in the number of governance units offering information since the immigration crisis. Also, the Oficina Precaria assists Spaniards in precarious working conditions, but they are less effective than in Germany because national institutions of the labour market do not support them.

However, the institutional isomorphism is indicated by the development of the same kind of institutions in all three countries. Some were developed in a process of coercive isomorphism enforced by the EU, such as NARIC or EURES, others spread out or increased due to mimetic or normative processes, such as the Oficina Precaria, private recruitment agencies and advisory services provided by a range of non-profit and for-profit organisations. The most important institutions in the field of labour integration and their activities are summarised in Table 15.

Table 15: Status quo of the British field of labour integration

Activities	NARIC	Companies	Migrant organisations	Labour, trade, professional unions
Labour integration measures	- Evaluation of comparability	- Training on the job - Welcome events - Mentoring	- provide contacts with others - provide information about employment law and social benefits	- public sector: information about labour market situation & employment law
Clients/ target group	- Immigrants - Employers - Institutional multipliers	Shortage occupations	Foreign workers in precarious working conditions	Shortage occupations
Collaborators	- NARICs abroad - Universities	- Recruiters	- Migrants, - Established Spanish immigrants	- Migrants
Myth, framings, perceptions	Signalling value of educational certificates	- Sink or swim	-Labour mobility as a chance	- Participation not relevant due to freedom of movement for workers

6.5 Right circumstances in the strategic action field of intra-EU mobility

All three countries faced a time of crisis, which destabilized the status quo in the field. In Spain it was the economic crisis, in Germany a demographic crisis and in the UK an immigration crisis. In this situation challengers of the status quo in the field of mobility were able to initiate field changes, which are outlined in this chapter. Afterwards, the governance units and their (re-)actions are focused to analyse the implementation of policy changes in the transnational field of labour mobility. Political framings for policy changes form the starting point to create or remove the *right circumstances* for intra-EU labour mobility. In order to cope with the ensuing changes in the field the reactions of incumbents from education, migration and the labour market are analysed as well as entrepreneurial actors that make profit by introducing new strategies to the field.

While a framing gets political legitimation from the government, subordinate governance units such as public employment agencies and other public services spread the *framings* and create the starting point for recruitment practices by establishing contacts and creating networks

Recruiters fulfil the bridging function connecting both labour markets transnationally. Soon after introducing the new recruitment policies, recruiters emerge, such as entrepreneurial actors keen to make money. In the UK they became incumbents during the last 15 years and established a dense recruitment industry.

Incumbents such as educational institutions, unions, language schools, migrant organisations and networks fulfil the function of an institutional filter by connecting Spanish job candidates and vacancies of employers abroad. In Spain, the incumbents preselect suitable job candidates and increase the matching of potential employees and employers. Abroad, incumbents offer labour integration measures and control the professional standards.

In steered forms of labour mobility a collective actor who challenges the status quo initiates field changes and governance units are able to trigger migration. However, in line with Massey, other institutions as incumbents of the field of mobility keep them going. As long as employers are willing to hire foreign professionals and foreign professionals are willing to immigrate for labour, the governments are not able to stop or reduce EU mobility in the common EU labour market. Besides, they are supported by incumbents in the field, such as recruiters, educational institutions, unions, language schools and migrant organisations.

Once recruitment relations are established, they are hardly reversible as incumbents have an inherent interest to keep the recruitment going seeing that it is existential for them. This is true for the incumbents offering new ways of international job search and fulfilling recruitment tasks. It is also true for those who fulfil tasks for matching and labour integration. Language schools offering individual matching services, unions and universities offering labour recruitment and integration measures for certain sectors and migrant organisations offering general information occupy a niche in the field of mobility which strengthens their survival capabilities as shown by Table 16.

Table 16: Right circumstances for intra-EU mobility

Right circumstances	Institutions	Function
Framing	-Challengers	-Initiate changes
	-Government	-Give political legitimation
Ways of international job search / recruitment	-Public employment agencies	-Establish networks
	-Public services	-Promote framing
	-Recruiters	-Transnational placement
Matching	-Language schools	-Individual matching
	-Educational institutions	-Matching for certain sector or profession
	-Unions	
	-Migrant organisations/ networks	-General information
Labour integration	- NARIC/ Trade associations	-Control qualificational standards
	-Companies	-Training on the job
	-Labour/trade/professional unions	-Labour protection
	-Migrant organisations	-General information

Important protagonists for labour integration in the destination country include NARIC and (trade-) associations that control the maintenance of qualificational standards, employers that provide training on the job, unions that - depending on their position in the labour market - offer assistance in enforcing standards of labour protection for foreign workers, and migrant organisations that offer information and contacts on living and working conditions as well as on the availability of benefits. The institutional analysis of the adjustments to create right

7. Right people: myth, motives and profiles

In the following chapter, various types of labour emigrants during the economic crisis are examined. Different types of Spanish labour emigrants are described and categorized according to their profession, age, skill-level, labour opportunities, the institutions involved in facilitating the job search as well as other contextual motivation to emigrate. Thus, insights into the profiles of the *right people* are provided and distinguished.

Statistics are intentionally left aside for various reasons. First of all, there are no statistics that offer the information provided by the experts. Secondly, intra-EU mobility is not registered due to the freedom of movement for workers. It is a voluntary step for EU migrants to register or deregister their stay. During the economic crisis Spain lost 10% of its inhabitants according to Bräuninger (2014), who refers to official statistics supplied by the Spanish Institute for National Statistics (INE). However, González Enriquéz (2014) claims that most of the population that emigrated was not autochthonous. She explains that the Spanish population had been extremely immobile since the end of the oil crisis in the 1970s, not only with regard to international mobility but also mobility within the country. Spanish employees were oriented locally giving priority to staying close to their family and friends. However, there is reason to believe that the official statistics neglect the amount of Spanish emigrants. Especially those Spaniards, who emigrated to other EU countries, did not necessarily need to register their emigration from Spain or their immigration into the other country. Most of the Spanish emigrants interviewed in the UK and Germany stated that they were still registered as residents in Spain. A majority of them did so to avoid losing unemployment benefits or health care coverage provided by the Spanish institutions. According to the emigrated Spaniards, their strategy is to use the unemployment benefits as initial capital for travel expenses, accommodation and means of subsistence until they find a proper job that earns their living. Furthermore, they are often unsure as to how long they are going to stay abroad and whether they will be able to meet their professional and personal targets there. So, they try to keep their privileges in Spain as long as possible. This is one of the reasons why the amount of intra-EU mobility of Spaniards might be underestimated.

The labour opportunities for Spaniards abroad depend strongly on the profession, the personal reasons for emigration and the destination country. Therefore, in the following section, different characteristics, opportunities and hurdles of intra-EU labour mobility will be analysed exemplified by four different professional groups. The first group is nurses, the second one is engineers, the third one is technicians and the fourth group includes graduates in humanities and arts, such as journalists, philologists,

C. Heimann, *Blessing and Curse of Intra-EU Mobility*, Studien zur Migrations- und Integrationspolitik, https://doi.org/10.1007/978-3-658-31486-6_7

philosophers, etc. These professions have been chosen to capture different motives, professional profiles and labour opportunities. The following sections show if and under which conditions engineers belong to a sought-after, internationally mobile elite as described by Favell (2008). In contrast, nurses and technicians, while in demand abroad, traditionally are not prepared for international mobility. So the focus is here on particular hurdles for professions on a medium-skill level that are usually regionally oriented (see Klopprogge, Ariño Mateo, & Heimann, 2016). The fourth group, the humanists, is added to show motives, profiles and opportunities for people that do not belong to the shortage occupations and therefore face different institutional hurdles and support systems, which they navigate strategically. Thus, this chapter shows how motives, profiles and opportunities determine migration projects and which strategies the migrants follow.

7.1 Labour situation in Spain: motives, profiles and chances

The first part of this chapter examines the labour situation of the exemplified professions in Spain in order to understand why they go for labour mobility. Firstly, the section about nurses shows how desperately especially the recently graduated nurses seek labour market entry, while international recruiters offer this chance abroad. Secondly, the section about engineers describes that these professionals seek career advancement and are attracted by more innovative tasks and higher salaries abroad. Thirdly, the section about technicians, shows that they are driven out of the country by the crisis in the construction sector and emigrate to find better living and working conditions to meet their breadwinner duties. Fourthly, the section about humanists describes that they mainly choose labour mobility in order to gain independence from their parents, while they seek adventure and personal development abroad.

7.1.1 Nurses: driven by opportunity

The first group, the nurses, are mostly not interested in living abroad if this was not the only opportunity for them to get a job and earn their own living. Spanish nurses undergo an education of a comparatively high standard in the EU, and there is a shortage of nurses in several other EU countries so that it is relatively easy for them to get recruited, as recruiters, public employment agencies and language schools stated.

Spanish nurses obtain an academic degree, as it is standard in many European countries. Nursing and other health care professions like physiotherapy are taught at university, where students additionally have the possibility to obtain a Master's degree or a PhD. This includes a four-year curriculum with several periods of practical work. Such programmes at universities are subject to strong government supervision in accordance with the Bologna regulations. Both public and private universities operate according to state-of-the-art standards. Supplementary qualifications can be obtained and are officially certified (see Klopprogge et al., 2016). After their graduation all diplomas are signed by the King to obtain validity. Moreover, the professional organization Colegio Oficial de Enfermería serves as a controlling authority to which every nurse has to register before being allowed to work in the profession (Noticias Jurídicas, 2018).

In Spain, there is a lesser risk of missing qualification or low quality of education than of overregulation and over-certification (see Amable, 2003; Klopprogge et al., 2016; OECD, 2010). The job profile of a nurse in Spain is based on holding a leading position, organizing the hospital ward and assisting the doctor, which includes instructing and controlling the auxiliaries that perform the care activities. According to nurses, professional unions and health care universities, they also perform minor surgeries and control the medication.
For nurses, the labour market has turned out to be very precarious in Spain ever since the onset of the economic crisis. Professional associations and universities state an oversupply of nurses in certain areas along with low regional mobility. Additionally, they mention drastic cuts in public health expenditure as the reasons for the high rates of un- and underemployment. Many of those who graduated during the crisis were not able to acquire a regular labour contract. As stated by nurses themselves and by labour unions, nurses without a contract mostly have to stand by and be available at very short notice. However, demand for working shifts as substitute stand-in is extremely low in general. Yet, employers continue to suggest that such work relations are the pathways into regular employment, which hardly ever turns out to be the case. Due to these exploitative working conditions, Spanish nurses have become increasingly desperate to find alternatives, even if it was abroad. The interviewed Spanish nurse 1 in the UK described her situation in Spain:

> *I submitted all my documents, my grades, working experience, courses and programmes I completed to the job exchange. Then, you receive a marking and you get your number in the ranking. Every community can have its own independent job exchange in the nursing sector. So it is very difficult (to get a permanent job), because when you enter the list, it is not to get a permanent job, but to act as a stand-in. (...) In fact, they only called me to fill in in summer, one day during Christmas or Easter holidays, basically only during major terms of holidays.*
>
> *(...) I could have stayed a long time in the ranking without climbing up. So, well, already many years have passed since I received my degree. Therefore, I decided to search for a stepping stone. (nurse, female, 33)*

According to the professional unions interviewed in Spain, such working conditions are standard among more recent graduates and are the major reason for Spanish nurses to consider employment in another country. Hence, their major reason for going abroad is to find labour market entry and self-sustained living and working conditions, as they are usually financially dependent on their parents in the family-oriented welfare system. They have good chances to find employment abroad because in Switzerland and several EU countries nurses are in demand, including the UK, Germany, Austria as stated by recruiters, labour unions and employment services.

These institutions reported that nurses are mostly female and in their early 20s and become aware of the labour opportunities abroad by mails and announcements received from professional unions, trade unions or their (former) university. These announcements are spread via these institutions by recruiters that select job candidates to recruit them in groups and do job interviews in one of the bigger cities in Spain. Most of the job candidates never planned to go abroad. The nurses are highly in demand but locally embedded in their social environment. Thus, one of the biggest hurdles in the recruitment process is not to get a job, but to eventually take the decision to leave friends, family, and pets to work in another country. They are highly qualified and demanded in other countries, but generally they do not have any additional interest in learning a new language, getting to know another culture or taking the adventure of experiencing life abroad. Recruiters, language schools, employers Spanish labour unions and Spanish nurses themselves confirmed these assessments.

The international mobility of nurses was driven by the objective of getting access to the labour market and living a self-sustained life independent of their parents, although they would prefer to stay in their local community.

7.1.2 Engineers: driven by career advancement

Instead of self-sustainment, as in the case of the nurses, engineers seek career advancement by going abroad. In comparison, they are relatively well prepared and more open-minded with regard to learning another language and entering a different cultural context.

According to recruiters, employers and trade unions from the industrial sector, engineers' training involves a five-year curriculum in Spain, which meets a relatively high standard compared to other EU countries. Engineering studies are theoretically oriented and regimented but also include practical work periods that are necessary to obtain the required ECTS points in accordance with the Bologna regulations. Recruiters, professional unions, public and private employment agencies gave the following information on the profile of emigrating Spanish engineers. Internationally mobile engineers are usually older (27-35 years) and better prepared than nurses. They apply individual job seeking strategies and are very well aware of their market value. Spanish engineers are well qualified especially in telecommunication, construction, the automotive industry and mechanical engineering, according to the statements of professional unions.

In 2009, the Spanish system of higher education was still criticised by the OECD for its low level of internationalisation. In the past few years, Spanish engineers and their study programmes have become more internationally oriented, as professional unions and recruiters state. They attend foreign language courses far more frequently than in the years before the crisis. According to the University of Technology in Spain, the recruiters and professional unions interviewed, the number of Spanish students doing foreign study periods or internships abroad has increased significantly. This kind of incremental preparation for international mobility is the most sustainable way to learn a language and gain access to a country, its culture and (later on) to the labour market. There seems to be a tendency to prepare for an international career, as employee 2 at a Spanish professional union for engineers explained, whose task is consultancy for labour emigration and intermediation for recruitment:

> *Since 2009, we have offered this service (consultancy and employment service). At the beginning, it was very difficult to find an engineer with German language skills and even their proficiency of English was low, and truly, a lot has changed. The other day, we (a colleague and me) discussed it after the job interviews. In the past, it was so difficult to find people with a good level of English for example, and now even among the recently graduated it is difficult to find the one, who has not worked on this aspect.*

On the one hand, the increasing international orientation of engineers and engineering students is an obvious response to the economic crisis, which had an enormous impact, especially on the manufacturing sector. The gross value added (GVA) of the manufacturing sector declined by 12.6% during the economic crisis, representing 86.1% of the decline in the total GVA (see Ferreiro & Serrano, 2012). On the other hand, the growing number of EU programmes and policies designed to facilitate the mobility of students and professionals encouraged internationalisation. Both developments have increased the awareness of labour opportunities abroad and led to higher demand and, consequently, to an increased availability of language courses, international career advice and international job portals at universities and professional associations. The range of services supporting the internationalisation of engineers was not only broadened but also more specified. For instance, universities offer language courses that concentrate on the technical terminology in German required in the automotive sector, or professional unions offer country-specific information events on international job search, recruitment, vacancies in certain sectors and regions, etc.

In the case of engineers, the motive of labour migration is more often driven by the wish to advance their professional career than by the mere wish to find a job in their field, as in the case of nurses. To a high extent, engineers were employed in Spain before they got a job abroad, as recruiters and professional unions reported. In contrast to nursing, international work experience and foreign language proficiency are valuable assets in engineering regardless of the country they work in. According to their own statements and the statements of recruiters, engineers carefully select their country of destination taking into account career opportunities, language and recognition requirements. Spanish engineer 1 interviewed in the UK said:

> *Well, I have always worked on improving my English as it is an asset in engineering. When the situation in my company got worse I looked for jobs abroad and in my field there are some interesting companies in the UK. After I sent my application to a job offer, the next day I had more than a dozen of missed calls and new job offers in my mailbox. The position I applied for was already occupied but they called me to offer other suitable positions to me. (engineer, male, 31)*

Similar stories were told by other highly-skilled engineers from Spain working abroad, which shows how sought after these professionals are by certain companies.

The engineers are especially interested in jobs in English speaking countries because of the language or German speaking countries because of the strong industry. However, older engineers and civil engineers prefer to look for a job in Latin America due to the convenience of the same language and similar culture, as is stated by Spanish professional unions and recruiters. Their main motives are to find interesting, more innovative jobs, higher salaries, better working conditions, and better employment contracts, as was explained by the Spanish engineers. They regularly emphasised in the interviews that they had a job matching their qualification before going abroad, but that their company started to perform economically worse. However, professional unions highlight the decreased demand in the industrial sector and the need for engineers to search jobs elsewhere. As the engineers interviewed seemed to be highly skilled and well prepared for an international career, they probably started to search employment and found a job abroad before they were laid off by their companies. It is likely that the engineers stress the point of career advancement and higher salaries because they want to distinguish themselves from poverty migrants and economic refugees, which do not match their self image and their international labour opportunities.

In summary, the engineers make use of intra-EU mobility in order to boost their careers by going abroad. Those emigrating are comparatively well prepared in terms of language skills and knowledge about the labour market abroad.

7.1.3 Technicians: driven by breadwinner duties

Another sought after profile of professionals is that of skilled technicians, such as plumbers, electricians, sanitation and heating technicians. As will be shown, labour mobility of those professionals is mainly driven by their bad situation on the Spanish labour market and their breadwinner duties:

The boom of the Spanish construction sector was also a boom for the skilled professionals, such as plumbers, electricians, sanitation and heating technicians. They easily found a job and had good earning opportunities. According to the statements of technicians who emigrated, most of them had a regular full-time job and, additionally, they earned extra money by illicit work they did during the weekends or evenings. The labour situation changed rapidly, when the crisis arrived in Spain and the construction sector declined. Technician 1 in Germany explained his situation in Spain:

> *I worked as a plumber in Spain from 2001 to 2010. In the beginning, I earned very well, when the construction sector was still flourishing. I could have worked 24 hours a day legally and illegally. Around the end of 2008, the first problems arose, that was when I lost my job for the first time. My wife is German and suggested to go to Germany because it would be easy to find a job as a plumber there. However, I was afraid to take this decision especially because of the language. So, I started to work self-employed, but finally my customers didn't pay me anymore. Then, I was ready to leave, when a friend offered me a job (in Spain). Only some months later, he told me that he couldn't pay my salary anymore. Then, I knew that I had no perspective in Spain anymore. (plumber, male, 35)*

As the technicians earned well during the boom and credits were cheap in Spain in those days, many of them raised a credit to buy a home with monthly loan instalments that were only affordable for them as long as they had their regular job and the illicit side-line activities, according to the statements of emigrated technicians, recruiters, labour unions and public job centres. The crisis then triggered a chain reaction. They lost their regular job and their side job, and they were no longer able to pay their loan.

According to foreign recruiters and employers, emigrating technicians have a relatively good education compared to those in other EU countries. The education covers 5 years of training at school combined with practical periods. Therefore, Spanish technicians have relatively good chances to get a job in other EU member states in which the construction sector is booming and craftsmen are in demand. Among these countries are Germany and the UK that have a demand for such professionals according to recruiters (see also Mangelberufe.de, 2018; UK Visa Bureau, 2018). Nevertheless, as in the case of nurses, the problem of language skills is most pronounced. The technicians are prepared for the practical tasks their job involves, but not for intercultural matters or communication in foreign languages. An electrician or a plumber is normally not planning or preparing an international career; instead they are mostly locally oriented. This means that they usually had no foreign language skills at the initial point of recruitment, as was explained by recruiters. The job candidates had forgotten the limited English skills taught at Spanish schools and they were not used to school-based learning anymore.

The technicians usually became aware of the labour opportunities abroad by mails, journals or TV, as was stated by recruiters and the technicians themselves.

The announcements were spread via these institutions by recruiters and by EURES. In this process, especially the trade unions seemed to be dedicated to spreading foreign job announcements in the communication media and to support recruiters by providing contacts with potential job candidates and office space for job interviews, as was explained by the interviewed recruiter. Therefore, the services of the trade unions that are most frequently demanded by their members are consultation services with regard to job seeking. Other services they provided before the crisis and before the latest labour market reforms are of minor importance now. This was why these trade unions were losing high numbers of members. On the one hand, supporting recruitment is a strategy to help professionals to find a job again. On the other hand, it is also a strategy of self-preservation for the trade unions.

According to the recruiters, most of the job candidates were middle-aged males, but younger and older technicians are also applying. The middle-aged candidates seemed to have a higher necessity to earn their own money than younger technicians and were therefore more likely to look for work in foreign countries. Mostly they were married, had a family and had to pay their loans. They are not alone to suffer from their unemployment, but their families were also affected. As the resources of parents and parents in law were limited, they were usually not able to support and accommodate the whole family. So the technicians have a strong motivation to find earning opportunities in order to provide the financial resources to care for their families and/or pay their loans. Therefore, they have a relatively high motivation to integrate themselves at the workplace and the location abroad as recruiters, employers and Spanish technicians themselves state. The interviewed German recruiter 4, specialised on recruitment of Spanish professionals in crafts and trades, said:

> *The order situation in Spain in these sectors (sanitary, heating, electric) related to the construction sector is so poor that only a minor part has had a job since the beginning of the crisis. That is why Spaniards are very motivated to find a good job in their profession.*

Generally, the type of emigrating technicians for labour opportunities are middle-aged men driven by their duties as breadwinners for their family.

7.1.4 Humanists: driven by a diffuse wish for self-realisation

Generally, graduates in the humanities and arts or social studies regard their labour situation in Spain as hopeless. Like elsewhere, labour market entry has always been difficult for them, even in the boom phase, but during the crisis it seemed to have become impossible.

Compared to the technicians, the humanists are normally referred to as highly skilled as they have obtained a degree that requires at least 5 years of university education. However, this should be relativized as the humanists are formally highly educated, but most of them do not have skills that are in demand for the broad labour market. So to speak, the technicians possess special skills but they are not necessarily highly educated, while most of the humanists are highly educated but hardly have any skills that are strongly requested in times of economic crisis. Humanists' skills are language-based, such as reading, writing and speaking, like in the case of journalists, philologists, social workers, etc. Therefore, a Spanish humanists' labour force is hardly transferrable into a country, which is not bound to the Spanish language. In their case, a diffuse mix of cultural interest and vague expectations drives labour emigration, while they earn their living with low-skilled jobs in restaurants, hospitality or retail. Due to unemployment and the family-based welfare regime in Spain, many interviewees did not have their own income and were financially dependent on their parents.

They hope that a stay abroad would grant them some independence, contribute to their personal development and improve their language skills to an extent that will help them find a job once they come back to Spain, as the Spanish humanist 4 said:

> *Among my close friends I was the only one who was fired during the crisis. Everybody was working, my boyfriend, my friends... it was just me who had nothing to do. Everybody's life was going on, but mine had stopped. So, I got really depressed and felt like a complete loser. Therefore, I decided to leave Spain and to go to the UK to gain new experiences, to learn English, to get to know a new culture just to make my life going on again. (female, 30, journalist)*

This statement indicates what many young Spanish humanists had to face at the time of the crisis: they do not pursue a concrete target or project, instead they flee from their depressing social environment and seek distraction (see also Tewes & Heimann, 2018). Other motives they mention are gaining international experiences, getting to know another culture, hoping to profit in some way from improved language skills. Just like several other interviewed institutions, these emigrants perceive international experience as a value in itself. Although it seems contradictory, the myth of intra-EU labour mobility as a chance is supported by the belief in the value of international mobility even if it does not lead to improving the labour situation. The perception of the value of international experiences diminishes the possibility of failing. Besides measurable salaries or career advancement, grown personal experience, self-realisation and international experience are evaluated as a major asset. These non-material aspects are legitimized personal aims in the affluent Spanish society for a single person that is not financially responsible for others. Jobs in hospitality abroad are socially accepted, because the aim is improving language skills, not being a waiter, cook's mate or cleaning lady.

A philologist, doing his PhD, working for a department for Romance studies at a Spanish public University, and who hardly ever gets paid for his work, explained the current situation in Spain during the economic crisis. He described his situation and the situation of his friends, all of whom studied languages, philology, performing arts, music or film science:

> *You know that I am from the posh quarter of Barcelona. My lifetime friends are the sons of upper class families. That means, they are unemployed, but they do not starve. They live in one of the flats their parents bought to invest capital. Every now and then they do occasional jobs or they get some money from their parents. However, they cannot afford to go out to a bar, restaurant, cinema, etc., but they have also lost their spirit and it is very hard to motivate them to do anything. Frequently, I say: „Hey, let's take our bikes and go to the beach, we can prepare some sandwiches, bring some water and we can enjoy the beach, the sea, the sun and it costs nothing." However, they don't do it. They prefer to stay at home and smoke pot. I guess it is even harder for my friends, who find themselves unemployed at the age of 30, while they had all the chances of good education and so on, and everybody in their family has a super successful career. Recently, one of my friends went abroad to France after having been unemployed for years. We learned French at primary school. For us it was quite easy to learn because it is similar to Catalan and we were children back then. Since he went to France, he has been the one who found a job abroad thanks to his exceptional language skills (smirking ironically) and his parents are so proud that the failure of the family finally forges ahead. Although, his job in France has nothing to do with the subject he studied or anything, but anyway... You know what? Whatever he is doing there, I guess it is much better than sitting in your flat, smoking pot and waiting for the days to go by. (male, philologist, 31)*

In this quote the contrast between personal expectations of young, well-educated graduates and labour market opportunities becomes obvious. Furthermore, it indicates several advantages of labour mobility even if it does not lead to improved employment conditions. If the graduates do low-skilled work that does not match their qualification in Spain they are perceived as failures by their social environment. However, if they do the same abroad it is legitimized by the skills they gain (personal experience, language skills) or have (language proficiency, intercultural experience). In the situation of missing occupational prospects, the chance of going abroad to learn another language and broaden one's horizon offers a socially accepted alternative. This became possible due to the diffusion of the *normative isomorphism* of international mobility as a value in itself fostering personal development, which displaces the perception of labour mobility as poverty migration. However, the motive of personal development could be overstressed to conceal a lack of personal and professional perspectives. Anyhow, going abroad became a strategy not only to improve working conditions, but also to improve their personal situation by gaining independence, experience something new and leave the depressive situation in a Spain in crisis behind.

As their type of labour emigration is only vaguely bound to their professional career, they normally follow the advice of friends or family instead of turning to recruiters or job offers to try their luck abroad. According to their own statements, if they got in touch with any institutions that facilitate emigration or integration, they got in touch with migrant organisations, online platforms of migrant groups on Facebook or mediating services. This was also confirmed by migrant organisations and Spanish networks.

Although, they have no clear aim about what to achieve by emigration, they expect their life to be better abroad. In Spain, they were mostly dependent on their parents and were exploited by employers offering unpaid internships or volunteering while raising their hopes to get a paid job in an indeterminate future; this situation continues until, finally, they do not see any perspective for themselves anymore in their home country.

7.1.5 Right people - myth, motives and chances

Comparing these four groups of professionals, it becomes obvious that there is not one single profile of the *right people* for intra-EU labour mobility. Instead, the question whether people are the *right people* varies depending on the profession and the skill level, the demand in their home country and abroad, the aim and motivation of intra-EU labour mobility, as well as the personal situation.

Generally, it shows that graduates who obtained a degree in an educational programme, which leads to a defined professional profile, are more successful in achieving a job matching their qualification. However, the success of labour mobility also depends on the aim and motivation of emigration. If the aim is to learn a foreign language and getting to know another culture or taking the adventure of experiencing life abroad, or if the motivation is to leave the parents′ house (which is a relatively big issue in the family-oriented welfare regime) or the depressing social context in Spain, labour mobility might still be evaluated as successful even when it leads to a precarious low-skilled job abroad as long as it enables a self-sustaining life. Additionally, the impression has been created that international and intercultural experience is an asset in itself, which is connected to the perceptions of opportunities of mobility in the globalized world. This myth legitimizes working in a precarious job abroad, but not in one's home country, because language skills are improved and valuable international and intercultural experiences are made in order to broaden the candidate's horizon. This argument was given regardless of the usefulness of language skills for a certain profession. It indicates that labour mobility is generally evaluated much more positively now than it was decades ago, when labour emigration was related to being an economic necessity for the socioeconomically weak Spaniards. This is an indicator for the *normative isomorphism* transported by different labour market institutions that promote international mobility.

Obviously, highly educated people having little opportunities with regard to finding a job matching their qualification express the narrative of adventure seeking as a motive for transnational mobility. This seems to apply, in particular, to humanists that are single and culturally interested. However, adventure-seeking or fleeing the depressive mood in Spain is not the main reason for emigration mentioned by everybody. Other professional groups that have better job opportunities abroad emphasise motives related to economic and professional reasons.

Table 17: Right people for emigration in Spain

Characteristics	Nurse	Engineer	Technician	Humanist
Education	medium	high	medium	high
Specific Skills	high	high	high	low
Employment status	unemployed	employed	unemployed	unemployed
Labour market situ abroad	High demand	High demand	High demand	Low demand
Personal situation in Spain	Age: early 20s, single, female, depend on parents	Age: late 20s, single	Middle-aged, men, married (with children), mortgage,	Age: early 20s to early 30s, single, depend on parents
Motivation[9]	Labour market entry and self-sustainment	Career advancement	Fulfil breadwinner duties	Personal experience, adventure and language skills
Expectation	Paid job that earns their living	Professional development	Good living conditions for the family	Personal development, language skills
Institutions contacted for labour mobility	Job announcement spread by recruiters, professional unions, educational institutions	Job announcement spread by recruiters, professional unions, educational institutions	Job announcement spread by recruiters, professional unions, educational institutions	Friends, family, migrant organisations, untrustworthy recruiters

→ Projects of labour mobility are different due to
- **Motives**
- **Profile**
- **Labour market situation at home and abroad**

Spanish nurses obtain an education, which is of a relatively high quality in the EU and there is high demand in other countries. They are desperate due to the bad labour market opportunities in Spain and perceive learning another language, getting to know another culture or experiencing life abroad as an unavoidable evil. Language skills or international experience are no transferable assets in this

9 In the interviews political corruption and lacking future perspective in Spain were also mentioned but were not highlighted as (main) reason to emigrate

profession. The mostly young, female singles use transnational mobility as an opportunity to find labour market entry in their profession and to achieve a self-sustaining life, which is not possible in the family-oriented welfare regime in Spain during the crisis.

In comparison, engineers choose intra-EU mobility to boost their careers by going abroad. They are relatively well prepared in terms of language skills and knowledge about the labour market in the destination country. Highly skilled professionals, such as the engineers, who are well prepared for labour mobility and in demand in many knowledge economies, seem to be mainly driven by career advancement, and not necessarily by economic needs.

The emigrating technicians are as poorly prepared as the nurses at the beginning of labour recruitment. However, they are mostly older and driven by their duties as breadwinners for their families. This is why they compensate for their lack of preparation quickly as they are highly motivated to work for their labour integration. The technicians might generally represent the needs and motivation of other middle-aged breadwinners.

Concluding, there are different types of projects linked to intra-EU labour mobility depending on the motives, profile and the labour market situation at home and abroad as summarised by Table 17. The labour market situation for the specific professional profile was mentioned as a motive in all four cases. While nurses sought for labour market entry abroad, engineers searched for career advancement, technicians for better living and working conditions to fulfil their breadwinner duties, while humanists hoped to gain independence from their parents as well as to make intercultural experiences.

7.2 Right people in Germany: myth, motives and chances

The good experiences made with Spanish guest workers in terms of integration raised the willingness to recruit people from Spain on the German side (see Thränhardt, 2014, see Section 4.2). While back then Spaniards were recruited for unqualified jobs in the secondary labour market, today they are recruited for qualified jobs in the primary labour market. Thus, the profile of the *right people* for labour mobility among the Spanish immigrants is different today. These may vary among the labour migrants, who do not necessarily match the recruitment criteria and shortage occupations defined by the German government. Therefore, in the following part the different institutional hurdles and incentives of labour recruitment and integration will be presented for the four professional groups, namely nurses, engineers, technicians and humanists. Firstly, it will be shown that nurses are highly demanded, so that they get a lot of support from recruiters and employers. However, they lack personal maturity and intercultural competences, which complicates their labour integration. Secondly, the engineers will be described as being sought-after, which means that those who have or develop the necessary intercultural competences will find career advancement. Thirdly, it will be shown that Spanish technicians search for decent living and working conditions in Germany and are willing to take the efforts to become settled. Fourthly, the case of humanists in Berlin will show a type of low-key lifestyle migration (see O´Reilly, 2014)in which they intentionally keep the aim and duration of their stay unpredictable. They seek intercultural experiences and personal development supported by welfare benefits in Germany. Additionally, the policies developed to retain especially medium-skilled EU immigrants will be addressed. Thus different projects of labour mobility and labour integration are found in which the migrants use the institutional services offered strategically.

7.2.1 Nurses: strongly demanded but not satisfied in Germany

Spanish nurses, who have been recruited mostly for German senior residences since the economic crisis, are taken as an example here. The Spanish nurses are an interesting case to illustrate three important obstacles to labour mobility. First of all, nursing is a regulated profession and mirrors all the chances and hurdles related to regulation. Secondly, the mobility of Spanish nurses showcases problems of the interconnectivity of EU labour markets arising from different educational systems and job profiles. Thirdly, this case underlines that offering labour opportunities and a broad range of integration measures is not enough to foster labour mobility successfully, if professionals do not accept the working and living conditions.

German recruiters have joined the recruitment industry for Spanish nurses only recently in the wake of the crisis and, even more often, since the German government has started to offer subsidies for recruitment. Most recruiters in Spain and Germany have or had closely related core competences before the economic crisis such as international business consultancy or national recruitment consultancy. They are mostly embedded locally in both countries and concentrate on certain regions. Most of them seized the opportunity of high unemployment rates among nurses in Spain, labour demand in the health care sector in Germany, and the subsidies offered in 2013 and 2014 within the programme MobiPro-EU (see Bundesagentur für Arbeit, 2013).

Many nurses applying for a job in Germany have never left Spain before. They are usually in their early twenties and lack professional experience. One of the interviewed recruiting agencies developed an adaptability and mobility test. Hundreds of job candidates for nursing took this test online. Afterwards, job candidates selected for a job interview were questioned personally in more detail. A large proportion of these job candidates had never experienced a stay abroad, neither for work nor even for holidays. They indicated that they had never gone somewhere by airplane, and many of them had never even driven their car to an unknown city in Spain (let alone abroad) or taken a train to another city. The test revealed that they had very little experience concerning mobility or building up new relations. Only few respondents said that they had ever been to a class (at school or in their spare time) or a sports club where they did not know anybody.

These statements were given despite the obvious desirability of such matters (see Klopprogge et al., 2016). This is one facet of the embeddedness in the local social communities and family ties in the family-oriented Southern European states (see Amable, 2003; Lessenich, 2013; Moreno, 1997). Without any doubt, the highest obstacle to labour mobility for nurses is to part from their family, friends and their social environment (see also Section 4.1).

Most of the nurses have never moved out from their parents' home before they went to Germany. The interviews with recruiters, language schools and the nurses themselves reveal that a considerable number of the nurses tended to lack independence, autonomy and personal maturity [10]. Several of them needed guidance by the recruiters to find their way to and around the airport, even in their home country.

Spanish nurses are usually recruited for the German labour market in groups in order to reduce transaction costs and to facilitate labour integration by offering them the opportunity to create a Spanish support network. The interviewed employers, recruiters and nurses describe the whole recruitment procedure and integration measures as follows: In some cases nurses have the chance to come to Germany and do a probationary period for some days in the recruiting facility before signing a labour contract. Before they start work in Germany, the recruited group of nurses usually takes part in intensive language courses of around 200 hours. The whole group is mostly recruited for the same facility or facilities that belong to the same organisation. Recruiting in groups is a measure of labour integration, as the Spanish nurses are supposed to support each other when taking the step of labour mobility and getting settled. Typically, all costs of travelling, language courses and the organisation of the journeys in Spain and Germany are covered by recruiters and employers. Once the nurses arrive in Germany, they are picked up at the airport by the recruiter, employer or another staff member. The employers usually provide affordable and convenient accommodation in a residential home for nurses, especially when the facility is located in a big city with a tense and expensive housing market. The recruited nurses profit from this way of recruitment because they do not have to invest their own money in language courses, relocation, etc. and save time and efforts, as the recruited male nurse[11] reported:

> *I chose Germany and the university hospital of XXX (name and location removed) after rejecting numerous offers from companies,*

10 To quote but a few examples: Some were not able to decide by themselves whether they could go to a job interview in another city but had to ask their parents' permission; Additionally, parents called recruiters to find out about the equipment of the nursing home and threatened not to allow their grown-up children to go abroad if no towels or bed linen were provided there.

11 This nurse was particularly in demand, because he was recruited for a hospital and male, while nurses are mostly female and recruited for senior residences. He was found because he became publicly active in the media and criticized prejudices against working as a nurse in Germany.

> *because there are loads of offers, but you need to select carefully. Then, I signed a contract with the German company XXX (name removed), which cared for securing a job for me, picked me up at the airport the day I arrived in Germany, searched accommodation for me until the hospital had arranged an apartment for me, provided financial assistance of 900€ for my relocation to Germany, paid a German teacher for me in order to achieve the B2 level which enabled me to work as a nurse. (nurse, male, 35)*

Despite the wide range of opportunities for nurses in Germany, Spanish nurses, German labour unions as well as professional forums and youtube tutorials advise to choose the employer carefully and to compare the offers, because recruiters and employers differ with regard to their level of professionalism, the service, the salary and the conditions they offer. A big German labour union especially warns against new mobile intensive care companies popping up as a profitable business model, which sometimes lack a certain degree of professionalism, but recruit intensively.

Even though - or probably because - labour mobility is facilitated to such a high extent, recruiters, employers and their colleagues partly report a demanding attitude of nurses. Probably due to the lack of experience of the Spanish nurses, their expectations are sometimes far from reality[12]. Recruiters and employers consider these issues most likely when subsidies and recruiters facilitate labour mobility to an extent that allows the job candidates to avoid more or less any responsibility, as the German recruiter 3 explained:

> *Well, I got the impression that if you make things too easy for professionals, this proves to be rather counterproductive. It is not productive to pay for the language course, organise the accommodation, and also hire a person, who always cares for everything. If you (the Spanish professionals recruited) have a problem, there will always be someone to solve it. In this way, you create an attitude of "I can take the liberty of doing everything I want and I have only rights but no duties anymore". If you establish a mediating service like that, then you will run the risk of not being the provider of a service or recruiter anymore, but you are more like the boss of the Club Robinson (=all inclusive touristic services): "today I (imitating the recruited Spaniard speaking) did not like the host and I make a call now and tell them I would like to have another*

12 For instance, Spanish nurses in Munich complained about their accommodation and demanded another one from their employer. The reason for this complaint was that the one-room apartment in the residential home for nurses they rented for 250€ per month, was located 20min by interurban train from the Munich city centre. They asked their recruiter and employer for an accommodation closer to the city centre. However, taking into account the tense and expensive housing market, the residential home for nurses was certainly located in a privileged area. Additionally, an apartment of the same size in the same area, furnished with a laundry room, would cost three times as much on the free housing market.

> *host, my washing machine is too small, I don't like it, (...)" This is a counterproductive story.*

Until the nurses have been fully recognized and allowed to work as qualified nurses, they work as auxiliaries. During that time, employers finance accompanying language courses and release them from work for these courses. Some employers pay them the salary of a fully qualified nurse during that period, as recruiters, employers and nurses stated. Along with the costs for recruitment, travel and accommodation, this involves high investments for employers depending on the region, country and provision of the recruiting services.

In accordance with the EU Directive 2005/36/EC (see European Commission, 2018e), the crucial formalities required in Germany for recognition from the responsible *Landesprüfungsamt* on Federal state level include a CV, ID, certified qualification and professional experience, certificate of good conduct or police clearance and the current professional status (see Bundesministerium der Justiz und für Verbraucherschutz, 2018). Although each candidate's certificates are individually reviewed, this general recognition procedure of the qualification is a formality rather than an assessment. Nevertheless, the Spanish nurses in Germany regularly need help from their employers or mentors to cope with the recognition procedure. Despite these issues, not a single incident of non-recognition was mentioned in the interviews with recognition bodies, employers, recruiters and nurses

The recognition bodies claim that the only obstacle is to obtain the King's signature on the certificate, which might take between one and a half and two years until delivery. Recently graduated nurses cannot be recognized in another EU member state unless they are certified as nurses in their home country. Indeed, some Spanish diplomas could not be recognized due to the King's missing signature.

In Germany, the recognition bodies for nursing are organized on the federal level with each of the Federal states having its own body in charge of recognition (see also Sommer, 2015). According to their own statements, these bodies have a high workload, which means, that there was a great number of foreign applicants seeking to be recognized. However, the major obstacle to obtaining recognition and the permission to work as a nurse in Germany is the language requirements. As the interview partner 1 from The German United Services Trade Union "ver.di" in Germany stated:

> *The problem for the colleagues (nurses) from EU countries is not the recognition of their diplomas in health care. Instead, the problem is the additional criterion that was introduced and is reasonable – the language proficiency.*

Being of fundamental importance when working with patients, relatively high language skills are required to work as a nurse. Therefore, a B2 proficiency in German is required to have diplomas recognized in Germany. However, foreign language skills in Spain are overall relatively low according to the interview partners (see Klopprogge et al., 2016; Santiago et al., 2009). Hence, those recruited for the German labour market tend to have no or only little language skills. The high pressure to learn German for receiving professional recognition was the biggest challenge and psychological burden for the Spanish nurses as described by the female Spanish nurse 2 in Germany:

> *At the beginning, I was worried about the language. There were people, who did not understand that I was a foreigner and that I did not speak German. And there is a mentality – which I do understand – that is: if you want to work in Germany then hurry up to learn the language. So, at the beginning I was in a situation of 'I want to but I am not able to'. (nurse, female, 27)*

Apart from the different language, Germany also boasts a different educational system and job profile for nurses. Nursing is part of the dual education system in Germany and consists of three years of vocational training, while it is a four-year academic curriculum in Spain. While nurses in Germany typically carry out all care tasks, nurses in Spain lead the hospital ward and partly assume tasks, which are exclusively done by doctors in Germany, as was reported by the nurses and recruiters. This is one of the reasons why Germany is less attractive for Spanish nurses than, e.g. the UK. Additionally, the fact that nurses are preferably recruited for geriatrics is another disadvantage. Employee 2 of a non-profit organisation, who analysed issues of labour integration of Spanish nurses in Germany to develop integration measures, explained:

> *Especially Spanish nurses often thought they were overqualified for work with German health care providers, especially in geriatrics, because they have to undergo a different education in Spain, an academic education, which does not match the job profile of the nurse in elderly care.*

In Germany, nurses need a requalification in order to be trained for care tasks that are not part of a Spanish nurse's job profile. Care tasks are either jobs done by auxiliaries or provided by relatives in Spain and in many other countries.

German nursing staff working with Spanish nurses explained that some Spanish nurses were unwilling to carry out care tasks, as they did not regard them as part of their duties. Also, nurses, professional unions and Spanish migrant organisations state that Spanish nurses feel downgraded by meeting the German job profile of a nurse in a senior residence and, even more so, in elderly care. The Spanish nurse 2 working in a senior residence in Germany said:

> *Well, as a nurse in Germany you are the girl Friday. You have to do a lot of tasks that are done by auxiliaries in Spain. You do not have your*

own office and the distance to the doctors in the hierarchy is greater. (nurse, female, 27)

The image of the job profile of a nurse as fulfilling mainly care tasks and tasks of auxiliaries spread among Spanish nurses and Spanish professional unions. However, the Spanish nurses' impression of the German job profile consisting mainly of care tasks seems exaggerated, because Spanish nurses are usually trained for work in hospitals but are mostly recruited for senior residences in Germany and have no working experience at all. For reasons of comparison, a Spanish nurse working in a hospital was searched for the interview, but was hard to find. This male nurse 1 (age 35) had worked in a Spanish hospital before and stated:

My daily tasks are the same as those I did in Spain. As the hospital I work at is a university hospital, it is true that there are sectors for internal medicine, such as cardiology, where only the doctors take blood or establish vascular access, but in other areas we (nurses) carry out these tasks, which is the same in Spain.

Additionally, Spanish nurses in Germany rate their workload as extremely high, according to labour unions, recruiters and employers, which is claimed to be one reason for the labour shortages. The workload is not only an issue for the Spanish nurses but also for their German peers. A representative of a labour union states that the high workload is the main reason for labour shortages in nursing in Germany. He explains that part of those who graduate in nursing change profession due to high time pressure and bureaucracy involved, which prevents them from fulfilling their actual care tasks with the patients in the adequate way they learned to do it. A major part also reduces working hours to part time because they feel unable to cope with the high workload in full time jobs.

Hospitals and senior residences that are most strongly affected by labour shortages are more likely to invest in recruitment. However, for varying reasons, these employers are often considered less attractive for employees, e.g. because they are located in 'unexciting' rural or, else, in expensive metropolitan areas or involve elderly care. Nevertheless, nurses often use these employers as a stepping-stone. They offer training, financial support and, most importantly, expedite recognition. As soon as the recognition has been formalized, they apply to a supposedly more attractive employer in a different city, region or hospital. The high labour shortage and the pressure on health care providers make it easy for nurses to find a job as soon as they are formally recognized.

In Germany, working conditions are considered little attractive due to the high workload and the fact that foreign nurses are mainly recruited for senior residences or other forms of elderly care. The interviewed recruiters and employers from the health care sector stated that in all cases of recruitment of Spaniards for senior residences they knew of, hardly any of the recruited nurses stayed with the employer who recruited them[13]. Nurses either stayed until it paid off for them when they had acquired recognition and changed to hospitals or, if they stayed longer, they mostly stayed for personal reasons. However, the Spanish nurses appreciate the salaries in Germany and the facility to gain a permanent employment contract, which offers financial and personal security they were not able to achieve in Spain.

Some employers concluded adhesion contracts with the internationally recruited staff to make sure their investments in recruitment, language courses, accommodation, training on the job, etc. will pay off. The contracts often needed to be fulfilled for one or two years. An earlier termination of the contract was penalized by some employers with a fine depending on the investments of the employer for labour integration, such as language courses and paid leave for these courses. Other employers did not pay the salary of a full nurse until recognition was achieved in order to reduce their financial loss if the nurse left after recognition, while travel costs, language courses etc. had been paid. In these cases nurses are advised to renegotiate after recognition, as YouTube tutorials, professional forums and labour unions state.

Spanish nurses gain working experience and are able to work in their profession as soon as they have acquired the necessary language proficiency and gained recognition. They are often recruited for elderly care and switch to hospitals or return to Spain whenever they can find a job there. Thus, recruitment hardly ever pays off for the recruiting senior residences. Additionally, they tend to cancel their labour immigration project at an early stage because they feel overburdened by the cultural shock and disillusioned about working and living conditions in Germany. As they lack working experience, intercultural competences and personal maturity, they tend to be overwhelmed by the requirements of the everyday working life, the pressure to gain B2 language skills and the fact of being far away from home. The fact that maturity is important for the success of labour integration is also underlined when recruiters, employers and migrants in the health care sector confirm that most of the recruited nurses are in their early or mid-twenties, while only interview partners at the age between 27 and 35 were found who actually stayed in Germany or the UK for several years. These interview partners evaluate their age and experience as an advantage over the younger ones as they consider themselves more robust to face the challenges of mobility, having a higher frustration tolerance, being less likely to fall prey to fraud and being more stable.

13 Although the interview partners were committed to offering exemplary labour conditions and measures of labour integration.

7.2.2 Engineers: seeking career advancement

As in Germany, the Spanish formation of engineers includes a five-year study programme, which is Bologna certified and of a relatively high standard when compared to other EU countries, as recruiters stated.

The interview partners involved in their recruitment explained that Spanish engineers who migrated to Germany during the economic crisis are mostly between 27-35 years old. Those who are relatively well prepared in terms of knowledge about the foreign labour market and language skills are able to apply individual job seeking strategies and are very well aware of their market value, as recruiters and professional unions state (see also Section 8.1.2). Spanish engineers are well qualified, especially in telecommunication, construction, the automotive industry and mechanical engineering, according to the statements of professional unions.

Germany, Austria and the Netherlands appear to be recruiting labour most actively in Spain according to the statements of Spanish professional and trade unions. First of all, these countries have a strong industrial sector and a high demand for well-qualified engineers. Secondly, they opt for targeted recruitment in Spain due to the availability of well-qualified engineers in that country. Thirdly, there is a higher language barrier than in the case of English-speaking companies and recruiters, not only for the job candidates but also for the employers and recruiters. Therefore, the hurdle for direct applications or recruitment is higher than in the case of English-speaking countries. It is easier for employers and engineers alike to receive assistance from Spanish labour market institutions, e.g. professional associations, public employment agencies, universities, etc. Especially in big multinational corporations, welcome parties are organized; assigned mentors are provided to the foreign newcomers, or rather formal induction events take place that inform them about the history and structure of the company and the German culture.

In the vast majority of cases, the recognition of diplomas does not constitute an obstacle to the transnational labour mobility of engineers because there are few formal regulations. Mechanical engineers, electrical engineers, IT engineers or mechatronic engineers, to name but a few, face very little formal impedance when applying for a job in another EU member country.

Apart from civil engineering, no other engineering profession requires official recognition of the foreign qualifications. It is possible to request an evaluation of their diploma from the central recognition body NARIC or to have the title engineer recognized. However, none of the interviews with counselling services, recruiters and engineers revealed even a single case (except for civil engineering) where an evaluation of a foreign diploma was requested.

Yet, the evaluation of foreign diplomas has obviously become more complicated as a consequence of the Bologna process, as was described by the Recognition Bodies, counselling services for recognition and employers. Before the Bologna reform, the diploma certificate stated the main or core discipline (e.g.

mechanical engineering, electrical engineering, etc.), listed the different specializations within the discipline (e.g. automotive technology, signal processing, etc.) and showed to what extent these special competences had been acquired. Today, in the wake of the Bologna process, a stark inflation of the number of specialized titles in a field was witnessed by the interviewed recruiters, employers, migrant organisations and professional unions, which makes the evaluation of both domestic and, to an even larger extent, foreign diplomas even more complicated. Therefore, a professional union for engineers in Germany explained that they specifically target this issue:

> *We are engaged in developing a transparent system for the recognition of qualifications. Due to the Bologna reform, introducing Bachelor and Master degrees, one could have believed that the process would be rather straightforward now. If I hold a Bachelor or Master degree – then everybody can assess my expertise; but unfortunately it is not like that. In Europe, we have a wide diversity of titles. Our aim is to increase transparency.*

This might be one of the reasons why factors such as work experience; international experience and the university programme seem to outweigh formal certification by means of diplomas, as recruiters explained. Focusing on former working experience and its informative value might be a strategy of recruiters and employers to overcome the obstacle of non-transparent diploma. German employers tend to pay special attention to the job candidate's work experience. This might refer to the relevance of the recruiting country's national standards. In Germany, more collaboration is practiced between universities and industrial enterprises, which implies a more 'practical' study programme than in other EU countries. Hence, employers may tend to focus more on a foreign job candidate's work experience.

Acquiring a job in Germany is perceived as a significant career advancement and valuable asset adding international work experience to the individual curriculum. Engineering jobs in Germany promise higher salaries, better employment protection, more innovative tasks and a higher degree of independence, autonomy and creative freedom for the Spaniards. The Spanish engineers appreciate a higher level of self-realisation in their job due to innovative tasks and flat hierarchies compared to the more patriarchal, authoritarian organisation in Spain.

Furthermore, experiencing the superior economic efficiency - not only in the organisation of work processes - is considered a significant personal and professional asset. As the Spanish engineer 1 working in Germany put it:

> *In Germany, everything is so efficiently organised and structured, also in the company where I work. In Spain, we can still learn a lot from the Germans about organisation, logistics and so on. () Then, once we go back*

to our country, we can improve our kind of organisation in order to increase efficiency. (engineer, male, 29)

In the perception of Spanish engineers, a major disadvantage is that open positions can usually be found in more rural areas instead of the attractive metropolitan areas. Additionally, many of these companies are small or medium-sized enterprises (SMEs) that are subcontractors or suppliers of bigger, more prestigious companies.

Therefore, Spanish engineers often find employment with a supplier that develops components in a more rural area. The recruiter 3 in Germany said:

Well, it is not BMW Munich that entrusts us with the recruitment of engineers. In this case, we would probably have more highly motivated job candidates than we could handle. No, there are small companies in Thuringia, Saxony or also in rural areas in Western Germany that cannot attract enough professionals because of their geographic location or because they do not pay as much as comparable companies in Stuttgart, Berlin, Munich or Hamburg.

The employing company might even be a world leader in its field, but it neither offers comparable prestige nor the glamour of a large city. Additionally, the engineers seem to prefer life in big cities because they want to spend their spare time in Spanish communities. One of the interviewed Spanish engineers had worked in Munich and Hamburg for 5 years already without speaking any German. A Spanish engineer answered the question about contacts and friends in Germany:

Well, we (a group of befriended Spaniards) work in an international environment. So we meet people from all over the world. However, we cherish our small Spanish oasis. (engineer, male, 28)

The vast and very important industrial sector in Germany produces high-tech products and offers a wide variety of challenging and interesting jobs. Lacking proficiency of German is less problematic in engineering since English is sufficient in many cases.

There is a high demand for electrical, mechanical, and mechatronic engineers for SMEs from the automotive industry in more rural areas. A considerable fraction of the Spanish engineers seems to perceive employment at an SME as a stepping stone into the German labour market, as has been witnessed by recruiters. Having enhanced their language skills and their work experience there, they apply for a more 'favourable' job. This is a common pathway of transnational career development. It goes without saying that some engineers are actually hired directly by their favoured employers, but these seem to be part of a small, highly skilled elite with outstanding grades, international experience and proficiency in at least two languages. Of course, these extremely highly skilled 'Eurostars' (see Favell,

2008) having intercultural competences and highly specialized skills in niche disciplines represent a small minority within the available work force.

Yet, another group of employees working for SMEs chooses to stay with the company, mainly due to the excellent match between the highly specialized skillset of the employee and an equally specialized or exotic product portfolio of the employing company.

7.2.3 Technicians: integration as a long-term project

Technicians usually learn about the labour market opportunities abroad by searching in Spanish job portals, or they receive job offers via EURES or labour, trade or professional unions.

Technicians were hit especially hard by the economic crisis as their position is directly or indirectly connected with the economic climate in the construction sector. The biggest hurdles for them when planning to go abroad are missing foreign language skills, no international experience and the wish to stay with the family, as was reported by recruiters, labour unions and technicians themselves (as explained in Section 8.1.3).

Nevertheless, German recruiters find more skilled Spanish professionals interested in job offers in Germany than employers that are willing to recruit and employ Spaniards. The employers and companies in Germany are careful with regard to international recruitment because they frequently lack experience with foreign employees. Furthermore, the investment in international recruitment, including travel costs, language courses, organisation of apartment, etc. involves high costs for the SMEs in crafts businesses, while it is still a risky process. However, there is a high demand for professionals and a readiness to recruit foreigners. One of the interviewed Spanish plumbers, who came to Germany on his own account together with his German wife, reported:

> *I do not regret my decision to go to Germany. Soon after I registered at the employment service (BA) I received several job offers although I did not speak any German, but I declined all of them because I wanted to terminate an integration course first to learn German and to learn more about Germany. (plumber, male, 35)*

Employers deciding to entrust recruitment agencies with the search for suitable professionals in Spain provide extensive personal assistance with regard to handling the bureaucracy, searching apartments, etc. Technicians are much more likely to be married - with or without children - than the other exemplified professions. Employers often help to find work for the wife or to search day care facilities for the children. Generally, several interviewed migrant organisations and Spanish immigrants witnessed that once the Spanish immigrants have children in Germany, they are less likely to return to Spain. The interview partners ascribe this effect to the better structural arrangements for families and children in Germany, such as child benefits, governmental arrangement and employment laws that facilitate the reconciliation of work and family life, the infrastructure of day care facilities, etc. The Spanish electrician 2 enthusiastically stated:

> *In Spain you can only dream of the German social system. Once you are in this system having a permanent job you have the right to receive all types of assistance for families for example. (He went on to praise maternity protection combined with wage replacement benefits as well as parental benefits and child benefits, a card that permits poor children to go to the cinema, theatre, library, etc.) (electrician, male, 30)*

Especially the Spanish immigrants with children highlight these institutional structures as a major advantage, as they are not provided to the same extent in Spain. For most of them earning and career opportunities were better in Germany than in Spain and are also important as material resources for their family.

Generally, technicians tend to have a long-term planning horizon. Therefore, according to recruiters, they show the lowest dropout rate of around 20-30% among all exemplified professions. They tend to stay permanently with the employer they were recruited for. Recruiters and immigrated Spanish technicians explain this by claiming that they were highly motivated to find a good job, a good place to live and a good home for themselves, their wife and their family. As they are usually older and more experienced, they seem to be clearer about their personal and professional goals and more realistic about the chances and obstacles of labour mobility than their younger compatriots. Additionally, they often have duties to fulfill concerning their dependents, so once they decide to migrate they have carefully thought about their future life in Germany. Due to their high motivation, they acquire the language skills needed for their job rather fast, and show a high degree of adaptability. Furthermore, as they are more settled people and move with their partner and/or children, they are more interested in a permanent stay and permanent personal contacts. Usually, their personal situation provides contact points at the work place, at school or a day care facility, or in the neighborhood. Additionally, as they frequently move with their family, they are not on their own but enjoy the support of relatives. In view of their personal situation, they are less driven by adventure-seeking and experiencing a vibrant multicultural environment.

They also tend to be more satisfied in rural areas and more willing to make an effort to make themselves feel at home and become part of the local community in Germany. The Spanish electrician interviewed explained:

> *At the beginning I was in XXX (name of city removed; it is a city with more than 100,000 inhabitants with a big university and a big multinational corporation). There, I was just one among many other foreigners, so nobody took any notice of me. Then I started to work for a small branch of the same company in a different city, which has only*

slightly more than 13,000 inhabitants. There, everybody is taking notice of me as I am the exotic foreigner. So, people are really interested in me and everybody asks what I am doing here and they show me their habits, invite me to eat their traditional food and to join traditional events, and they explain everything to me. They are also really interested in learning what it is like in my home country, the traditional holidays, events and cultural particularities we have, etc. To be honest, it was much easier to make friends here and I enjoy being in Germany far more now in the small town than I did in the big city. Of course, you also need some kind of open mind. I know a lot of Spaniards in Germany living in Spanish communities, not bothering to learn German; and they are always complaining like that "the food here is worse, the people are so cold, the weather is not nice,...". Then I think: "So what are you doing here, you can go back home if you dislike everything and if you are not willing to make the slightest efforts to become settled here." (electrician, male, 30)

In order to get integrated in the labour market, recognition might be an issue for technicians depending on the way they are recruited, the profession they work in and the company they work at.

If a specialized recruiter recruits technicians on behalf of an employer, normally no assessment of equivalence is needed. Employers trust in the recruiters and their knowledge about the labour market and the educational system abroad as well as in their expertise in evaluating skills and qualifications of the job candidates, as was stated by employers and recruiters. If Spaniards apply directly to job offers in Germany, a certificate of equivalence increases the likeliness of being hired by around 50% (see Vollmer, 2015) due to its signaling value and the transparency it offers. However, the signaling value of this certificate depends on the specific profession and the work experience of the professional. In certain security-related professions or sectors, the assessment of equivalent is also important to guarantee the competences and authorization of the job candidate to work in this particular profession. For others the certificate of equivalence becomes relevant to receive the negotiated standard wage (see also Section 6.3.4).

Employers, recruiters and Spanish technicians in Germany state that work itself is generally the same in both countries, but there are different tools and different techniques the technicians need to familiarize with. Knowing about these differences, a professional and specialized recruiter prepares the technicians for handling these differences in Spain already. The German recruiter 4 specialized on the recruitment of Spanish professionals in crafts and trades explained:

They (technicians) need an individual language course. I have a German plumber and a German electrician, who have lived and worked in Spain for 7 and 11 years respectively. They spent the majority of their professional life in Germany and received their education there. They know how work is done in Germany and how it is done here. We show them the main differences and teach them the terminology for material, tools, working stages, climate, water quality, high-value materials used

> *in Germany. They get a vocabulary list containing 100 words. (...) So once they have started working in the crafts business, they have seen and touched most of it and they can understand the stuff and reproduce it. This is very important, because the person working with the Spaniards needs patience at the beginning. It's like that, but in most companies it works well.*

These labour integration measures seem to prepare the technicians very well for labour mobility to Germany, as the plumber 2 stated:

> *I still remember that I was really excited when I had my first working day (at the employer in Germany), but it went better than expected because I think I had no problems at all to accomplish the tasks I was given. Well, admittedly my German is not yet fluent, but my colleagues are patient and helpful explaining the work that needs to be done to me (male, plumber, 35).*

As their priorities include mainly having a permanent job and a new home for themselves and/or their family, as along with the fact that the very act of labour mobility is thoroughly planned and thought through, technicians seem better prepared and more motivated to make an effort to integrate, and they seem more robust to overcome the obstacles of labour mobility. This fact seems to be supported by their age, working and living experience and their personal maturity. Additionally, once arrived in Germany, they usually do not have to face the new situation alone but are accompanied by their partner and/or family.

7.2.4 Humanists: subsidized low-key lifestyle mobility

The Spanish labour migrants gathered in this sample who fit into this type have graduated in fields that either do not offer a clear career path outside academia, such as philology, philosophy, sociology, political sciences, arts, or have a very small and shrinking labour market in times of crisis, such as journalism as reported by migrants themselves, migrant networks, language schools and non-profit organisations. Their choice of destination was not made with regard to any professional goal, but instead they were attracted to the metropolitan city of Berlin and seized opportunities such as being offered accommodation in Berlin, having friends there, etc. They mainly want to escape from living with and being dependent on their parents, their depressing social environment in Spain and their bad labour market opportunities there. Having to face all these issues in Spain, they seize the opportunity to go abroad for some adventure using the freedom of movement of workers, as could be derived from the interviews (see also Section 8.1.4).

However, although they mention the crisis and the bad labour market situation in Spain as a major reason for leaving Spain, they are not applying labour mobility in the strict sense. They are hardly prepared for labour mobility nor do they inform themselves about the labour market as such and the chances of labour market entry in Berlin. They are not informed about how to find or apply for a job or how to have their qualification recognized, and they tend to have no German language skills before their arrival. There are also partner migrants among the humanists, who followed their partner abroad. Thus, they are not prepared as it was not their own migration project that brought them to Germany. However, for most of the humanists the crucial motive for coming to Berlin is the cultural experience of living in a foreign and interesting environment. Nevertheless, this does not necessarily mean that they are interested in German culture at all, but simply in living in the multicultural metropolitan region, enjoying the cultural events, etc.

Although, they themselves mention motives like learning the language or broaden their horizon by getting to know another country, they seem to avoid contact with locals and speaking the language. They mostly live in their own subculture, which could be located in any big European city. Even after stays of one year or more, they often have acquired very little language skills only and established very few contacts with Germans. Instead, they have established friendships within the Spanish community, brought about by Facebook, migrant organisations or random contacts. According to some well-integrated Spanish immigrants and migrant organisations, many of those, who initially came to Germany with the goal of learning another language and enjoying intercultural experiences in mind avoid the challenges of learning a new language and getting in touch with the German culture. They take part in language courses, but are afraid to speak the language and therefore avoid opportunities when they could practice German, which is why their language skills do not advance. Interviewed Spanish migrants, educational institutions and migrant organisations confirmed the explanation of an expert from a migrant organisation:

> *We Spaniards are not that good at languages. For many Spaniards it is really difficult to learn German. Most people never came in touch with German before their arrival. () I think they also lack the motivation to learn and they are relatively impatient. They feel intimidated when they are not able to express themselves or when people talk to them and they are not able to answer rapidly. I heard that in many conversations.*

Despite the language issues, Berlin seems to be among the most popular destinations for young Spaniards (see Faraco-Blanco, 2014; González Ferrer, 2013; OECD, 2013). Berlin is reputed for being the most multicultural, culturally vivid, innovative, liberal and still affordable of the European capitals. Thus, young Spaniards develop an intrinsic thirst for experience and adventure, which motivates them to leave their home country. In this case, they show a form of low-key lifestyle migration (see O´Reilly, 2014; Tewes & Heimann, 2018). As the head of a Spanish migrant organisation in Berlin said:

They just come. They register in blogs and say I want to go to Berlin. We observe this every day. I would like to go to Berlin, I do not speak German, but how are your experiences, how can I get a job...? Of course they ask for hospitality and cleaning jobs, ancillary activities or work as removal men, all these little jobs. However, as they are not able to speak the language, they do not look at German websites. Well, I know hardly anybody without a job. There are companies that have operated in Spain and helped people here. It is a bit adventurous and the adventure has a negative connotation, but they (Spanish immigrants) have to blame themselves for their conditions.

In this last statement, the head of the migrant organisation refers to the low level of preparation and information of the Spanish immigrants. However, the high attractiveness of Berlin led to a fast growing Spanish community there. The networks created by Spaniards in Berlin increased the city's appeal and the Spanish community grew even more by word of mouth recommendation. Most Spaniards were inspired and attracted to go to Berlin by random social contacts, loose ties and indirect social relations. They heard about friends of friends or friends of relatives, who are or were in Berlin and followed their example. The Spanish immigrant in Berlin stated:

In the summer I had a job as a waiter in a beach bar in Barcelona. () At work I met some Germans and I got on very well with them. Also, Spanish friends, who were in Berlin, were very enthusiastic about the city. I remembered these two occasions, when I was tired of the situation in Spain and I bought a ticket to Berlin. There, I had some Spanish friends, who helped me to find accommodation. (artist, male, 35).

These immigrants have a short-term planning horizon since their plans have been accomplished with the very act of migration. Although these migrants relocate their entire centre of life to go to the one destination Berlin, their migration project is more similar to the concept of *liquid migration* or the Visa category of *working holidaymakers* (in the UK and Australia for instance) than to pure forms of work-related mobility. They share apartments and rooms, change their address rather often and take on temporary jobs in bars or shops in order to finance their living, while interpreting their mission as acquiring valuable experiences for their personal development.

During this period, they are willing to do occasional jobs, mini-jobs and illegal work, which they would most probably reject in Spain, as was explained by the head of a Spanish migrant organisation in Berlin:

I think in Spain, they would not necessarily work in hospitality, but here (Berlin) they do, as long as they are a bit able to learn the language and to orient themselves about what to do with their life. Well, where do I find a language course or where can I apply for an internship? This is not only an occupation but also helps a bit to finance their living at the beginning. So they do not always have to rely on the Spanish side, if they have a mini-job. This makes life in Berlin easier for them and their stay can be extended.

They do not have a clear-cut plan with regard to time or personal or professional aims. They show a lack of reachable steps and reasonable goals while seeking independence, which fits the category of liquid migration. They apply labour migration as a temporary but unpredictable stay in terms of duration and goals. As they seek independence from their families, self-development and cultural experience, they are an indicator for the individualisation that has taken place among the younger generation of Spaniards. They seek mainly low-wage jobs to cover their living expenses. As qualified employment and stable, safe working conditions seem unattainable, they are particularly vulnerable to marginal and exploitative employment. This situation is not new for most of them, as they have already worked in precarious working conditions and done illegal work in Spain before. However, partly they would like to return as soon as they see a chance for acceptable working and living conditions in Spain, which means finding a job more or less matching their qualification. In this context, their stay in Berlin is evaluated as a personal experience of staying abroad until the labour market situation in Spain improves.

Therefore, these Spaniards are often occupied in the low-skilled sector doing illegal work or mini-jobs up to a salary of 450€ and working up to 13 hours a week, as the minimum wage in Germany is 8,50€, while paying hardly any taxes. However, 450 € is usually not enough to cover the living expenses of the Spanish immigrants. Additionally, as soon as they earn more than 450 € taxes must be paid. In order to build up a maximum of amount financial resources and spare time and to avoid having to pay taxes, they usually prefer to top up earnings from a minimum job with illegal work or social benefits. Spanish migrant organisations such as *Oficina Precaria* or *GAS* offer concrete information and assistance with applying for social benefits. On their web pages, they describe that in Germany all EU citizens, who have a job or are self-employed and earn at least 144 € per month working at least 6 hours per week are entitled to obtain social benefits (see Oficina Precaria, 2015). They explain how to get housing benefits and how to apply for assistance in topping up a mini job until having reached the subsistence level. This information is spread in the Spanish community. The Spanish interview partners in Berlin explain that right after their arrival in Berlin the immigrants learn about the option to apply for social benefits from their Spanish friends and get instructions on how to apply for these benefits. They explain that they applied for housing benefits and social benefits to top up their mini job. Although they received job offers for part time or full time work, they preferred the mini job to be entitled to the social benefits. Among the reasons given for their decision, they mentioned the chance to attend a language course for free and have more time and energy left to learn German and to enjoy the city and its nightlife. Some view this period as a chance to learn the language and become better integrated, as the following example of a Spaniard in Berlin shows, who rejected a 50% part-time job in a skilled position as a social worker matching her qualification to be eligible for social benefits:

> *I have all my papers ready to go to the job centre to apply for help from the state. Because there is one (help), if you are under twentysomething or thirty and you have a mini-job, and there are some conditions that you have to meet. Not everybody can apply for this, you have to be in a concrete situation and it's exactly mine. I'm studying German and I have a mini-job. I think they pay you like the rent and they give you like 300 euros per month. During six months. Only. So this is perfect, because it's the time you need to start to be better integrated, you know? To learn German a bit and all these kinds of things. And, yeah, to apply for this help, you need to have worked in a mini-job for at least three months. When you have accomplished these three months, which I did just now in November - I've been in the catering for three months with a contract - when you have stayed at one place for three months, then you can apply for this help and they give it to you for six months. Yeah. And yeah, this money will be really good (female, social worker, 27).*

Others use the benefits only to enjoy their spare time, even if they came for professional reasons, as one of the Spanish immigrants stated:

> *First, I did an internship and, in addition to my salary, I got a scholarship (EU-subsidized, probably Erasmus + or Leonardo Da Vinci) and I had a good life. During the week I worked and at the weekends – party! After the internship, I applied for Hartz IV (social benefit in Germany). When I got the letter of acceptance, I was cheering loudly. I got money and could learn German for free – and the party went on. After six months, my Hartz IV was cut. Since then, I have been working three days a week in the bar of a nightclub (female tourist manager, 25)*[14]

This is an example of one of the main advantages of being in Berlin mentioned by the Spanish immigrants. Due to the social benefits it is much easier for the young Spaniards to become independent from their parents in financial terms and to leave their area of influence and their social control. One of the interview partners explicitly mentioned that the public employment agency in Germany (BA) replaced the role of his mother in giving him financial support, while requiring less than his mother. Although, none of the Spaniards stated that they actually came to claim social benefits, they found out about this option right after coming to Germany as other Spaniards told them. Then, they prepared

14 Although this migrant did not study humanities arts or social sciences, she was categorised as humanist due to the characteristics of her migration project. This indicates that being a humanist is not determined by the profession, but is rather a mindset.

strategically for being eligible, including avoiding a higher amount of working hours and higher salary, because they found claiming social benefits as a rational option more convenient. Thus, it seems that the possibility of claiming benefits creates benefit tourists.

None of the humanists, social scientists, etc. aimed at obtaining an assessment of equivalence of their university degrees or even thought about applying for it. This might have several reasons: Firstly, the assessment of equivalence is not a precondition for working in these professions. Secondly, it is not sure that a certificate of equivalence would be an advantage, as these jobs are not considered shortage occupations. There are enough local job candidates in this field without any language issues. Thirdly, most of the humanists do not strive to achieve a long-term career in Germany.

Thus, the picture of exploited Spaniards being trapped in precarious working conditions in Berlin that is painted by GAS, Oficína Precaria and 15M seems to be part of the story at best. The Spaniards in Berlin rather seek mini jobs and illegal work in order to profit from social benefits and or prefer precarious working conditions in Berlin instead of moving to other parts of Germany that feature considerable labour demand or to miss the opportunity to get Hartz 4 and language courses for free. They seek a low-key lifestyle migration supported by welfare benefits. Their stay is temporary and intentionally unpredictable in terms of outcome and duration. First of all they want to experience an adventure and gain cultural as well as personal experiences. Thus, although the right for freedom of movement for workers offers them the possibility to do so, they are not the type of labour migrants that immigrate for professional reasons. In this context, the transition of mobile EU citizens categorised as partner migrants, adventurers or benefit tourists is fluid.

7.2.5 Interim conclusion: right Spaniards in Germany

The exemplified professions differ with regard to their profile, aim of labour mobility and their chances and problems on the German labour market.

For Spanish nurses, a job in Germany is a chance to work in their profession and gain independence from their parents. As most of them do not seek the experience of going abroad, they rather feel forced to leave than of being offered a chance to work in Germany in order to find **labour market entry**. Their planning horizon is, therefore, short or unpredictable. However, it is rather easy for them to get recruited due to the high demand for nurses and the subsidies available in Germany where there is a high **shortage** for these professionals. They are mostly young, female singles who do not have any German language skills at the beginning of their recruitment. However, recruiters and employers organize and finance language courses in Spain and in Germany for groups of recruited Spanish nurses. They are under high pressure to learn German, because it is necessary for them to obtain the professional recognition by the responsible

Landesprüfungsamt, which is the precondition to work in their job. Recruiting hospitals, recruiters and language schools provide various integration measures for nurses, such as language courses, welcome events, mentoring and training on the job. However, they are often recruited for senior residences and feel downgraded in Germany seeing that their job is not university-trained in Germany and they have to take over care tasks. As they are young and **lack maturity** as well as **intercultural competences** it is especially hard for them to cope with the circumstances in Germany.

The main motivation for Spanish engineers to go to Germany is **career advancement**. Therefore, they have a medium-term planning horizon, as they expect to need some years to achieve their professional goals. They are mostly in their late 20s or early thirties and are single males. Depending on their professional profile, English might be sufficient for their job in Germany or, else, they need to learn German. Generally speaking, the better skilled they are and the less contacts they have with technicians, the more speaking English will be sufficient. They have the chance to apply for a certificate of equivalence from NARIC, but in the interviews none of the Spanish engineers, employers or recognition bodies mentioned a concrete case of application for the certificate. According to recruiters, the more highly skilled the engineer is and the more attractive the company, the more directly will the recruitment procedure run, which means, that there is no need for recruiters to fulfil a bridging function between the labour markets. Thus, the highly-skilled engineers are part of a **transnationally mobile elite**. In bigger companies, there might be welcome parties or mentors organized by the company, but generally there are only few integration measures, which are often limited to training on the job. Language skills as well as other **intercultural competences** are usually acquired individually by the job candidate.

Technicians come to Germany in order to find better living and working conditions for themselves and their dependents. They form a relatively small group among all Spanish labour immigrants. They are usually between their late 20s and up to 40 years old and mostly live in a stable relationship or are married with or without children, which is different from the other exemplified professions. Thus, they do not only bring **certain professional skills** that are in demand but also working and living experience that accounts for personal **maturity**. On the one side, their family bonds complicate labour emigration. On the other side, once they take the step of labour emigration their decision is carefully thought through and they are willing to take the efforts. At the beginning of their recruitment, they usually have no German language skills at all. However, they learn fast, as they are **highly motivated** to work for finding better living and working conditions in Germany. Generally, they do not need any recognition of their qualification as a precondition for working in their profession. Nevertheless, this might be reasonable in security-related professions or to gain the negotiated union wage. Generally, labour integration is often provided by personal contacts with the employer and the colleagues than formally organised as the technicians are regularly recruited for SME´s.

Humanists in Berlin use labour mobility to gain independence and experience an adventure abroad. They tend to be singles and between 20 and 30 years old.

Table 18: Right people for labour integration in Germany

	Nurse	Engineer	Technician	Humanist
Motives	Labour market entry Independence	Career advancement	Better living and working conditions	Independence Adventure
Planning horizon	Undefined, short	Medium-term	Long-term	Undefined, short
Personal situation	Single, female young	Late 20s or early thirties, single, male	Male, married, with or without family, middle aged	Single, more females, young to middle-aged
Language skills	Low at the beginning, but pressure to learn fast – learn fast	Medium English or German	Low at the beginning Learn fast due to high motivation	Low – medium
Responsible recognition body	Landesprüfungs-amt	NARIC	IHK-FOSA	NARIC
Application for recognition	Necessary for professional entry	None	Not necessary but may bear advantages	None
Labour integration measures	-Language courses -Recruitment in groups -Mentors -Training on the job	-Training on the job (-language courses)	-Training on the job -Language courses -Mentors	-Language courses - Illegal work
Labour integration measures by	Language schools Hospitals Recruiters	Company Language school	Language schools Company	-Migrant organisations -Language schools
Myth, framings, perception	Overestimated attractiveness of German senior residences for Spanish nurses; Underestimated differences in job profile and prestige of nurses	Myth of unlimited resources of high potentials abroad; myth of unlimited top jobs for engineers	Realistic, thoroughly thought about decision of employers and employee	Myth of personal development through experience and adventure abroad; myth of exploited economic refugees

Their planning horizon is undefined and **intentionally unpredictable** because they want to stay for a **temporary** period as long as they enjoy Berlin. They are attracted mainly by the multicultural lifestyle in Berlin via informal networks. In addition, their decision for **labour mobility** is a rather spontaneous one, which is often financially supported by welfare benefits, such as Hartz 4 and language and integration courses for free. They do not prepare for labour mobility in terms of seeking information about the labour market in Berlin or gaining language skills before coming to Germany and often become benefit tourists by opportunity. The boundaries between the categories of adventurers, benefit tourists and partner migrants seem fluid among humanists.

These exemplary professions indicate that the *right people* for labour mobility seek adventure, labour market entry, or career advancement or wish to find better living and/or working conditions. Furthermore, they need to be willing and able to overcome the hurdles on their way to professional integration. This group is ready to learn German and take the efforts of the recognition procedure. In particular, in professions in which labour shortages were detected, such as in the health care sector, international recruitment was facilitated by financial support to relocation, language courses, travel and other labour integration measures. Nevertheless, the high amount of offers and the high degree of support bears risks for both employers and job candidates, if their selection process of staff or company is not thoroughly thought through.

Another aspect is that the higher degree of social benefits in Germany seems to attract Spanish immigrants who do not necessarily seek employment opportunities but are rather a mix of adventure-seekers and benefit tourists. However, the assistance the Spanish immigrants receive from labour unions, non-profit organisation and from the state, including welfare benefits, show that a certain degree of transnational solidarity has developed among EU citizens.

The *right people* with regard to successful labour integration are those who show a certain degree of independence, who gather information, prepare to be able to evaluate their chances on the host labour market realistically, and plan their professional goal taking into account the steps that need to be taken.

However, from a employers' point of view, for some companies the *right people* for labour recruitment obviously do not exist regardless of what they offer in terms of (labour) integration and/or salary, such as senior residences in the health care sector or SMEs in rural areas for engineers. In most of these cases the Spaniards took advantage of their services with regard to recruitment and labour integration and searched for a better job as soon as they had achieved professional recognition, professional experience and/or acquired advanced language skills.

Hence incentives for recruitment and labour integration also offered by employers in sectors of high demand do not ensure successful recruitment and labour integration.

Table 18 summarises the chances and hurdles for labour integration of the different professionals in Germany.

7.3 Right people in the UK: myth, motives and chances

Independently from the political aim to reduce immigration, recruitment is an established practice in the British labour market. In the following part, the four different exemplifying groups of professionals are examined in order to understand its conditions for recruitment and job search as well as labour integration. Hereby, the job- and sector-specific procedures will be analysed in more detail. The profile of the *right people* for labour mobility is a matter of chances and demand as well as a matter of perceptions and motivations. Thus the following part will show that nurses seek labour market entry in the UK but are often overburdened by the daily work routine, the language and intercultural changes, which is why only very few stay with the British employer that recruited them. Instead, Section 8.3.2 will describe that highly-skilled engineers obtaining intercultural competence and professional maturity are likely to find career advancement during their temporary stay in the UK. Section 8.3.3 underlines that Spanish technicians rarely chose to emigrate to the UK because high language skills and intercultural competences are a precondition to achieve a good job. Section 8.3.4 will describe that Spanish humanists in London seek personal and cultural experiences as well as development, while they work in low-wage jobs to sustain their living. Hence, the different migration projects in the UK and the strategies of Spanish migrants will be distinguished.

7.3.1 Nurses: highly demanded in British hospitals

British recruiters are particularly well experienced, having recruited large numbers of labour force on an international level in the first decade of the 21st century (see Hopkins & Levy, 2012); today, one third of the nurses working in Britain are foreign-trained (see Buchan, Wismar, Glinos, & Bremner, 2014). In the UK, there have been two waves of active recruitment of nurses. The first one occurred around 2003 and targeted English-speaking non-EU countries such as India, the Philippines, and Australia. The second one concerned the recent recruitment targeted to EU countries, especially Spain, Portugal, Italy and Greece which featured high unemployment rates, as scientific experts, labour and trade unions stated. A general shortage of nurses was detected, but the situation was especially tense in Greater London due to the high living costs. Nevertheless, this multicultural metropolitan city seems to be especially attractive for foreign nurses. The ageing society is mentioned only as a secondary reason for the high amount of international recruitment; more importantly, cuts in funding for home-based training are highlighted by labour and trade unions. So the numbers of nurses being trained domestically dropped, while demand was increasing. As the government funded all the training of new nurses in the UK, it was able to decide how many new nurses would be trained every year. In order to respond quickly to the demand arisen, international recruitment was fostered.

Recruiters in the UK are highly specialised concerning nurses from a broad range of countries, also from third countries such as the Philippines according to the interviewed recruiters, labour and trade unions and Spanish nurses in the UK. British companies and recruiters use online job portals, including foreign ones, and the labour and trade unions as well as the Spanish nursing and midwifery council to announce vacancies and promote their services.

In the UK, education of nurses is a study program as it is in Spain. There are more vacancies in hospitals, which are often considered to be more attractive than the jobs in senior residences. In general, there are good chances for career advancement due to opportunities for further training and specialization. These working conditions are highly appreciated by the Spanish nurses in the UK. Relatively high English skills are already required at the point of recruitment compared to Germany. It is easier for British recruiters to set higher language requirements, because of two reasons. On the one hand, there are more people in Spain acquiring at least basic English language skills (than people who have German language skills). On the other hand, British recruiters are not focussed on the Spanish labour market, instead, they also recruit from states, in which English is the native language or English as a foreign language is widespread. Nevertheless, in the wake of the economic crisis British recruiters increased their activities on the Southern European labour market significantly due to opportunity. Thus, in the wake of the economic crisis a high number of Spanish nurses was recruited for the British health care sector (see Adams, 2013; Kassam, 2015; Mowafi, 2018).

Usually, both British hospitals and the German ones recruit nurses in groups. This practice offers the advantage of lower transaction costs for the recruitment of each nurse and the nurses are able to provide their own support network in the phase of labour integration.

One of the interviewed nurses has worked in the UK for three years and ran a youtube tutorial for Spanish nurses in the UK as well as a facebook group and a network of Spanish nurses in the UK to support each other. She (Spanish nurse 1 in Britain) provided the broadest and deepest information of all interviewed nurses as she had comprehensive insights into the cases of many other nurses. Therefore, in the following part her statements are cited exclusively, but the information she gave was also confirmed by trade and professional unions as well as the other nurses interviewed.

The Spanish nurse 1 in Britain explained:

> *Of course, it is hard. Well, as we all are more or less in the same situation, it's useful. It helps you a lot to have people, who are supportive and who listen to you and share their experiences with you. So you do not feel that alone. Yes, I think something like a collective feeling developed as we are all in the same situation. Some suffer more, because their level of English is worse, others less, because their language skills are better or they feel better at work. There are others, who do not get on well with their position and they do not like it... and there is all of that on all levels, to be honest. But yes, yes, it helps a lot, it helps a lot to have fellows from Spain. (nurse, female, 33)*

The employers in the UK do not generally compensate for language courses or removal costs. Some employers fund travel costs and organize accommodation, others do not offer these services. In recent years, due to the high labour shortages, the offer of these services arose and increased as was reported by the Spanish nurses in the UK, labour and trade unions and recruiters.

However, in the case of British hospitals a higher level of language skills is required to get recruited and also to get recognized as a nurse. As specified by EU law, the recruited nurses are only allowed to work as qualified nurse once the nurses are fully recognized. Therefore, they work as auxiliaries in the beginning and hereby face the same kind of dilemma as the nurses in Germany between constrained competences, high workload under the conditions of limited language skills, as one of the interviewed nurses 1 described:

> *In the beginning you can do a bit of work as an auxiliary of nursing instead of nursing, because here you have to qualify for certain competences to develop the technique, such as taking blood. We (Spanish nurses) are trained in these clinical basics since we graduated, but here this is not the case. Here these competences are optional. You qualify for these techniques if you need them. Well, it was... you feel a bit, not frustrated, but yes, I'd say less independent. Now it is the nursing we are getting used to. Well, but I think this depends on the attitude of the persons, because there are people, who are very negative and in the beginning you can feel very frustrated. Also, you can get the impression that you are shot across the bows, but here is such a shortage of persons. There are a lot of services, which are overloaded and they need people and have the money to employ people, but they do not find people who come here to cover all the work and then, of course, therefore, you feel overburdened. (nurse, female, 33)*

In this context, she mentioned that the mostly significantly younger nurses had more problems to cope with this situation and were more likely to give up and return to Spain at an early stage. She stated that her age and experience helped her to face the challenges of labour mobility and labour integration. From her point of view, she had a more realistic attitude and was better able to discuss upcoming issues openly before they turned out to become problematic and to seek support. Therefore, she is convinced that she succeeded in the UK and is satisfied with her job there because she felt more stable in her personality due to her maturity than the younger nurses.

At this point it is up to the employer and the Spanish nurse to ensure that labour integration works. In contrast to many German recruiters, the responsibility for recruitment and labour integration of the British recruiters ended after recruitment. Afterwards, employers and the individual professional were responsible for successful labour integration. In the first week, the hospitals offer a general induction for the newly hired foreign nurses, in which the policies of the hospital, regulations on patient safety and hygiene standards, etc. are introduced. Nevertheless, the day-to-day practices and its focus in the UK are not part of the induction. This part is provided by a mentor in the hospital ward, who is a senior nurse. As in Germany, the daily tasks of a nurse in the hospital ward differ from the ones in Spain. In this context, basic care tasks were mentioned again, as the interviewed nurse explained:

> *To be honest, in the UK the focus on nursing is different. I think, they are more focussed on the basic care. Here they have another type of, for example, the social assistance, we give them. In Spain this is not covered to the same extent as it is here. The patients, when they are in hospital, they are sent to many types of fields, such as a dermatologist to look at the skin or they wash it to see that there is no ulcer, they weigh the patients to test the nutritional, ... this detailed look at the patient is better than in Spain, where we leave that out. Maybe these techniques of basic care are as bad in Spain because there is no time, basically, you don't have the time. It's impossible to evaluate the overall constitution of the patient because we do not have nutritionists in the hospital wards in Spain. Here, they have them. Here is a dietician in the ward, who cares for a nutritional plan for the patient. Depending on the weight, they change the diet. So, this type of basic care is much better developed here. (nurse, female, 33)*

Until the nurses achieve official recognition and are able to work on their own, they have to get used to the different tasks, although these are not assessed by the recognition procedure. According to the EU Recognition Directive 2005/36/EC a recognition requires a CV, ID, certified qualification and professional experience, certificate of good conduct or police clearance and the current professional status. Each candidate's certificates are reviewed individually at the Nursing and Midwifery Council, which is the centrally organized, authorised recognition body. The organisational arrangements are similar between the Spanish and the British central body for the registration of nurses, which are the Colegio Oficial de Enfermería and the Nursing and Midwifery Council (see also Klopprogge et al., 2016).

As in the case of Germany the major hurdle, which needs to be taken in order to get recognised and to be allowed to work as a qualified nurse are the language requirements. Due to the necessity of being able to communicate with the patients, language skills are an indispensable requirement for nurses. Therefore, the English level B2 was introduced as a requirement in the UK, which is the same level of language skills that is required in Germany. However, recently the required English level was raised to C1 proficiency for nurses, which is a rather strict requirement, taking into account that the same level of English proficiency is required to study at one of the prestigious British universities. Professional unions and recognition bodies in the UK stated that these changes were introduced during the government of David Cameron in order to achieve the political goal to diminish immigration. Therefore, it became increasingly difficult for nurses from other EU member states - mostly from non-English speaking countries - to achieve recognition in the UK, as it is the most important precondition to find work. As one of the interviewed recruiters in the UK most vividly put it:

> *There are three requirements a nurse needs to meet in order to get hired. Recognition, recognition and recognition.*

Generally, in the UK, education is more similar to the Spanish system than in Germany, as it is a university study programme. Additionally, professional unions in Spain and the UK confirm that there are more vacancies in hospitals, which are often considered as more attractive than the jobs in senior residences. In general, the salaries are relatively high for nurses in a worldwide comparison and there are good chances for career advancement due to opportunities for further training and specialization. These working conditions are appreciated by the Spanish nurses in the UK.

For the Spanish nurses working in the UK is seen as a short-term project. Therefore, in the UK as well as in Germany, hospitals partly conclude adhesion contracts with the internationally recruited staff to make sure their investments in recruitment, training on the job, etc. pay off. The contracts often need to be fulfilled for at least one yeas. An earlier termination of the contract is penalized with a fine depending on the investments in recruitment and labour integration. This measure is part of the labour contract with some employers to diminish the high fluctuation rates, which were reported by the trade unions, employers and nurses. The nurse 1 gave an example of fluctuation of foreign nurses in the hospital she was hired for:

> *Although the majority, many of those, who were with me in XXX (name of hospital removed) left. I can tell you, because we met in a big community in the beginning and we were around 150 nurses, only from Spain. And I can tell you that only 10% of those stayed. A lot of them, I know because I am still in contact, they went to Spain. Another part of them decided that they do not want to be here anymore because they have gained enough experience. Those, who worked here do not need to register in the job market. They had been here long enough so that their market value rose and they could find work in Spain.* (nurse, female, age 33)

Spanish nurses gain working experience and are able to work in their profession as soon as they have acquired the necessary language proficiency and gained recognition. However, they also have to invest a lot of effort in learning a new language, getting acquainted with a different culture, etc., although their planning horizon is only short-term as their aim is to develop their skills and experience to be able to enter the Spanish labour market. They are mostly young and graduated recently, so they were not able to get established in the labour market during the crisis. These young nurses are likely to return to Spain soon after their recruitment for the British labour market as they lack professional and personal maturity and intercultural competences.

7.3.2 Engineers: attracting the best and the brightest

Internationally mobile engineers are usually around 27-35 years old, apply individual job seeking strategies and are very well aware of their market value, as described by recruiters and professional unions. The interviewed Spanish engineers were very well prepared for labour mobility to the UK, which means they had good education, language skills and practical experience. These qualifications are sought after and the interviewed Spanish engineers had a lot of labour opportunities in the UK.

British companies and recruiters almost exclusively used online job portals to announce vacancies and promote their services, also on Spanish job portals. They are not solely focused on the Spanish labour market as they advertise vacancies on an international scale and, in particular, also in the former Commonwealth states, especially India, as was stated by trade unions and recruiters. In one of the most attractive metropolitan areas, Greater London, there is no industry at all. Therefore, recruitment is focused on engineers for consulting jobs in that part of the country. However, in other parts of the UK different kinds of vacancies are available for engineers.

No official recognition of the foreign qualification is required EU-wide (except for civil engineering). It is possible to request an evaluation of their diploma at the central recognition body NARIC, which comprises more than just a mere translation of the diploma as it is assessed according to the national standards of the evaluating member state, but as in Germany, none of the interviews with Counselling Services, recruiters and engineers revealed a single case (except for civil engineering) where an evaluation of a foreign diploma was requested.

This might be one of the reasons, why factors such as work experience, international experience and the university programme seem to outweigh the formal certification by means of diplomas, as stated by recruiters. In the UK, employers respectively recruiters seem to pay slightly more attention to the university the job candidate graduated from (at least in the case of recently graduated candidates), while German employers tend to pay more attention to the job candidate's work experience. This might be an indication of the relevance of the recruiting country's national standards. In Germany, there is more collaboration between universities and industrial enterprises, which implies a more 'practical' study programme than in other EU countries as stated by professional unions and recruiters. For this reason, employers may tend to focus more on the work experience of a foreign job candidate. The negligible relevance of the evaluation of diploma itself, not only by formal recognition bodies, but also by employers, was illustrated most explicitly by one of the Spanish engineer 2 working in the UK:

> *'In fact, if you have the experience and you can prove that you know what you know in the job interview, I think it (formal evaluation of diploma by the Recognition Body NARIC) is not important. () I was told (by the employer) to hand in a copy of my Master degree, and I handed it in, but I actually handed in the Catalan version. They did not say anything and they do not know what it says because it is in Catalan (laughing). So, I do not think they looked at it (...).' (engineer, male, 32)*

The Spanish engineers perceive acquiring a position in the UK as a significant career advancement and valuable asset in the curriculum. International competitiveness, international work experience and language skills give an added value to an engineer's human capital in the labour market. The positions Spanish engineers found in the UK usually offer higher salaries, more innovative tasks and a higher degree of independence, autonomy and creative freedom. These aspects were highly appreciated by the Spanish engineers working in the UK. Moreover, experiencing a higher level of economic efficiency in the UK and Germany, though not only in the organisation of work processes, is considered a significant personal and professional asset. The higher level of self-realisation at the workplace issuing from the innovative work content and the more egalitarian relations between boss and employee as compared to the strict hierarchy in Spain is highlighted as a major advantage. The Spanish engineers 1 interviewed in the UK explained:

> *In Spain, the boss is pretty much the boss and gives orders. There is no way of arguing. Here, I am much more part of a team in which we work together, and my boss appreciates my own ideas and encourages me to express them.' (engineer, male, 29)*

In general, Spanish engineers seem to have a longer planning horizon in Germany than in the UK due to the more favourable working conditions in Germany. The interviewed Spanish engineers seem to belong to a highly-skilled elite, which is very attractive for employers. Engineering is a shortage occupation in the UK (see UK Visa Bureau, 2018), but nevertheless, there is high international competition for engineering jobs.

Regarding the discrepancy in the attractiveness Greater London was mentioned to be the most popular destination in the UK. However, the industrial production is located in the more rural areas or close to smaller cities. Therefore, Greater London offers only few jobs in engineering and if so, these are mostly consulting jobs that do not cover the core competences of engineers. Additionally, Spanish engineers compete with engineers from the English-speaking Commonwealth countries with which the UK maintains strong historical and economic ties. Hence, most recruited job candidates in the field of engineering still come from India as explained by recruiters and professional unions.

This is not least of all due to the excellent engineering universities in India along with the historical ties and the hardly existing language issues between the two countries. Often, Indian engineers are directly recruited from the Indian Institutes of Technology (IITs). Spanish engineers state that, despite having been established in the British labour market, most of them view their employment as a medium-term commitment and professional stepping stone. Although they are satisfied with their jobs, they tend to return to Spain, marketing their international experience as an asset, or moving on to the next career step in another country. Professional unions confirm the use of these strategies especially for those engineers who belong to a highly-skilled elite obtaining intercultural competences, such as language skills.

7.3.3 Technicians: sought-after and Polish

Although a high amount of the technicians in the UK are immigrant workers, only few of those seem to be Spanish, as interviews with technicians, labour and trade unions and the analysis of Spanish professional forums confirmed. Only sporadically cases of Spanish technicians in the UK were found, so only few data could be collected as they seemed to be very small in number. Those cases that have been found covered males in their mid-thirties, which matches the profile found with regard to Spanish technicians emigrating and Spanish technicians in Germany.

Especially, in trades and crafts there has been a skills shortage that offered chances for immigrant workers in crafts and trades. Several reasons led to this development as trade unions, recruiters and educational institutions explained. Firstly, the traditional trades and crafts have been depreciated as well as the industry and construction sector in general since the British economy has focussed on creating a knowledge-based service economy as stated by trade and labour unions. Additionally, in the wake of the economic crisis, the number of apprenticeships offered by companies in this sector declined. Once the economy recuperated from the crisis, a skill shortage arose, which was amongst others eased by hiring migrant workers. However, already before the crisis migrant workers accounted for a large proportion of skilled workers in crafts and trades, especially plumbers, bricklayers and electricians. Since the Eastern Enlargement of the European Union particularly immigrants from Poland and other Eastern European countries filled the vacancies in crafts and trades, which the natives did not want to take over. The Polish plumber became a proverbial symbol for this development (see Asthana, 2005; Deutsche Welle, 2016; Dick, 2014; Frayer, 2016; Sciolino, 2005). Polish immigrants established an ethnic transnational community, which supports the recruitment procedure. They are very successful due to the high demand and the good image the Polish plumbers received with private customers, companies and even governmental entities as stated by a trade union in the construction sector.

Customers have the impression that Polish technicians are more easily available, do the jobs quickly and in good quality, while British technicians have the fame of not responding to calls, delaying appointments and not bothering to perform well as there is such a high demand for technicians anyway that they do not need to care for their image, as was stated by the interviewed experts. Furthermore, the private households prefer the lower costs due to undeclared work. However, companies similarly make use of the willingness of Polish workers to do a good job for lower salaries. This was caused by lower job and earning opportunities of Polish workers in Poland. Therefore, self-sustaining informal structures of recruitment of Polish technicians in crafts and trades developed as trade unions and migrant organisations confirmed.

In comparison, there seem to be only few Spanish technicians in the UK, although the crafts and trades were hit especially hard by the Spanish economic crisis. While there are many professional forums, Facebook groups, youtube tutorials giving advice for emigration and labour integration in the UK for nurses and engineers or Spaniards, who seek low-skilled jobs, there are only few for technicians. This might have several reasons, which were deduced from the collected information. Firstly, British companies seem not to advertise their job announcement in Spanish job portals. Secondly, there is only little information available on how to get a job in the UK as a Spanish technician. Thirdly, foreign technicians in the UK need very good English language skills to find good working conditions as will be explained in the following part.

According to immigrated Spanish technicians, they need a certificate of equivalence of their qualification at NARIC and they have to apply for a CSCS (Construction Skill Certificate Scheme) card to achieve a skilled job and decent working conditions in construction, trades and crafts. An exam about profession related safety standards has to be taken to receive the CSCS card. Although neither the certificate of equivalence nor the CSCS are a legal precondition to work as a technician, such as plumber, electrician, sanitation and heating installer), the Spanish technicians in the UK state that they are necessary to be hired as a skilled professional. The Spanish Plumber 1 in London said:

> *In order to work as a plumber they (employers) demand the CSCS card. You can achieve this card if you take an exam at the authorised places. (Explaining what the exam looks like, amount of questions, content, etc., which are different depending on the profession and skill level). It is a multiple-choice test, but in English. Without this card nobody will ever hire you (technicians). If you do not know enough English to read a paragraph, understand it and read different possible answers understanding them and to respond to an amount of questions adequately, then there is no need for you (technicians) to come to London. (plumber, male, 34)*

Although according to the EU recognition directive, the member states are not allowed to assess language skills as a requirement to recognise the qualifications of technicians in crafts and trades (see European Commission, 2018e), English is a precondition to receive the CSCS card. However, the exam for the CSCS card is not an English test, first of all, the CSCS card shows that the professional is knowledgeable in the particular security standards and its requirements. A similar card can be received by taking an exam about safety standards in Spain, which is called "Tarjeta Profesional de Construcción (TPC)" (see Fundación Laboral de la Construcción, 2018). A Spanish professional union in the construction sector recommends that the CSCS could be replaced by the TPC. The professional union stated that they were surprised why none of the technicians using their consultation services ever did that. However, a Spanish electrician (male, 35) in the UK states, the CSCS was not only a formal requirement because the British safety standards were different from Spanish ones. Independently from what might be the valid pathways to achieve, the CSCS card, it seems a necessary asset to get hired as a skilled professional. This necessity is also confirmed on the website of the CSCS (see CSCS, 2018), which says:

> *Holding a CSCS card is not a legislative requirement. It is entirely up to the principal contractor or client whether workers are required to hold a card before they are allowed on site. However, most principal contractors and major house builders require construction workers on their sites to hold a valid CSCS card.*

In this regard all professions related to the construction sector, such as plumbers, electricians, heating and sanitation installers, bricklayers, are considered to be construction workers. The professionals are able to apply for CSCS cards in different colours depending on the skill level and the profession. Therefore, the certificate of equivalence issued by NARIC in the UK, a (translated) copy of the original qualification and a completed CSCS application form is necessary to apply for the CSCS card (CSCS homepage). The Spanish technicians interviewed in the UK evaluate the recognition of their qualification and the application for the CSCS card as paying off. The Spanish plumber states that he earns 1000-2000 pounds a week, which according to this Spaniard is as much as or even more than an engineer would earn. He says that he partly works also late in the evenings and on Saturdays and he could earn even more with regard to the order situation.

So living and working conditions as well as earning opportunities seem very attractive in the UK, however, the Spanish construction sector and its professionals do not seem to be aware of the chances they would have in the UK. Additionally, the practical hurdle of language skills that needs to be taken seems to be too high for the vast majority of Spanish technicians, anyway, while Polish immigrants seem to dominate the sector.

7.3.4 Humanists: between adventure, independence and survival

The humanists in London are in search of making their own living, to become independent from their parents and to flee from the bad economic and social climate in Spain as stated in the interviews. They come to learn English, either as an asset to find a job on the Spanish labour market after returning to Spain or going elsewhere or to find a job in the UK.

Mostly they became aware of the possibilities of intra-EU mobility by friends, family or friends of friends, so the information they have about the British labour market are based on hearsay, which is the same as in the case of Spanish immigrants in Berlin. Furthermore, they use Facebook groups of the Spanish community in London to find apartments, work and information or just a sofa as an accommodation in the beginning or while they are facing a hard time. These informal support networks in the Spanish (-speaking) community are especially important in the UK, as none of the Spanish immigrants or migrant organisations knows about any social benefits or subsidised labour integration measures, such as language courses, etc. the Spaniards were eligible for. The only support with regard to labour integration are the Job Centre Plus (EURES) and a non-profit organisation offering information and assistance on how to write an adequate CV in the UK.

The Spanish humanists in Britain state that they did not deregister, when they left Spain because they were afraid of losing health care benefits and/or unemployment benefits. All the interviewed humanists were working in at least one job and requested a social security number in the UK. Mostly, they worked in fast food chains, catering, hospitality, or in one of the Spanish fashion stores in London, such as Bershka, Zara, Mango, Stradivarius, etc. The Spanish immigrants in London have only little spare time and work many hours to afford their living according to their own statements. This is necessary as the living costs in London are among the highest in any European capital (see Expatistan, 2018).

Therefore, working full-time at least seems to be indispensable for the humanists in London, which are mainly working in the low-skill and low-wage sector. All of them state that they came to London having a financial cushion to survive in the first month(s). Thus, referring to her own experiences and those of other Spaniards she knows in London one of the interviewed Spanish immigrants assumed:

> *Those who come here are not the poorest of the poor because you already need quite some money to come here and get started. Those who do not have money or do not have parents who are able to support them financially cannot come here. (PhD student in anthropology, social worker, 25)*

In the interviews the motive of cultural interest and interest in the metropolitan city of London is much less present than among the Spanish immigrants interviewed in Berlin. Instead, the aim of learning the language is much more dominant as well as getting established on the labour market. Additionally, they have to work hard from the very beginning in order to cover their living expenses. Therefore, they accept low-skilled jobs in fast-food chains, fashion stores, catering and hospitality while they improve and practice their English skills. In contrast to the Spanish immigrants in Berlin, all of the interview partners in London already had at least basic English skills before they came to England. However, most of them - especially the humanists - state that they are still struggling with the English language.

At the moment of the interview the humanists saw no chance to find qualified employment, neither in the UK nor in Spain. However, they evaluated this situation as temporary and hoped to achieve qualified employment either in Spain once the economic situation would recover or in the UK once their English was good enough. However, this was more a diffuse wish because they had no strategy how to achieve a qualified job as they did not plan to take any concrete steps. Just like the Spanish immigrants in Berlin, they were very poorly informed about the labour market in London and employment laws in the UK. Therefore, it seems, they were especially vulnerable to marginal employment and exploitative employment relations compared to the other types of migrants. Nevertheless, not only the lack of knowledge of the British labour market, but also their situation in the Spanish labour market makes them more likely to fall prey to exploitation or even to accept exploitative working conditions.

Due to the high unemployment rates and the bad economic situation in Spain the humanists were used to exploitative working conditions, which were much more common in Spain than in Germany or the UK. One of the interview partners worked for different magazines as a journalist in Madrid before she immigrated to London. She explained that she wrote articles and took photos using the equipment she bought herself, but she sometimes only earned 20€ a month. In London, so far she only found a job at a fast-food chain and is in an exploitative work relationship again. She had a zero-hour employment contract and was regularly working double shifts and/or working 6 or 12 days in a row before having a day off. Nevertheless she said in a convinced manner:

> *I am still better off in London than in Madrid. (female, 27, journalist, working in a fast-food restaurant in London)*

The examples of the interviewed immigrants show that the emigrating Spaniards, who graduated in humanities, social sciences, etc. mainly work in the low-skilled sector abroad at least until increasing their language skills and getting established on the foreign labour market. Nevertheless, the living and working conditions in the UK as in Germany are considered to be better than in Spain. However, the extent of preparation for the host labour market just like the level of language skills was very low, but seems to be crucial for a successful labour market entry. Their stay is temporary and unpredictable in terms of aims and duration. They use free labour mobility in order to achieve a self-sustaining life and gain intercultural competences, so they show the type of individualisation of liquid migration.

7.3.5 Interim conclusion: right Spaniards in the UK

The exemplified professions differ with regard to their profile, aim of labour mobility and their chances and problems on the British labour market.

Nurses are highly demanded on the British labour market and their recruitment is facilitated by a competitive recruitment industry. The Spanish nurses seize the opportunity to get recruited in order to **achieve labour market entry**, which they are unable to gain in Spain. Working in the UK is a chance to get independent from their parents' home and financial resources. As their main motive is seeking independence and labour market entry, they plan to stay as long as their employment conditions are better in the UK than in Spain. Thus, their planning-horizon is mostly short-term until they developed skills and gained working experience in order to be able to enter the Spanish labour market. They already need relatively high English language skills to get recruited and mostly learn the language individually due to interest and/or in preparation for labour mobility. A high level of language skills was required (formerly B2, currently C1) to receive professional recognition. Formal recognition at the Nursing and Midwifery Council is a mandatory prerequisite to work as a nurse in the UK. Due to the high demand for (foreign) nurses on the British labour market, employers and recruiters are involved in targeted recruitment and labour integration. Additionally, as the health care sector in the UK is public, there are strong labour and trade unions, which also support recruitment and labour integration of foreign nurses. However, the Spanish nurses mostly return relatively soon after their recruitment. They are highly frustrated because they **lack intercultural competences and maturity**.

Generally, engineers seek first of all **career advancement** on the British labour market. Their planning horizon is medium-term because the engineers plan to gain professional experience in an innovative environment but do not plan to stay in the UK. The temporariness of their stay is determined either by the plan to return once they achieve a good job either in Spain or move on elsewhere. The Spanish engineers in the UK are mainly single males in their late twenties or early thirties and possess advanced language skills they already obtained before they emigrated. They can apply for a certificate of equivalence at NARIC in the UK, but work experience seems to have a higher signalling value. Due to their **intercultural competences**, their working experience and their **sought-after profile** they fit into the category of **elite migrants** or **self-initiated expatriates**. Job seeking is mainly an individual path of Spaniards, which means the employers and the job candidate are solely responsible for recruitment and labour integration. However, there are also recruiters specialized for engineers, but they are usually not specialized on foreigners or nationalities, apart from the recruitment of Indians.

Only few data could be collected about Spanish technicians, who emigrated to the UK. So, solely sporadic cases were found and labour or trade unions could only give general information on recruitment and labour integration but not about Spanish technicians in particular because they seem to be very small in number. Those cases that have been found concerned males in their mid-thirties, who planned to stay in the UK at long- or medium-term. Hence, in terms of working and living experience they show a certain degree of **maturity**. This was also a common profile found with regard to Spanish technicians emigrating and Spanish technicians in Germany. Their low number seems to be attributable to the hurdles of high language skills to enter the British labour market and few information in Spanish and at Spanish professional associations and forums. employment security, which requires high English skills, are not legal but practical preconditions for being hired as a technician. Thus, compared to the Spanish technicians in Germany, the technicians in the UK need high language skills and **intercultural competences**. These represent high hurdles and Spanish technicians need to be **willing to take the efforts**, which is one of the reasons why they are rather few in number in the UK.

The Spanish humanists in the UK seek independence from their parents, international experience, improving language skills and adventure. They tend to have hardly any obligations apart from earning their living as they are young (in their twenties) and single. Thus they seek **individualisation** for a free and independent life. However, they do not plan to take certain steps of (personal or professional) development or have a clear goal they want to achieve, so the timeframe of their stay is **unpredictable**. Most of them pursue **labour migration** and work in low-wage jobs, but this situation is perceived as **temporary**. All of them have at least basic language skills, which seem to determine their labour opportunities, in contrast, none of them applied for a certificate of equivalence. Their information is provided by hearsay in informal transnational networks in Facebook groups or lose ties, such as friends of friends or friends of the family. A summary is provided by Table 19.

Judging from these exemplifying professions, the *right people* for labour mobility seem to be those, who have some financial resources for the first period of living abroad, speak English, seek adventure and/or labour market entry or career advancement. Additionally, they need to be willing to take the efforts of labour integration, such as improving their language skills, taking the hurdles related to professional recognition. Especially, in professions in which labour shortages were detected, international recruitment was still on going in the UK despite the political aim of reducing net migration.

Thus, the UK still seemed to be the right place for labour immigration as long as there are better working and living conditions than in the home country and as long as international recruitment and informal transnational networks provide the right circumstances within the framework of free movement of workers in the EU. Therefore, labour integration policies were used in order to narrow down the group of EU citizens for which the UK offers the right circumstances for labour immigration. In particular, this was achieved by setting up higher hurdles in terms of required language skills to achieve labour integration

Table 19: Right people for labour integration in the UK

	Nurse	gineer	Technician	Humanists
Motives	Labour market entry independence	Career advancement	(Better living and working conditions)	Independence Adventure
Planning horizon	Short-term	short-term	(Medium to Long-term)	unpredictable
Personal situation	Single, female young	End of 20s to early thirties, single, male	(Male, Middle aged)	Single, more females, in their twenties
Language skills	Advanced and pressure to achieve high language skills	Advanced	Advanced level necessary to work in skilled jobs, Not required for low-skilled jobs	basic – advanced
Responsible recognition body	Nursing and Midwifery Council	NARIC	NARIC	NARIC
Application for recognition	Legal requirement for Professional entry	None	Not a legal requirement, but necessary to get hired	None
Labour integration measures	-language courses -Recruitment in groups -Mentors -Training on the job during work as auxiliary	-Training on the job	CSCS exam	CV training
Labour integration measures provided by institutions	- Labour- and trade union - employers - recruiters - professional forums - youtube tutorials -facebook groups	recruiters employers professional forums (facebook groups)	(- professional forums)	-migrant organisation - non-profit orgas - facebook groups
Myth, framings, perception	- international recruitment legitimized for the British labour market, despite the political goal of reducing net migration		- labour immigration in depreciated blue collar work	personal development through experience and adventure abroad

8. Institutional Analysis

The following part analyses the institutions, their roles, their actions and the diffusion processes in the strategic action fields for each country. Thus, it shows how the institutional arrangements in the EU member states Spain, Germany and the UK were implemented to benefit from the common EU labour market.

8.1 Institutional analysis of the Spanish case

In general, Spain is the **right place** for intra-EU labour mobility as it is a member state of the EU. Based on a **coercive process,** freedom of movement is guaranteed for workers, the university system is part of the European Higher Education Area and professional recognition of qualifications obtained in another member state is stipulated, and EU workers are eligible for social benefits.

8.1.1 Spanish field of intra-EU labour mobility

The freedom of movement for workers in the common labour market allowed for the strong influx of immigrants, who came to Spain at the beginning of the 21st century, at a period of economic boom. There was a high need for workers, and Spain opened its labour market for Eastern European citizen as early as in 2004 developing liberal labour immigration policies. This was followed by a huge inflow of EU migrants in Spain, as employers readily recruited foreign professionals. Thus, Spain became an immigration country by attracting foreign workers from abroad. These migration flows involved institutional structures of immigration and integration, such as migrant organisations, business contacts, public, private and non-profit organisations offering integration measures. The **governance units** supported this development by introducing liberal labour immigration policies and **incumbents** such as employers helped putting labour mobility into practice by recruiting foreigners. Although mobility from Spain to other EU countries was quite low during that period, highly skilled Spaniards already made use of intra-EU mobility due to the limited job opportunities the Spanish labour market offered them.

However, this boom was mainly based on cheap credits for investments in companies and construction that created jobs. Therefore, Spain was especially vulnerable once the US financial crisis, which was an **external crisis,** hit the country and the housing and investment bubble burst. This resulted in high general **unemployment** rates between 20% and 25% and enormous youth unemployment rates of over 50% between 2011 and 2015. The latter, in particular, rose even more

C. Heimann, *Blessing and Curse of Intra-EU Mobility*, Studien zur Migrations- und Integrationspolitik, https://doi.org/10.1007/978-3-658-31486-6_8

due to the educational expansion but only few labour opportunities for skilled and highly skilled professionals and a difficult labour market entry and precarious working conditions for newcomers. In addition, the **depressive environment** ensuing from unemployment and political corruption drove workers out of Spain. Hence, these negative conditions in Spain triggered labour mobility. While unemployment rates were constantly rising, the already established institutions for labour immigration and integration could offer their services to facilitate labour emigration. Hence, when the economic boom in Spain turned into an economic crisis, Spain switched from being a **Right Place** for intra-EU labour immigration to being the **Right Place** for intra-EU labour emigration.

As a result, **challengers** of the status quo emerged that were mainly young Spaniards, who were unemployed or in precarious working conditions. They appealed to the **governance units** to create labour opportunities. In response, the Spanish Ministry of Employment developed labour emigration policies to support labour emigration practices. In this context, the Ministry of Employment established recruitment relations with other EU countries. They created the framing of intra-EU mobility as a chance to find suitable jobs. Although the opposition objected that the government was supporting a brain drain, intra-EU mobility as a chance became the **dominant framing**.

On behalf of the Ministry, the public employment services, such as the European Employment Service (EURES), the Spanish Employment Service (SEPE) and municipal service were in charge of facilitating labour mobility from Spain to other EU labour markets and putting recruitment relations into practice by offering advisory and mediating services. Additionally, they created networks with different **incumbents** from the fields of education, migration and the labour market, such as language schools, unions, universities and migrant organisations, in order to promote their activities with regard to international placement efforts. Accordingly, in a **coercive process** the Ministry used its power to implement an institutional environment designed to foster mobility in the common EU labour market. By doing so, the **governance units** spread the **framing** of labour mobility as a chance for the unemployed. The media supported the creation of the **myth** that labour mobility was a chance for everybody.

Thus, those who were in precarious working conditions or unemployed reached out to the **incumbents** of education, migration and the labour market, such as language schools, unions, universities and migrant organisations seeking assistance. The unemployed demanded that these institutions use their specific expertise to provide support for labour mobility. Due to this **normative pressure** they developed advisory services and/or contacts with entrepreneurial recruiters and employers from abroad. This means that they all developed similar kinds of services producing *mimetic isomorphism*, especially counselling and mediating, in order to take part in the new field and secure their survival.

Figure 6: The diffusion process in the Spanish field of labour mobility[15]

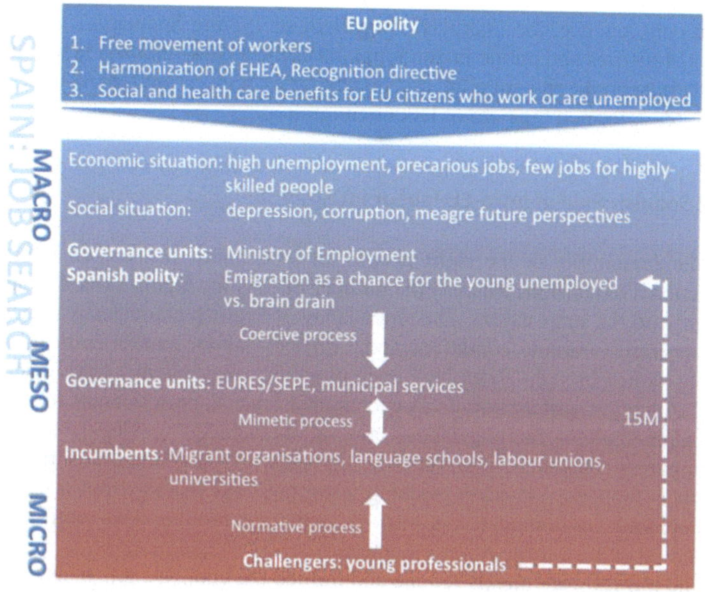

This figure was created by the author and is based on own research.

Depending on their expertise they specialised in a certain sector or profession (unions, universities), certain cultural and social skills (language schools) or EU law on health care, insurances, professional recognition (migrant organisations). Private language schools as well as universities and unions in Spain often cooperated with the entrepreneurial actors, in other words the **recruiters**. Private language schools used the opportunity to earn money during the economic crisis as language skills became necessary to work abroad. Thus, professionals - and partly employers, too, especially those from Germany - spent high amounts of money on language courses in Spain to prepare for intra-EU labour mobility. Due to the poor economic situation and the established institutional structures providing the **right circumstances** facilitating labour emigration, a significant number of Spaniards chose to find employment opportunities abroad, which led to a loss of 10% of the Spanish population. During this wave of labour emigration, migrant networks and formal and informal institutions of Spanish migrants were established and supported by social media, which triggered peers to follow. All

[15] In the strategic action fields of all countries coercive isomorphism was most prominent on the macro-level; mimetic processes were most prominent on the meso-level and normative processes on the micro-level. For reasons of visualization, these are only present in the first figure of the structural analysis. This figure was created by the author

these institutions fostered migration and spread the framing of labour opportunities abroad as shown by Figure 6.

In consequence, the interplay of challengers (young Spaniards), governance units (Ministries and public institutions), incumbents (universities, labour unions, language schools and migrant organisations) as well as entrepreneurial actors (recruiters), formed the field of labour emigration.

8.1.2 Spanish field of intra-EU labour integration

The availability of the **right people** for labour mobility was ensured by an educational expansion, whereas the number of jobs for highly skilled people did not grow to the same extent. The redundancy of Spanish graduates was increased by precarious working conditions and a difficult labour market entry for young people, which brought about high unemployment rates among the younger ones. In this situation, different motives encouraged Spanish professionals to emigrate. The main motives fuelling labour emigration included seeking labour market entry, career advancement or better living and working condition for themselves and their families. However, seeking adventure and fleeing from a depressive sociocultural environment was also an important motive. The motives varied depending on the profile of the emigrants.

The **nurses** were mostly female and formed the youngest group, as they were usually in their early twenties and graduated only recently. They were presented with the best labour opportunities abroad as nurses were sought after in many EU countries in Central, Western and Northern Europe. Therefore, it was relatively easy for them to be hired by a **foreign employer** via a **recruiter**. Partly, **incumbents** like their (former) universities, professional unions or language schools put them in contact with these entrepreneurial actors. Since they were desperate, as they could not find a job after their graduation, the main aim of labour mobility for them was to finally obtain labour market entry in their profession.

The **technicians** form the oldest group including usually 27-45 year-old males who are most likely to be married and have children. Usually **incumbents** in their sector, such as their former educational institute and/or informal networks raised their awareness for labour opportunities abroad and established contacts with recruiters. Partly, informal networks also encouraged labour emigration of technicians, when personal contacts reported of job opportunities abroad. As these technicians were often the breadwinners of their families, their main motive was to find better living, working and earning conditions for themselves and their families abroad.

The **engineers** were usually males in their late twenties to early thirties and were most likely to apply directly for a job abroad without using intermediaries since they were the group that was best prepared for an international career. Additionally, the professional unions and universities spread job announcements, and offered advisory service on working and living conditions to engineers to inform and prepare them for labour mobility.

Especially the highly skilled graduates found work in Germany and the UK relatively easy. They reported about being sought after, obtaining immediately several job offers when they began to search for a job abroad. In contrast, less skilled engineers were more likely to take advantage of mediating services offered by **entrepreneurial actors** such as recruiters. The reason for engineers to go abroad was mostly career advancement as they look for more innovative tasks and higher salaries. There is a diffusion of the **norm** that an engineer should possess some international experience, which supports the intra-EU labour mobility; this signals a normative isomorphism as the driving force of preparation for mobility among engineers.

Figure 7: The diffusion process of the Spanish field of labour mobility

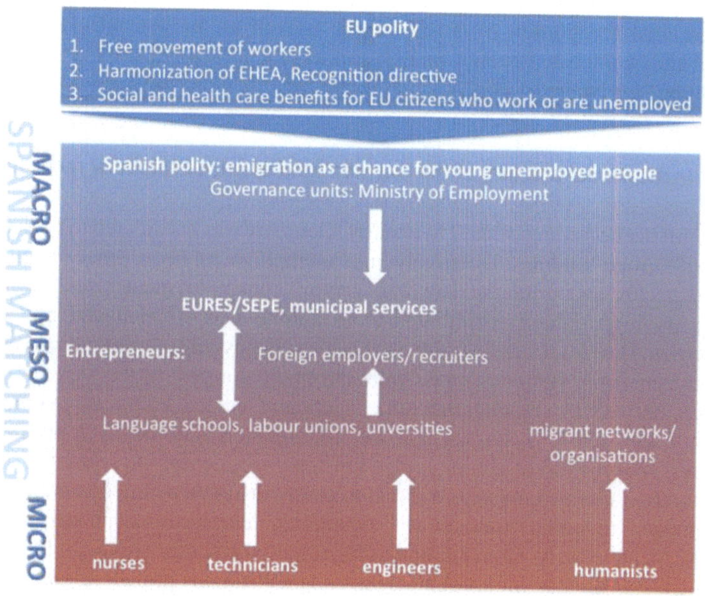

This figure was created by the author and is based on own research.

The **humanists** were between their early 20s and their early 30s and were generally the least prepared for labour mobility in terms of acquiring language skills and information about living and working conditions in Germany and the UK. Usually, they were inspired by friends, family members or random encounters to seize the opportunity of labour mobility. Some use the advisory services of **incumbents** from the field of migration or education, such as **migrant organisations** or other **non-profit organisations**, telling them that it will be difficult for them to find a decent job without good language skills and/or other skills in demand. Their main reasons for labour mobility were escaping from their depressive social environment, corrupt politics and seeking adventure. Therefore, they were usually attracted by living in vibrating metropolitan cities such as London or Berlin.

These examples show how much the profiles, motives and institutional contacts of those practising labour mobility vary as shown by Figure 7.

8.2 Institutional analysis of the German case

As a member state of the European Union, Germany is the **right place for intra-EU labour mobility** because of the institutional setting provided by EU law, which had to be implemented in a *coercive process*. The principle of freedom of movement for workers, the harmonization of education combined with granting professional recognition of qualifications as well as the general eligibility for social and health care benefits for EU citizens in employment, provide favourable conditions for labour mobility.

8.2.1 Institutional analysis of the German field of intra-EU labour recruitment

Until the beginning of the 21st century, Germany was considered to be the "sick man of Europe" and faced relatively high unemployment rates. Since the oil crisis in the 1970s and until the late 20th century, unemployment rates have been relatively high, labour recruitment from abroad was stopped and emigration facilitated. Besides, German politicians refused to govern an immigration country. EU citizens from Eastern Europe were not granted access to the German labour market until 2011. During that time, Germany denied being an immigration country and (due to historical reasons) immigration was mainly a privilege of asylum seekers, who could apply for legal residency. In contrast, labour immigration was perceived as a threat to prosperity. The main counterarguments were related to welfare tourism, wage dumping, decrease of social standards and employment security. **Governance units** of both the conservatives and the social democrats as well as **incumbents** such as labour unions promoted this framing. Therefore, hardly any recruitment structures were developed.

This situation has changed more recently when an economic boom produced relatively low unemployment rates. Combined with an ageing society, the availability of employable people on the labour market dropped. Therefore, it became more difficult for employers to fill vacancies and labour opportunities arose for foreign professionals. The innovative industrial sector, crafts and trades, and the health care sector show a high demand for (foreign) professionals. In this situation, employers associations acted as **challengers** of the status quo and lobbied the government, which reacted by developing international recruitment policies, such as MobiPro-EU. Employers argued that international recruitment was important to fill vacancies and meet customer orders to help them stay competitive in the global market. In this context, their arguments demonstrate the **normative isomorphism** of a liberal labour market supporting international recruitment and the importance of being competitive in the global market, which are in line with the aims of EU2020.

Figure 8: The diffusion process in the German field of labour recruitment

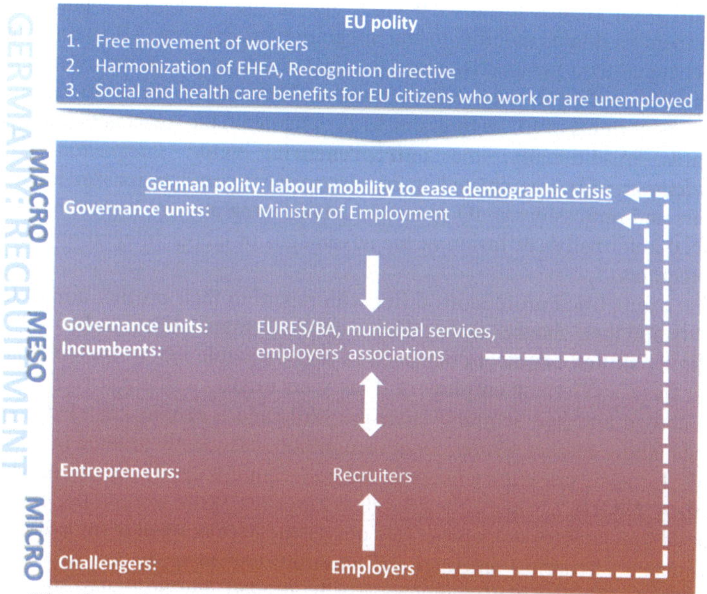

This figure was created by the author and is based on own research.

The **right circumstances** for labour immigration from other EU countries were legitimized by **the framing** of international labour recruitment as a measure to reduce the effects of the demographic crisis. Consequently, **governance units** used their **power** to start a **coercive process** providing subsidies and entrusting the public employment agencies with the task of facilitating recruitment. Thus, the national employment agency BA developed a shortage occupation list in order to identify the professionals most urgently needed on the labour market, and EURES facilitated their incoming. Private recruitment agencies emerged as an **entrepreneurial actor** and supported the recruitment, mediating between the German and the foreign labour markets. The interplay of institutions is summarised by Figure 8. Other governance units and **incumbents** from the fields of labour market, education and migration were less involved in recruitment but in labour integration, as will be explained in the following part.

8.2.2 Institutional analysis of the German field of intra-EU labour integration

Certain **governance units** supported labour integration for foreign professionals by providing an institutionalized Culture of Welcome and Recognition, such as federal recognition bodies, NARIC and municipal integration councils. These institutions were developed in a **coercive process** as they were in charge of implementing the Recognition Directive on the national and the federal level. Additionally, incumbents, such as (Spanish) migrant organisations that have (in part) been created already 50 years ago in the wake of the guest worker recruitment facilitated mobility to and integration in Germany. Also, labour unions have changed their perspective since the Eastern European citizens were granted free access to the German labour market. They rather prefer to defend the employment rights of EU immigrants so as to maintain the social and employment standards. Additionally, the **entrepreneurial actor** *Integration through Qualification (IQ)* was created to accelerate labour integration for all foreign workers and professionals. IQ promoted labour integration in their networks and enforced a normative diffusion of the advantages of labour integration measures for foreigners.

The exemplified professions differ with regard to their profile, aim of labour mobility and their chances and problems on the German labour market.

Highly skilled engineers managed to find a suitable job by applying directly for vacancies of German **employers**. They were usually well prepared for seeking a job abroad and had acquired language skills and a certain knowledge of the German labour market. Professional recognition was mostly granted on the basis of their former work experience and did not require a certificate of equivalence issued by **NARIC**. In part, their English language skills were sufficient to get recruited for German companies. This proves the development of an international environment favouring international mobility by *institutional isomorphism*. Hence, the highly skilled engineers hardly needed any assistance from other institutions for labour mobility, while less skilled engineers needed private **recruitment agencies** and their bridging function to find a job abroad.

As far as the **nurses** are concerned, recruiters usually provided a carefree package on behalf of German employers, as German language skills and mobility/working/international experience were poor among Spanish nurses. As nursing is a **regulated profession,** the nurses had to get recognized and registered at the **Federal Recognition Body**. In this context, employers and recruiters often helped them to achieve recognition. Major challenges for them were to meet the language requirements for professional recognition and to live in a culturally and socially different environment.

The Spanish **technicians** searching a job in Germany were a rather small group compared to the nurses. They were either attracted by personal contacts in **informal networks,** or **recruitment agencies** recruited them. Generally, they did not need a certificate of equivalence to pursue their profession, however, in some cases it was helpful to achieve a salary at union rate or to be hired in security and safety-related sectors. The **incumbent** *Chamber of Commerce (IHK)* provided the certificate of equivalence. Language skills were not a big issue. Instead, professionals were often hired with very little language skills but learned quickly from their German fellow workers while doing their job.

Personal relations and informal migrant networks mainly attracted **Spanish humanists** to Berlin and its vibrant cultural and party scene. In their case, mobility was encouraged by the ***myth*** *of international experience* as a value in itself. They mostly found work in mini-jobs or registered as self-employed Spanish teachers, which made them also eligible for social benefits. Informal Spanish networks and Spanish migrant organisations as well as labour unions offered language courses and information on the labour market and employment rights in Germany. These also helped the Spanish humanists to make strategic use of loopholes in the welfare system in order to be able to claim benefits.

Summarizing, the **right people** with regard to successful labour integration are those who show a certain degree of independence, who gather information beforehand, prepare to be able to assess their chances on the host labour market realistically, and plan their professional goals accordingly.

Figure 9: The diffusion process of the German field of labour integration

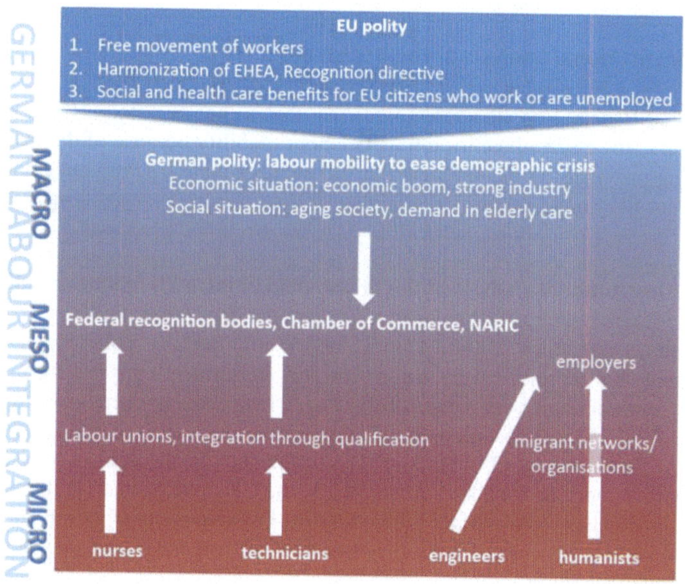

This figure was created by the author and is based on own research.

The great number of institutions created to provide labour integration measures is proof of the structural inefficiency of international recruitment in Germany. The federal organization of education and recognition, the highly specialized and standardized national job profiles as well as the hurdles of the German language and the fact that Germany is not a fluid labour market, form a setting that ensures the high quality of German products yet does not make transnational labour integration smooth. Therefore, in the case of Germany, intra-EU labour mobility and international recruitment lead to a self-reinforcing process of *decoupling*. The inconsistencies when it comes to implementing EU regulations concerning the common EU labour market, such as Bologna and the recognition directive, repeatedly require the development of well elaborated institutions offering integration measures to make labour mobility feasible. Thus, different labour market institutions such as labour unions, IQ, federal recognition bodies, the Chamber of Commerce, employers, the Federal Office for Migration and Refugees, migrant organisations and other non-profit organisations develop and provide information and labour integration measures in a *mimetic process* as shown by Figure 9. By doing so, they reproduce the myth of a common EU labour market offering chances for everyone along with the advantages of international recruitment. Hence, by trying to deal with the described inconsistencies they legitimize the practice of international recruitment.

8.3 Institutional analysis of the British case

The British case illustrates explicitly that a member state of the European Union is the **right place** for intra-EU labour mobility because of the institutional setting provided by EU law, even if the member state's governance units try to prevent EU immigration.

8.3.1 Institutional analysis of the British field of intra-EU labour recruitment

Since the early 2000s, liberal labour immigration policies and intense international recruitment by employers and recruitment agencies have attracted foreign immigrants very successfully. The British economy kept growing steadily after World War II. In line with its liberal ideology, it was the first EU country to follow the US model of international recruitment in an attempt to keep pace in the global competition for talent. Accordingly, the UK developed an immigration law and opened its labour market for the Eastern Europeans as early as in 2004. Thus, recruitment agencies, migrant networks and organisations developed and facilitated labour mobility.

After millions of foreigners had immigrated within a period of 20 years, parts of society have obviously become tired of immigration. Therefore, right-wing rhetoric and politics began to rise among citizens and was bundled in the United Kingdom Independence Party (UPIK), which **challenged** the status quo of immigration policies and practices. Due to the rhetoric claiming that immigration was a threat the challengers appealed to the government to care for the citizens' demand to reduce immigration. In response to this development, the conservative government adopted some of UKIP´s arguments and promised to reduce net immigration. Subsequently, **governance units** as employment services removed and limited the *right circumstances* for labour immigration they had provided so far, such as offering advisory service for foreigners and assisting international recruitment. Additionally, in professions featuring particularly high immigration levels, the language skills for required recognition were increased significantly. In this context, the *right circumstance* of a universal language was reduced for EU immigrants, who have usually other mother tongues. Nevertheless, the **governance units** did not achieve a decrease of net immigration as employers and recruiters went on to hire professionals from abroad, who continued to immigrate for professional reasons and job opportunities. As Figure 10 shows, the British economic actors maintained their usual routine of international recruitment within the framework of freedom of movement for workers that had been established by **coercive isomorphism**.

Figure 10:
The diffusion process of the German field of labour integration

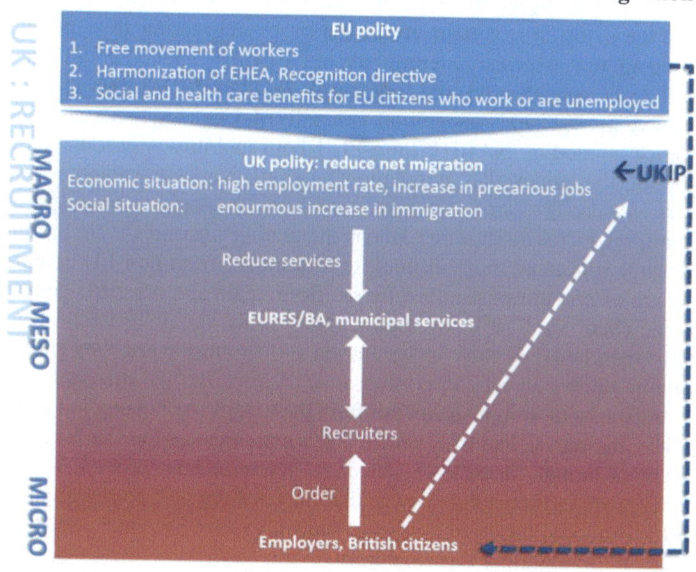

This figure was created by the author and is based on own research.

It was impossible for British **governance units** to make their promise come true because the relevant **incumbents**, such as employers, recruiters and foreign workers, did not act accordingly. In this situation, these economic actors are supported by the EU, which has been an economic union by definition ever since its foundation with its basic principles of free movement of workers, goods, capital and services aiming at market liberalisation. Thus, protectionist national forces are structurally disadvantaged in the EU. This led to a point at which questions of national sovereignty arise and abetted to an EU exit in the case of the UK.

In the next section, the exemplifying professionals and their recruitment and labour integration will be described to demonstrate how institutional actors kept facilitating labour mobility, which undermined the efforts of governance units to reduce net immigration.

8.3.2 Institutional analysis of the British field of intra-EU labour integration

On the British labour market centralized institutions fulfil the task of professional recognition. The centralized organization seems to make it easier for migrants to find out which recognition body is responsible. However, the level of required language skills increased and became more and more a hurdle to intra-EU labour mobility.

Highly skilled engineers had good chances to find employment by directly applying for a job at a certain **employer** or by registering their profile at a **recruiting agency**, which are **incumbents** in the British labour market. They were prepared well enough and did not need assistance by other institutions; furthermore, professional recognition generally did not require a certificate of equivalence granted by **NARIC**. Intra-EU labour mobility is encouraged by the diffusion of the **norm** that international experience is a valuable asset for engineers.

For **nurses** increasingly more labour integration measures were provided in the UK since it became more difficult to hire nurses from non-EU countries. A broad range of **recruiters** searched nurses from Spain and other EU countries in their home countries. The better their English skills, the more likely it was for them to be recruited. Once the nurses arrived at their **employers**, they got in touch with **unions** during an induction process and generally had the opportunity to receive assistance or training measures from the unions. As nursing is a **regulated profession,** the nurses had to get recognized and registered at the **Nursing and Midwifery Council**. Increased language requirements proved by official certificates were introduced to ensure that nurses were able to thoroughly fulfil their tasks. However, these requirements might also have been increased to reduce the number of immigrating foreign nurses.

Spanish **technicians**, who took the step of searching employment in the UK, had to obtain a certificate of equivalence from **NARIC** and a **GSCS card** to prove their familiarity with security and safety standards. Especially for achieving the GSCS card, relatively high language skills were required, which might be a reason why Spanish technicians rarely took the step to search work in the UK. Other reasons might be that international experience is not a merit per se for technicians and the fact that British recruiters do not actively search for technicians in Spain. Additionally, the niche of crafts and trades is mainly occupied by Polish professionals, who achieved an exceptional reputation and became **incumbents** in this sector.

Spanish **humanists,** who went abroad, were mainly attracted by personal relations and informal migrant networks and chose preferably the metropolitan cities, such as London or Edinburgh. Personal development and improving language skills were their main motives to come to the UK, besides escaping the bad situation in Spain. In their host country, they found work in the low wage sector and were vulnerable to exploitation. In this context, they received support from local informal **entrepreneurial actors** forming **Spanish networks** and **Spanish migrant organisations**, such as Oficina Precaria and Facebook groups, while British organisations such as unions did not provide considerable points of contacts. The diffusion process in the British field of labour integration is illustrated by Figure 11.

Figure 11: The diffusion process in the British field of labour integration

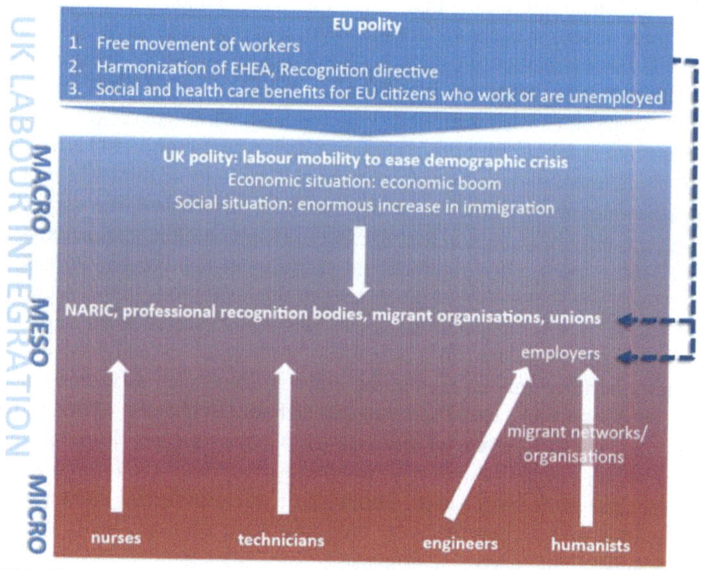

This figure was created by the author and is based on own research.

Thus, the right people for labour mobility to the UK are independent, skilled and highly skilled professionals who are willing to learn English very well alongside people who are prepared to fill in vacancies in the low-skilled and low-wage sector.

8.4 Necessary institutional conditions versus favourable circumstances

In all three cases, the economic situation was crucial in initiating the implementation of new policies for labour mobility and labour integration. This happened in a historically important situation when free movement for workers was expanded and favourable conditions were created by harmonizing the educational systems and guaranteeing professional recognition and welfare benefits to EU citizens. This is why the UK and Spain opened their labour markets for Eastern European citizens in 2004 already, while Germany only started to do so after the country had to grant access to these citizens and when the German economy boomed.

However, the fact that the implementation of policies facilitating intra-EU labour mobility coincided with an economic growth and rising labour demand in all three countries should not mistakenly lead to the conclusion that the economic situation had been the only or the main driver. Instead, the freedom of movement for workers, the Bologna reform, the recognition directive and the availability of welfare benefits for EU citizens had to be implemented EU-wide, so it was a coercive process. It is rather the extent of support provided by the different institutions and the point in time that varies due to the economic situation.

In all three cases, it becomes obvious that once the legal framework of the common EU labour market has been implemented, it cannot be reversed easily. Only if employers stop hiring foreign EU citizens and/or foreign EU citizens stop labour immigration, can labour mobility be reduced, while governance units are not able to prevent labour mobility. Thus, employers and mobile EU citizens are the main challengers and protagonists in the policy field of intra-EU mobility. Additionally, once a recruitment industry has been established, the incumbents facilitating mobility have an inherent interest in maintaining it, as it is existential for them. Furthermore, once international recruitment has become an essential feature in a specific sector of the labour market, the institutions in this sector tend to see no alternatives to this habit anymore. This was indicated in the case of the recruitment of nurses in the UK, where neither employers and recruiters nor professional and trade unions mentioned other options, such as higher salaries, better working conditions, etc. The issue was different in the case of Spain, when the economic situation changed because employers did not hire foreigners anymore. Instead, due to their precarious working conditions the foreign workers were among the first to be released. Furthermore, the established institutions for labour migration and recruitment kept providing their services, while reversing them and secured their survival in doing so.

The described cases therefore show that once the EU framework for labour mobility has been implemented, intra-EU labour mobility takes place regardless of whether governance units support it or not as summarised in Table 20. As long as employers support intra-EU recruitment and EU citizens immigrate for labour, the institutions involved support intra-EU labour mobility.

Table 20: Institutions providing the right circumstances

European Union - Freedom of movement for workers - Harmonisation of education → professional recognition - Access to social benefits → non-discrimination principle			
Member state	**Spain**	**Germany**	**UK**
Policy agenda	Un(der)employment	boom	Saturation of immigration
Governance units: Governmental and public institutions	+	+	–
challengers: Professionals Employers	+	+	+
incumbents: Migrant organisations, recruiters, **labour unions language schools**	+	+	+
Intra-EU labour mobility	+	+	+

Hence, the willingness of employers and workers to exercise labour mobility is a **necessary condition**, while the services and actions of all other institutions in the field are merely **sufficient conditions**. As they facilitate labour mobility they are rather **intervening variables**. This is true for intra-EU labour mobility only as long as the framework of the common EU labour market is implemented by the member states.

8.5 The three right factors

8.5.1 Right place for the right people

The questions as to whether a place is the right place for intra-EU labour mobility and whether there are the right circumstances at a certain place and who might be the right people for labour mobility, are interrelated. Therefore, they have to be analysed and evaluated in relation to each other. The right people are evaluated in relation to the right place from a destination-country perspective, which depends on the socioeconomic structure of the country in question and does not necessarily match the perspective of the people. As shown in Chapter 3, the perspectives and parameters for the evaluation of intra-EU mobility in the member states are developed in a normative debate. In relation to the normative debates and standards, people can be assessed as the right people not only if they choose intra-EU labour mobility as suggested by the scope, but also if they are favoured immigrants in a certain place. The same is true for places and circumstances. In accordance with the profile of immigrants and their expectations as well as the aims of fostering or preventing intra-EU mobility matching the labour market needs, places and circumstances can be assessed as right or wrong from a normative perspective.

From this viewpoint, the highly-skilled engineers and the skilled technicians from Spain seem to be the *right people* at the *right place* in the UK and Germany, because they are in demand on these labour markets and satisfied with their labour situation abroad. Three factors seem to make their labour mobility particularly successful. Firstly, they were willing to take the efforts of labour integration, such as acquiring language skills and informing themselves about the labour situation. Either they prepared over years (such as the engineers) or in due time while taking the steps of labour mobility (such as the technicians). Secondly, they had a clear goal related to labour migration, which was either career advancement in the case of the engineers or better living and working conditions for the technicians and their families. Thirdly, a certain extent of work and life experience helped them estimate challenges and have realistic expectations.

The wrong people in the right place seem to be the nurses and the less skilled engineers. Though there is a demand for these employees, they mostly did not seem to be satisfied with their working and living conditions in the UK and Germany. Thus, they frequently leave their employer before the recruitment pays off. In the case of Germany, nurses were often recruited for elderly care but generally preferred to work for hospitals. However, in the case of the UK, Spanish nurses were mainly recruited for British hospitals, which offered further education and promotion, but these hospitals had similarly made bad experiences with recruitment. Compared to the engineers and technicians, nurses tended to be younger, more inexperienced and generally less prepared for intercultural experiences. Overall, the recruitment of Spanish nurses must be evaluated as an enormous misinvestment as most of them stayed only temporarily in the recruiting country and worked even less time for the recruiting employer. In the case of the less skilled engineers, the problem was that they aimed for high salaries at a prestigious employer in a metropolitan area. However, they usually found work in more rural areas and were therefore dissatisfied and returned to their home country or sought work elsewhere. They are not able to meet their unrealistic expectations and are therefore considered as the wrong people in the right place.

Generally, if people are the right people is at the same time a matter of balance between supply and demand or expectations and possibilities. This is also true in the case of humanists. There are people who aim at working in hospitality and/or catering to afford a living in a place of interest for a while and/or want to learn a language and do not mind working in the low-wage sector during this period. This means, they might be the right people in the right place if they are in a metropolitan area with a high demand for low-wage workers in this sector. This situation is different, when people aim at finding skilled work sooner or later but are not able to acquire such a position. However, the myth of personal development through migration offers an excuse so that labour mobility need not be considered a failure even if expectations are not met. Thus, the motive of personal development might be over-applied.

Table 21: Matching of people and place for labour mobility

Place / People	Wrong People	Right People
Right Place	Skilled/ high incentives **Nurses**	(Highly-) skilled / demand **Engineers, Technicians** low skilled / demand **Low-wage workers in metropolitan areas**
Wrong Place	No transferable skills / no demand **Humanists**	Skilled / no demand **Humanists**

Another part of the humanists is categorised as the wrong people in the wrong place as summarized in Table 21. This includes those whose skills are tightly connected to the Spanish language, such as journalists. Any country, which is not Spanish-speaking, will be the wrong place for them, while they will always be the wrong people in any non-Hispanic country because they are not able to offer any transferable skills. However, many humanists in Berlin might be the right people in the wrong place as they might possess the relevant transferable skills, but they are not willing to move away from Berlin, which has a relatively high unemployment and underemployment rate compared to other regions in Germany.

However, it is not only the places and the people that decide about the right match. Instead, institutions offer selection and adjustment mechanisms and thereby provide certain favourable or impeding circumstances. Thus, the relation between circumstances and people will be highlighted in the following chapter.

8.5.2 Right circumstances for the right people

Despite the framework of the EU policies and the economic differences between EU member states, there are still other circumstances that trigger or foster mobility. These are especially created by institutions that facilitate mobility/recruitment and labour integration. In Table 22 the circumstances are evaluated in relation to the migration projects of people from a destination-country perspective, which do not necessarily match each other.

In the case of highly skilled engineers, the right circumstances for the right people were created, as international recruitment seemed rather easy due to the fact that the engineers were relatively well prepared and stayed at least for some years. The technicians also stayed permanently, although they had to learn the language rather quickly. However, they were highly motivated and personal contacts in rather small companies seemed to help them while integrating. Hence, the favoured professionals are not only those who exercise the freedom of movement for workers, but from a destination countries' and employers' perspective are those who stay at least for some years (medium-term), as could be derived from the interviews.

Table 22: Providing adequate circumstances for the appropriate people

Circumstances / People	**Wrong People**	**Right People**
Right Circumstances	Subsidies for recruitment & labour integration Do not stay permanently **Nurses, less skilled Engineers**	Relatively easy to recruit High demand Stay permanently **Technicians, highly skilled Engineers**
Wrong Circumstances	Benefit tourism **Humanists** in Berlin	Subsidies for recruitment & labour integration No commitment **Professionals** never came

The reasons why the wrong circumstances for the right people were created in the case of the nurses are as follows: It was mentioned that it became too easy for nurses to get recruited. Employers or recruiters bridged typical hurdles that normally need to be taken. These hurdles seem to include necessary steps, which prepare for living and working in another country. In the case of the nurses, a large number lacked this kind of preparation. Thus, they were not informed about living and working conditions, employment laws, or cultural particularities, which is combined with low work and life experience. Once they have arrived in the destination country, the cultural shock and the exigencies of managing daily life abroad overburdened them. Additionally, they lack a reason for going abroad apart from seeking labour market entry. That makes them likely to return whenever they feel like it as their investments were low and they are young and unbound, which means they can easily try out labour mobility.

In the case of Germany, the wrong circumstances were created for the wrong people, as benefit tourism was seized as an option instead of working to sustain living in Germany or living with the parents in Spain. Although none of the Spanish immigrants stated that he or she had come to Germany with the intent to claim benefits, they reported to be instructed on how to claim benefits immediately upon arrival, as Spanish migrant networks and organisations give advice on strategies how to exploit the loopholes and twilight zones in the welfare system to a maximum. Thus, obviously the mere option of being able to claim benefits seems to foster benefit tourism.

Also, the wrong circumstances for the right people were created in the case of Germany, when Spanish professionals got 200 hours of language classes to prepare their labour integration in Germany, but they never came to Germany as there was no mechanism to commit or sanction them.

Hence, there is not an easy answer to what the right or wrong circumstances are to attract the right people. And it is not straightforward to decide who are the right people for labour mobility either. It depends on the perspectives of the migrants, the home and destination countries.

8.5.3 Enhancing the scope of the three right factors

After having evaluated the right people, right places and right circumstances from a normative perspective, the scope will be extended to a theoretical approach by concluding objective and abstract categories and hypothesis.

Place Generally, all EU member states are the right place for EU mobility due to the freedom of movement for workers, EHEA, the recognition directive, etc. and other institutions created by coercive and normative isomorphism. Economic differences in development and performance are most decisive for the direction of migration flows in the EU. However, the institutions involved depend on the type of market economy, educational system and migration history of the member state.

Different institutional structures affect the way recruitment and labour integration are organised. In a liberal market economy like the UK, less institutional adjustments are necessary for intra-EU recruitment and labour integration. This leads to the following hypothesis:

1. The more open a labour market is, the less institutional adjustment are necessary for the integration of foreign professionals.
2. The more universal (anglosaxon, twofold) an educational system is, the less institutional adjustments are necessary for labour integration.
3. The more general skills are in demand, the less integration measures are necessary for labour integration.
4. The more transnational migrant networks exist, the more they facilitate the immigration of more people.
5. The more a country is in an economic boom phase, the more it attracts mobile EU citizens.
6. The more social benefits are available in a member state for mobile EU citizens, the more it will attract foreigners to seek benefits.

Conversely, it can be said that the more coordinated a market economy is, the more institutional adjustments are necessary for labour integration. That means, in the case of coordinated market economies the first three hypotheses are reversed.

Circumstances Besides the structure of the specific member states, certain circumstances are favourable for intra-EU mobility.

Circumstances for intra-EU mobility, may they be in favour or not, need legitimation before they can be created. In times of crisis, such as the economic crisis in Spain, the demographic crisis in Germany or the immigration crisis in the UK, challengers may initiate changes of intra-EU mobility. The challengers may be different collective actors in different member states, but they always need the support of other institutions. They may be able to influence societal perceptions on their own, but in order to gain political legitimation for their aims they need governance units. Governance units, such as public employment services, municipal youth services, etc. are also important to promote the framing with regard to intra-EU mobility. Consequently, the fact whether or not the framing favours intra-EU mobility affects the institutional behaviour. Several arguments for and against intra-EU mobility have been highlighted (see Chapter 4-7). It is shown that these debates are not only driven by rational argumentation, but also by emotional aspects. In general, they negotiate the normative standards of a society on who should be granted access to their labour market and welfare system.

Entrepreneurial actors - the recruiters in the case of Spain and Germany - fostered the establishment of a recruitment industry and became themselves incumbents like in the UK.

Also other incumbents, such as educational institutions, language schools and migrant organisation participated in establishing and maintaining a recruitment industry in order to increase their survival capabilities. Hence, once established institutions have an intrinsic motivation to keep the industry going and spread the framing by normative and mimetic processes. The following hypotheses could be derived with regard to circumstances:

1. The more favourable perceptions and framings are towards mobility, the more likely become steered forms of labour mobility.
2. The more favourable perceptions and framings are, the more likely are new international ways of job search or recruitment services created.
3. The more international ways of job search or recruitment services are created, the more likely it is for matching services and labour integration measures to be developed.
4. The more a comprehensive recruitment industry is established, the less likely it is reversible (even if perceptions and framings change).
5. If perceptions and framings turn negative, integration measures and matching of public services are likely to be reduced and/or standards are increased.

As a result, institutions of the labour market, education and migration concerned with intra-EU mobility play a major role for providing the *right circumstances* for the right people.

Table 23: Right place, right circumstances and right people

Factors	Characteristics	
Right place	-Open labour market -Twofold educational system -General skills in demand -Migration relations - economic boom - matching of nationals and vacancies - social benefits	Structure: - educational system - labour market - migration history and policy - welfare system → EU harmonization leads to coercive and normative isomorphism
Right circumstances	- favourable perceptions/framings (labour demand, tax contributors - recruitment/ international ways of job search - labour integration measures/ matching services	Institutions - collective actor promoting mobility (challengers) - governance units legitimizing political framing -recruitment industry maintained by institutions of the labour market, education and migration (incumbents) → normative and mimetic isomorphism leads to structural inefficiencies
Right people	-matching of demand (which cannot be filled by nationals) - professional and personal motives - personal maturity	Profile: - motives - educational degree - family status - working and living experience → normative myth of the value of international experience

People As there is not one single distinct profile of the *right people*, a major advantage of the concept of the right people is its ability to capture a multitude of motives for migration projects. These include career advancement of highly-skilled professionals (see Alaminos-Chica & Santacreu-Fernandez, 2010; Favell, 2008), reluctance of societal anomy (Bygnes, 2017; see Okolski & Salt, 2014) and political corruption (see Triandafyllidou & Gropas, 2014), the thirst for adventure (see Eade et al., 2007; Engbersen, 2015), precarious working conditions, search for better living and working conditions (East-West migration in the EU), such as increased career perspectives, and the self-realisation of elites (see Bygnes, 2017; Favell, 2008). They can be categorized as either personal motives, such as avoiding political corruption, the thirst for adventure, search for better living conditions, self-realisation, or professional motives, such as career advancement or the search for better working conditions.

Generally, the following hypotheses could be drawn from the data with regard to the right people, who are mobile EU citizens:

1. Personal maturity increases the likeliness of a successful mobility project.
2. If mobile EU citizens pursue professional and personal reasons, the likeliness of a successful mobility project increases.
3. The more the matching between professionals and vacancies fits, the more will the likeliness of a successful mobility project rise.

As the analysis of the exemplified professionals shows, profiles are highly diverse among mobile EU citizens in times of crisis. Firstly, it depends on the initial motive to opt for intra-EU labour mobility and the objective pursued both by workers and recruiting countries. These differ between workers and between member states. Additionally, the intentions of mobile EU citizens do not necessarily match the purpose of the recruiting member states. Also, on the micro-level, the normative isomorphism becomes obvious, as many mobile EU citizens have internalized the value of international mobility to increase their human capital and their personal development, which for a significant part of mobile graduates turns out to be a myth. A summary is shown by Table 23.

9. Conclusions and Outlook

This study provides insights into the practical implementation of EU policies, which were derived from opening the blackbox of institutional actions. In addition, labour migration projects of different professionals were examined. Furthermore, the normative debates legitimizing or delegitimizing intra-EU mobility were analysed.

The present book examines the crucial policies and institutional processes of transnational labour recruitment and integration along with the political framings legitimizing them in the case of Spanish mobility to Germany and the UK. In addition, New Institutionalism made it possible to analyse the implementation process of EU policies on the national level. In this context, different institutional settings, discourses and economic climates on the national level have defined the interplay of institutions, its policies, practices and its impact on labour mobility.

Coming back to the focal research question of how steerable intra-EU mobility actually is, this study shows that there are certain policies and institutional mechanisms that may foster or reduce intra-EU mobility. The policies and practices developed in Germany, Spain and the UK tried to steer labour mobility in accordance with the various countries' economic and social situation. However, the common EU labour market and the freedom of movement for workers provide a framework in which intra-EU mobility is not controllable. Recent efforts of harmonization in the European Higher Education Area, the recognition directive and programmes fostering mobility, such as ERASMUS or Your First EURES Job foster the practicability of freedom of movement. Therefore, once implemented and well-received by professionals and employers, they become practically irreversible as long as employers and professionals make use of the option of international job search/recruitment as is demonstrated by the case of the UK.

Nevertheless, the direction of actual migration flows is determined by the economic situation of the member states, which was underlined by all Spanish migrants, even those who did not - or at least not primarily - come to the UK or Germany for labour-related reasons. This does not implicate, however, that all workers are willing to benefit from the option of labour mobility to achieve better working and living conditions, as is shown in the case of Spain; and there are certainly also other motives that might trigger labour mobility. Hence this study concludes that economic conditions, in particular, define the right place, while free labour movement is steerable to a certain extent only. Intra-EU migration can be fostered, but its flows alone do not even out imbalances of the national labour markets. As a short-term measure, and in addition to other institutional changes, it is able to take away some pressure from the member states so as to ease acute labour market deficits. Mismatches, labour shortages or unemployment can be reduced by fostering mobility, but not if they are the measure to conceal structural deficits of national labour markets only.

C. Heimann, *Blessing and Curse of Intra-EU Mobility*, Studien zur Migrations- und Integrationspolitik, https://doi.org/10.1007/978-3-658-31486-6_9

In all three cases, a mismatch was detected produced by an oversupply of university graduates, while more practical skills were in need. If intra-EU mobility is used extensively, as in the UK, it might foster precarious working conditions and wage dumping. The case of nurses revealed that nurses from abroad were mainly needed in metropolises requiring high living costs. Additionally, zero-hour contracts (in the UK) and mini jobs (in Germany) were applied extensively to exploit foreign workers. In both cases, mobile EU citizens were used to keep wages, social and employment standards low. If intra-EU recruitment leads to social erosion, it is likely to lead to a refusal of mobility sooner or later, as has been shown in the case of the UK.

Nevertheless, this is just one side of the coin. Intra-EU mobility bears chances for employers and employees alike. It offers opportunities for professionals in search of better living and working conditions, cultural exchange, career advancement, adventure or to gain independency from their parents by receiving welfare benefits. This study shows that mobile EU citizens seize the chances they are offered strategically. With regard to welfare benefits, they detect grey and twilight zones rapidly and know how to bend them in their favour. However, the availability of benefits to top up a salary beneath the poverty line in Germany gained by a mini job seems to be the economically cheaper alternative in the social market economy than to offer adequate salaries, working hours above underemployment as well as social and employment standards in the low-wage sector.

The beneficial use of intra-EU labour mobility is mainly applicable to economies with an acute difference in economic performance but a comparable degree of economic development. Nevertheless, the degree of economic development and the economic performance of the member states are (still) extremely diverse. Hence, a highly developed economy like Germany or the UK (as long as it is part of the EU), while in crisis, would still be attractive for foreign professionals from comparatively weaker states in terms of their national economy. In this case, the success of intra-EU recruitment could lead to discussions on national sovereignty in the European Community, as has happened in the case of Great Britain. As the basic principles of the European Union provide for market liberalisation of the common EU labour market, protectionist policies on the national level are undermined. Aspirations to put them into practice may therefore only leave the option of EU exit as a last resort. However, this does not only account for the freedom of movement of workers, but also for the free movement of goods, services and capital that could create sovereignty issues.

The theoretical, institutional, and practical contributions open up several avenues for future research and the development of recommendations for action. Especially the multi-faceted and holistic approach shows many connection options that might be pursued.

One focus of the study is on the description and evaluation of political framings and underlying myths that reinforce labour market liberalisation. However, especially the UK and BREXIT showcase that there are significant counter-movements at work. A worthwhile theoretical research endeavour may revolve around a more detailed description, analysis, and interpretation of reverse myths to labour migration, i.e., how bottom-up tendencies of renationalization counteract top-down internationalization efforts. In addition, the development in the UK has shown that no universal transnational solidarity among EU citizens has developed as a result of free labour movement. Quite the contrary, when in doubt UK citizens questioned the legitimacy of the availability of their national public goods, e.g., public housing, social benefits, education and health care services for their EU "compatriots". An interesting research question would be the assessment of the degree of transnational solidarity in the context of the EU and of the factors that determine the willingness to share national wealth and benefits with non-nationals, whose potential contribution to the said wealth and benefits is uncertain.

Furthermore, applied research could be conducted in order to assess the adequacy and effectiveness of recruitment strategies and labour integration measures in more detail and also include other professions than those highlighted above. Many of them still suffer from either inefficiency or various degrees of impracticability as is shown in this study. To this end, rigorous analyses and evaluations of present measures must be followed by a detailed implementation of novel strategies based upon the premise of mutual benefits. Research obviously identifies a noticeable discrepancy in the expectations of employers and employees, which is in part due to exaggerations and misconceptions stemming from institutional myths. Hence, increased transparency in communication, advertising, and the recruiting process itself need to replace the currently dominant promotion of advantages of intra-EU mobility. To this end, adequate recruiting and matching procedures must first be identified and then implemented. The main institutions providing the *right circumstances* – such as job centres, recruitment agencies, policy makers, unions and employers - could assume responsibility for informing the employees and employers about typical issues and hurdles to reduce inefficiencies of transnational mobility.

Another open question is to what extent return migration is preferable in terms of career advancement after having left the country of origin for a (temporarily) advantageous career step. Along with the theoretical contributions, this book also supplies answers to practical issues. The data analysed can be used as an approach to providing a broader picture of intra-EU mobility and capturing policies, institutions and migrants as well as their particular facets. It shows typical hurdles that have to be taken and names the relevant institutions and strategies that can help to overcome them.

Furthermore, it informs about recruitment agencies and existing integration measures, their relevance and their impact on successful job placement. Additionally, it takes into account the importance of profiles and motivation of immigrants. In this context, there are different issues of recruitment and labour integration in each sector and profession that need to be considered. Besides, it offers insights into structural inefficiencies and gives hints on how to reduce these.

All this information can be used for policy consultancy in order to inform policy-makers on how to foster or prevent mobility, to improve institutional inefficiencies and create labour integration measures. Furthermore, the findings can be used to offer professionals and employers insights into how they can best navigate the system of labour mobility and which institutions provide support for various issues. These contributions can be used for business consultancy as well as for the development of labour integration measures for mobile EU citizens. Additionally, the findings can be used to develop more efficient assessments for the selection of job candidates.

In summary, we can say that member states need to develop suitable adjustment mechanisms if they aim at benefitting from the common EU labour market. This study shows that the type of mechanism that is best suited for this purpose differs from country to country, its economic situation and its institutional structure. Additionally, it has to be taken into account that labour mobility is only steerable to a certain extent in the EU.

Literature

20minutos. (2013, April 17). Báñez dice que la fuga de jóvenes en busca de trabajo no es nueva y la llama 'movilidad exterior'. Retrieved 6 July 2018, from https://www.20minutos.es/noticia/1788690/0/fatima-banez/empleo-jovenes/movilidad-exterior/

Adams, S. (2013, June 2). NHS hires record number of Spanish and Portuguese nurses while refusing Britons because of slashed training budgets | Daily Mail Online. Retrieved 6 July 2018, from http://www.dailymail.co.uk/news/article-2334587/NHS-hires-record-number-Spanish-Portuguese-nurses-refusing-Britons-slashed-training-budgets.html

Alaminos-Chica, A., & Santacreu-Fernandez, O. (2010). La emigración cualificada española en Francia y Alemania. *Revista de Sociologia, 95*(1), 201–2011.

Aldrich, H. E. (1979). *Organizations and environments*. Englewood Cliffs, NJ: Prentice-Hall.

Alichniewicz, J., Geis, W., & Nintcheu, J. M. (2014). *Willkommenskultur*. Köln: IW Medien.

Allen, J., & Velden, R. K. W. van der (Eds.). (2011). *The flexible professional in the knowledge society: new challenges for higher education*. Dordrecht ; New York: Springer. Retrieved from http://dx.doi.org/10.1007/978-94-007-1343-6

Allen, K. (2015, August 19). UK graduates are wasting degrees in lower-skilled jobs | Business | The Guardian. Retrieved 12 March 2018, from https://www.theguardian.com/business/2015/aug/19/uk-failed-create-enough-high-skilled-jobs-graduates-student-debt-report

Allmendinger, J., & Ebner, C. (2006). Arbeitsmarkt und demografischer Wandel. *Zeitschrift Für Arbeits- Und Organisationspsychologie A&O, 50*(4), 227–239. https://doi.org/10.1026/0932-4089.50.4.227

Amable, B. (2003). *The diversity of modern capitalism. [electronic resource]*. Oxford : Oxford University Press, 2003.

Aneca. (2013). Analysis of Health Sciences Study Plans - Aneca. Retrieved 29 March 2018, from http://www.aneca.es/eng/Press-service/News/2013/Analysis-of-Health-Sciences-Study-Plans

Anerkennung in Deutschland. (2018). Spanien. Retrieved 5 July 2018, from https://www.anerkennung-in-deutschland.de/html/de/welcome_center_madrid.php

C. Heimann, *Blessing and Curse of Intra-EU Mobility*, Studien zur Migrations- und Integrationspolitik, https://doi.org/10.1007/978-3-658-31486-6

Arditti s, S., Lewis, R., & Manchip, C. (2005). From Rome to the Hague: European Union policy-making on asylum. Institute for Public Policy Research, www.ippr.org. Retrieved 20 May 2018, from www.ippr.org/files/ecomm/files/migration6eu.pdf?noredirect=1

Arghyrou, M. G., & Kontonikas, A. (2011). *The EMU sovereign-debt crisis: Fundamentals, expectations and contagion*. Brussels, Belgium: European Commission, Directorate-General for Economic and Financial Affairs. Retrieved 29 March 2018, from http://ec.europa.eu/economy_finance/publications/economic_paper/2011/pdf/ecp436_en.pdf

Arosa, B., Iturralde, T., & Maseda, A. (2010). Ownership structure and firm performance in non-listed firms: Evidence from Spain. *Journal of Family Business Strategy*, *1*, 88–96. https://doi.org/10.1016/j.jfbs.2010.03.001

Asthana, A. (2005). Focus: Polish plumbers and the EU constitution | World news | The Guardian. Retrieved 6 July 2018, from https://www.theguardian.com/world/2005/may/29/france.immigration

Aurora Humanitarian Index. (2017). 2017 Aurora Humanitarian Index. Retrieved 15 March 2018, from https://auroraprize.com/en/aurora/article/dialogues/10769/2017-aurora-humanitarian-index

Autofácil. (2015). Qué fabrica Seat en España. Retrieved 29 March 2018, from http://www.autofacil.es/seat/2015/02/18/fabrica-seat-espana/23399.html

Bauman, Z. (2000). *Liquid modernity* (1. publ., reprinted). Cambridge [u.a.]: Polity Press [u.a.].

Bauman, Z. (2013). *Moral blindness* (1. publ.). Cambridge [u.a.]: Polity Press.

BBC News UK. (2016, June 20). Immigration target 'impossible' in EU. Retrieved 29 March 2018, from https://www.bbc.co.uk/news/uk-politics-eu-referendum-36573220

BBC News UK. (2018). Short History of Immigration. Retrieved 29 March 2018, from http://news.bbc.co.uk/hi/english/static/in_depth/uk/2002/race/short_history_of_immigration.stm#1914

BDA. (2010). *Fachkräftemangel bekämpfen Wettbewerbsfähigkeit sichern: Handlungsempfehlungen zur Fachkräftesicherung in Deutschland.* (Bundesvereinigung der Deutschen Arbeitgeberverbände, Ed.). Berlin.

BDA. (2015). Fachkräftemangel bekämpfen – Wettbewerbsfähigkeit sichern. Handlungsempfehlungen zur Fachkräftesicherung in Deutschland. Retrieved 26 March 2018, from https://www.arbeitgeber.de

Beas, D. (2011). How Spain's 15-M movement is redefining politics | Opinion | The Guardian. Retrieved 3 April 2018, from https://www.theguardian.com/commentisfree/2011/oct/15/spain-15-m-movement-activism

Beck, U. (1986). *Risikogesellschaft* (1. Aufl., 2. Dr., Erstausg.). Frankfurt am Main: Suhrkamp.

Beduwe, C., & Planas, J. (2003). *Edex Educational Expansion and Labour Market: A Comparative Study of Five European Countries--France, Germany, Italy, Spain and the United Kingdom with Special Reference to the United States. Cedefop Reference Series*. Bernan Associates.

Beetham, D. (1991). *The legitimation of power* (1. publ.). Basingstoke u.a.: Macmillan.

Berger, P. L., & Luckmann, T. (1967). *The social construction of reality : a treatise in the sociology of knowledge*. Garden City, N. Y. : Doubleday, 1967, c1966.

Bernhard, S., & Bernhard, S. (2014). Arbeitnehmerfreizügigkeit und Diskriminierung auf dem deutschen Arbeitsmarkt * europäische Politik, transnationaler Mobilitätsraum und nationales Feld., *H. 2*. Retrieved 29 March 2018 from http://www.iab.de/389/section.aspx/Publikation/k140714302

Birsl, U. (2005). *Migration und Migrationspolitik im Prozess der europäischen Integration?* Opladen: Budrich.

Blinder, S. (2017, July 18). Naturalisation as a British Citizen: Concepts and Trends. Retrieved 8 March 2018, from http://www.migrationobservatory.ox.ac.uk/resources/briefings/naturalisation-as-a-british-citizen-concepts-and-trends/

Bodvarsson, Ö. B., & Van den Berg, H. (2013). *The economics of immigration. [electronic resource] : theory and policy*. New York, NY : Springer, c2013.

Booth, R. (2016, November 15). More than 7m Britons now in precarious employment. Retrieved 12 March 2018, from http://www.theguardian.com/uk-news/2016/nov/15/more-than-7m-britons-in-precarious-employment

Bortz, J., & Döring, N. (1995). *Forschungsmethoden und Evaluation* (2., vollst. überarb. und aktual. Aufl.). Berlin [u.a.]: Springer.

Braun, D. (2012). Einheitlicher, transparenter, effektiver? Das Verfahren zur Bewertung von im Ausland erworbenen Qualifikationen im Wandel | bpb. Retrieved 7 July 2018, from http://www.bpb.de/gesellschaft/migration/kurzdossiers/141828/bewertung-von-im-ausland-erworbenen-qualifikationen

Bräuninger, D. (2014, July 14). The dynamics of migration in the euro area. Retrieved 17 November 2017, from https://www.dbresearch.de/PROD/RPS_EN-PROD/The_dynamics_of_migration_in_the_euro_area/RPS_EN_DOC_VIEW.calias?rwnode=PROD0000000000435631&ProdCollection=PROD000000000044494

Breitenbach, B. von. (1985). *Italiener und Spanier als Arbeitnehmer in der Bundesrepublik Deutschland*. München : Mainz: M. Grünewald, Mainz.

Brown, J. D. (2001). *Using surveys in language programs*. Cambridge, U.K. ; New York : Cambridge University Press, 2001.

Brücker, H., Brunow, S., Fuchs, J., Kubis, A., Mendolicchio, C., & Weber, E. (2013). Fachkräftebedarf in Deutschland * zur kurz- und langfristigen Entwicklung von Fachkräfteangebot und -nachfrage, Arbeitslosigkeit und Zuwanderung. Retrieved 17 November 2017, from http://www.iab.de/537/section.aspx/Mitarbeiter/455#j2013

Brussig, M., Dittmar, V., & Knuth, M. (2009). *Verschenkte Potenziale. Fehlende Anerkennung von Qualifikationsabschlüssen erschwert die Erwerbsintegration von ALG IIBezieher/ innen mit Migrationshintergrund*. Universität Duisburg Essen: Institut für Arbeit und Qualifikation.

Buchan, J., Wismar, M., Glinos, I. A., & Bremner, J. (2014). *Health professional mobility in a changing Europe. New dynamics, mobile individuals and diverse responses* (European Observatory on Health Systems and Policies No. 2). World Health Organization. Retrieved from 29 March 2018 http://www.euro.who.int/en/publications/abstracts/health-professional-mobility-in-a-changing-europe.-new-dynamics,-mobile-individuals-and-diverse-responses-2014

Bundesagentur für Arbeit. (2013). Förderprogramm MobiPro - EU - www.arbeitsagentur.de. Retrieved 5 July 2018, from https://www3.arbeitsagentur.de/web/content/DE/dienststellen/rdnrw/paderborn/Agentur/Detail/index.htm?dfContentId=L6019022DSTBAI529388

Bundesagentur für Arbeit. (2014). *Der Arbeitsmarkt in Deutschland. Fachkräfteengpassanalyse – Juni 2014*. Nürnberg.

Bundesamt für Migration und Flüchtlinge. (2011). Broschuere Anerkennung Zugang Ingenieure. Retrieved 17 November 2017, from https://www.scribd.com/document/216573194/Broschuere-Anerkennung-Zugang-Ingenieure

Bundesamt für Migration und Flüchtlinge. (2013). BAMF - Bundesamt für Migration und Flüchtlinge - Publikationen - Bestimmung von Fachkräfteengpässen und Fachkräftebedarfen in Deutschland. Retrieved 26 March 2018, from https://www.bamf.de/SharedDocs/Anlagen/DE/Publikationen/EMN/Studien/wp64-emn-bestimmung-fachkrafteengpaesse-und-bedarfe.html

Bundesamt für Migration und Flüchtlinge. (2015). *Anerkennung Ihres Berufsabschlusses. Ein Schritt auf Ihrem Weg zum Arbeiten in Deutschland.* Paderborn: Bonifatius GmbH Druck-Buch-Verlag.

Bundesministerium der Justiz und für Verbraucherschutz. (2018). BQFG - nichtamtliches Inhaltsverzeichnis. Retrieved 6 July 2018, from http://www.gesetze-im-internet.de/bqfg/

Bundesministerium des Innern. (2018). Demografie. Retrieved 5 July 2018, from http://www.bmi.bund.de/DE/themen/heimat-integration/demografie/demografie-artikel.html;jsessionid=AE70923531DD51B8458EDC4AB020E6E7.1_cid287?nn=9394666

Bundesministerium für Arbeit und Soziales. (2011). *Fachkräftesicherung. Ziele und Maßnahmen der Bundesregierung.* Retrieved 29 March 2018, from https://www.bmas.de/SharedDocs/Downloads/DE/fachkraeftesicherung-ziele-massnahmen.html

Bundesministerium für Arbeit und Soziales. (2013). Arbeitsmarktprognose 2030. Eine strategische Vorausschau auf die Entwicklung von Angebot und Nachfrage in Deutschland. - Bundesministerium für Arbeit und Soziales. Retrieved 29 March 2018, from https://www.bmas.de/DE/Presse/Meldungen/2016/arbeitsmarktprognose.html

Bundeszentrale für politische Bildung. (2005). Deutsche Migrationsgeschichte seit 1871 | bpb. Retrieved 6 March 2018, from http://www.bpb.de/gesellschaft/migration/dossier-migration/56355/migration-1871-1950

Bundeszentrale für politische Bildung. (2014). Aktuelle Entwicklungen und zukünftige Herausforderungen | www.bpb.de. Retrieved 6 July 2018, from http://www.bpb.de/gesellschaft/migration/laenderprofile/198213/aktuelle-entwicklungen?type=galerie&show=image&i=198677

Burrell, K. (2006, March 2). Moving Lives | Narratives of Nation and Migration among Europeans in Post-War Britain | Taylor & Francis Group. Retrieved 12 March 2018, from https://www.taylorfrancis.com/books/9781351916554

Bux, U. (2017). The citizens of the Union and their rights | EU fact sheets | European Parliament. Retrieved 28 November 2017, from http://www.europarl.europa.eu/atyourservice/en/displayFtu.html?ftuId=FTU_2.1.1.html

Bygnes, S. (2017). Are They Leaving Because of the Crisis? The Sociological Significance of Anomie as a Motivation for MigrationSociology - Susanne

Bygnes, 2017. *Sociology*. Retrieved 29 March 2018, from http://journals.sagepub.com/doi/pdf/10.1177/0038038515589300

Bygnes, S., & Erdal, M. B. (2017). Liquid migration, grounded lives: considerations about future mobility and settlement among Polish and Spanish migrants in Norway. *Journal of Ethnic and Migration Studies*, *43*(1), 102–118. https://doi.org/10.1080/1369183X.2016.1211004

Cartwright, D., & Zander, A. F. (1953). *Group dynamics, research and theory;* Evanston, Ill., Row, Peterson [1953].

Casillas, C. (2013, January 25). España ha destruido más de tres millones de puestos de trabajo en cinco años de crisis. Retrieved 29 March 2018, from http://www.finanzas.com/noticias/empleo/20130125/espana-destruido-tres-millones-1691555.html

Castillo-Castilla, E. (2014). Anlaufstellen für spanische Einwander/-innen in Berlin. In C. Pfeffer-Hoffmann (Ed.), *Arbeitsmigration nach Deutschland* (pp. 17–105). Berlin: Mensch & Buch Verlag.

CCOO. (2011). www.1mayo.ccoo.es. Retrieved 29 November 2017, from http://www.1mayo.ccoo.es/nova/NBdd_LstDocumentos?cod_primaria=1185&cod_secundaria=100145

Cebolla Boado, H., & González Ferrer, A. (2008). *La inmigración en España (2000-2007) de la gestión de flujos a la integración de los inmigrantes*. Madrid: Centro de Estudios Políticos y Constitucionales.

CEDEFOP. (2009, September 22). European qualifications framework (EQF). Retrieved 21 May 2018, from http://www.cedefop.europa.eu/en/events-and-projects/projects/european-qualifications-framework-eqf

CLASS. (2014, March 21). Why immigration is good for all of us | Publications | CLASS. Retrieved 7 July 2018, from http://classonline.org.uk/pubs/item/why-immigration-is-good-for-all-of-us

Cerna, L. (2011). Selecting the Best and Brightest. Retrieved 11 March 2018, from http://www.migrationobservatory.ox.ac.uk/resources/primers/selecting-the-best-and-brightest/

Chong, D., & Druckman, J. N. (2007). Framing Theory. *Annual Review of Political Science*, (10), 103–126.

Clark, T. (2014). Ukip support plummets to push Tories back into the lead. *The Guardian*.

Clemente, Y. (2015). Evolución del desempleo (1975 - 2015) | Actualidad. Retrieved 27 March 2018, from https://elpais.com/elpais/2015/11/18/media/1447871942_778264.html

Coleman, J. S. (1990). Foundations of Social Theory. The Belknap Press of Harvard University Press: Cambridge, Massachusetts, London.

Consejo de la Juventud de España. (2013). OBSERVATORIO DE EMANCIPACIÓN. Retrieved 15 March 2018, from http://www.cje.org/es/publicaciones/novedades/observatorio-de-emancipacion/

Conti, F. (2011). *Leaving or Staying – An Analysis of Italian Graduates' Migratory Patterns.* Sussex: University of Sussex.

Costa, M. T., & Duch, N. (2004). La renovación del sector textil-confección en España: proceso de ajuste y contenido tecnológico. *Economía industrial*, (355), 263–272.

Council of Europe. (2014a). Higher Education and Research. Retrieved 21 May 2018, from https://www.coe.int/t/dg4/highereducation/recognition/lrc_EN.asp

Council of Europe. (2014b). The Lisbon Recognition Convention. Retrieved 18 November 2017, from https://www.coe.int/t/dg4/highereducation/recognition/lrc_EN.asp

Crouch, C., & Streeck, W. (1997). *Political Economy of Modern Capitalism: Mapping Convergence and Diversity*. London. https://doi.org/10.4135/9781446217849

Cruz-Martin, M. C. (2012, January 21). La crisis dispara la demanda de cursos de idiomas. Retrieved 6 April 2018, from http://www.rtve.es/noticias/20120121/conocimiento-ingles-herramienta-clave-para-encontrar-empleo/490498.shtml

CSCS. (2018). Construction Skills Certification Scheme | Official CSCS Website - About CSCS. Retrieved 6 July 2018, from https://www.cscs.uk.com/about/

Czepek, J., Dummert, S., Kubis, A., Leber, U., Müller, & A., Stegmaier, J. (2015). *Betriebe im Wettbewerb um Arbeitskräfte: Bedarf, Engpässe und Rekrutierungsprozesse in Deutschland* (1st ed.). Nürnberg: wbv Media.

Daugherty, H. G., & Kammeyer, K. C. W. (1995). *An Introduction to Population: Second Edition* (2 edition). New York: The Guilford Press.

De Lange, N., Geiger, M., Hanewinkel, V., & Pott, A. (2014). *Bevölkerungsgeographie* (1st ed.). Paderborn: UTB GmbH.

Dehesa, G. de la. (2009). *La primera gran crisis financiera del siglo XXI: orígenes, detonantes, efectos, respuestas y remedios* (1. ed). Madrid: Alianza Editorial.

Delgado, C. (2011, June 9). Ingenieros españoles hacen cola para irse a Alemania | Edición impresa | EL PAÍS. Retrieved 31 March 2018, from https://elpais.com/diario/2011/06/09/economia/1307570409_850215.html

Denzin, N. K. (2006). *Sociological methods : a sourcebook*. New Brunswick, N.J. : Aldine Transaction, [2006].

Denzin, N. K. (2014). *Triangulation*. John Wiley & Sons, Inc.

Department of Education. (2018). Further and higher education, skills and vocational training - GOV.UK. Retrieved 15 March 2018, from https://www.gov.uk/education/further-and-higher-education-skills-and-vocational-training

Deutsche Welle. (2016). Can the UK live without the Polish plumber? | DW | 17.05.2016. Retrieved 6 July 2018, from http://www.dw.com/en/can-the-uk-live-without-the-polish-plumber/a-19263835

Deutscher Gewerkschaftsbund. (2018). Fair Mobility. Retrieved 12 March 2018, from http://www.faire-mobilitaet.de/en/

Dick, L. (2014). Exploding the myth of Polish plumbers – POLITICO. Retrieved 6 July 2018, from https://www.politico.eu/article/exploding-the-myth-of-polish-plumbers/

DiMaggio, P. J. (1988). Interest and Agency in Institutional Theory. In L. G. Zucker, *Institutional patterns and organizations*. Cambridge, Mass.: Ballinger Publ.

DiMaggio, P. J., & Powell, W. W. (1983). The Iron Cage Revisited: Institutional Isomorphism and Collective Rationality in Organizational Fields. *Schlüsselwerke Der Wirtschaftssoziologie*, 195.

Dominiczak, P. (2013, November 28). Most immigrants to the UK now come from China, figures show. Retrieved 29 March 2018, from https://www.telegraph.co.uk/news/uknews/immigration/10480785/Most-immigrants-to-the-UK-now-come-from-China-figures-show.html

Dominiczak, P. (2014, May 13). David Cameron: Foreigners fleeing eurozone countries pushing up UK net migration. Retrieved 29 March 2018, from https://www.telegraph.co.uk/news/uknews/immigration/10828770/David-Cameron-Foreigners-fleeing-eurozone-countries-pushing-up-UK-net-migration.html

Durkheim, E. (1982). *Rules of Sociological Method*. Simon and Schuster.

Dustmann, C., & Frattini, T. (2013). The Fiscal Effects of Immigration to the UK. *Center for Research and Analysis of Migration-Discussion Paper Series*, (22).

Eade, J., Drinkwater, S., & Garapich. (2007). Class and Ethnicity: Polish Migrant Workers in London [html]. Retrieved 29 November 2017, from https://www.surrey.ac.uk/cronem/projects/polish/class_and_ethnicity_polish_migrant_workers_in_london.htm

El Mundo. (2007). Zapatero afirma que España juega en la 'Champions League' económica | elmundo.es. Retrieved 5 July 2018, from http://www.elmundo.es/mundodinero/2007/09/11/economia/1189506158.html

El Mundo. (2013, April 17). Báñez dice que la salida de jóvenes de España 'se llama movilidad exterior'. Retrieved 6 July 2018, from http://www.elmundo.es/elmundo/2013/04/17/espana/1366192479.html

elEconomista.es. (2013, December 4). Las sombras de corrupción sobre UGT y CCOO agravan la crisis del sindicalismo español - EcoDiario.es. Retrieved 6 April 2018, from http://ecodiario.eleconomista.es/politica/noticias/5368774/12/13/Las-sombras-de-corrupcion-sobre-UGT-y-CCOO-alejan-a-Espana-del-sindicalismo-solo-un-34-de-ciudadanos-estan-implicados-en-su-lucha.html

Engbersen, G. (2012). Migration Transitions in an Era of Liquid Migration. In M. Okólski (Ed.), *European immigrations: trends, structures and policy implications* (pp. 91–106). Amsterdam: Amsterdam University Press.

Engbersen, G. (2015, 30-01). *Liquid Migration in Europe: Contemporary Patterns of Mobility and Diversity in Europe.* Presented at the EUI/IMISCOE conference Mobility in Crisis', Florence, Italy.

Ernst&Young. (2016). EY - Pressemitteilungen. Retrieved 5 July 2018, from https://www.ey.com/de/de/newsroom/news-releases/pressemitteilungen

Esping-Andersen, G. (1998). *The three worlds of welfare capitalism* (Reprint.). Princeton, NJ: Princeton Univ. Press.

Eurodesk. (2018). Eurodesk | Informing all young people about ways to experience the world. Retrieved 31 March 2018, from https://eurodesk.eu/

European Commission. (2006). European Commission - PRESS RELEASES - Press release - FAQ on the Commission's free movement of workers report. Retrieved 6 July 2018, from http://europa.eu/rapid/press-release_MEMO-06-64_en.htm?locale=en

European Commission. (2011). *First European Survey on Language Competences*. Retrieved 29 March 2018, from https://www.fundae.es/Pages/default.aspx

European Commission. (2014a). Evaluation of the Your first EURES job preparatory action Executive summary: findings, recommendations & policy options for the future. Retrieved 18 November 2017, from http://ec.europa.eu/social/main.jsp?langId=en&catId=1160&newsId=2136&furtherNews=yes

European Commission. (2014b). Homepage –. Retrieved 28 November 2017, from http://ec.europa.eu/youthonthemove/

European Commission. (2016, June 14). Agriculture in the European Union and the Member States - Statistical factsheets [Text]. Retrieved 29 March 2018, from https://ec.europa.eu/agriculture/statistics/factsheets_en

European Commission. (2018a). Erasmus+ | EU programme for education, training, youth and sport. Retrieved 1 July 2018, from https://ec.europa.eu/programmes/erasmus-plus/node_en

European Commission. (2018b). Europe 2020 strategy. Retrieved 20 May 2018, from https://ec.europa.eu/info/business-economy-euro/economic-and-fiscal-policy-coordination/eu-economic-governance-monitoring-prevention-correction/european-semester/framework/europe-2020-strategy_en

European Commission. (2018c). Investing in Europe's youth - Employment, Social Affairs & Inclusion - European Commission. Retrieved 20 May 2018, from http://ec.europa.eu/social/main.jsp?catId=950&langId=en

European Commission. (2018d). Move2Learn, Learn2Move - Mobility and Transport - European Commission. Retrieved 1 July 2018, from /transport/themes/social/move2learnlearn2move_en

European Commission. (2018e). Recognition of professional qualifications in practice - Growth - European Commission. Retrieved 6 July 2018, from /growth/single-market/services/free-movement-professionals/qualifications-recognition_en

European Commission. (2018f). Your first EURES job: EC publishes evaluation report. Retrieved 31 March 2018, from http://ec.europa.eu/social/main.jsp?langId=en&catId=1160&newsId=2136&furtherNews=yes

European Commission. (2018g, June 30). The European Credit system for Vocational Education and Training (ECVET) - Education and training - European Commission. Retrieved 30 June 2018, from https://ec.europa.eu/education/policy/vocational-policy/ecvet_en

European Committee of the Regions. (2017). CoR - The Lisbon Strategy in short. Retrieved 19 November 2017, from https://portal.cor.europa.eu/europe2020/Profiles/Pages/TheLisbonStrategyinshort.aspx

European Employment Services. (2018). EURES - EURES - The European job mobility portal - European Commission. Retrieved 21 May 2018, from https://ec.europa.eu/eures/public/homepage

European Youth Portal. (2018). Home | European Youth Portal. Retrieved 1 July 2018, from https://europa.eu/youth/EU_en

Expatistan. (2018). Cost of Living Ranking in Europe. Updated Jul 2018. Retrieved 6 July 2018, from https://www.expatistan.com/cost-of-living/index

Faist, T. (1997). Migration und der Transfer sozialen Kapitals oder: Warum gibt es relativ wenige internationale Migranten? In L. Pries (Ed.), *Transnationale Migration* (1. Aufl.). Baden-Baden: Nomos-Verl.-Ges.

Faist, T. (2000). Transnationalization in international migration: implications for the study of citizenship and culture. *Ethnic and Racial Studies*, *23*(2), 189–222. https://doi.org/10.1080/014198700329024

Faraco-Blanco, C. (2014). Neue Migration: Junge Spanier/-innen in Berlin. In C. Pfeffer-Hoffmann (Ed.), *Arbeitsmigration nach Deutschland* (pp. 17–105). Berlin: Mensch & Buch Verlag.

Favell, A. (2008). *Eurostars and Eurocities: free movement and mobility in an integrating Europe*. Malden, MA: Blackwell Pub.

Favell, A. (2014). The fourth freedom: Theories of migration and mobilities in 'neo-liberal' Europe. *European Journal of Social Theory*, *17*(266–289).

Fellmer, S. (2013). *Vergemeinschaftung von Zuwanderungspolitik in der Europäischen Union*. LIT Verlag Münster.

Ferreiro, J., & Serrano, F. (2012). The Economic Crisis in Spain: Contagion Effects and Distinctive Factors. In P. Arestis & M. C. Sawyer (Eds.), *The Euro crisis* (pp. 235–268). Houndmills, Basingstoke, Hampshire ; New York, NY: Palgrave Macmillan.

Flick, U. (2002). *Qualitative Sozialforschung* (vollst. überarb. und erw. Neuausg., (6. Aufl.), Orig.-Ausg.). Reinbek bei Hamburg: Rowohlt-Taschenbuch-Verl.

Fligstein, N. (2001). Social Skill and the Theory of Fields. *Sociological Theory*. 19(2), 105-125.

Fligstein, N., & McAdam, D. (2011). Toward a General Theory of Strategic Action Fields. *Sociological Theory*, *29*(1), 1–26.

Flock, E. (2011). Spanish 'revolution': Thousands gather in Madrid's Puerta del Sol Square [VIDEO] - The Washington Post. Retrieved 3 April 2018, from https://www.washingtonpost.com/blogs/blogpost/post/spanish-revolution-thousands-gather-in-madrids-puerta-del-sol-square/2011/05/18/AFLzpZ6G_blog.html?utm_term=.2e7155bbac5e

Fontanella Khan, J., Wiesmann, G., & Warrell, H. (2013, March 7). UK seeks EU support over 'benefits tourism'. Retrieved 7 July 2018, from https://www.ft.com/content/8cf287a8-8749-11e2-bde6-00144feabdc0

Forbes. (2018). The World's Biggest Public Companies List. Retrieved 29 March 2018, from https://www.forbes.com/global2000/list/#tab:overall

Frayer, L. (2016). If Britain Leaves The EU, What Happens To The 'Polish Plumber?' Retrieved 6 July 2018, from https://www.npr.org/sections/parallels/2016/05/14/477685487/if-britain-leaves-the-eu-what-happens-to-the-polish-plumber

Fromm, A. (2013, October 16). Spanische Arbeitslose: Gestrandet in Erfurt. *Die Zeit*. Retrieved 29 March 2018, from https://www.zeit.de/gesellschaft/zeitgeschehen/2013-10/auszubildende-spanien-arbeitsvermittler

Full Fact. (2018). EU immigration to the UK. Retrieved 7 July 2018, from https://fullfact.org/immigration/eu-migration-and-uk/

Fundación Laboral de la Construcción. (2018). Trabajo en Construcción. Retrieved 6 July 2018, from http://www.trabajoenconstruccion.com/?AspxAutoDetectCookieSupport=1

Fundae. (2018). Fundación Estatal para la Formación en el Empleo - Fundae. Retrieved 5 July 2018, from https://www.fundae.es/Pages/default.aspx

Gamson, W. A., & Modigliani, A. (1987). The Changing Culture of Affirmative Action. *Research in Political Sociology*, *3*, 137.

Ganz, M. (2000). Resources and Resourcefulness: Strategic Capacity in the Unionization of California Agriculture, 1959-1966. *American Journal of Sociology*, *105*(4), 1003–1062.

Garapich, M. P. (2016). *London's Polish Borders: Transnationalizing Class and Ethnicity among Polish Migrants in London*. Columbia University Press.

García-Montalvo, J. (2007). Wage Inequality among Higher Education Graduates Evidence from Europe. In *Fundación BBVA*.

Geißler, R. (2014). Bundeszentrale für politische Bildung - Bildungsexpansion und Bildungschancen | bpb. Retrieved 27 March 2018, from http://www.bpb.de/izpb/198031/bildungsexpansion-und-bildungschancen?p=all

General Medical Council. (2018). Home - GMC. Retrieved 6 July 2018, from https://www.gmc-uk.org/

Glaser, B. G., & Strauss, A. L. (1979). *The discovery of grounded theory* (10. printing). New York: Aldine.

Glaser, B. G., & Strauss, A. L. (1998). *Grounded theory*. Bern [u.a.]: Huber.

Gläser, J., & Laudel, G. (2010). *Experteninterviews und Qualitative Inhaltsanalyse*. VS Verlag.

Glick-Schiller, N., Basch, L., & Blanc-Szanton, C. (1992). Transnationalism: A New Analytic Framework for Understanding Migration. *Annals of the New York Academy of Sciences*, *645*(1), 1–24. https://doi.org/10.1111/j.1749-6632.1992.tb33484.x

González Ferrer, A. (2013). La nueva emigración española. Lo que sabemos y lo que no. Retrieved from https://digital.csic.es/handle/10261/93167

Gonzalez-Enriquez, C., & Martinez-Romera, J. P. (2014). España: Emigración de los españoles autóctonos durante la crisis - Elcano. Retrieved 29 March 2018, from http://www.realinstitutoelcano.org/wps/portal/rielcano_es/contenido?WCM_GLOBAL_CONTEXT=/elcano/elcano_es/zonas_es/GonzalezEnriquez-MartinezRomera-Espana-emigracion-espanoles-crisis-Spain-migration-crisis

Goss, J., & Lindquist, B. (1995). Conceptualizing International Labor Migration: A Structuration Perspective. *The International Migration Review*, (2), 317. https://doi.org/10.2307/2546784

Government Digital Service. (2018). Tax credits - GOV.UK. Retrieved 6 July 2018, from https://www.gov.uk/browse/benefits/tax-credits

Green, L. A. (2006). The impact of asylum and possible amnesty on social housing. Retrieved 11 March 2018, from http://www.migrationwatchuk.com/briefing-paper/document/57

Green, L. A. (2014). A summary history of immigration to Britain. Retrieved 8 March 2018, from http://www.migrationwatchuk.com/briefing-paper/document/48

Grossarth, J. (2010). Deutschland stirbt aus: Wir und die Kinder. *FAZ.NET*. Retrieved from http://www.faz.net/1.596473

Guilmoto, C. Z., & Sandron, F. (2001). The Internal Dynamics of Migration Networks in Developing Countries. *Population: An English Selection*, (2), 135.

Hall, P. A., & Soskice, D. (2001). *Varieties of Capitalism: The Institutional Foundations of Comparative Advantage*. Oxford University Press.

Hammersley, M., & Atkinson, P. (1983). *Ethnography, principles in practice*. London ; New York : Tavistock, c1983.

Hansen, R. (2000). *Citizenship and Immigration in Postwar Britain*. Oxford University Press, USA.

Harris, C., Moran, D., & Bryson, J. R. (2014). Polish Labour Migration to the UK: Data Discrepancies, Migrant Distributions, and Indicators of Entrepreneurial Activity. *Growth and Change*, *46*(2), 196–217. https://doi.org/10.1111/grow.12087

Hassel, A. (2014). Adjustments in the Eurozone: Varieties of Capitalism and the Crisis in Southern Europe, *LEQS Working Paper No. 76*. Retrieved 29 March 2018, from http://www.ankehassel.de/downloads-1/index.php

Haug, S. (2008). Migration Networks and Migration Decision-Making. *Journal of Ethnic & Migration Studies*, *34*(4), 585–605. https://doi.org/10.1080/13691830801961605

Heidemann, W. (2012). Zukünftiger Qualifikations- und Fachkräftebedarf. Handlungsfelder und Handlungsmöglichkeiten. Retrieved 29 March 2018, from https://www.boeckler.de/pdf/mbf_pb_fachkraeftemangel_heidemann.pdf

Heimann, C., & Wieczorek, O. (2017). The Role of Argumentation and Institutions for Labour Migration in the European Union – Exemplified by Spanish labour migration to Germany. *International Migration*, *55*(S1), 69–85. https://doi.org/10.1111/imig.12338

Herbert, U. (2001). *Geschichte der Ausländerpolitik in Deutschland*. München: Beck.

Hessel, S. (2012). *The Power of Indignation: The Autobiography of the Man Who Inspired the Arab Spring*. New York: Skyhorse Publishing.

Hinrichs, J., & Giebel-Felten, E. (2002). Die Entwicklung des Arbeitsmarktes 1962-2001, (82). Retrieved 29 March 2018, from www.kas.de/wf/doc/kas_467-544-1-30.pdf?030610110803

Hollifield, J. F., & Brettell, C. B. (2000). *Migration theory : talking across disciplines*. New York ; London : Routledge. Retrieved 29 March 2018, from https://trove.nla.gov.au/version/7620526

Hopkins, L., & Levy, C. (2012). Simply the Best? Highly-skilled migrants and the UK's knowledge economy. The work foundation; Lancaster University.

Huntington, S. P. (1968). *Political order in changing societies*. New Haven : Yale University Press, c1968.

Instituto Nacional de Estadistica. (2017). Encuesta de población activa. Retrieved 29 November 2017, from http://www.ine.es/CDINEbase/consultar.do?mes=&operacion=EPA.+Resultados+trimestrales&id_oper=Ir

Instituto Nacional de Estadistica. (2018a). INEbase / Mercado laboral /Actividad, ocupación y paro /Encuesta de población activa / Últimos datos. Retrieved 27 March 2018, from http://www.ine.es/dyngs/INEbase/es/operacion.htm?c=Estadistica_C&cid=1254736176918&menu=ultiDatos&idp=1254735976595

Instituto Nacional de Estadistica. (2018b). INEbase/ Mercado laboral / Actividad, ocupación y paro. Retrieved 29 March 2018, from http://www.ine.es/dyngs/INEbase/es/categoria.htm?c=Estadistica_P&cid=1254735976595

Instituto Nacional de Estadistica. (2018c). Población extranjera por Nacionalidad, sexo y año. Retrieved 27 March 2018, from http://www.ine.es/jaxi/Tabla.htm?path=/t20/e245/p08/l0/&file=02005.px&L=0

Integration durch Qualifizierung. (2018). Netzwerk IQ: Förderprogramm IQ - Startseite. Retrieved 6 July 2018, from https://www.netzwerk-iq.de/

Integration up North. (2018). Integration up North : Migration Yorkshire. Retrieved 7 July 2018, from http://www.migrationyorkshire.org.uk/integrationupnorth

Jacobs, M. (2017). United Kingdom | OECD READ edition. Retrieved 12 March 2018, from http://www.keepeek.com/Digital-Asset-Management/oecd/education/education-at-a-glance-2017/united-kingdom_eag-2017-71-en

Jasso, G., & Rosenzweig, M. R. (1989). Sponsors, Sponsorship Rates and the Immigration Multiplier. *The International Migration Review*, (4), 856. https://doi.org/10.2307/2546465

Jepperson, R. (2012). Institutions, Institutional Effects and Institutionalism. In W. W. Powell & P. J. DiMaggio, *The New Institutionalism in Organizational Analysis*. University of Chicago Press.

Kassam, A. (2015, February 24). Meet the Spanish nurses desperate for a job in the NHS | Society | The Guardian. Retrieved 6 July 2018, from https://www.theguardian.com/society/2015/feb/24/spanish-nurses-job-nhs-health

Kettner, A. (2012). *Fachkräftemangel und Fachkräfteengpässe in Deutschland: Befunde, Ursachen und Handlungsbedarf*. Technische Universität Berlin, Berlin. Retrieved 27 March 2018, from https://d-nb.info/1022885774/34

Klopprogge, A., Ariño Mateo, E., & Heimann, C. (2016). Erfahrungen mit der Rekrutierung von Pflegekräften in Spanien. In S. Arend & T. Klie (Eds.), *Wer pflegt Deutschland?: Transnationale Pflegekräfte - Analysen, Erfahrungen, Konzepte* (1st ed.). Hannover: Vincentz Network.

Knuth, M. (2012). In A. Bolder, R. Dobischat, G. Kutscha, & G. Reutter (Eds.), *Beruflichkeit Zwischen Institutionellem Wandel und Biographischem Projekt* (2012th ed.). Wiesbaden: VS Verlag für Sozialwissenschaften.

Koslowski, R. (1998). European migration regimes: Emerging, enlarging and deteriorating. *Journal of Ethnic and Migration Studies*, *24*(4), 735–749. https://doi.org/10.1080/1369183X.1998.9976663

Kowalewski, S. (2015). Berufsbezeichnung - Wann ist ein Ingenieur ein Ingenieur? Retrieved 7 July 2018, from https://www.deutschlandfunk.de/berufsbezeichnung-wann-ist-ein-ingenieur-ein-ingenieur.680.de.html?dram:article_id=331721

Kraatz, S. (2018, May). Free movement of workers | Fact Sheets on the European Union | European Parliament. Retrieved 30 June 2018, from http://www.europarl.europa.eu/factsheets/en/sheet/41/free-movement-of-workers

Kreienbrink, A. (2006). Länderprofil Spanien, in: Focus Migration - Länderprofile, hg.v. Bundeszentrale für politische Bildung / Netzwerk Migration in Europa / Hamburgisches Weltwirtschaftsinstitut.

Kreienbrink, A. (2010). Vom Auswanderungsland zum Einwanderungsland | bpb. Retrieved 4 March 2018, from http://www.bpb.de/gesellschaft/migration/laenderprofile/57893/migrationsgeschichte

La Vanguardia. (2011). Más del 80% del empleo destruido por la crisis lo ocupaban jóvenes. Retrieved 16 March 2018, from http://www.lavanguardia.com/economia/20111103/54237468974/mas-del-80-del-empleo-destruido-por-la-crisis-lo-ocupaban-jovenes.html

Lamnek, S. (1988). *Qualitative Sozialforschung*. München [u.a.]: Psychologie-Verl.-Union.

Lamnek, S. (1995). *Qualitative Sozialforschung*. Weinheim: Beltz Verlagsgruppe.

Lamnek, S. (1998). *Gruppendiskussion*. Weinheim: Beltz Psychologie-Verl.-Union.

Lennartz, C., Arundel, R., & Ronald, R. (2016). Younger Adults and Homeownership in Europe Through the Global Financial Crisis. *Population Space & Place*, *22*(8), 823–835. https://doi.org/10.1002/psp.1961

Lessenich, S. (2013). *Wohlfahrtsstaat, Arbeitsmarkt und Sozialpolitik in Spanien: Eine exemplarische Analyse postautoritären Wandels*. Springer-Verlag.

Loeffelholz, H. D. (2013). Arbeitsmigration nach und aus Deutschland im Zuge der Finanzkrise in Südeuropa sowie der wirtschaftlichen Transformation und Erweiterung der EU in Osteuropa. Situation, Möglichkeiten, Probleme, Perspektiven. *2*.

Lorca-Susino, M. (2011). The Economic Cycle and the Unemployment Rates: Spain and the Brain Drain. In J. Roy & M. Lorca-Susino (Eds.), *Spain in the European Union: The First Twenty-Five Years (1986-2011)* (pp. 211–230). Miami-Florida: Miami-Florida European Union Center/Jean Monnet Chair,.

Maciejewski, M., & Dancourt, L. (2017, November). The internal market: general principles | EU fact sheets | European Parliament. Retrieved 20 May 2018, from http://www.europarl.europa.eu/atyourservice/en/displayFtu.html?ftuId=FTU_2.1.1.html

MacMillan, I. C. (1978). *Strategy formulation: Political concepts.*

Mangelberufe.de. (2018). Mangelberufe in Deutschland. Retrieved 4 July 2018, from http://www.mangelberufe.de/

Massey, D. S. (1990). Social Structure, Household Strategies, and the Cumulative Causation of Migration. *Population Index*, (1), 3. https://doi.org/10.2307/3644186

Massey, D. S. (1998). *Worlds in motion : understanding international migration at the end of the millenium.* Oxford : Clarendon Press ; New York : Oxford University Press, 1998.

Massey, D. S., Arango, J., Hugo, G., Kouaouci, A., Pellegrino, A., & Taylor, J. E. (1994). An Evaluation of International Migration Theory: The North American Case. *Population and Development Review*, *20*(4), 699–751. https://doi.org/10.2307/2137660

Mayring, P. (1993). *Einführung in die qualitative Sozialforschung* (2., überarb. und neu ausgestattete Aufl.). Weinheim [u.a.]: Beltz.

Meyer, J. W. (2005). *Weltkultur* (1. Aufl.). Frankfurt am Main: Suhrkamp.

Meyer, J. W., & Rowan, B. (1977). Institutionalized Organizations: Formal Structure as Myth and Ceremony. *American Journal of Sociology*, *83*(2), 340–363.

Mieg, H. A., & Näf, M. (2005). *Experteninterviews*. Skript, Institut für Mensch-Umwelt-Systeme, ETH Zürich.

Migration Observatory. (2015). Net migration, the genie and the bottle: Where next for the net migration target? Retrieved 15 March 2018, from http://www.migrationobservatory.ox.ac.uk/resources/commentaries/net-migration-the-genie-and-the-bottle-where-next-for-the-net-migration-target/

Ministerio de Economía. (1977). *Programa de saneamiento y reforma económica: Pacto de la Moncloa.* Madrid: Secretaría general técnica, Ministerio de Economía.

Ministerio de Empleo y Securidad Social. (2013, May 21). Ministerio de Empleo y Seguridad Social - Gabinete de comunicación - Ministra -. Retrieved 31 March 2018, from http://prensa.empleo.gob.es/WebPrensa/noticias/ministro/detalle/1934

Monaghan, A. (2014). China surpasses US as world's largest trading nation | Business | The Guardian. Retrieved 4 July 2018, from https://www.theguardian.com/business/2014/jan/10/china-surpasses-us-world-largest-trading-nation

Montero-Lange, M. (2014). GRUNDLAGEN: DIE NEUE ARBEITSMIGRATION AUS SPANIEN Innereuropäische Mobilität am Beispiel der neuen spanischen Arbeitsmigration nach Deutschland. In C. Pfeffer-Hoffmann (Ed.), *Arbeitsmigration nach Deutschland* (pp. 17–105). Berlin: Mensch & Buch Verlag.

Moreno, L. (1997). The Spanish development of Southern welfare. Retrieved 29 March 2018, from https://digital.csic.es/handle/10261/2025

Mowafi, M. (2018). NHS recruits Spanish nurses | Daily Mail Online. Retrieved 6 July 2018, from http://www.dailymail.co.uk/news/article-6087/NHS-recruits-Spanish-nurses.html

Mruck, K., & Mey, G. (2000). Qualitative Forschung. In F. Jacobi (Ed.), *Klinisch-psychologische Forschung*. Göttingen [u.a.]: Hogrefe, Verl. für Psychologie.

Müller, A. (2012, April 12). Wirtschaftskrise: Spaniens verlorene Generation ergreift die Flucht. *Die Zeit*. Retrieved 29 March 2018, from http://www.zeit.de/wirtschaft/2012-04/spanien-verlorene-generation

Müller-Wacker, M. (2017). 'Wenn der Bildungstransfer nicht gelingt, vergeuden wir wertvolles Humankapital.' | bpb. Retrieved 7 July 2018, from http://www.bpb.de/gesellschaft/migration/kurzdossiers/245797/interview-mit-martina-mueller-wacker

Münch, R. (1984). *Die Struktur der Moderne* (1. Aufl.). Frankfurt am Main: Suhrkamp.

Münch, R. (2012). *Inclusion and exclusion in the liberal competition state* (1. publ). London [u.a.]: Routledge.

Nardelli, A. (2015, October 20). Tax credits: what are they and who benefits? *The Guardian*. Retrieved 29 March 2018, from http://www.theguardian.com/money/2015/oct/20/tax-credits-what-are-they-and-who-benefits

NARIC. (2018). NARIC - UK NARIC. Retrieved 6 July 2018, from https://www.naric.org.uk/naric/

Neurer, D. (2011). Fachkräfte-Anwerbung: Ökonomen bejubeln Röslers Job-Initiative. Retrieved 5 July 2018, from https://www.wiwo.de/politik/deutschland/fachkraefte-anwerbung-oekonomen-bejubeln-roeslers-job-initiative/5923030.html

Noticias Jurídicas. (2018). Ley 2/1974, de 13 de febrero, sobre Colegios Profesionales. Retrieved 23 September 2018, from http://noticias.juridicas.com/base_datos/Admin/l2-1974.html

Nursing and Midwifery Council. (2018). NMC. Retrieved 6 July 2018, from https://www.nmc.org.uk/

O´Reilly, K. (2014). What Is Lifestyle Migration? | bpb. Retrieved 6 July 2018, from http://www.bpb.de/gesellschaft/migration/kurzdossiers/198255/what-is-lifestyle-migration

Office for National Statistics. (2017). International student migration research update - Office for National Statistics. Retrieved 7 July 2018, from https://www.ons.gov.uk/peoplepopulationandcommunity/populationandmigration/internationalmigration/articles/internationalstudentmigrationresearchupdate/august2017

Office for National Statistics. (2018a). Migration Statistics Quarterly Report Statistical bulletins - Office for National Statistics. Retrieved 29 March 2018, from https://www.ons.gov.uk/peoplepopulationandcommunity/populationandmigration/internationalmigration/bulletins/migrationstatisticsquarterlyreport/previousReleases

Office for National Statistics. (2018b). Unemployment - Office for National Statistics. Retrieved 5 July 2018, from https://www.ons.gov.uk/employmentandlabourmarket/peoplenotinwork/unemployment

Oficina Precaria. (2015, February 10). ALG II (Hartz IV). Retrieved 6 July 2018, from http://oficinaprecariaberlin.org/ayudas-sociales/alg-ii-hartz-iv/

Okolski, M., & Salt, J. (2014). Polish Emigration to the UK after 2004; Why Did So Many Come? | CEEMR. *Central and Eastern European Migration Review*, *3*(2), 11–37.

Olligschlaeger, A. M. (1986). *Neoclassical economics and labour migration theory : a Canadian perspective*. University of British Columbia. https://doi.org/10.14288/1.0097140

OECD. (2009). Education at a Glance 2009 - Survey. Retrieved 27 March 2018, from http://www.oecd.org/education/skills-beyond-school/educationataglance2009-survey.htm

OECD. (2010). OECD Economic Surveys: Spain 2010 | OECD READ edition. Retrieved 27 March 2018, from https://read.oecd-ilibrary.org/oecd/economics/oecd-economic-surveys-spain-2010_eco_surveys-esp-2010-en

OECD. (2013). International Migration Outlook 2013. Retrieved 6 July 2018, from https://www.oecd-ilibrary.org/social-issues-migration-health/international-migration-outlook-2013_migr_outlook-2013-en

OECD. (2016). *United Kingdom | READ online* (Education at a Glance). Paris: OECD. Retrieved from http://dx.doi.org/10.1787/eag-2016-85-en

OECD. (2017). Statistics / Education at a Glance. Retrieved 12 March 2018, from http://www.oecd-ilibrary.org/education/education-at-a-glance_19991487

Petz, F. (2013, April 7). 'Agenda 2010' - Reform mit Wirkungen und Nebenwirkungen. Retrieved 8 July 2018, from https://www.tagesschau.de/inland/agendazwanzigzehn-hintergrund100.html

Pichler, E., & Gruner, P. (1997). *Migration, Community-Formierung und ethnische Ökonomie: Die italienischen Gewerbetreibenden in Berlin*. Berlin: Berliner Inst. f. Vergl. Sozialforschung.

Pries, L. (2007). Transnationalism: Trendy Catch-all or Specific Research Programme? A Proposal for Transnational Organisation Studies as a Micromacro-link. In Fak. für Soziologie, Centre on Migration, Citizenship and Development (COMCAD) (Ed.). Bielefeld: COMCAD Working Papers 34. Retrieved 29 March 2018, from http://www.ssoar.info/ssoar/bitstream/handle/document/51144/ssoar-2007-pries-Transnationalism_Trendy_Catch-all_or_Specific.pdf

Prognos. (2013). Zukunftsatlas-Regionen. Retrieved 5 July 2018, from https://www.prognos.com/publikationen/zukunftsatlas-regionen/

Publico. (2013, April 17). Fátima Bañez llama a la fuga de cerebros 'movilidad exterior'. Retrieved 6 July 2018, from http://www.publico.es/actualidad/fatima-banez-llama-fuga-cerebros.html

Rahona-López, M., & Pérez-Esparells, C. (2013). Educational Attainment and Educational Mismatch in the First Employment in Spain. *Article ID 850827*, 7.

Recchi, E., & Favell, A. (Eds.). (2009). In *Pioneers of European integration*. Cheltenham [u.a.]: Elgar.

Rodríguez Rodríguez, V. (1999). Los inmigrantes europeos jubilados en Andalucía: rasgos sociodemográficos, motivaciones para migrar y modo de vida. Retrieved from https://digital.csic.es/handle/10261/45957

Roth, J. (2011, November 21). Spanische Fachkräfte in Deutschland - 'Angela Merkel hat gesagt: Wir brauchen euch' - Karriere - Süddeutsche.de. Retrieved 31 March 2018, from http://www.sueddeutsche.de/karriere/spanische-fachkraefte-in-deutschland-angela-merkel-hat-gesagt-wir-brauchen-euch-1.1193210

Sachverständigenrat für Wirtschaft. (2013). Jahresgutachten 2012/13. Retrieved 26 March 2018, from https://www.sachverstaendigenrat-wirtschaft.de/jahresgutachten-2012-20130.html

Santiago, P., Brunner, J. J., Malo, S., Pietrogiacomo, P. di, & Haug, G. (2009). *OECD Reviews of Tertiary Education. Spain.*

Santos-Ortega. (2013). Fuga de cerebros y crisis en España: los jóvenes en el punto de mira de los discursos empresariales. *Revista Internacional de Ciencias Sociales*, (23), 125–137.

Schatzman, L., & Strauss, A. L. (1973). *Field research*. Englewood Cliffs, N.J.: Prentice-Hall.

Schengen VISA Information. (2018). Die Länder des Schengen-Raums. Retrieved 21 May 2018, from https://www.schengenvisainfo.com/de/staaten-des-schengen-raums/

Schleicher, A. (2012). Preparing Teachers and Developing School Leaders for the 21st Century, OECD. https://doi.org/10.1787/9789264174559-en

Schmid-Drüner, M. (2017). Free movement of workers | EU fact sheets | European Parliament. Retrieved 19 November 2017, from http://www.europarl.europa.eu/atyourservice/en/displayFtu.html?ftuId=FTU_3.1.3.html

Sciolino, E. (2005). Unlikely Hero in Europe's Spat: The 'Polish Plumber' | YaleGlobal Online. Retrieved 6 July 2018, from https://yaleglobal.yale.edu/content/unlikely-hero-europes-spat-polish-plumber

Scott, W. R., & W., R. S. (2014). W. Richard SCOTT (1995), Institutions and Organizations. Ideas, Interests and Identities. *M@n@gement*, (2), 136.

Secretariat of the Bologna Follow-Up Group. (2017). Home - European Higher Education Area and Bologna Process. Retrieved 18 November 2017, from http://www.ehea.info/

Servicio Público de Empleo Estatal. (2012). Servicio Público de Empleo Estatal. Trabajamos para ti. Retrieved 31 March 2018, from https://www.sepe.es/contenidos/que_es_el_sepe/publicaciones/sobre_el_sepe/informe_anual.html

Shah, D. V., Watts, M. D., Domke, D., & Fan, D. P. (2002). News Framing and Cueing of Issue Regimes: Explaining Clinton's Public Approval in Spite of Scandal. *The Public Opinion Quarterly*, (3), 339.

Siebert, H. (1997). Labor Market Rigidities: At the Root of Unemployment in Europe. *Journal of Economic Perspectives*, *11*(3), 37–54. https://doi.org/10.1257/jep.11.3.37

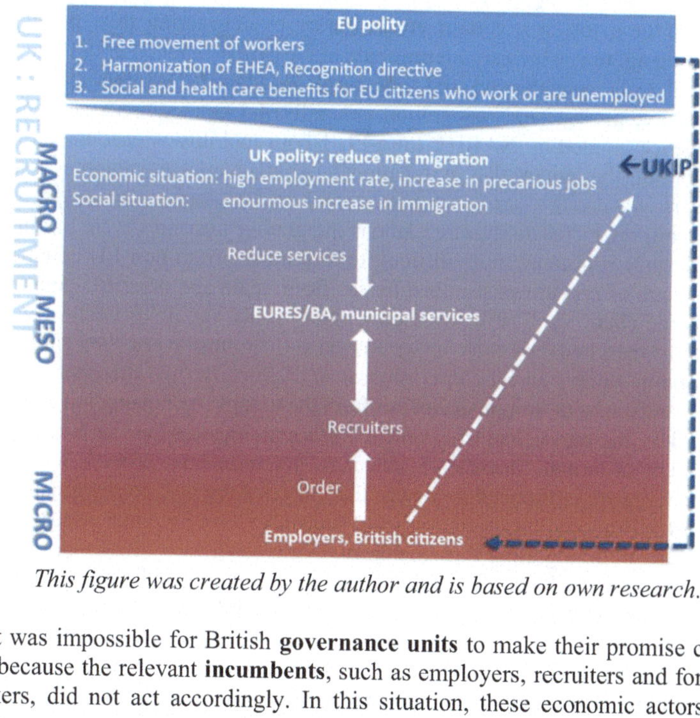

Smith, M. P., & Favell, A. (Eds.). (2006). *The human face of global mobility: international highly skilled migration in Europe, North America and the Asia-Pacific*. New Brunswick, N.J: Transaction Publishers.

Sommer, I. (2015). *Die Gewalt des kollektiven Besserwissens: Kämpfe um die Anerkennung ausländischer Berufsqualifikationen in Deutschland*. transcript Verlag.

Sparrow, A. (2013). 'Go home' campaign against illegal immigrants could go nationwide. *The Guardian*.

SPD. (2012). Positionen. Retrieved 19 November 2017, from http://www.spdfraktion.de/themen/positionen

Spiegel Online. (2012). Wegen Euro-Krise: Spanier stürmen Deutschkurse in Goethe-Instituten -. Retrieved 5 July 2018, from http://www.spiegel.de/wirtschaft/soziales/wegen-euro-krise-spanier-stuermen-deutschkurse-in-goethe-instituten-a-853317.html

Spiegel Online. (2013). Bertelsmann-Studie: Deutschland schrumpft und vergreist bis 2030 - SPIEGEL ONLINE. Retrieved 26 March 2018, from http://www.spiegel.de/wissenschaft/mensch/deutschland-bevoelkerung-schrumpft-bis-2030-um-halbe-million-a-1042605.html

Springford, J. (2013). *Is immigration a reason for Britain to leave the EU?* Centre for European Reform.

Stark, O., & Wang, Y. Q. (2002). Migration Dynamics. *Economics Series*.

Statista. (2018a). Arbeitslosenquote - Arbeitslosigkeit in Deutschland bis 2018. Retrieved 29 March 2018, from https://de.statista.com/statistik/daten/studie/1224/umfrage/arbeitslosenquote-in-deutschland-seit-1995/

Statista. (2018b). Lebenserwartung in Deutschland - Durchschnittsalter nach Geschlecht bis 2060. Retrieved 5 July 2018, from https://de.statista.com/statistik/daten/studie/273406/umfrage/entwicklung-der-lebenserwartung-bei-geburt--in-deutschland-nach-geschlecht/

Statistisches Bundesamt. (2015). Staat & Gesellschaft - Geburten - Alter der Mutter - Statistisches Bundesamt (Destatis). Retrieved 5 July 2018, from https://www.destatis.de/DE/ZahlenFakten/GesellschaftStaat/Bevoelkerung/Geburten/Tabellen/GeburtenMutterAlterBundeslaender.html

Statistisches Bundesamt. (2018a). Economic Sectors - Industry, Manufacturing - Federal Statistical Office (Destatis). Retrieved 29 March 2018, from https://www.destatis.de/EN/FactsFigures/EconomicSectors/IndustryManufacturing/IndustryManufacturing.html

Statistisches Bundesamt. (2018b). Economic Sectors - Service, financial services - Federal Statistical Office (Destatis). Retrieved 29 March 2018, from https://www.destatis.de/EN/FactsFigures/EconomicSectors/Service/Service.html;jsessionid=6AFD675D3ADD420579BC30D85C33CCAF.InternetLive1

Statistisches Bundesamt. (2018c). Staat & Gesellschaft - Geburten - Zusammengefasste Geburtenziffer nach Kalenderjahren - Statistisches Bundesamt (Destatis). Retrieved 26 March 2018, from https://www.destatis.de/DE/ZahlenFakten/GesellschaftStaat/Bevoelkerung/Geburten/Tabellen/GeburtenZiffer.html

Stegbauer, C. (2009). Wikipedia - Das Rätsel der Kooperation. Bielefeld: VS Verlag.

Streitwieser, B. (2014). *Internationalisation of Higher Education and Global Mobility*. Symposium Books Ltd.

Sturm, R. (2009, February 27). Wirtschaftssystem und Wirtschaftspolitik | bpb. Retrieved 12 March 2018, from http://www.bpb.de/izpb/10553/wirtschaftssystem-und-wirtschaftspolitik

Suárez-Corujo, B. (2017). The 'Gig' Economy and its Impact on Social Security: The Spanish example. *European Journal of Social Security, 19*(4), 293–312. https://doi.org/10.1177/1388262717745751

Tewes, O., & Heimann, C. (2018). Reasons for Moving in Times of Crisis: The Motives Behind Migration of Highly-Skilled Spaniards to Berlin and London. Retrieved 26 July 2018, from https://escholarship.org/uc/item/6rc6m4rj

The Economist. (2009, April 8). Big in America? *The Economist*. Retrieved from https://www.economist.com/node/13447445

The Guardian. (2017, May 25). Majority of Britons think minorities threaten UK culture, report says. Retrieved 13 March 2018, from http://www.theguardian.com/world/2017/may/25/majority-of-britons-think-minorities-threaten-uk-culture-report-says

The Week. (2015, January 24). EU referendum: what does David Cameron want from Europe? | The Week UK. Retrieved 6 July 2018, from http://www.theweek.co.uk/brexit/64153/eu-referendum-what-does-david-cameron-want-from-europe

Thelen, K. (2004). *How Institutions Evolve: The Political Economy of Skills in Germany, Britain, the United States, and Japan*. Cambridge University Press.

Thomas, W. I., & Znaniecki, F. (1958). *The Polish peasant in Europe and America*. New York: Dover Publications.

Thränhardt, D. (2005). Spanische Einwanderer schaffen Bildungskapital: Selbsthilfe-Netzwerke und Integrationserfolg in Europa. In D. Thränhardt & K.

Weiss (Eds.), *SelbstHilfe: Wie Migranten Netzwerke knüpfen und soziales Kapital schaffen*. Freiburg im Breisgau: Lambertus.

Thränhardt, D. (2014). GRUNDLAGEN: DIE NEUE ARBEITSMIGRATION AUS SPANIEN Innereuropäische Mobilität am Beispiel der neuen spanischen Arbeitsmigration nach Deutschland. In C. Pfeffer-Hoffmann (Ed.), *Arbeitsmigration nach Deutschland* (pp. 17–105). Berlin: Mensch & Buch Verlag.

Tobin, L. (2015, August 4). Love or money? High tuition fees lead students to vocational degrees | Education | The Guardian. Retrieved 12 March 2018, from https://www.theguardian.com/education/2015/aug/04/love-money-tuition-fees-student-vocational-degrees-jobs-university-business

Tortella Casares, G., & Núñez, C. E. (2014). *El desarrollo de la España contemporánea: historia económica de los siglos XIX y XX*. Madrid: Alianza. Retrieved from http://cielo.usal.es/Record/Xebook1-3461

Triandafyllidou, A., & Gropas, R. (2014). “Voting With Their Feet”American Behavioral Scientist - Anna Triandafyllidou, Ruby Gropas, 2014. *American Behavioral Scientist*, *58*(12), 1614–1633.

Triper, J. M. (2015, July 27). CCOO y UGT pierden durante la crisis el 44% de los afiliados, hasta 1,4 millones - elEconomista.es. Retrieved 6 April 2018, from http://www.eleconomista.es/economia/noticias/6900078/07/15/CCOO-y-UGT-pierden-durante-la-crisis-el-44-de-los-afiliados-hasta-14-millones.html

Tuchman, G. (1978). *Making news : a study in the construction of reality*. New York : Free Press, c1978.

UK Visa Bureau. (2018). Shortage Occupations List: UK Visa Bureau. Retrieved 4 July 2018, from http://www.visabureau.com/uk/shortage-occupations-list.aspx

Varsavsky, M. (2011, May 26). ‘Spanish Revolution’ of 2011 Explained. Retrieved 3 April 2018, from https://www.huffingtonpost.com/martin-varsavsky/spanish-revolution-of-201_b_867156.html

Vertovec, S. (1999). Conceiving and researching transnationalism. *Ethnic and Racial Studies*, *22*(2), 447–462. https://doi.org/10.1080/014198799329558

Vilar Ramírez, J. B., & Vilar, M. J. (1999). *La emigración española a Europa en el siglo XX*. Arco Libros.

Vollmer, M. (2015). Bestimmung von Fachkräfteengpässen und Fachkräftebedarfen in Deutschland. Fokus-Studie der deutschen nationalen Kontaktstelle für das Europäische Migrationsnetzwerk (EMN). Retrieved 29 March 2018, from https://www.bamf.de/SharedDocs/Anlagen/DE/Publikationen/EMN/Studien/wp64-emn-bestimmung-fachkrafteengpaesse-und-bedarfe.html

Weber, M. (1925). *Wirtschaft und Gesellschaft* (2., verm. Aufl.). Tübingen: Mohr.

Weber, M. (1968). *Economy and Society: An Outline of Interpretive Sociology*. Bedminster Press.

Wehrhahn, R., & Sandner Le Gall, V. (2011). *Bevölkerungsgeographie*. Darmstadt: WBG.

Wilpert, C. (1992). The use of social networks in Turkish migration to Germany. In M. M. Kritz, L. L. Lim, & H. Zlotnik (Eds.), *International migration systems : a global approach*. Oxford : Clarendon Press ; New York : Oxford University Press, 1992.

Witzel, A. (1985). Das problemzentrierte Interview. In G. Jüttemann (Ed.), *Qualitative Forschung in der Psychologie*. Weinheim [u.a.]: Beltz.

Zeit Online. (2017, January 3). Arbeitslosenquote: Arbeitslosenzahl sinkt auf Rekordtief. *Die Zeit*. Retrieved 29 March 2018, from http://www.zeit.de/wirtschaft/2017-01/arbeitslosenquote-bundesagentur-fuer-arbeit-rekordtief

The manufacturer's authorised representative in the EU is Springer Nature Customer Service Centre GmbH, Europaplatz 3, 69115 Heidelberg, Germany. If you have any concerns regarding our products, please contact ProductSafety@springernature.com

Printed and bound by CPI Group (UK) Ltd, Croydon, CR0 4YY
22/09/2026
02221059-0001